W9-BIY-501

BOTTOM LINE'S

Treasury *of* Home Remedies & Natural Cures

1,001 Surprising, Doctor-Approved Healing Secrets

JOAN WILEN AND LYDIA WILEN

BottomLineBooks

BottomLineInc.com

Bottom Line's Treasury of Home Remedies and Natural Cures
By Joan Wilen and Lydia Wilen

Adaptation © 2016 by Bottom Line Inc.

Some remedies in this book adapted from:
Folk Remedies That Work © 1992, 1996 by Joan Wilen and Lydia Wilen.
Published by arrangement with HarperCollins Publishers, Inc.

Grateful acknowledgment is made for the use of excerpts from *Folk Remedies That Work*, originally appearing in *Healing Visualizations* by Gerald Epstein, MD.
Copyright © 1989 by Gerald Epstein, MD. Used by permission of Bantam Dell, an imprint of Random House, Inc.

10 9 8 7 6 5 4 3 2

ISBN 0–88723–750–9

Bottom Line Books® is a registered trademark of Bottom Line Inc.
3 Landmark Square, Suite 201, Stamford, CT 06901
www.BottomLineInc.com

Bottom Line Books® is an imprint of Bottom Line Inc., publisher of print periodicals, e-letters and books. We are dedicated to bringing you the best information from the most knowledgeable sources in the world. Our goal is to help you gain greater wealth, better health, more wisdom, extra time and increased happiness.

Printed in the United States of America

Cover designed by Aimee Zaleski

Contents

About the Authors

The Wilen Sisters—Joan and Lydia—are energetic and enthusiastic health investigators. In a career that's spanned decades, they have uncovered thousands of amazing "cures from the cupboard," which they share through their best-selling books, including *Bottom Line's Secret Food Cures* and *Bottom Line's Household Magic*, dozens of magazine articles and with appearances on many national television talk shows, including NBC's *Today Show* and *CBS This Morning* and countless radio shows.

Joan and Lydia grew up in a family where natural healing was a way of life. If you had an ailment, their bubby (grandmother) had a remedy. Once their first book was in print and they did a weekly TV spot, bubbies, nanas, nonnas, yayas and just about everyone who ever had a grandmother was sharing his/her remedies with them.

The Wilens' goal for writing their books is to give their readers the safest, simplest and smartest ways to help themselves feel and be their best. And so, they've searched and researched and found this incredible collection dedicated to your good health. ■

Welcome from the Wilen Sisters

Hello dear person who is reading this page. Congratulations for wanting to take care of yourself, and thank you for selecting this book.

About this book...we received such positive response from our first Bottom Line book of home remedies, *Bottom Line's Healing Remedies*, and so many requests for *more* natural treatments that we felt compelled to put together another book which we titled *Bottom Line's Treasury of Home Remedies and Natural Cures*. We're very excited to bring you these remedies.

In addition to the A-to-Z (*well*, W) listing of ailments, there are a few chapters with all kinds of eye-opening revelations, life-changing suggestions, health-restoring treatments, innovative therapies and incredible products that you may not (but should) know exist.

The chapters we'd like to call your attention to are...

- **Today's Alternative Treatments and Remarkable Age-Old Therapies**
- **It Does a Body Good**
- **Healthful Hints**
- **Home Health Hints**

In these chapters and throughout the rest of this book, we quote medical experts who were willing to share their expertise, experience and wisdom with you. Look for Dr. Ben Kim's recipe for delicious *Energy Boosters* (page 86), Master Herbalist Richard Schulze's *All-Natural Antibiotic Tonic* (page 232), the *Remarkable Gin-Soaked-Raisins Arthritis Remedy* (on page 5), holistic-living authority Jane Alexander and her *Smudging* secrets (page 270) and veterinarian Dr. Jill Elliot's *Pet Advice* (page 300).

We'd also like to call your attention to the "Word from the Wise..." articles you will come across. Don't miss this important information from leading experts in their fields, which includes further information on a topic—sometimes illustrations or sometimes a recent study.

While reading through the pages of this book, you will see some brand names pop up. Since it's impossible for us to investigate and report on many hundreds of supplement and food companies on the market and online, we stick to telling you about the few outstanding companies we trust. Please know we are not on anyone's payroll. We write about companies because we believe in their ethics, integrity and the quality of their products, hoping they will help our readers, as they've helped us.

One more important point: Remember to always listen to your inner voice, especially about knowing when to go to a doctor.

Neither of us has medical credentials and we're *not prescribing* treatment or medication. We're writers and researchers and we're *reporting*. Before starting any self-help treatment, consult with your health professional…one who is familiar with your medical history. If your doctor is not open to alternative or integrative treatment, it may be time to shop around for another doctor. We know this is easier said than done, particularly with health insurance considerations. If that's the case, give some thought to arming yourself with the appropriate pages from this book related to your specific health challenge, and show them to your doctor. You will not be the first patient who does this, particularly in this age of the Internet. And, your doctor may surprise you by starting a dialogue about new ways to approach your health problem.

We ask one more thing of you…imagine each of us giving you a big hug (everyone should have at least three hugs a day, and we're starting you off with two).

In addition to the hugs, this brings every good wish from both of us.

Joan and Lydia
(The Wilen Sisters)

Today's Alternative Treatments and Remarkable Age-Old Therapies

When we set out to do this book, we decided it would be an assortment of the latest alternative treatments as well as age-old remedies. But, the more research we did, the more we realized that in many instances, "the latest" is actually "age-old," rediscovered and given new names.

And so, in this book, we touch on rediscovered therapies in the hope of opening up a whole new healing horizon to you. If you spark to something in particular, we urge you to follow your interest.

There are organizations, associations and foundations eager to share their information. There are wonderful Web sites, books, DVDs and tapes available where you can find everything you'd ever want to know about almost anything. We provide helpful resources throughout this book and in the "Sources" section. But also check libraries and bookstores. There are also classes, seminars and workshops of all kinds. Not only can you broaden your knowledge, but it's a great way to meet people with shared interests. Check local schools for adult education courses, and health food stores for guest speakers giving lectures, and for free publications and flyers advertising what's out there for you.

Here, then, with brief explanations to get you started, is an introduction to some of the alternative and/or age-old therapies mentioned throughout this book...

ACUPRESSURE

Most of us think of acupressure as acupuncture without needles. And it is... sort of. Both are derived from traditional Chinese medicine. Both involve specific trigger points on the body along pathways called "meridians." With acupressure, pressure is applied utilizing thumbs, fingers, palms or electronic devices. The pressure stimulates points that correspond to the troubled area of the body and engages the body's natural self-curing abilities.

Shiatsu is the most well-known from of acupressure. With his/her thumbs, fingers and palms, a Shiatsu therapist will use massage techniques such as tapping, squeezing, rubbing and applied pressure along the appropriate meridians to clear energy blockages allowing the optimal flow of chi (energy).

There are a few schools of thought as to why acupressure works...

● **It releases muscle tension,** promotes the flow of energy, unblocks energy and rebalances energy, which results in healing.

● **Applied pressure may block transmission of pain signals.**

● **It may release endorphins,** *opioids* and/or *neurotransmitters* which are our natural pain reducers.

Whatever the reason, acupressure works well and is fairly easy to do. You can even use it on yourself. Now that you have a better understanding of it, when you come across it as a remedy for a challenge you're having, give it a try. If you're pleased with the results, sign up for an acupressure course and learn how to maintain good health by keeping your body in balance the acupressure way.

A Word from the Wise...

Relief at Your Fingertips

Acupressure can alleviate many physical, mental and emotional problems in only a few minutes—and it is free.

The acupoints often have ancient descriptive names, such as *Joining the Valley* and *Mind Clearing*.

Here are the acupressure techniques for various health problems. Unless otherwise noted, daily acupressure sessions, three times a day, are the best way to relieve a temporary or chronic problem.

Arthritis Pain

Joining the Valley is a truly amazing acupoint because it can relieve arthritis pain anywhere in the body.

Location: In the webbing between the thumb and index finger, at the highest spot of the muscle where the thumb and the index finger join together.

What to do: Rhythmically squeeze the acupoint. As you're squeezing, place the side of your hand that is closest to the little finger on your thigh or a tabletop. Apply pressure in the webbing as you press downward. This allows you to angle more deeply into the point, increasing the benefits.

Also helpful for: Headache, toothache, hangover, hay fever symptoms, constipation.

 CAUTION: This point is forbidden for pregnant women because its stimulation can trigger premature contraction in the uterus.

Memory Problems

The *Mind Clearing* acupoints are for improving recall instantly—for example, when you have forgotten a name or gone to the supermarket without your shopping list.

Location: One finger width (that's about one-half inch) directly above the center of each eyebrow.

What to do: Gently position your right thumb above your right eyebrow and your middle fingertip above the eyebrow on the left side. Hold very gently. You should feel a slight dip or indentation in the bone structure—the acupoints on both sides are in the dip. Press the indentation very lightly, hold and breathe deeply. After a minute or two, you'll experience more mental clarity and sharper memory.

Lower Back Pain

To help prevent and relieve lower back pain, practice this exercise for one minute three times a day. You can do it standing or sitting.

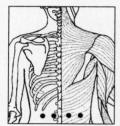

Location: Position the backs of your hands against your lower back, about one inch outside the spine.

What to do: Briskly rub both your hands up and down—about three inches up and six inches down—using the friction to create heat in your lower back.

If you're doing the technique correctly, you'll need to breathe deeply to sustain the vigorous rubbing, and you'll break out in a slight sweat.

Also good for: Food cravings, especially sugar cravings, chronic fatigue, sexual problems, chills, phobias as well as fibromyalgia symptoms.

Emotional Upset

The *Inner Gate* acupoint can reduce emotional upset—such as anxiety, depression and irritability—in two to three minutes.

Location: On the inner side of the forearm, three finger widths up from the center of the wrist crease, in between two thick tendons.

What to do: Place your thumb on the point and your fingers directly behind the out-

side of the forearm between the two bones. Squeeze this slowly and firmly, hold for two to three minutes, while breath-

ing deeply. Repeat on the other arm for the same amount of time.

Also good for: Carpal tunnel syndrome, insomnia, indigestion and nausea.

Insomnia

The acupoints *Calm Sleep* and *Joyful Sleep*—on the outer and inner ankles—can help relieve insomnia. Use these acupressure points whenever you want to deeply relax and sleep better.

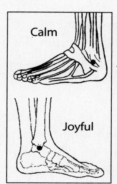

Location: *Calm Sleep* is in the first indentation below the outer anklebone. *Joyful Sleep* is directly below the inside of the anklebone, in a slight indentation.

What to do: Position your thumb on one side of your ankle and your fingers on the other, and press firmly. If you're on the right spot, it will be slightly sore. Hold for two minutes, breathing deeply. Repeat on the other ankle. Do this again if you still are having trouble sleeping or if you wake up.

Headaches

The acupoints *Gates of Consciousness* relieve a tension headache or migraine.

Location: Underneath the base of your skull to either side of your spine, about three to four inches apart, depending on the size of your head.

What to do: Using your fingers, thumbs or knuckles, press the points under the base of your skull.

Illustrations courtesy of Michael Reed Gach, Phd.

At the same time, slowly tilt your head back so that the angle of your head relaxes your neck muscles. Press forward (toward your throat), upward (underneath the base of your skull) and slightly inward, angling the pressure toward the center of your brain. Continue to apply pressure for two minutes, breathing.

Also good for: Neck pain, insomnia, high blood pressure.

Acupressure Basics

Unless otherwise noted, use your middle finger, with your index and ring fingers for support. Firmly and gradually, apply stationary pressure directly on the acupoint for three minutes.

● **Firmly** means using an amount of pressure that will cause a sensation between pleasure and pain—or pressure that "hurts good." If the pressure is applied too fast or too hard, the point will hurt. If the pressure is too soft, you won't get the full benefit.

● **Gradually** means moving your finger into and out of the point in super-slow motion. Applying and releasing finger pressure allow the tissue to respond and relax, promoting healing.

● **Stationary** means you are not rubbing or massaging the area.

● **Directly** means at a 90-degree angle from the surface of the skin. If you are pulling the skin, the angle of pressure is incorrect.

● **When you apply pressure,** lean your weight toward the point. If your hands are weak or it hurts your fingers when you apply pressure, try using your knuckles. You also can use a tool, such as a golf ball or pencil eraser.

● **Breathe** slowly and deeply while you apply pressure. This helps release pain and tension.

Michael Reed Gach, PhD, founder of the Acupressure Institute in Berkeley, California. He is author of self-healing instructional DVDs and CDs and many books, including *Acupressure's Potent Points* (Bantam), *Acupressure for Lovers* (Bantam), *Arthritis Relief at Your Fingertips* (Warner) and coauthor of *Acupressure for Emotional Healing* (Bantam). His Web site is *www.acupressure.com*.

AFFIRMATIONS

"*Pleasant words are as a honeycomb. Sweet to the soul and health to the bones.*" (Proverbs 16:24)

Words have power...great power.

A simple example from Joan: I had to do something for someone and resented it. It took me away from what I wanted to be doing. I walked around feeling angry and annoyed and soon developed a stiff neck. This made me even more angry and annoyed. When I ran into a friend on the bus, I asked to change seats with him, explaining that I had a stiff neck and couldn't look in his direction unless he sat on the other side of me. He immediately asked me what was happening in my life that was making me unhappy. Without thinking, I told him what I was doing, adding, "And it's a real pain in the neck."

Aha!, our subconscious mind acts on words and thoughts without discrimination. We have to be careful about what we *think* and *say.*

Start listening to yourself and stop programming yourself negatively: "All that traffic makes me sick to my stomach." "When she talks, I turn a deaf ear." "It's back-breaking work." "I get a headache at the thought of preparing my taxes for the accountant." Does this sound familiar?

Instead, affirmations are *positive* statements that phrase a desire or wish as though it is *already* true. For example, suppose you have a painful back condition. A simple affirmation could be, "I am living free of pain." All affirmations are positive, in the present tense and specific. An affirmation is positive programming for the subconscious and, as a bonus, it makes you feel better *consciously*, too.

Start by assigning an appropriate affirmation to yourself. (There are affirmations at the end of most of the sections in this book.) Write it down on an index card and read it over and over—at least seven times in a row, out loud if possible—time and time again throughout the day. Think about the meaning of it and when you say it, mean it. But even if you memorize it and then just say it by rote, it will make a proper impression on your subconscious.

Here's an example of an affirmation to keep repeating when you stroll down the street: *I walk through life with joy and ease.*

Once you have a better understanding of how deeply affected you are by your words and thoughts, you can create your own affirmations by pinpointing your physical problem and the underlying cause of it.

AROMATHERAPY

Debra Nuzzi, Master Herbalist and creator of essential-oil inhalers, observes that our sense of smell is unique in that the olfactory nerve receptors are the only receptors in direct contact with the outside world.

■ Recipe ■

How to Prepare Your Own Perfume

- **Sterilize a bottle** (colored glass is preferable for perfume) and its cap in the dishwasher or carefully in just-boiled water.
- **Pour ¼ cup of vodka (the higher percentage of alcohol, the better) into the bottle.** Vodka is used because during its distillation process the alcohol is purified creating a neutral substance that stabilizes a perfume's scent and prevents essential oils from spoiling.
- **Add a total of 22 to 25 drops of essential oils.** As you add the oil, one drop at a time and one oil at a time, be sure to write down the formula you're creating. For example, you may want to use 7 drops of ylang-ylang and 10 drops of lavender and 5 drops of chamomile.

Mix and sniff until you have the recipe that makes you hum.

- **To allow the oils to mingle and age the fragrance, cap the bottle** and put it in a cool, dark, out-of-the-way place for at least 48 hours, but not for more than a month.
- **Once you have decided that the perfume has aged enough, dilute it** with 2 tablespoons of distilled or spring water. Then add about 5 drops of glycerine to help preserve the fragrance.
- **Create a name for your perfume and label the bottle.** If you are not using a colored glass bottle, protect the perfume from the light by wrapping aluminum foil around it.

Located just beneath the brain, level with the bridge of the nose, these sensitive "hairs" pick up the fragrant molecules, transporting their message directly to the limbic system, bypassing the blood brain barrier. The limbic system is the cerebral core of emotion and memory. It controls the entire endocrine system of hormones that regulate body metabolism, stress, caloric levels, balance of insulin, sexual arousal and much more.

For aromatherapy to be effective, use only natural essential oils (not synthetic or artificial), and look for the words "true," "absolute" or "concrete" on the label. The oils are potent, so use them sparingly.

A Word from the Wise...

Scents That Heal

Aromatherapy safely eases many ailments, my research shows, by triggering release of brain chemicals that affect physical and emotional well-being.

Best: Hold a food, flower, essential oil or naturally scented toiletry one-half inch away from your face and level with your lips. Inhale for three minutes…take a five-minute break…repeat up to two dozen times.

- **For anxiety,** try lavender.

It may work by: Increasing the alpha brain waves that promote a relaxed, meditative state.

To use: Inhale lavender essential oil… light a lavender-scented candle…or place a lavender eye pillow over your eyes.

- **For fatigue,** try jasmine.

It may work by: Boosting the beta brain waves that improve alertness.

To use: Close one nostril with a finger and deeply inhale a jasmine oil or jasmine-scented toiletry…repeat with other nostril. Continue alternating for five minutes. This single-nostril technique prolongs the effects.

- **For headache,** try green apple (sliced).

It may work by: Triggering the release of brain chemicals, such as *endorphins* and *serotonin*, that inhibit pain sensations and alleviate tension.

To use: To reduce migraine or tension-headache pain and duration, inhale the apple scent as soon as you feel a headache coming on. This seems to work best for people who like the smell of green apple.

- **For low libido,** try Good & Plenty candies plus cucumber or banana.

It may work by: Stimulating the arousal centers of the female brain, reducing inhibitions and promoting alertness.

To use: Best results are achieved by simultaneously smelling the candy and either of the other foods—so hold both up together.

- **For any menopause-related memory problems,** try flowers.

It may work by: Acting on the connection between the olfactory nerve and the parts of the brain involved in memory.

To use: Whenever you want to retain new information, smell mixed scents to increase learning speed. Try a bouquet of fragrant mixed flowers or a floral-scented perfume.

- **For menstrual cramps,** try green apple (sliced) plus any personal favorite scent.

It may work by: Easing muscle contractions (the apple)…and lifting mood.

To use: Select an aroma you particularly enjoy—a favorite scent helps to banish the blues by distracting you from pain.

- **For overeating,** try banana or green apple (sliced) or peppermint.

It may work by: Stimulating the satiety center of the brain that registers when your stomach is full.

To use: To reduce food cravings, deeply inhale three times in each nostril, alternating sides. Alternate among fragrances monthly to help prevent weight-loss plateaus.

- **For sadness,** try baked goods.

It may work by: Evoking happy memories of childhood.

To use: Bake or buy a favorite pie, cake or other fragrant treat—the aroma alone will help you feel better. If your diet permits, take a few bites for an extra boost in mood.

Alan Hirsch, MD, founder and neurological director of the Smell & Taste Treatment and Research Foundation in Chicago, *www.smellandtaste.org.* A neurologist and psychiatrist, he has published more than 300 articles on smell and taste disorders and is author of eight books, including *Life's a Smelling Success* (Authors of Unity).

CHROMOTHERAPY (COLOR THERAPY)

Color therapists treat medical conditions with specific colors to correct energy imbalances believed to be the underlying cause of disease. The practitioner applies the color in the form of gemstones, candles, wands, prisms, fabrics, glasses, lenses or lights, on appropriate chakras (the seven main spiritual centers of the body located along the spine). By introducing the proper color, the healing should begin. *Here is a description of each chakra, its corresponding color and the medicinal uses of each...*

- **First Chakra—red.** Located at the base of the spine. Used to stimulate the body and mind and to increase circulation.
- **Second Chakra—orange.** Pelvis area. Used to heal the lungs and to increase energy levels.
- **Third Chakra—yellow.** Solar plexus. Used to stimulate the nerves and purify the body.
- **Fourth Chakra—green.** Heart. The balance point for all of the chakras governing relationships and interactions with others.
- **Fifth Chakra—blue.** Throat. Used to soothe illnesses and treat pain.
- **Sixth Chakra—indigo.** Lower part of the forehead. Used to alleviate skin problems.
- **Seventh Chakra—violet.** Top of the head. Used to stimulate inspiration, creativity and spirituality.

GEM THERAPY (CRYSTAL HEALING)

Gemologists Connie Barrett and Joyce Kaessinger from Beyond the Rainbow, share with us their understanding of why and how stones can help heal.

People and stones are said to have electromagnetic energy fields. Our energy fields are constantly shifting—going in and out of balance. Stones vibrate at a perfectly symmetrical, steady and harmonious frequency. It's the nature of the universe for everything to seek balance. When we put ourselves in direct contact with the energy of stones, we allow that energy to unblock our own energy and bring balance where there was imbalance.

The most effective way of healing yourself with a stone is to lie down on your back, with your head to the north (aligning your spine with the earth's axis and the earth's magnetic energy), and the stone taped to the problem area. Stay in that position and meditate, or say an affirmation, or just relax for at least 20 minutes. If you can't lie down, just hold the stone and rub it. When you're not actively working with the stone, wear it or carry it with you in a pocket, pocketbook or briefcase. A half-inch stone projects energy for up to three feet around.

When stones are in jewelry, the silver or gold conductive encasements enhance the energy of the stone. Silver is a soft, flowing receptive energy and gold is considered to be very active and energizing.

Stones are said to get you in touch with your own intuition (also known as your "higher self" or that little inner voice). To select a stone, use that intuition and choose the one that seems to call out to you. Size and cost do not count. They don't have to be big and expensive to be effective. In fact, some small stones with deep, rich colors or designs are more powerful than their muted-colored big daddies.

Traditionally, certain stones are known to be good for specific ailments. But if you feel that a specific stone, other than the suggested one, is going to help you, use the one of your choice. Trust your intuition, even if it means overriding tradition. When you have a physical problem, the root of the problem may not be what the symptom is. Your higher self may direct you to the stone that's going to get to the root of the problem.

It all gets back to: Listen to that little voice inside. However, if you don't want to leave any stone unturned, you may want to use the

stone you were attracted to, as well as the one recommended for your particular problem. That's fine. In fact, the more the merrier. There's no such thing as overdosing on stones.

After using a stone for healing, run cold water over it for 15 seconds, allowing the negative energy to flow off the stone and down the drain. While you're at it, rinse your hands and wrists under the cold water, too.

HERBS

There are some do's, don'ts and general rules that you should know about herbs to get their full benefit.

• **Store herbs in airtight, amber-colored (if possible), glass containers.** *Glass* containers are best because herbs have volatile oils that react with plastic.

• **Keep herbs away from direct sunlight and heat.**

• **Do not keep herbs in the refrigerator.** They need to be kept in a dry place and the fridge is a moist environment.

• **Be sure to label and date your herbs.** The consensus of opinion among herbalists is that it usually takes about a year before herbs start to lose their potency.

• **The general rule for herb preparation is to *steep* leaves and flowers and to *boil* roots, barks and seeds.** To make a tea from gingerroot, for example, you would bring the water and ginger pieces to a boil, then simmer for 15 to 20 minutes, then strain and drink.

• **Whenever possible, use a glass or porcelain pot** if you're going to boil roots, barks and seeds, and for boiling water in which to steep the herbal leaves and flowers.

● **Herbs can be powerful.** Be as cautious with herbs as you know to be with prescription drugs. In most cases, *more is not better.*

● **If you have a history of allergies, be especially careful about taking herbs.** Start ever so slowly, allowing yourself to test for an allergic reaction. If there's any sign or symptom whatsoever, forget using it! Find a nonherbal remedy for your problem.

● **Herbs usually mix well with each other.** If you have more than one problem, you can prepare a tea using two or three different herbs. As herbalist Maria Treben puts it, "The medicinal herbs in God's garden know their way around the human body, and they always go to the place where they are needed."

● **Always sip tea slowly rather than gulping it down.** As you're sipping, you might want to give some thought to the herb's healing energy.

● **An herbal poultice is used to apply soothing moist heat to an affected area.** Prepare the poultice by steeping a tablespoon of an appropriate herb in hot water for five minutes. Strain out and keep the water, then wrap the herb in cheesecloth (using two or three thicknesses of the cloth), or in a piece of white cloth or unbleached muslin, and apply. As soon as the poultice is dry, dip it into the herbal water again and reapply the moist poultice to the affected area.

● **Occasionally, treat yourself to a soothing herbal bath.** For at least five minutes, steep a half-cup of your favorite herb(s) in two quarts of just-boiled water. Strain, and pour the liquid into your warm bath water.

Another way to prepare an herbal bath is to fill a cloth pouch with herbs and let it dangle under the faucet as it fills your tub with hot water.

● **Tinctures are made with fresh herbs and ethyl alcohol.** The alcohol draws out and preserves the healing properties of the herb. Fortunately, a wide variety of prepared herbal tinctures are available at most health food, vitamin and herb stores, and (of course) on the Internet. Unless you have a problem with alcohol, tinctures are convenient to use; you can carry the little jar with you. You can put drops of tincture in water or juice, or you can take it straight—under your tongue—and it will be absorbed into the bloodstream quickly. About five drops of tincture is equivalent to one cup of herbal tea. Dosage varies according to the tincture. Check the label for the manufacturer's suggested amount.

 CAUTION: Pregnant women and children should be treated with herbs only under the supervision of an herbal health professional!

Also, people with a history of alcoholism should avoid alcoholic tinctures. However, if the tincture is mixed with hot water, the steam will "blow off" most of the alcohol.

HOMEOPATHY

In 1796, the German physician Samuel Hahnemann established the fundamental principles of homeopathy. He was the first physician to prepare medicines in a specialized way; proving them on healthy human beings, to determine how these medicines acted to cure diseases. That earned Dr. Hahnemann the title "Father of Experimental Pharmacology."

In the practice of homeopathy, patients are treated with extremely diluted preparations that can *cause* symptoms in a healthy person, but can *alleviate* similar symptoms in a person sick with these symptoms. Huh? To better understand Dr. Hahnemann's philosophy, the main principle of homeopathy is best summed up by the Latin phrase *Similia similbus curentur* or *Like cures like*.

Homeopathic veterinarian Dr. Jill Elliot says, "A homeopath's goal is to find a substance that produces in a healthy person (or animal) the same symptoms the patient is suffering from. When the correct remedy is given...you'll swear it's MAGIC!!!"

Homeopathic remedies, made from plant, animal and mineral products, are prepared by serial dilution with shaking by forceful striking, which homeopaths term "succussion," after each dilution under the assumption that this increases the effect of the treatment. This process is referred to as "potentization," and is continued until certain potencies are reached. Homeopathic remedies come in different potencies (6C, 30C, 6X, 30X, etc.).

 CAUTION: Keep your homeopathic remedies away from any appliance that has an electromechanical field, like refrigerators, microwaves, cell phones, etc. Homeopathic remedies are considered an energetic medicine. Other strong electromechanical fields can "knock off" the energy of the homeopathic remedies. Homeopathic remedies will not work on a patient who is going for radiation treatments for this reason.

Also, when using homeopathic remedies, do NOT drink coffee or have strong aromatic substances like mints, including mint toothpaste, at the same time. Doing so will make homeopathic treatment ineffective.

MAGNETIC THERAPY

The late Dr. Alvin Bakst, a thoracic and cardiovascular surgeon, was a magnetic pain-relief pioneer (*www.drbakstmagnetics. com*). His research led him to rediscover the ancient, Far Eastern technique of strategically placing strong, unipolar magnets on areas of the body affected by pain and discomfort.

Dr. Bakst's theory on how a person feels pain: There is no such thing as pain if it doesn't reach the brain. When a pain impulse is initiated, it must reach the brain to be determined as pain. The nerve impulse is carried to the brain in a manner that is similar to the flow of electricity along a wire. Simplified, the pain impulse is transmitted to the brain via a flow of positively charged magnetic particles called ions.

Blocking the pain: There are several ways to block the transmission of the pain impulse to the brain. One is the use of an anesthetic block. A second is the use of drugs which act on the hypothalamus of the brain to dull the pain. The third is the use of magnetic therapy to impede the flow of the nerve impulse.

How magnets work: By placing a highly powerful negative magnetic field over the nerve, the magnetically, positively charged ions will be attracted to the negative magnetic field, thus impeding the flow of the positively charged ions along the nerves to the brain. Of course, some of the positive ions will escape, thereby allowing continued sensation. However, research reveals that the longer the magnets are in place over the affected site, the more effective the negative magnetic field will become.

About magnets: Magnetic strength is measured in gauss. The higher the gauss rating, the stronger and more effective the magnet will be.

The magnetic field has the ability to penetrate through the skin. Different magnets have different depths of penetration through the skin. A ceramic magnet might have a depth of penetration of 1 to 1.5 inches. If a nerve is superficial (near the surface of the skin), a ceramic magnet will be sufficient to control the pain impulse of that nerve. If the affected nerve is 2 to 4 inches deep, a ceramic magnet will be of little value. Only a neodymium magnet has the ability to penetrate that deeply.

Other benefits from magnets: Magnets also have been scientifically proven to have a profound effect on a basic cellular level. It has been demonstrated that they increase circulation to the area within the magnetic field, which aids in the healing of tissue and speeds the healing of fractures. So, although magnets themselves do not heal an injury, they increase circulation to the affected area, helping the body to heal more quickly.

Veterinarians have also been using magnets to help alleviate pain and swelling in horses.

REFLEXOLOGY

While the art of reflexology dates back to Ancient Egypt, India and China, it wasn't until 1913 that Dr. William Fitzgerald introduced this therapy to the West as *zone therapy*. He noted that reflex areas on the feet and hands were linked to other areas and organs of the body within the same zone.

In the 1930s Eunice Ingham further developed zone theory into what is now known as *reflexology*. She observed that congestion or tension in any part of the foot is mirrored in the corresponding part of the body.

The Association of Reflexologists in Great Britain (*www.aor.org.uk*) defines reflexology as a complementary therapy that works on the feet or hands (ears, too), enabling the body to heal itself. Following illness, stress, injury or disease, it is in a state of "imbalance," and vital energy pathways are blocked, preventing the body from functioning effectively. A reflexologist's sensitive, trained hands can detect tiny deposits and imbalances in the feet, and by working on these points, the reflexologist can release blockages and restore the free flow of energy to the whole body, encouraging the body to heal itself, often counteracting a lifetime of misuse.

More information: We describe a few do-it-yourself reflexology remedies in this book. If you want to take it a step further and go to a professional reflexologist, check the Web site of the American Reflexology Certification Board (ARCB) for a referral. Visit *www.arcb.net* and click on "Find an ARCB Reflexologist."

A Word from the Wise...

So Much More Than a Foot Massage!

Reflexology has long been thought of by many Americans and medical professionals as little more than a foot massage.

Now: Recent scientific studies show that chronic pain, digestive disorders and other common health problems can be alleviated through the use of this practice. Reflexology involves applying pressure to specific areas—known as "reflex points"—located on the feet, hands and ears.

How it works: When a body part is injured or stops functioning properly due to disease, irritating chemicals accumulate in distant but related nerve endings in the feet, hands and ears. Various studies have repeatedly shown that when certain parts of the feet, hands and ears are worked on with touch techniques, relief results in corresponding parts of the body.

Bonus: You can perform many basic forms of reflexology on yourself or a partner.

For best results, work on all of the reflex points described in this article for at least five minutes twice a day, four or more times a week. Relief can be experienced within minutes, but it sometimes takes days or weeks of repeatedly working on the appropriate reflex areas to get results.

 CAUTION: Do NOT work on bruises, cuts, sores, skin infections or directly on areas where you have damaged a bone or strained a joint during the preceding three to six months. If you've had surgery or suffered a bone fracture, ask your surgeon when it's safe to perform reflexology on these areas.

The main technique used on most parts of the feet and hands, including those points described below, is the "thumb roll."

What to do: Place gentle pressure with the pad of your thumb against the area on which you wish to work. Maintaining this pressure and moving slowly, bend the knuckle in the center of the thumb in an upward direction and roll your thumb from the pad toward the tip, moving it forward. Next, reverse the movement of the knuckle, so that once your thumb is flattened you can do another thumb roll, each time moving forward in the direction the thumb is pointing.

Reflex points that correspond to common complaints…

Heartburn

What to do: While sitting in a chair, place your left foot on your right knee. Use your left thumb to locate the "diaphragm line," which separates the ball of your foot and your instep, where the skin color changes between the pad and soft part of the sole. On this line, about an inch from the inner edge of the foot, press gently with the tip of your thumb while squeezing gently with your index finger on top of the foot for five to 10 minutes.

Next, place the tip of your right thumb on the soft part of your left palm at the point between the base of the knuckles below your index and middle fingers. While the fingers of your right hand gently squeeze the back of your left hand, apply gentle pressure using the tip of your right thumb for five to 10 minutes.

Headache

What to do: Start with the hand corresponding to the side of your head where the pain is most noticeable. On the back of that hand, locate a point about an inch below the base knuckle of your index finger in the fleshy web between your index finger and thumb. Place the tip of the thumb of your other hand on this point and the tip of your index finger of the other hand on the palm side of this point, squeezing to find a spot that's slightly thicker and more tender than the surrounding region. While maintaining steady pressure, gently move the tip of your thumb in small circles over this spot. (This movement is different from the thumb roll.) It usually takes about five minutes of work to alleviate a tension headache, and up to an hour to reduce or eliminate a migraine headache.

 CAUTION: This point should not be worked on during the first trimester of pregnancy, as it could have an adverse effect on the fetus. Instead, work only on the related point on the ear, as described here.

After you have completed the hand reflexology, locate the small, hard flap of cartilage at the top of your earlobe, then feel where this flap and the earlobe meet. With the tip of your thumb on the front of the ear and the tip of your index finger behind the ear, gently squeeze this point between your index finger and thumb, feeling for a spot that's slightly thicker and more tender than the surrounding area. Squeeze both ears at once, holding for five to 10 minutes, while resting your elbows on a table or desk.

Irritable Bowel Syndrome

What to do: While sitting, place your left foot on your right knee. With the fingers of your left hand, gently grasp the top of the foot. Using the thumb roll technique in repeated overlapping strips, work across from the inner edge to the outer edge of the foot, on all of the soft part of the sole and the entire heel, for 10 minutes. Repeat, using your right thumb on the bottom of your right foot.

After you have completed the foot reflexology, use your right thumb to perform the thumb roll technique on your left palm. Work from the outside to the inside of the palm, starting just below the base of the fingers and progressing toward the wrist. Repeat, using your left thumb to work on the right palm.

Illustrations by Shawn Banner.

Neck Pain and Stiff Neck

What to do: Move your finger slightly above the cartilage flap described in the headache section, and find a ridge of cartilage running up and down the ear. Place the tips of your index fingers on the lower inch of this ridge on both ears while resting your elbows on a table or desk. Squeeze gently but firmly between your index fingers and thumbs, with your thumbs behind the ears. Continue for five to 10 minutes.

Bill Flocco, a reflexology teacher and researcher and the founder and director of the American Academy of Reflexology, based in Los Angeles. He is the author of several books on reflexology, including *Reflexology Research: Anatomy of a Reflexology Research Study* (William Sanford).

VISUALIZATION (GUIDED IMAGERY)

Your mind is an active and powerful tool. The average person is said to have an estimated 10,000 thoughts racing through his/her mind every day (at least half of them are negative). Visualization—a variety of visual techniques using mental images—can harness the positive energy of your imagination to promote relaxation and changes in attitude and behavior. It also encourages physical healing.

Gerald N. Epstein, MD, psychiatrist and one of the foremost practitioners of integrative health care for healing and transformation, and director of the American Institute for Mental Imagery (*www.drjerryepstein.org*), poetically describes the way in which visualization, or mental imagery, can be used to help heal yourself and create your own good health.

"I look at our individual lives as gardens that need to be tended. We are all essentially gardeners caring for our own reality-garden. As gardeners, we have special functions, primarily weeding, seeding and of course, harvesting.

"Gardens that are full of weeds cannot be harvested properly. Weeds will overrun the seeds and prevent them from taking root and blossoming. Illness, disease and negative beliefs are weeds that we have allowed to grow in our personal gardens. Emotions such as anxiety, depression, fear, panic, worry, and despair are also weeds. Negative beliefs and emotions are intimately connected with illness and disease. It is not a surprise to anyone who recognizes the basic unity of the body/mind that researchers have found a correlation between negative emotions and lowered immunity. Similarly, positive beliefs bring us positive emotions such as humor, joy and happiness, and researchers have shown that positive emotions are tied in with healthy immune responses.

"Mental imagery is a technique for clearing out the old, negative weed-beliefs and replacing them with new, positive seed-beliefs. By becoming a gardener of your own reality, self-healing becomes possible."

A Word from the Wise...

Meditation for People Who Don't Like to Meditate

We have heard all about the benefits of meditating. For decades, studies have shown that meditation helps with depression, anxiety, tension, insomnia, pain, high blood pressure, self-esteem, self-control, concentration and creativity. Yet for many people, meditation seems daunting. Maybe you find it hard to sit still...to clear your mind...to make the time...or to stick with it long enough.

Key to success: Choose a technique that suits your personality, schedule and level of experience, then do it consistently. *Twenty minutes or more daily is a good goal, but even five minutes is helpful if you do it every day...*

If You Are a Beginner...

These methods are effective yet simple enough for a novice. Start with just a few minutes, and work your way up.

➤ **Single-Tasking.** Our time-crunched society encourages multitasking—so you sort mail while on the phone. What you may not know is that the simple act of focusing fully on a single task is a meditative exercise. It improves your powers of concentration, alleviates stress and boosts mood by enhancing your appreciation of the here-and-now.

Try: Once or twice each day, give your complete attention to just one activity. *Example:* When you fold the laundry, don't turn on the TV—just enjoy the soft fabrics and the rhythm of your hand motions.

➤ **Focused Breathing.** Sit in a quiet place, on the floor or in a chair, keeping your back straight so your lungs can expand. Pay attention to your breathing. Feel the air moving through your nostrils as you slowly inhale and exhale...feel your abdomen rise and fall. Then choose either of these sites (nostrils or abdomen) and focus fully on the sensations there. Soon you may notice that your mind has wandered. Don't berate yourself—this can happen even to experienced meditators. Simply return your attention to the breath.

➤ **Centering Prayer.** Choose a phrase or a word that is spiritually meaningful for you, such as *God is love* or *shalom*. With each breath, repeat it silently to yourself. Again, if your thoughts start to stray, just calmly return to your prayer.

If You Hate to Sit Still...

Some people can't stop squirming when they try to meditate. *Solution:* Moving meditation.

➤ **Qigong, Tai Chi or Yoga.** These practices combine specific movements with a contemplative focus on the body, so you exercise while you meditate. Many health clubs, adult-education centers and hospitals offer classes in these techniques.

➤ **Mindful Eating.** Eat a meal alone, in silence, savoring the experience. Enjoy the colors and aromas of the food. Chew slowly. How do the taste and texture change? What sensations do you perceive as you swallow? Surprise! You are meditating. Continue to eat each bite as consciously as you can, never rushing.

If You Can't Find the Time...

Some days you may not have even five minutes to meditate—but you can take just a moment.

➤ **Three Breaths.** Whenever you feel tense, take three long, deep breaths. Even a few conscious inhalations and exhalations will calm you. Also use cues in your environment as regular reminders to focus and breathe deeply. *Example:* Take slow breaths every time you hang up the phone or walk through a doorway.

➤ **Beauty in the Moment.** Three times a day, look around you and notice something lovely—the scent of someone's perfume, the happy sound of children playing. Explore the experience with your full attention. *Example:* A light breeze is blowing. Watch the graceful way it makes the grass sway...listen to it as it moves through the trees...feel its gentle touch. Notice your emotions of appreciation—and carry them with you through your day.

Roger Walsh, MD, PhD, professor of psychiatry and human behavior in the School of Medicine, and of anthropology and philosophy in the School of Humanities, both at University of California, Irvine. He has done extensive research on Asian philosophies, religion and the effects of meditation and received more than 20 national and international awards. He is author of *Essential Spirituality: The 7 Central Practices to Awaken Heart and Mind* (Wiley), which contains a foreword by the Dalai Lama.

A Word on
Our Remedies

No one passes along or shares a remedy that doesn't work. Of course, we realize that not every remedy will work for every person. But these remedies are easy to use, inexpensive and have no side effects. In other words, while they may not always help—they certainly wouldn't hurt. *Which brings us to a very important point…*

An esteemed doctor has reviewed the remedies in this book and deemed them SAFE. But you have to do your part for your own well-being—please check with a health professional whom you trust prior to trying any self-help treatment, including the remedies contained in this book.

Also, if you are pregnant or nursing, have any allergies and/or food sensitivities, or have been diagnosed with any serious illness or chronic condition—please!—talk to your physician, nurse/midwife, dentist, naturopath or other health specialist before trying any of these remedies. And keep in mind that most of these remedies are NOT meant for children. Please see "Childhood Ailments" (starting on page 27)

for healing suggestions appropriate for the wee ones in your life.

Also, please heed all the "NOTE"s and "CAUTION"s found throughout the book. They stress the fact that our home-remedy suggestions are scientifically unproven and should not take the place of professional medical evaluation and treatment. Some remedies can be dangerous for people who are taking prescription medication or who suffer from a specific illness or condition.

Effective, proven, traditional health care is available for almost all of the conditions mentioned in this book. You may need to see your physician for certain ailments and/or persistent symptoms. These natural remedies should be used in addition to—but never as a substitute for—professional medical help.

Please know that we do not have formal medical training and we are not prescribing treatment. We're writers who are reporting on what has worked for many generations of people who have shared their remedies with us. For your own safety, please consult your doctor before trying any self-help treatment or natural remedy.

1

Conditions A to Z
(*well, W*)

APPENDICITIS

If you think the pain you're experiencing is really gas, but you are not sure, and you're afraid it may be your appendix, we have a simple test…

Stand up straight, bring your right knee up toward your chest, stopping at your waist. Then, quickly, jut your right leg forward as though kicking something in front of you. If you get a sharp, unbearable pain anywhere in the abdominal area, you may have an inflamed appendix. If that's the case, *get medical attention immediately!*

CAUTION: This test is NOT a substitute for a professional diagnosis—especially if pain persists longer than your usual gas pains have in the past.

Appendicitis Prevention

BMJ (formerly the *British Medical Journal*) reported the findings of studies that were conducted at England's University of Southampton.

It seems that by liberally lacing your diet with tomatoes and a variety of green vegetables, you may reduce the chance of having appendicitis.

It is thought that there is a particular fiber in those foods that helps prevent inflammation of the appendix.

ARTHRITIS

At an awards presentation, the late great comedian Jack Benny was quoted as saying, "I don't deserve this award, but I have arthritis and I don't deserve that either."

No one deserves arthritis, but according to the Centers for Disease Control and Prevention (*www.cdc.gov/arthritis*), an estimated 46 million Americans reported that their doctor told them they had arthritis.

There are at least a hundred different forms of arthritis—some involve connective tissues, most involve inflammation of one or more joints, and just about all involve pain.

With the exception of remedies for gout, it's hard to know which remedies work best for each form of arthritis.

Follow your instincts. Read through the remedies below and listen for that little voice inside to say, "Yes!" Then check with your doctor for his/her assurance that the remedy is safe for you to use. You may have to settle for a polite shrug since some doctors don't believe in home remedies.

Arthritis Remedies

➤ **Alfalfa Remedy.** Alfalfa seeds and sprouts have trace minerals that seem to be lacking in people with common kinds of arthritis. Grind alfalfa seeds (available at health food stores) in a blender or a coffee bean grinder and eat a tablespoon of the ground seeds with each meal. There are alfalfa tablets, too, but it would take 15 to 20 tablets a day to equal the value of the ground seeds.

➤ **Cabbage Leaves Make Pain Leave.** For relief from pain, take a few cabbage leaves and steam them for 10 minutes, until they're limp. While the steamed cabbage leaves are cooking, lightly massage a little olive oil on the painful area. As soon as possible, without burning yourself, place the warm cabbage leaves on the oiled area. Cover with a heavy towel to keep in the heat. Repeat the process an hour later with new cabbage leaves.

➤ **Shark Cartilage.** Dr. I. William Lane, in his book *Sharks Don't Get Cancer* (Avery), reports researchers have found that shark cartilage (available at health food stores) is successful in reducing pain in approximately 70% of osteoarthritis and 60% of rheumatoid arthritis cases.

Dr. Lane reports, "Experience suggests that arthritis pain can be alleviated through ingesting one gram (1,000 milligrams [mg] equal one gram) of dried shark cartilage for every 15 pounds of body weight, taken daily. Investigators have found this most effective when divided into three equal doses, each taken about 15 minutes before a meal."

Reduce the dosage to one gram for every 40 pounds of body weight when the cartilage begins taking effect.

According to Dr. Lane, "If major pain relief is not noted after 30 days of continuous and correct use, the cartilage will probably not work at all with your system or problem."

Look for unadulterated 100%-pure shark cartilage. It's pricey, but if it works, it's worth it.

 CAUTION: According to the late Dr. Ray Wunderlich, Jr., respected physician and pediatrician in St. Petersburg, Florida, children, athletes and people with compromised circulation should be wary of prolonged usage of shark cartilage. Be sure to check with your health professional before starting this self-help program.

➤ **A Need for Seaweed.** We Americans are not used to the taste of seaweed. But if you have arthritis, it's a good idea to acquire the taste for it. It can be extremely beneficial. Start with a half-teaspoon of kelp powder (it's available at health food stores or Asian markets) in a cup of warm water. Drink it every night at bedtime. Gradually, add kelp, in piece form, to your food—soup, stew, salad. Kelp pills are also available. Follow the directions on the label.

➤ **Mix an Elixir.** Since arthritis is a major challenge, and not everything works for everyone, we want to supply a substantial variety of remedies, especially the ones for which we received positive feedback. One such remedy is this ginger-tea recipe that appeared in our

■ Recipe ■

Remarkable Gin-Soaked-Raisins Arthritis Remedy

Of all the remedies in all of our books, we've received the most positive feedback from this gin-soaked-raisins remedy. We've gotten letters that tell us, "As a last resort, I tried this and it worked!" E-mails that say things like, "My wife prepared a jar of raisins, so I thought I'd humor her and take it. I can't believe the difference it's made."

If you're wondering why we're repeating the remedy in this book, it's simply too good to leave out.

Ingredients

1 box of Golden Raisins (or a pound of golden raisins bought loose at a health food store)
Gin (about 1 pint)
Glass bowl (Pyrex is good; not crystal)
Glass jar with lid that will hold the raisins

Instructions

Spread the golden raisins evenly on the bottom of the glass bowl, and pour enough gin over the raisins to completely cover them. Let them stay that way until the raisins have absorbed as much gin as possible. It takes five to seven days, depending on the humidity in your home. (If there's a dust or fruit fly problem, *lightly* cover the bowl with a paper towel.) To make sure that all of the raisins get gin-soaked equally, occasionally take a spoon and turn the raisins over so that the ones on top get to sit in the gin on the bottom of the bowl.

As soon as all the gin has been absorbed, transfer the raisins to the jar, put the lid on, and keep it closed. DO NOT REFRIGERATE. Each day, eat nine raisins...EXACTLY AND ONLY NINE RAISINS A DAY! It seems easiest to eat them in the morning with breakfast.

 CAUTION: Joe Graedon, author of *The People's Pharmacy* (St. Martin's), had the raisins tested for alcohol content, and the result was that less than one drop of alcohol was left in nine raisins. Even so... be sure to check with your health professional to make sure that this remedy will not conflict with a medication you may be taking or present a problem for any health challenge you may have, particularly an iron-overload condition. Also, people who are recovering from alcoholism should avoid this remedy.

My friend told her parents about this remedy for their minor joint and back aches and pains. Her folks followed the instructions. One day, while the mixture was marinating, the couple were baking strudel and realized they were short of raisins. Well, there went the remedy. But it was the best strudel they ever made. Wait—that's not the end of the story. They had shared the remedy with a neighbor who is a skier and was scheduled for knee surgery. He prepared the remedy and ate it on a daily basis. When last we heard, the neighbor was pain-free and his surgery had been put off indefinitely.

Some people have had dramatic results after eating the raisins for less than a week, while it has taken others a month or two or more to feel results. As with all remedies, this doesn't work for everyone. Since it's easy, inexpensive and delicious, it's worth a try. Be consistent—eat the raisins every day. Expect a miracle...but have patience!

book, *Bottom Line's Household Magic*.

In March of 2009, we got a letter from Martha who lives in Texas and cared for her husband who had arthritis in his hands and couldn't make a fist, and her sister who was in severe pain and couldn't walk without a cane.

Martha prepared the tea for them daily, and within three weeks, her husband had mobility in his pain-free hands, and her sister no longer needed a cane and became almost pain-free. Martha writes, "My sister says she wants to shout it to the world about how much better she feels."

To give credit where credit is due, we got this remedy from Bruce Fife, ND, director of the Coconut Research Center in Colorado Springs, Colorado (*www.coconutresearchcenter.org*).

Use as much fresh ginger (available at green grocers and in the produce section of most supermarkets) as you like. In fact, the more ginger, the better—it helps to reduce inflammation.

To make the tea, bring one-half cup water to a boil. Cut ginger into thin slices, add them to the hot water and simmer for five minutes. Remove the pan from the heat and discard the ginger. Stir one-quarter teaspoon of powdered turmeric and one tablespoon of unflavored gelatin (both available at your supermarket) into the water. Add one tablespoon of coconut oil (available at health food stores), and continue to stir until the gelatin is dissolved. Then add one-half to one cup of calcium-enriched orange juice. Drink this tea once or twice a day.

 CAUTION: Ginger acts as a blood thinner, so check with your doctor before using it if you are taking a prescription blood thinner. Also, stop using ginger three days before any surgery.

 Hawaiian Nectar. Some nutritionists feel that pineapple's enzyme, *bromelain*, can help decrease joint inflammation in some arthritic conditions. If you're not concerned with counting carbs, and you're not allergic to pineapple, drink a glass of pineapple juice after lunch and after dinner. Fresh juice is best; second best is bottled juice without additives or preservatives.

 CAUTION: Bromelain is NOT recommended for people with a pineapple allergy, or with gastritis or active gastric or duodenal ulcers. Also, people taking anticoagulant drugs such as *warfarin* should consult with their doctor before taking bromelain.

If bromelain is taken with food, it will act more like a digestive enzyme than an anti-inflammatory.

NOTE: Be sure to read about cherries as an anti-inflammatory and pain reliever in the "It Does a Body Good" chapter, page 236.

 Cat Sitting. Have a cat sit on your knees, or wherever you have arthritic pain. Just like a Chihuahua is said to somehow chase away allergies from its owner (see page 108), so is a cat said to rid its owner of arthritis, according to German folklore. If you have arthritis and if you have a cat…here kitty, kitty.

Take Herbal Tea and See. Certain herbal teas can help relieve pain. Our four faves are yarrow tea, willow bark tea, dandelion tea and burdock (roots or leaves) tea. These are available at health food stores and herb shops. Steep a heaping teaspoon of these herbs in a cup of just-boiled water for 10 minutes. Strain and drink two or three cups a day.

NOTE: Yarrow tea has an unusual taste, so you may want to add honey.

➤ **Cut Out Coffee or Anything with Caffeine.** Even caffeinated tea. Caffeine seems to heighten pain for some (not all) arthritis sufferers.

➤ **Assault with Pepper.** Named after Cayenne, the South American region where it was originally grown, cayenne pepper is red, hot and effective.

There seems to be a big payoff with this treatment, but you pay a price. The treatment takes time and patience and the pain gets worse before it gets better or disappears completely. We're reporting this remedy because we think it's well worth the effort.

Check with your doctor before starting this and do it with his or her guidance. Take one or two cayenne pepper capsules three or four times a day, every day, consistently. Remember, at first the pain will probably increase for a short while and then it will subside considerably, maybe even completely.

Over-the-counter topical cayenne creams are also available and can be very effective.

 CAUTION: Do NOT use cayenne capsules if you have heartburn, gastritis, ulcers or esophagitis.

➤ **Celery Tonic.** Celery is known to neutralize uric acid and other excess acids in one's system. On a daily basis, eat fresh celery, drink celery juice and/or celery seed tea. The more, the better …within reason. Oh, and keep in mind that celery is a natural diuretic, so be sure you have access to a nearby bathroom.

➤ **Sex Can Help You to Flex.** There's good news and *more* good news. The good news is that sex can relieve arthritis sufferers from pain for up to six hours at a time. The theory is that sexual stimulation increases and releases the production of cortisone. More good

news is that self-stimulation works as well as having sex with a partner.

➤ **Oily Solution.** Warm a tablespoon of peanut oil, and when it's cool enough, massage your inflamed joints with the oil. Do this several times a day and give it a few days to make a difference.

➤ **What's Shakin'?** Salt causes water retention and swelling, so it stands to reason that it might put more pressure on joints and add to the pain. Restrict your salt intake. If you must use salt, check out Original Himalayan Crystal Salt (*www.himalayancrystalsalt.com*). If you add salt *after* preparing food rather than during, you'll need only half the amount without compromising the taste. (See page 19 for salt substitutes.)

➤ **Garlic to the Rescue.** Garlic—daily doses in any way, shape or form—can strengthen your immune system, rid you of pain, maybe even clear up your arthritic condition—and earn you the nickname "salami breath."

Actually, if you finely mince a clove of garlic and put it in orange juice or water and drink it down without chewing the garlic bits, the smell will not stay on your breath.

Supplement the raw garlic with a good, strong garlic capsule. There are many *odorless* garlic capsules out there that, according to reports, are as effective as the supplements that cause the smell of garlic to stay with you.

 CAUTION: Having garlic on an empty stomach can cause nausea. Be sure to have some food in your stomach before eating garlic or taking capsules. And, be cautious with garlic if you have gastritis.

➤ **Pack Up Your Troubles.** Many doctors, naturopaths and the legendary medical clairvoyant healer Edgar Cayce have recommended castor oil packs for relief from arthritis pain.

Because this remedy takes some effort to do, it seems to be a kind of test of how much you really want to let go of your condition. Hmmmm, that should give you something to think about. While you're thinking, continue reading about the castor oil pack.

For this remedy you will need...

• **A hot water bag or a microwaveable feed corn heating bag.** To order a corn bag, go to *www.corn-bags.com*.

• **A piece of white wool flannel cloth** (or cotton flannel will do) large enough to cover the affected area four times

• **Two pieces of soft plastic**—one for under your body to protect your linens and one for the affected area

  • **A heavy towel**
  • **A bottle of castor oil**
  • **A washcloth**
  • **Baking soda**

Once you have all of the ingredients, start by folding the flannel in four thicknesses and douse it with castor oil. Put the plastic on your bed and lie down on it. Put the oiled flannel directly on your skin, where you have the pain. Next, put the other piece of plastic on the flannel, and place the hot water bottle or heating bag on top of the plastic. Throw the towel over the whole shebang and stay that way for an hour or two. You should find it very relaxing as the hour or two seems to fly by.

Once you remove the pack, prepare a mixture of one teaspoon of baking soda in a pint of room-temperature water, dip the washcloth in it and use it to wash the castor oil off your skin.

Using the same flannel cloth (dousing it with castor oil each time you use it), do the pack

four nights on—at about the same time each night—and three nights off, four nights on, and three nights off. Notice a pattern forming here? Also notice how your pain subsides.

► **Dr. Jarvis's Old Standard.** We keep getting letters from people telling us how this famous New England remedy (apple cider vinegar and honey) from the late (1881–1966) country doctor D.C. Jarvis gave them a new lease on life, usually within a month.

Mix two teaspoons of raw honey and two teaspoons of apple cider vinegar in a glass of warm water and drink it down before each meal and at bedtime.

The pain may disappear and don't be surprised if you shed a few pounds in the process.

 CAUTION: Do NOT use this honey/vinegar remedy if you have heartburn, gastritis, ulcers or esophagitis.

► **Morning Stiffness Prevention.** Sleep in a sleeping bag. There's no need to rough it on the floor. Place the sleeping bag *on* your bed and zip yourself in for the night. Your own body heat gets evenly distributed and it seems to be much healthier than an electric blanket or a heating pad. You save on electricity, and you should notice more ease-of-movement in the morning.

► **Gem Therapy.** When gemologist Connie Barrett was the proprietor of a gem shop in New York City, she would see people come in, look around and with arthritic fingers, instinctively reach for a carnelian. Connie believes that just by following our instincts, we find what we need. And yes, carnelian is one of the stones for arthritis sufferers, since it represents fluidity in every way including fluidity of movement.

Another stone that's used successfully by people with arthritis is green calcite. The inexpensive stone helps release mental rigidity which, in turn, releases physical rigidity.

Clairvoyant, teacher and author Barbara Stabiner says that when you take a bath, keep a piece of coral in the tub with you and it can help alleviate arthritic pain. A nice warm bath may do that too.

➤ **Visualization.** Upon rising and at bedtime, sit up in bed (if you prefer, sit on a hard-back chair) and close your eyes for a two- to three-minute visualization.

Start by breathing out all of the air in your lungs, then slowly breathing in. As you exhale, visualize a huge theater marquee with bright lights flashing the number "3" three times. Take another slow, deep breath, and as you exhale, visualize the number "2" flashing three times. Take one more deep breath, slowly, and when you exhale, see the number "1" flashing three times.

Now that you are totally relaxed, visualize yourself going into a high-tech laboratory. Look around at the sophisticated equipment. As you're looking around, you spot a machine with your name on it. You walk up to it and see that it's a huge vacuum cleaner. Look at the hose. It branches out so that there are two sections of hose. Follow it to its beginning and see that the opening of each hose is in the shape of a foot. Pull up a chair, sit down, and attach each hose to the bottom of each of your feet. Now reach over and press the "ON" button. The vacuum cleaner is working. Visualize each area of your body as the vacuum cleaner pulls out all the waste products and every one of the crystallized deposits that causes the pain. Once you feel that your body is completely free of toxins, press the "Off" button.

Slowly count from one to three. Opening your eyes, stretch and feel refreshed.

More information: Log on to the Arthritis Foundation Web site at *www.arthritistoday.org* and sign up for its *Arthritis Today* e-newsletter. It has the latest information, insight and inspiration, and it's free.

If you have questions about arthritis, or want to locate the Arthritis Foundation in your area, call 800-283-7800.

AFFIRMATION

Repeat this affirmation first thing in the morning, then for every person you deal with during the day and last thing at night…

I let go of anger and replace it with understanding, compassion and love. The love is returned and I feel very loved.

A Word from the Wise…

Chinese Herb Eases Joint Pain

Rheumatoid arthritis patients took 60 mg three times daily of an extract of the herb *Tripterygium wilfordii Hook F* (TwHF)…a control group took 1,000 mg twice daily (a typical dose) of the anti-inflammatory drug *sulfasalazine*. After 24 weeks, 65% of TwHF users and 33% of drug users had a 20% or greater improvement in symptoms. But, many TwHF products are not standardized for strength—only use under a doctor's guidance.

Raphaela Goldbach-Mansky, MD, MHS, acting chief of translational autoinflammatory disease, National Institute of Arthritis and Musculoskeletal and Skin Diseases, Bethesda, Maryland, and leader of a study of 62 people.

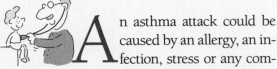

ASTHMA

An asthma attack could be caused by an allergy, an infection, stress or any combination of these issues. Pay careful attention to your patterns so you can figure out what exactly triggers an attack. That's a big step toward knowing how to control the condition.

Finding the Trigger

If, typically, the asthma starts acting up once you're in bed, an allergy to your detergents, fabric softener and other laundry supplies used on your linens may be the cause.

Or, maybe you've gone to bed too soon after eating. Stomach acidity-backup can trigger an attack in some people. If you think you have a problem with stomach acid, be sure you don't eat right before bedtime. When you do go to bed, use an extra pillow so that you're almost sitting up.

One more nighttime troublemaker for some asthmatics is a working fireplace. If you're in a room that's using a wood-burning fireplace, make sure some windows are open—you don't want to be inhaling the particles released by the wood burning in the fireplace.

Let's face it, most of us don't have a fireplace in our bedroom. But how many of you burn candles? With *anything* burned, microscopic particles are released into the air, and there you are, looking beautiful in the candlelight, as you breath in those particles, along with carbon monoxide. Not good for anyone; especially not good for asthmatics.

Trade in the romantic atmosphere for an asthma-free sleep.

CAUTION: Acute and dramatic asthma symptoms need to be treated with prescription medications for immediate relief. Asthma symptoms that are mild in nature can be treated with more gentle remedies like those below.

At the Onset of Asthma Symptoms

➤ **Cranberry Juice.** Drink a couple tablespoons of concentrated cranberry juice (available at health food stores). You can also prepare your own mixture. Boil one pound of cranberries in one pint of water until the berries are very soft. Bottle and refrigerate the mixture. At the first sign of an asthma attack, take the chill out of the cranberries and take two tablespoons of it.

➤ **Cold Water.** Put your hands in a basin of ice-cold water. If you feel that it's helping, let your hands soak for up to 15 minutes.

➤ **Garlic.** At the very first sign of an asthma attack, peel and finely mince a clove of garlic, add it to a tablespoon of raw honey, and swallow it down. The combination of garlic and honey may quell an attack.

CAUTION: Having garlic on an empty stomach can cause nausea. Be sure to have some food in your stomach before eating garlic or taking capsules. And, be cautious with garlic if you have gastritis.

Asthma Symptom Prevention

➤ **Aloe Vera.** Consume aloe vera juice (available at health food stores)—an ounce after every meal.

➤ **Tabasco Sauce.** According to Dr. Isadore Rosenfeld, professor of clinical medicine, Weill Cornell Medical College, drinking a glass of water containing 10 to 20 drops of Tabasco sauce on a regular basis will reduce the frequency and severity of attacks. (The same drink

Let There Be Light!
If you have asthma and candles are important to you, battery-operated candles may be the healthy alternative. For a huge selection, visit *www.batteryoperatedcandles.net* or call 800-879-0537.

also eases the symptoms of chronic bronchitis and the common cold.)

CAUTION: Do NOT use this Tabasco remedy if you have heartburn, gastritis, ulcers or esophagitis.

➤ **Vitamin B-6.** Studies show that vitamin B-6 (100 milligrams [mg] to 150 mg daily) can help prevent asthma attacks.

CAUTION: Do NOT take more than 150 mg of vitamin B-6 a day, as it can be toxic.

➤ **Carrot Juice and Ginger.** The combination of carrot juice and ginger works wonders for preventing attacks and also for getting rid of mucus. Prepare or buy fresh carrot juice. Grate fresh gingerroot, put it in cheesecloth and squeeze out a tablespoon of ginger juice. Add it to six ounces of carrot juice and drink it in the morning and whenever you feel congested.

CAUTION: Ginger acts as a blood thinner, so check with your doctor before using it if you are taking a prescription blood thinner. Stop using ginger three days before any surgery.

More Asthma Help

➤ **Respiratory Strengthener.** Start playing a wind instrument. Wind instruments range from the bugle, clarinet, flute, French horn, recorder, saxophone, trombone, trumpet and tuba to the kazoo and harmonica. Aside from the kazoo, the harmonica is the least expensive and the easiest to learn. Discipline yourself to practice every day for at least a half-hour. It's beneficial for all respiratory problems. The Hohner Harmonica Company sent us letters that they've received through the years from people whose conditions have greatly improved as a result of playing the harmonica. Yes, music hath charm to soothe the asthmatic chest.

➤ **Clearing Up Mucus.** Fenugreek seed tea (available at health food stores) seems to clear up mucus that's part of the asthmatic condition. Drink a cup of the tea first thing in the morning, after every meal and at bedtime.

➤ **Gem Therapy.** Rhodochrosite's well-known for relieving anxiety, relaxing the muscles of the diaphragm area, and bringing oxygen into the system—all directly related to asthma.

A five-year-old boy and his mother went into Crystal Gardens, a gem shop that used to be in New York City. The boy picked up a piece of rhodochrosite and said, "Mommy, buy me this stone." The mother told her son to put it down and wait for her outside. Then she said to the shop's proprietor, "I need something for my son. He has a terrible case of asthma." As you may have guessed, the most appropriate stone for the young boy was the one he had picked out.

The shop owners tell that story to emphasize the point that we should follow our instincts and go with the stones we're drawn to.

Citrine is a beautiful yellow stone that's also said to help quell asthma attacks.

AFFIRMATION
Repeat this affirmation 10 times, first thing in the morning and each time you make a decision, no matter how insignificant the decision…

I welcome today as a day of independence. It's a choice that's right for me. I can now breathe easy.

BACK PAIN

It is estimated that 80% of all Americans have or will have at some time in their lives some kind of back problem, ranging from occasional discomfort to chronic back pain.

Many health professionals feel that the neuromuscular imbalance that triggers most chronic back pain may be an *emotional* problem rather than a *structural* one.

Dramatic positive changes can take place when one changes his or her attitude and mental frame of mind. Studies show, for instance, that falling in love can make back pain disappear. *Until you fall blissfully in love, try one or more of these substitutes...*

• **Sign up for Alexander Technique lessons.** Learn about it in the "It Does a Body Good" chapter, page 229, and you'll see why you should consider it. While you're at it, check out tai chi as well, page 274.

• **Say affirmations, starting with the one at the end of this section.**

Do whatever it takes to expand your thinking, enlarge your beliefs, give you a more optimistic outlook, put you in control of you and ultimately the result will be neuromuscular balance that will eliminate your back pain.

Meanwhile, here are some additional suggestions that can give you relief along the way.

For Relief from Back Pain

➤ **Cabbage Press.** Take a few cabbage leaves and steam them for 10 minutes, until they're limp. While the steamed cabbage leaves are cooling, lightly massage a little olive oil on the painful area of the back. As soon as possible,

without burning yourself, place the warm cabbage leaves on the oiled area. Cover with a heavy towel to keep in the heat, and stay that way for an hour. Then repeat the process with new cabbage leaves. After these two hours, you should feel some relief.

➤ **Herbal Capsules.** White willow bark capsules (available at health food stores) contain *salicylate*, which is the active anti-inflammatory ingredient in aspirin. Follow the recommended dosage on the label and be sure to take the capsules right *after* meals.

 CAUTION: Do NOT use white willow bark capsules if you have heartburn, gastritis, ulcers or esophagitis.

➤ **Foot Bath.** In Asia, it is believed that soaking your feet in a big basin of hot water for 20 to 30 minutes can bring relief from back pain and spasms. If you don't have a big basin, use two plastic shoe boxes (one for each foot).

➤ **Floor Relaxation.** When you have the feeling that your back is about to go out, you need to take the stress off that part of your body. Gather enough books to equal about a seven-inch stack and carefully lie down on the floor. Rest your head on the books and raise your knees so that your feet are flat on the floor, about a foot apart. Put your heels as close to your *tush* as possible. Now relax that way for 15 minutes. You might want to use this time to do a visualization and/or affirmations.

When 15 minutes has gone by, stand up by rolling over on your side and slowly lifting yourself by letting your hands and arms do most of the work, instead of putting the pressure on your back.

➤ **Reflexology.** If your back pain seems due to stress (and most back pain is caused by stress) trigger the reflexology point that connects to your spine. Starting with your left foot, use your thumbs to apply firm pressure along the inner sole from the big toe to the heel. Then do the same with your right foot. If relief isn't instant, repeat the procedure again, or until the pain eases.

➤ **Yarrow Tea.** Add a teaspoon of yarrow to a cup of just-boiled water. Let it steep for 10 minutes. Strain and drink a cup before each meal and a cup at bedtime. It can help pain fade away.

 NOTE: Yarrow tea has an unusual taste, so you may want to add honey.

➤ **Color Therapy.** If you have lower back problems, blue is for you. It represents sky and water and is a soothing, anti-inflammatory color. Wear a blue shirt or blouse. Surround yourself with blue things—use blue bed linens, a blue tablecloth, a blue glass or mug. If you're willing to treat yourself to some quiet time during the day, get a blue lightbulb, put it in a lamp, then completely relax under that lamp for 20 minutes. Consider saying an affirmation for at least part of that time.

Stay away from the red clothes in your wardrobe until your back is back to normal.

➤ **Gem Therapy.** Gemologist Connie Barrett had severe lower back pain. She went to a chiropractor, got an adjustment and was told to come back two days later. She was doubled over and could hardly walk out of his office. On her painful trip home, Connie decided to work with stones. *She used...*

● **Smoky quartz** which teaches pride in our physical bodies and physical existence. It's excellent for depression and fatigue.

● **Aventurine,** which is considered by many to be the best all-purpose healing stone. It is especially good for soothing the emotions and creating a feeling of balance and well-being.

● **Green tourmaline,** which is a stress reliever and strengthens the nervous system.

● **Hematite,** which increases self-esteem and helps ground a person. It also helps separate your emotions from those of others.

● **Eilat stone** (composed of azurite, chrysocolla, malachite and turquoise) helps us blend the various elements of our being peacefully and harmoniously.

Intermittently, Connie meditated with the stones and kept them on her back for periods at a time. Forty-eight hours later, when she returned to the chiropractor, she was standing up straight, feeling as though she had never had a problem. (We wonder why she even went back to the chiropractor.) See "Sources," page 311, for gem companies.

► **Ridiculous, Yet Worth a Try.** To ease back pain, sleep with a champagne cork under your mattress. The person who gave us this remedy swears by it. We are wondering whether that person was in the habit of emptying out the champagne bottle before the cork went under the mattress.

Commonsense Do's and Don'ts

► **Let the Shoe Designers Wear the High Heels!** Wear comfortable low- or medium-heeled shoes (this goes for men, too).

► **The Best Way to Lift.** If you have to lift something heavy, bend your knees, keep your back straight and hold that heavy something close to your body.

► **Push Things, Don't Pull Them,** particularly if they're big and heavy.

► **Sleep on Your Side** in the fetal position.

► **Don't Sleep on Your Stomach with your head on a pillow,** unless you raise your back by putting a pillow under your stomach.

► **Don't Sleep on a Mattress That Sags in the middle.** A plywood board between the mattress and box spring can prevent sagging.

► **Don't Cradle the Telephone in the crook of your neck** during long phone conversations. It can cause muscular tension all the way to your lower back.

A Helpful Tip

► **Nothing to Sneeze At.** If you have back trouble, brace yourself when you sneeze to avoid compounding the problem. If you're standing, bend your knees a little and put one hand on a nearby table. If nothing is nearby, then place your hand on your thigh. If you're seated, put your hand on a table or on your thigh. Okay, you're ready to "Achoo!"

Recommended Reading

► *Healing Back Pain: The Mind-Body Connection* by John E. Sarno, MD (Wellness Connection). We've been recommending this book in its many incarnations for years. It is excellent! Dr. Sarno believes that your pain is most probably caused by repressed emotions. It's a lot to take in and go through, but it can result in dramatic results...the elimination of pain! Dr. Sarno has helped thousands of people become pain free, including each of us.

AFFIRMATION

Repeat this affirmation at least 12 times a day—first thing in the morning, each time you handle money and last thing at night...

I let go of fear and replace it with a secure feeling, knowing everything I need is here for me now.

A Word from the Wise...

The Right Bed Can Ease Back Pain

People with back pain often think that a very firm mattress is best. Not true. In a study published in *The Lancet*, 313 individuals with low-back pain slept on either a firm or a medium-firm coil mattress. After 90 days, the participants with the medium-firm mattresses had less pain in bed, upon rising and during the day than those with firm mattresses. *Other misconceptions about beds and back pain…*

Misconception: Everyone with back pain feels the pain when he/she first wakes up—so you can't tell if the mattress is a problem or not.

Fact: Most back pain is mildest in the morning, before you get out of bed and begin moving. If you wake up stiff and sore, your mattress may be to blame. Try sleeping on a different mattress—in the guest room, at a friend's, in a hotel—and see if you notice an improvement when you get up.

Misconception: Heavier people with back pain need soft beds.

Fact: Everyone needs sufficient support during the night to keep the spine in a normal position. If the spine sinks into a sagging bed,

SOMETHING SPECIAL

An Incredible Back-Up!

The late Dr. Alvin Bakst was a thoracic and cardiovascular surgeon for 40 years and was one of the pioneers in heart surgery.

Performing thousands of surgeries while bending over the operating table, Dr. Bakst developed back problems that at times were incapacitating. After he rejected back surgery and stopped the medications, Dr. Bakst began researching the feasibility of a nonsurgical, drug-free method of pain relief.

The doctor's research led him to rediscover the ancient, Far Eastern technique of strategically placing strong, unipolar magnets on areas of the body affected by pain and discomfort. After strategically placing and using neodymium magnets on his own back, Dr. Bakst finally found total relief for his back pain.

He then designed and created his first magnetic back belt. Based on his design, Dr. Bakst applied for and received a United States Patent for Reducing Sensation in a Human Body Part Using Magnetism.

Magnatech Labs, Inc., founded by Dr. Bakst in 1994, has been dedicated to researching and developing effective methods of alleviating and eliminating pain in the body without the use of drugs or invasive medical procedures.

The product line includes a Magnetic Back Support, a Compact Back Device and the (more expensive) Super Back Belt. Consider the Super style if you have severe discomfort in the back area. The magnetic or "gauss" power is more than eight times stronger than the regular belt. This is the only belt on the market made with 28 high-powered neodymium unipolar magnets, strategically and anatomically positioned.

 CAUTION: Do NOT use these magnets if you wear a pacemaker or any implanted electronic device. Do NOT use if you are pregnant. Do NOT place next to charge cards with a magnetic strip. Do NOT place on a color TV or computer.

More information: Go to *www.drbakst magnetics.com* or call Magnatech Labs at 800-574-8111.

the muscles are strained. Heavier people and those who sleep on their backs tend to need firmer mattresses. Side and stomach sleepers need softer beds.

Misconception: A foam pad or an entire mattress made of foam helps relieve back pain.

Fact: There are two kinds of foam generally available—egg-crate and memory foam. Egg-crate foam creates a layer of softness but does not change the support beneath. Memory foam is sensitive to temperature and conforms to the body. However, there is no scientific evidence that either kind of foam reduces back pain.

Misconception: Adjustable beds can ease back pain.

Fact: Some adjustable beds are filled with air or water that can be pumped in or out. Other types have joints that allow parts of the bed to be propped at different angles. There are no authoritative studies showing that adjustable beds help reduce back pain.

Misconception: You can't tell in the store if the mattress is right for you.

Fact: Trying out a mattress in the store can help you determine if it's comfortable. Lie on each mattress for at least five minutes. Start on your back, without a pillow. Your hand should fit snugly in the small of your back. Lying on your side, you shouldn't notice significant pressure on your hips or shoulders. Choose a retailer that will allow you to return a mattress if it isn't comfortable. These include Sleepy's and 1800Mattress.com. (You may have to pay an exchange fee.)

Baljinder Bathla, MD, cofounder of Chicago Sports & Spine, a pain-management practice. He is certified in physical medicine, rehabilitation and pain management. His Web site is *www.chicagosportsspine.com.*

BLISTERS

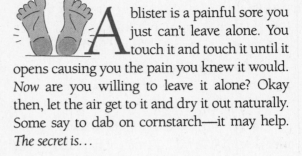

A blister is a painful sore you just can't leave alone. You touch it and touch it until it opens causing you the pain you knew it would. *Now* are you willing to leave it alone? Okay then, let the air get to it and dry it out naturally. Some say to dab on cornstarch—it may help. *The secret is...*

Blister Prevention

➤ **Grease Up.** When you're going to be walking a lot and/or when wearing new shoes, grease up the areas of the feet where you're most likely to get blisters. Use petroleum jelly or any *thick* ointment to help resist a blister. Or dab on egg white and let it thoroughly dry before putting on socks and shoes.

➤ **Wear Acrylic Socks.** They're layered, and instead of your feet absorbing the friction as you walk, the socks do it for you.

➤ **Or There's Lamb's Wool.** Ballerinas wrap it around their toes to soften the impact and to prevent blisters while on toe. Backpackers also use it for the same reasons.

If you're wondering why use expensive lamb's wool and not inexpensive absorbent cotton, it's because lamb's wool (available at pharmacies and at dance shops) is wonderfully soft and substantial. Absorbent cotton doesn't hold together and doesn't offer adequate protection. If a blister has already formed or has broken open, be sure to put a Band-Aid over the area before using the lamb's wool. You don't want lambs-wool fibers to get in the blister.

➤ **Plantain Plant.** Pick the leaves of the plantain plant and put them in your shoes. They should prevent blisters. It is also said that they will dry up blisters you already have.

Legend has it that the plantain plant sprang from the body of a maiden sitting by the roadside, waiting for her lover to return. That is supposedly why plantains grow at the edge of the road. You must have seen them hundreds of times. Visit *www.prairielandherbs.com/plantain.htm* for an excellent picture of the plant. Once you see it, it will be like seeing an old friend…who is green and has seed spikes!

BLOOD PRESSURE

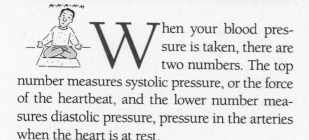

When your blood pressure is taken, there are two numbers. The top number measures systolic pressure, or the force of the heartbeat, and the lower number measures diastolic pressure, pressure in the arteries when the heart is at rest.

Are You Sure You Have High Blood Pressure?

Do you really have high blood pressure, or are you suffering from "white-coat apprehension"? White-coat apprehension, or fear of the doctor and nervousness at being tested for high blood pressure, quite often *raises* one's blood pressure.

There are several other factors that could make it seem as though you have high blood pressure. *For best results, keep these tips in mind…*

• **Do not drink a lot of liquids before going to the doctor.** Having more water in your system than is normal for you can cause your blood pressure to be higher than normal.

• **Drinking coffee right before having your blood pressure taken can also influence the reading.** Studies show that the caffeine in two to three cups of coffee can raise your blood pressure up to 15% within an hour. So, before your doctor's visit, no coffee…no

SOMETHING SPECIAL

Breathe Easy!

RESPeRATE is a nondrug portable electronic device that adapts to your unique breathing rate and pattern, and interactively guides you to reduce your breathing rate. Your blood pressure is lowered by gently relaxing constricted blood vessels through the power of your paced breathing. It is simple to use, takes 20 minutes a day and has been proven effective in helping lower blood pressure if used on a daily basis.

More information: To see a demonstration, go to *www.resperate.com*, or if you have questions, call 877-988-9388.

over-the-counter drugs that contain caffeine …no nasal decongestants.

• **Be sure your doctor has the proper-size cuff** if you're bigger or smaller than the average-sized adult. Using the wrong-size cuff can lead to an inaccurate reading. Ask about the size of the cuff in relation to your size. If the doctor poo-poos the fact that you need a large-sized or extra-small cuff, you may want to find a more responsible doctor.

• **One of every four people tested seemed to have high blood pressure,** according to a Canadian research project. But when tested again and again, those same people actually had normal pressure.

Ask the person who will take your blood pressure—doctor or nurse—to take your pressure after you've had a chance to calm down. If your pressure is high, ask for it to be taken again, at the end of your examination.

It's also a good idea to have your pressure taken the day after your doctor's appointment,

17

once you've *really* calmed down. There are some discount chains that have blood pressure machines in their pharmacy department. Or, if you promise not to drive yourself crazy taking your blood pressure every two minutes, you can buy an at-home blood pressure monitor. They're sold in discount-store pharmacy sections, or visit *www.omronhealthcare.com*.

When You're Sure You Have High Blood Pressure

If you are one of the estimated 70 million Americans with high blood pressure, it's time to do something about it.

Studies show that vegetarians have lower blood pressure than meat eaters. Studies also show that smoking cigarettes, drinking alcoholic

SOMETHING SPECIAL

Get a Grip!

Zona Plus is another nondrug medical device that has been clinically proven to help lower blood pressure.

A battery-powered, computer-controlled device that fits in the palm of your hand, Zona Plus takes you through a 12-minute therapy session five times a week. You will see a measurable drop in your resting systolic blood pressure after about four to five weeks and maximum benefit in six to eight weeks.

Zona Plus actually changes the physiology of your body. Zona Plus therapy leads to an increased production of nitric oxide, a powerful vasodilator, which relaxes blood vessels in your arterial system and allows blood to flow more freely.

We decided to try Zona Plus for ourselves. It's easy (the hardest part was opening the battery housing to insert the battery.) And it's a lot more convenient, less time-consuming and far less tiring than aerobic exercise. In fact, clinical studies consistently showed that Zona therapy, performed as recommended, is three to four times more effective at lowering blood pressure than 30 minutes of vigorous aerobic exercise performed three times a week. And there's no warm-up, you can do

it anywhere, anytime and it doesn't matter what you wear.

The science behind Zona Plus was first discovered when cardiopulmonary physiologist Dr. Ronald L. Wiley was working on an unrelated fighter-pilot problem (G-force blackout) for the Air Force. Using isometric handgrip therapy, Dr. Wiley not only solved the blackout problem, he also discovered that it offered an important side benefit—for pilots with slightly elevated blood pressure, the therapy actually lowered their blood pressure.

Working in several university laboratories over the next two decades, Dr. Wiley eventually developed the ideal isometric therapy to safely and effectively lower blood pressure. He then tested this therapy in multiple controlled studies conducted by physicians and cardiac rehabilitation centers, and found it produced dramatic results in just weeks.

More than 90% of people who use Zona Plus are able to lower their blood pressure naturally. If you use it properly—12 minutes a day, five days a week—for 60 days and you do not see a reduction in your blood pressure, the company will refund the purchase price.

More information: Visit *www.zona.com* or call 866-669-9662.

beverages and overeating can raise your blood pressure. Enough with the studies! *Let's concentrate on ways to lower your blood pressure…*

➤ **Some Basics.**

• **Start by cutting down on the amount of red meat you eat.** Each week reduce the number of times you have red meat meals. And remember, a portion should be the size of a deck of cards.

• **Stop smoking**…even if you don't have high blood pressure.

• **Is drinking alcohol that important to you?** Make one drink last an entire evening. Eventually, you may not even want that one drink. What? We're taking all the fun out of life? At least you'll have a life!

➤ **Avoid Being A-Salted.** The first thing a doctor tells a patient with high blood pressure is to cut down or eliminate salt. Dr. Mark Stibich, PhD, who writes about longevity for the Web site *www.about.com* has this clear explanation of how too much salt affects blood pressure levels: "Normally, the kidneys control the level of salt. If there is too much salt, the kidneys pass it into urine. But when our salt intake levels are very high, the kidneys cannot keep up and the salt ends up in our bloodstream. Salt attracts water. When there is too much salt in the blood, the salt draws more water into the blood. More water increases the volume of blood, which raises blood pressure."

While we require about 500 milligrams (mg) of salt for our body to function, most people have about 10 times that amount daily. People with high blood pressure should not exceed about 1,500 mg a day. Less is better!

To help keep your sodium count down if you use canned foods—beans and vegetables in particular—put the contents of the can in a

■ Recipes ■

Salt Substitutes

When it's appropriate—according to the foods or drinks being prepared—lemon juice can be used as a good substitute for salt. *You can also add spice to your life with McCormick & Company's three salt-substitute recipes…*

• **For salads or salt shakers:**
  2 teaspoons thyme
  2 teaspoons ground savory
  1 teaspoon sage
  2 teaspoons basil
  1 tablespoon marjoram

• **For soups, stews, poultry or pot roast:**
  1 tablespoon thyme
  1 teaspoon sage
  2 teaspoons rosemary
  1 tablespoon marjoram

• **For cooked vegetables, beef or added table seasoning:**
  1 teaspoon celery seeds
  1 tablespoon marjoram
  1 tablespoon thyme
  1 tablespoon basil

Mix ingredients for the blend you choose and grind together in a blender or using a mortar and pestle. Store in a tightly covered dark glass jar, and be sure to label.

strainer and rinse under cold water for at least a minute. This can reduce the salt content by more than 50%.

At mealtimes, add salt after you prepare your food. That way, you'll use half as much salt without compromising taste.

► **Kiwi and Company.** A kiwi a day helps keep high blood pressure away. This furry little fruit is rich in potassium and is a natural diuretic—two reasons people with high blood pressure should eat them as well as other foods high in potassium, such as ripe bananas, raw or steamed leafy green vegetables, oranges, avocadoes and unsalted sunflower seeds.

► **Sing Hallelujah! Come On, Get Happy.** University researchers have found that people's emotional states directly affect how high or low their blood pressure goes. When you're feeling happy, your systolic blood pressure goes down; when you're filled with anxiety, your diastolic pressure rises. Happy is better! And the good part is that your emotional state is entirely up to you. Abraham Lincoln summed it up best when he said, "Most people are about as happy as they make up their mind to be."

► **Hopeful Hawthorn.** The hawthorn tree is a symbol of hope. Drinking hawthorn berry tea twice a day—in the morning and afternoon or evening—*hopefully* can help lower your blood pressure. Give it a few weeks to see results. Hawthorn is available in several forms (powdered, cut or whole), and also in capsules. Health food stores should have a selection.

► **Louisiana "Sole" Food.** This is a regional folk remedy that came to us from a woman in Louisiana, where Spanish moss grows on trees. Take pieces of Spanish moss, sometimes referred to as "old man's beard," and walk around with them in your shoes. This may sound far-fetched, but it's said to bring down one's blood pressure.

► **Aromatherapy.** Dr. Alan R. Hirsch, founder and neurological director of the Smell & Taste Treatment and Research Foundation (*www.smellandtaste.org*), says that some scents can significantly decrease blood pressure. The smell of the seashore is one, lavender is another, and the seemingly most effective is the smell of spiced apples. These scents are available in spray form at health food stores.

► **High or Low Blood Pressure.** Aloe vera juice (available at health food stores) is said to strengthen blood vessels and stabilize blood pressure. Drink an ounce after breakfast and an ounce after dinner.

AFFIRMATION

This is a longer-than-most affirmation. It's an important one and should be repeated at least 10 times, starting first thing in the morning, and every hour that begins with the letter "t"—ten, twelve, two, three—and last thing at night...

I take comfort in knowing that where I am is exactly where I should be, and whatever is best for me will come to me. I love myself and I love my life.

BODY ODOR

For some time now, there has been lots of speculation and research on the long-term side effects of antiperspirants and deodorants that contain aluminum and zirconium.

Incidentally, an *antiperspirant* is classified by the Food and Drug Administration (FDA) as an over-the-counter *drug* because it retards the flow of perspiration. A *deodorant*, on the other hand has no physiological effect and is therefore considered a *cosmetic*.

Until we know for sure about those side effects, you might have more peace of mind using these nonchemical alternatives...

➤ **Baking Soda for That Odor.** Baking soda is an inexpensive deodorant. Some people combine one part baking soda to two parts cornstarch or rice starch. You can also add a dried herb to give it a pleasant scent.

Sprinkle the mixture on your underarms right after a bath or shower and/or before getting dressed in the morning. It's our deodorant of choice, and it works.

➤ **Believe It or Not, Vinegar.** Vinegar is effective protection against bacteria and body odor. Mix distilled white vinegar with an equal amount of water. Then dip a cotton ball in the mixture and dab on. The vinegar smell will disappear within minutes.

➤ **When Smell is Baddish, Use Radish.** Juice up a few bunches of radishes. If you don't have a juicer, put the radishes in a food processor, then squeeze the juice through a piece of cheesecloth. Pour the juice into a jar, refrigerate it and use it daily as an underarm deodorant.

➤ **Fennel Tea-riffic!** Fennel tea is a deodorant that works from the inside out. Boil one teaspoon of fennel seeds (available at health food stores) in a cup of water. Simmer for 15 to 20 minutes. When it's cool, after at least five minutes, strain and drink. Have fennel tea in the morning and late afternoon. It should promote odorless perspiration.

➤ **Nuke with a Cuke.** Cucumber can be used to wash and deodorize body parts. Cut a big succulent cuke in quarters and wash your perspired areas with it. Let your skin dry naturally. Cucumbers are rich in magnesium, which is said to be a natural deodorant.

➤ **Get Stoned.** If you prefer to buy a natural deodorant, check out the Thai Crystal Deodorant Stone (available at health food stores and pharmacies). This is a perfect example of a *new alternative product* that's really *age-old.*

For centuries, the people of Thailand have been using this natural crystal as deodorant. It is made from potassium sulfate and other mineral salts, crystallized over a period of months, then shaped by hand and smoothed. This deodorant does not contain perfumes, emulsifiers, propellants, aluminum chlorhydrate or any other harmful chemicals.

The Deodorant Stone leaves an invisible layer of protection that prevents odor-causing bacteria from forming wherever you put it on your body—underarms and feet, too.

Just one Thai Crystal Deodorant Stone is equivalent to about six cans of deodorant spray. That means the average person will be able to use it for close to a year.

➤ **Glad Rags.** Clothing can play a part in preventing or promoting odors. One hundred percent cotton is best.

Synthetic fabrics seem to stop the circulation of air, causing you to perspire more than usual. Certain synthetics, usually in conjunction with the fabric's dyes, produce a strong, unpleasant smell as soon as you start to perspire. You'll know soon enough which ones they are when you wear them. Again, stick with cotton whenever possible.

BRUISES

However you got that nasty bruise, we have got some remedies for you to try…

➤ **Black Eye.** Every couple hours, gently massage castor oil on the delicate eye area. It is said to ease the pain, lessen the swelling and minimize the discoloration.

Or: Get out the ice! Put the cubes in a wet washcloth or plastic bag and place it on the eye area.

No ice? Then use a package of frozen vegetables, or that movie cliché, a steak. Just make sure it's very cold and is wrapped in plastic wrap so that it doesn't touch your skin.

Find a routine that's comfortable, e.g. on for five minutes, off for 15 minutes. The cold ice, veggies or steak should numb the pain and keep down the swelling and discoloration.

➤ **Black-and-Blue Mark Remover.** This is an amazing Chinese remedy for getting rid of a black-and-blue mark. You'll need an egg and a large coin that's mostly silver. Quarters, half dollars and dollars minted before 1965 are 90% silver. Half-dollars from 1965 to 1969 are 40% silver. Quarters and dollars minted in 1965 and later have no silver in them.

Hard-boil the egg and peel off the shell. Then hold the egg vertically and slip the coin into the egg vertically until the edge of the coin is flush with the egg. While still warm, but cool enough not to burn the skin, place the egg with the coin on the black-and-blue mark. Leave it there for at least a half-hour while it somehow draws out the discoloration of the bruise.

➤ **Preventing Black-and-Blue Marks.** As soon as you bruise yourself, wet the fingers of one hand and dip them in the sugar bowl. Then rigorously massage the injured area with your sugar-coated fingers. Make sure you reach the outer edges of the bruise. This will reduce the scope of the broken capillaries and help prevent a black-and-blue mark from forming.

Or: Immediately after you bruise yourself, take a couple of tablespoons of arrowroot, add a little water to make a paste, and rub it on the area. When it dries and crumbles off, there should be no sign of a bruise. If you're not famil-

iar with arrowroot, it's a starch used in cooking as a thickener, and can usually be found in the supermarket baking section.

➤ **A Slammed Finger or Toe.** Oh, the pain! If part of the finger is dangling, or bone is jutting out, call 9-1-1 for emergency help.

If it's just a nasty, painful slam, use CPR. No, not Cardiopulmonary Resuscitation. Our CPR stands for **C**old, **P**ressure and **R**aise it. As soon as possible after the slam, dunk the digit into ice or ice-cold water. If there's bleeding, this will stop the bleeding, internally as well as externally. Keep it there until the *cold* becomes painful—not much longer than half-a-minute. Then, for 30 seconds put *pressure* on the finger by squeezing it, also to help stop the bleeding, but not tight enough to stop all circulation. While you're squeezing the injured finger, *raise* it above your head to slow the flow of blood. Repeat the entire one-minute procedure over and over—two, three, four dozen times. It may save you from pain, swelling and a black fingernail.

➤ **Bruising and Swelling.** Steep a heaping tablespoon of oregano in a cup of just-boiled water for 10 minutes. Strain out and save the liquid, then put the moist oregano in cheesecloth and make a poultice. Place it on the bruised area. When the oregano dries up, moisten it with the warm liquid. An oregano poultice can relieve the pain and help bring down the swelling.

Or: Make a grated raw potato poultice and put it on the bruised area. Within two hours, there should be considerably less and maybe no soreness.

➤ **Bruised and Swollen Knees.** Finely grate raw cabbage—enough to cover the whole knee. Wrap it securely in cheesecloth and place it on the knee. Then wrap plastic wrap around the knee, and around that, wrap a big towel.

Keep the cabbage wrap on as much of the day as possible. Change the cabbage every night before you go to bed and sleep with it that way. There should be great improvement by the fourth day.

AFFIRMATION

The second you get a bruise, do whatever you can to ease the pain and prevent swelling, while repeating this affirmation over and over, at least two dozen times…

I recognize my goodness and my bright inner light. I love me.

BURNS

Burns are categorized in degrees. It is easy to remember the degree of severity of each if you think of it this way…

• **First-degree burns damage the *first* layer of skin.** They're minor burns that don't blister.

• **A second-degree burn damages the first and *second* layers of skin.** They blister and can be serious. *Don't break the blisters*. It's Mother Nature's bandage. When the blisters break, there's danger of infection. If that's the case, you need professional health care.

• **Third-degree burns are certainly serious.** Obviously, they're deeper than first- and second-degree burns. Call for professional help immediately. Meanwhile, get the burned area under gently running cold water. If you need to go for help, put cold water on the burned area, then carefully cover it with the cleanest cloth available.

Now that you know what to do for second- and third-degree burns, look over the

page and select the ingredient(s) that you have available to use as a remedy for a minor, first-degree burn…

 CAUTION: NEVER put ice on a burn. It can do more harm than good. According to the Mayo Clinic, ice can damage the skin and may even cause frostbite.

➤ **Aloe Vera.** The classic folk remedy for first-degree burns is the gelatinous juice from the succulent aloe vera plant. This perennial plant is a potted first-aid kit that's easy to grow. It doesn't need direct sunlight or much water.

The aloe plant is inexpensive and can usually be found wherever plants are sold. The most effective juice is from a plant that's at least two to three years old and has leaves with little spike-like bumps on the edges.

If you burn yourself and happen to have an aloe plant, cut off the top of one of the lower leaves. Either peel the skin off the leaf to get at the gel, or squeeze out the healing gel and spread it on the burned area.

Aloe gel is available in health food stores. It's a good idea to keep a bottle of it in your refrigerator for burns and other uses described in this book.

➤ **Carrots.** Grate carrots and wrap them in cheesecloth or a white handkerchief to make a poultice. Then place the poultice on the burn. If you prefer using fresh carrot juice, soak gauze or a white washcloth with the juice and apply it to the burn. Either one of these treatments should draw out the heat, lessen the pain and promote healing.

➤ **Brown Paper Bag and Vinegar.** Cut a piece of paper from a clean brown paper bag, dip it in distilled white vinegar, and apply it to the burn.

➤ **Mushrooms.** The fungus among us can help heal a burn. Put mushroom slices on the affected area.

➤ **Radishes.** Throw cleaned, cold radishes into a blender or food processor and purée them. Place the purée pulp on cheesecloth or a white handkerchief to form a poultice and put it on the burned area.

➤ **Baking Soda and Egg White.** As soon as you burn yourself, mix enough baking soda with the white of an egg to make it a creamy solution. The sooner you apply it to the burn, the better chance you have of preventing it from blistering.

➤ **Burned Fingertips.** Have you ever reached for the wrong side of a plugged-in iron? Or, how often have you touched a too-hot-something in the oven? On the stove?

A friend of ours shared Grandma Bessie Mae's remedy with us for burned fingertips—it's one of our favorites. Simply hold your earlobe—place your thumb on the back side of the lobe and the burned fingertips on the front side of the lobe. Stay that way for one minute. It works like magic.

➤ **Oil Splatter Burn.** Honey has very healing enzymes. Put a thin layer of honey on the burned area.

Another Type of Burn

➤ **Hot Pepper Mouth Burning.** After you've eaten hot peppers and your mouth feels like it's on fire, rinse your mouth with milk or yogurt or sour cream. It should take about seven minutes for the burning to subside. If you don't have any of these dairy products, chew a mouthful of white bread. (If you don't have white bread, use sourdough, rye or whatever type of bread you have.)

AFFIRMATION

Repeat this affirmation over and over while treating the burn...

I am calm and cool and surrounded by healing energy.

CANKER SORES (MOUTH ULCERS)

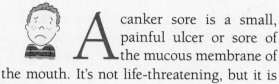

A canker sore is a small, painful ulcer or sore of the mucous membrane of the mouth. It's not life-threatening, but it is painful.

About one in every five Americans gets canker sores—mostly when they're between the ages of 10 and 20, and twice as many females as males—and no one seems to know for sure what causes these viral infection flare-ups. *Educated guesses are...*

- **Vitamin deficiency,** specifically B-12, iron and folic acid; or vitamin C intolerance.
- **Excess acid from foods like tomatoes and vinegar.**
- **Food allergies from eggs, milk, cabbage, turnips, pork, coffee and tea, citrus fruits and walnuts.**
- **Emotional stress.**
- **Tissue injury.**
- **A sharp tooth surface or dental appliance like braces.**

NOTE: After a month, if the canker sore has not gone away, see a dentist.

Canker Sore Prevention

➤ **With a Brush.** A fascinating experiment was conducted on people who get canker sores. Pinpricks were made in their mouths and that's where the canker sores formed—on the exact spots where the pinpricks were made.

Use a soft toothbrush to brush your teeth so that you don't scratch or pierce the inside of your mouth where canker sores form. This can help cut down your chances of getting these painful mouth ulcers.

➤ **With Toothpaste.** Check your toothpaste for the ingredient *sodium lauryl sulfate* or *SLS.* Studies show that canker sore sufferers are up to 80% less likely to get a breakout if they use toothpaste that does not have SLS in it. If your toothpaste has SLS, replace it immediately with a purer product. We use Tooth Soap (*www.toothsoap.com*) because it has ingredients we trust.

Canker Sore Remedies

➤ **Apple Remedy.** Eat an apple after every meal and let its potassium, pectin and other healing-promoting properties clear up your canker sore in three or four days. If you don't have organic apples, check "Healthful Hints," page 283, for how to clean fruit so you can eat the peel and reap the benefits from it without any of the down sides (and pesticides).

➤ **Relieve the Pain.** Gently rinse your mouth with a mixture of one teaspoon of baking soda in one-half cup of warm water. This rinse can help neutralize bacteria and relieve pain.

➤ **Myrrh for Sure.** Students of the Bible or Scrabble players are familiar with myrrh. It's available at health food stores and some pharmacies, in powder form, capsules and in a tincture (an alcohol solution). The latter seems to be most effective for canker sores. Dip a cotton swab in the tincture and dab the center of the sore with it. It may smart for a second, but after that, the pain will be a thing of the past, and soon the sore will be too.

➤ **Speed the Healing.** Touch the center of the sore with a styptic pencil to help hasten the healing.

25

➤ **Mustard Power.** Moisten the tip of your just-washed index finger with water. Dip it into dry mustard powder. Then hold the finger on the sore for five minutes. Do this three times a day. It's a painful treatment, but it works. The canker sore should be gone within 48 hours. If you let a canker sore run its normal course, it can take up to three weeks to clear.

NOTE: To put mustard powder on a canker sore, instead of using your finger to hold the powder in place, it may be easier and more efficient to put a dab of peanut butter on a little piece of bread and then put the mustard powder on the peanut butter. Herbs and spices stick to peanut butter better than to one's finger.

AFFIRMATION

Repeat this affirmation first thing in the morning, last thing at night, and each time a painful throb of the canker sore seems to be pounding on your heart…

I release all regrets now, and enjoy the best things in life.

CELIAC DISEASE

 Celiac disease is a chronic, hereditary, autoimmune digestive disorder, characterized by a toxic reaction to gluten. Gluten is a protein found in wheat, barley, rye and contaminated oats.

According to Beyond Celiac (formerly the National Foundation for Celiac Awareness) (*www.celiaccentral.org*), one out of every 141 Americans has celiac disease. Because of the many symptoms that manifest in different ways

for each individual, 95% of celiacs are undiagnosed or misdiagnosed with other conditions.

Since we realize the importance of *awareness*, we've included this entry in our book, even though we don't have remedies for this condition. Right now, the only existing treatment for celiac is a 100% gluten-free diet.

We do offer good advice and a recommendation. First the advice—if you have a history of digestive problems, and suspect that you may have celiac disease, the first step is to go to your doctor and have the celiac panel. It's a blood test, and while it cannot give a conclusive celiac diagnosis, it can rule out celiac disease, or determine where you are on the risk spectrum.

If celiac is not ruled out, your doctor will probably proceed with an endoscopy and small tissue biopsy.

Now the recommendation. Anyone who has celiac, or is in the process of being diagnosed, or anyone who wants to be gluten-free, should know about *The G Free Diet: A Gluten-Free Survival Guide* by Elisabeth Hasselbeck (Center Street), former co-host of ABC-TV's *The View*.

For years, Elisabeth couldn't figure out what was making her sick. She asked doctors and consulted nutritionists, but no one seemed to have any answers. It wasn't until she was a contestant on the TV reality show *Survivor* and spent 39 days living off the land in the outback of Australia that her symptoms disappeared, and she felt good. Elisabeth realized that there was something she was eating at home that caused her to feel awful.

When she returned home, she was determined to pinpoint the food that made her sick. We'll spare you the details of all that she endured. Finally, in 2002, five years after the onset of her symptoms, she stumbled upon some information about gluten intolerance and celiac disease, and knew that was her problem—gluten, the binding element in wheat.

By eliminating it from her diet, she is able to enjoy a completely normal, active, healthy life.

And so, Elisabeth wrote an excellent, user-friendly book, *The G Free Diet: A Gluten-Free Survival Guide*. It tells you everything you need to know to start living a gluten-free life, including defining gluten, where to find it, how to read food labels, targeting gluten-free products, creating shopping lists, sharing recipes and managing gluten-free living with family and friends.

Elisabeth says that anyone can enjoy the health benefits from a gluten-free diet—from weight loss and increased energy to even the alleviation of the conditions of autism.

CHILDHOOD AILMENTS

Infants—Newborn to Age Two

 uddle, cradle, caress, hold, hug and love your baby! Studies show that babies who are hugged and loved are healthier, grow faster, cry less and are more active.

> **CAUTION:** We know you know this, but we couldn't sleep nights if we didn't say it anyway—*check with your pediatrician* before trying any of the following remedies on your baby.

➤ **Air Travel.** In an airplane, takeoff and landing can be particularly painful to baby's sensitive small ears. To help make the flight as comfortable as possible, especially during takeoff and landing, feed your baby a bottle of whatever he/she prefers to drink. The constant swallowing can help equalize ear pressure.

➤ **Colds/Chest Congestion.** In a pan, combine one slice of white bread with a quarter-cup of milk and a pinch of catnip. Heat it for a minute or two. Then put it in a white cotton sock. Make sure it's cool enough to put on the baby's chest to help clear up the congestion and the cold.

➤ **Cradle Cap.** Puncture a vitamin E capsule, squeeze out the oil, and gently massage it on the baby's scaly scalp. If one application doesn't clear up the condition, repeat the treatment the next day.

➤ **Low-Fat Diets.** Children who are under two years old should not be on a low-fat diet, even when it comes to milk. In other words, skim milk or low-fat milk should not be fed to your baby or toddler. A fat-restricted diet can lower their defenses against gastrointestinal infections and hamper normal growth and development.

➤ **Honey a No-No.** NEVER give honey to a child under one year old. The spores can cause botulism in babies.

Colic

There are dozens of reasons and any number of combinations of reasons that cause colic. There are also many treatments or combinations of treatments for it. Use that inner voice to help you decide which would work best for your baby.

➤ **Nursing Schedule.** If you are nursing, you may be feeding the baby too often, not allowing enough time for proper digestion. Try for longer intervals between nursing sessions and see if that makes a difference.

➤ **Cow's Milk.** If baby is on cow's milk, add one teaspoon of acidophilus (available at health food stores) to the bottle. Make sure the label says there are one to two billion viable acidophilus cells.

➤ **Vacuum.** The noise from a vacuum cleaner may calm the colicky baby, especially if you vacuum while carrying your child in a front carrier. Even if your baby doesn't stop fussing, at least you'll have a clean home.

➤ **Sweet Onion Water.** Put a small slice of onion in a half-cup of water and let it boil for a minute. Then add a quarter-teaspoon of sugar and let it cool. Take out the onion and give the sugared onion water to the baby. Within a half hour the colic may be gone.

➤ **No Noise Is Good Noise.** Turn your radio to a station that's not broadcasting but still has the dead-air sound called *white noise.* Or try turning on the stove fan. This white noise has been known to calm colicky kids.

➤ **Take a Drive.** If you're really desperate for a break from the crying, buckle baby up in his/her car seat and go for a drive. The vibration and hum of the car works like magic.

➤ **Dill Seed Tea.** This has been known to relieve colic and prevent it from recurring. Prepare the dill seed (available at health food stores) by boiling a half-teaspoon in water. Simmer for 15 to 20 minutes. Stir, then strain. When it's cool enough, give the baby two to four ounces of the dill tea.

➤ **Extra Virgin Olive Oil (EVOO).** Heat up a teaspoon of EVOO. Making sure it's warm, not hot, massage the oil on the baby's stomach in a gentle, soothing, clockwise motion. Next swaddle a towel around the oily midsection and for extra relief, bring the baby's knees up toward the midsection. If the baby seems comfortable and happier that way, keep him in that position for a few minutes.

Diaper Rash

➤ **Bottoms Up!** There are harmless bacteria that live on skin and feed on *urea,* the nitrogen that's in urine. Their waste product is ammonia, which causes diaper rash. These bacteria are *anaerobic.* That means that oxygen kills them. When babies are bundled up with a diaper and diaper cover, air can't get in and so the bacteria thrive, producing ammonia, which, as you now know, causes diaper rash. The answer is to let air get at the baby's skin. That means, lose the plastic covering! Treat a severe case of diaper rash by letting the baby romp around bare-bottom as much as possible, until the condition clears up.

➤ **Flour Power.** There's an old folk remedy for diaper rash, and if it worked way back when, there's no reason it shouldn't work now. Pour three cups of flour in a heavy fry pan, over a medium-to-high flame. Stir it with a wooden spoon until it turns a darkish brown, without burning. Bottle it and use it in place of talcum powder every time you change baby's diaper.

If you don't have flour for the remedy above, and you do have corn starch, put corn starch on the diaper. It can help make baby more comfortable and clear up the rash, too.

Diarrhea

➤ **Vinegar.** Lots of classic folk remedies require that an ingredient be placed on the soles of the feet. Since the pores on the bottom of a baby's feet are four times larger than anywhere else on the body, you can see how fast-acting an appropriate application might be.

One remedy is to smear the soles of baby's feet with distilled white vinegar. If the condition isn't cleared up in a couple of hours, smear the soles one more time.

➤ **Carob.** Carob has also been used for ages to fight bouts of diarrhea—in adults as well as children. Add one teaspoon of carob powder to baby's water bottle or to applesauce. Carob is sweet and baby will like it. If diarrhea doesn't stop right away, continue the treatment throughout the day. Don't overdo it. Too much carob can cause constipation.

➤ **Lime Juice.** Add a half-teaspoon of fresh lime juice to two ounces of warm water, and if the baby will drink it, the diarrhea may quickly disappear.

Hiccups

➤ **Seeing Red.** Take a little piece of red thread—it must be red—and wad it up in your mouth. Put the wadded red thread on your baby's forehead and the hiccups will stop. Have we ever lied to you?

➤ **Gem Therapy.** To stop the baby's hiccups, put a piece of rhodochrosite (available at gem stores or see "Sources," page 311) on baby's tummy for a few minutes. Be sure to place the gem gently and watch carefully. Better the hiccups than getting scratched by a stone.

Teething

➤ **Cold Cure.** Cold numbs baby's painful, swollen little gums. Let the baby chew on a frozen bagel. The bagel lasts longer than a mushy teething biscuit and can help relieve the pain.

➤ **Teething Misconception.** Teething does not cause a fever. If your baby is running a fever higher than 101°F, chances are the baby is sick, not just teething.

Children—Ages Two to 12
Asthma

➤ **Breathing Exercise.** Children who use the muscles of the shoulders and chest to breathe are not breathing in a relaxed way. It's important for asthmatic children to learn to do deep breathing so that they can be and feel more relaxed. It can go a long way to reduce the frequency and severity of asthma attacks.

The information below has been adapted from *Controlling Asthma* by the American Lung Association...

If you aren't sure how your child is breathing, try this—ask him/her to lie down with his back on the floor. Knees should be bent, feet on the floor and arms at the sides. Place a book just above the belly button and ask your child to breathe deeply a few times.

As air is taken in, if breathing is relaxed and deep, the belly should swell out like a balloon. As air is exhaled, the belly should go flat. The book will move up and down with the deep breathing motions, or it may fall off. The chest should remain motionless.

If breathing is shallow (the book doesn't move much), your child is filling and emptying only the top part of the lungs. By learning how to fill the lungs from the bottom and exhale completely, your child should feel more relaxed and breathe more easily. The following exercise can really help.

If the doctor agrees, your child should do the exercise for five minutes every day. It can be done lying down, sitting or standing.

Start by asking your child to put his hand just above his belly button to feel the motion of the breathing.

Next, tell your child to think of the chest and belly area as a container for air. As your child breathes in through the nose, tell him to

29

slowly fill the bottom of the container first and to keep filling it until the belly feels puffed out and swollen like a balloon. His hand can feel this and will move with the motion.

Then ask your child to exhale calmly through the mouth as slowly as possible. Emphasize that the container must be completely empty and the stomach as flat as it can be before slowly inhaling again.

To complete the exercise, repeat the inhale and exhale process 12 times.

(Adult asthmatics can also benefit from this deep-breathing exercise.)

Autism

See "Celiac Disease," page 26.

Bed-Wetting Remedies

➤ **Give Your Honey Honey.** A teaspoon of raw honey at bedtime can help your child sleep better and wake up with a dry bed. Be sure the honey is raw and, if possible, from a local source.

 CAUTION: NEVER give honey to a child under one year old. The spores can cause botulism in babies.

➤ **Got a Minute?** That is how long it takes to apply acupressure, which can eliminate bed-wetting. With your palm facing you, look at your pinky. See the two lines that separate the two joints? Those are the acupressure points. At bedtime, when you're about to tuck in your child, explain exactly what you're doing, as you take his pinkies and, with your thumbnails, put pressure on each of those four lines for 30 seconds each. Take special care if your nails are especially long.

➤ **No-Nos for Bed Wetters.** For dinner and until bedtime, do not give carrots to your child who has a bed-wetting problem. Carrots are a diuretic that seems to have a powerful negative effect on bed-wetters.

Another no-no is television. According to research conducted in Japan, watching TV before going to bed, particularly watching violent shows, promotes bed-wetting. It is suggested that the child be assured some peace of mind for at least an hour before bedtime. That means no TV, no loud rock music and certainly no violent video games. Quality time with a parent is best.

 NOTE: Bed-wetting can be caused by food allergies, so think about getting your child tested.

Lice

It happens, and it's no reflection on the care you give your child. *Here are three remedies, all using oil...*

➤ **Tea Tree Oil.** Get rid of the lousy lice by adding 20 drops of tea tree oil to your child's shampoo. Shampoo the hair and wait 10 minutes before thoroughly rinsing. Repeat the procedure in a week.

 CAUTION: Be sure to keep tea tree oil out of your child's eyes.

➤ **Coconut Oil.** Add two teaspoons of coconut oil to your child's shampoo. Wash the hair fastidiously, then rinse and wash and rinse one more time. Put a towel turban-style around your child's head and leave it on for a half hour. Once you remove the towel, comb the hair with a nit comb. And again, wash the hair with the shampoo/coconut oil mixture and thoroughly rinse.

➤ **Severe Case of Lice.** If you've tried various remedies and nothing has helped, you may need to smother the lice with this long, overnight process that usually works after everything else has failed. If you and your child are up to it, you'll need olive oil, plastic wrap, a plastic shower cap, three clean towels, gentle shampoo, a nit comb, a mixing bowl and rubber gloves.

Have your child sit down—the bathroom is probably the best place—put a towel around his shoulders, and put on the rubber gloves. Work a generous amount of olive oil through your child's hair. More is better. Once all of the hair and head are saturated with the oil, cover the head with plastic wrap, making sure all of the hair is tucked under the plastic. Then cover the plastic wrap with the shower cap. Finish it off by tightly wrapping a clean towel around your child's head, tucking it in so that it will stay in place overnight.

Put another towel on your child's pillow, and have him sleep on it. In the morning, reseat your child, remove the towel and put it on his shoulders. Remove the shower cap and the plastic wrap. (You may want to put on rubber gloves again.) Use the mixing bowl to catch whatever stuff (dead lice and oil) comes off as you comb-comb-comb your child's hair with the nit comb.

When there's no more to comb out, wash his hair with gentle shampoo once or twice, or more, until the hair seems clean.

If you didn't smother all of the nits and lice, you may have to repeat the procedure in a day or two.

More Childhood Matters

➤ **Chicken Pox.** To soothe chicken pox sores and promote scarless healing, let a cup of bran steep in just-boiled water until cool enough to touch. Strain out the water and put the soggy bran in cheesecloth. Tie it securely so the bran doesn't fall out and become messy. Then let the cheesecloth sit on the sores for 10 seconds. Once you've patted all the sores, rewet the bran and repeat the process. Do this several times a day. It can really help.

Or, stop the chicken pox itching and prevent scarring with pea water. Buy half a pound of peas, shell them, put them in a pint of water and let them boil for about five minutes. When it cools, strain out the peas and sponge down your child with the liquid. If it stops the itching, continue the process a few more times until the itching completely subsides.

➤ **A Virus-Based Cold.** Antibiotics will not help the common cold if it is viral...and most colds are caused by a virus. (An antibiotic would be appropriate only if there is a bacterial infection, along with the cold.)

You may want to try a homeopathic remedy for your cold. Homeopathic remedies are safe, effective, almost fun to take and are available at health food stores. (To obtain a better understanding of homeopathy, check it out in "Today's Alternative Treatments and Remarkable Age-Old Therapies," page xi.)

Use a 6X potency, three to four pellets at a time, three to four times throughout the day, for a few days.

Match the symptom with the pill...

• **Thick mucus secretions**—*Kali muriaticum.*

• **Runny nose**—*Allium cepa* (onion).

• **Influenza and neck stiffness**—*Kali carbonicum.*

• **Red face, dry throat and throbbing headache**—*Belladonna.*

• **Feeling week or in the first stage of inflammation**—*Ferrum phosphoricum* (iron phosphate).

• **An abrupt onset, fear and anxiety around the illness, restlessness and no sweating**—*Aconite*. If sweating begins, stop Aconite.

 CAUTION: Keep your homeopathic remedies away from any appliance that has an electromechanical field, like refrigerators, microwaves, cell phones, etc. Homeopathic remedies are considered an energetic medicine. Other strong electromechanical fields can "knock off" the energy of the homeopathic remedies. Homeopathic remedies will not work on a patient who is going for radiation treatments for this reason.

Also, when using homeopathic remedies, do NOT drink coffee or have strong aromatic substances like mints, including mint toothpaste, at the same time. Doing so will make homeopathic treatment ineffective.

➤ **Allergy Helper.** Teddy bears as well as other cuddly creatures are magnets for dust mites that can trigger allergic reactions such as asthma attacks. To kill dust mites, simply put the stuffed toy in a plastic bag and leave it in the freezer for 24 hours once a week. Explain to your child that her stuffed toy joined *Stars on Ice* and must be "on ice" every Monday or whenever.

➤ **Constipation.** Aside from using the adult constipation remedies on page 43, in smaller doses of course, depending on the age and size of your child, you might also try rubbing his stomach with warm olive oil. Use a clockwise circular motion for about five minutes. Then wash it off with warm water.

 CAUTION: If your child's constipation is more often than *occasional,* consult your pediatrician or other health care professional.

SOMETHING SPECIAL

What's Nu?

Occasional constipation is common in children during toilet training, or the toddler years, or during the stress of going to school. Rather than give your child laxatives or fiber products that are loaded with artificial, chemical and other questionable ingredients, you can give them a fiber-filled NuGo Bar. They come in an appealing variety of flavors, and are an all-natural, effective way to help with the challenge of your child's occasional constipation.

The American Heart Association Eating Plan recommends that children older than two get the majority of their calories from complex carbohydrates high in fiber. They recommend the "age plus five" formula to figure dietary fiber amounts for young children. For example, a six-year-old should eat six (their age) plus five grams (g) of fiber, which equal 11 g of fiber daily. As a child consumes up to 1,500 calories daily, he or she can tolerate 25 g or more of dietary fiber.

Toss a NuGo Bar in the lunch box, or have it handy as a snack. Even if your child does not have occasional constipation, this treat is a safe, delicious way for your child, and you too, to actually enjoy getting a dozen grams of dietary fiber.

More information: For stores in your area that carry NuGo Bars, visit *www.nugofiber.com* and click on "Find a Store" or purchase online.

 CAUTION: If your child has any sensitivity to wheat, psyllium, peanuts/tree nuts, do NOT give him/her a NuGo Bar.

➤ **Hiccups.** When your child gets the hiccups, tell him to form a gun with each of his hands. If you don't understand what we mean, it's okay, kids know how to do that. Next, tell the child to stretch out his arms and point the two guns at each other (in other words, the two index fingers should be facing one another). Finally, tell the child to slowly bring the guns together as close as they can get without touching. By the time that's done, the hiccups should be gone and forgotten.

If you don't want your child playing with *hand guns*, you can use any of the adult hiccup remedies, page 119.

➤ **Warts.** Take a piece of tracing paper or tissue paper, put it on the child's wart, and with a pencil, trace the wart. Take your child and the tracing paper into the bathroom. Then make sure you impress upon the child that *only Mommy or Daddy should do this*. While she watches, burn the tracing paper in the sink, then flush the ashes down the toilet. Within a week, the wart will begin to disappear.

➤ **Minor Boo-Boos.** Laura Silva Quesada, healer, international lecturer and president of The Silva Method (*www.silvamethod.com*), teaches children to use their own healing energy to help themselves.

Laura has young people shake out their hands, then rub them vigorously together to feel the heat and the energy. She explains that they can project a beam of blue-white energy from their right hand and collect it in their left hand. The right hand is the projector; the left hand is the collector.

When a child has a minor injury, he should shake out his hands, rub them together and put them over—close, but not touching—the hurt area. Then he should imagine the right hand projecting a beam of blue-white

energy and the left hand collecting it as the hurt goes away and he feels better and better.

P.S. It works.

P.P.S. Adults can do this too.

➤ **Saving a Tooth.** If your child's permanent tooth is knocked out, put the tooth in a container of milk and take it, along with your child, to the dentist. If you act fast and have a skilled dentist, he may be able to save the tooth.

➤ **Bad Dreams.** If your child has nightmares and, after thorough investigation, you are absolutely convinced that the child is not suffering from any emotional or physical abuse, you might try a century-old remedy. At bedtime, rub the soles of the child's feet with a peeled clove of garlic, cover the feet with a pair of socks. Finally, tell him that this will put an end to those bad dreams, and kiss him goodnight. (Don't forget to wash his feet in the morning.)

 CAUTION: Garlic can irritate the skin. You can dilute garlic with olive oil to minimize this effect. Also, avoid putting garlic on areas where there are cuts.

➤ **Separation Anxiety.** When you are getting ready to leave your child at home, try this helpful tip before he starts to act up. Tell him that there's a surprise for him, and that as soon as you touch the doorknob on your way out, he has to give you a kiss and you will give him a hint as to where (or what) it is. Chances are, your child will be eager for you to leave so that the treasure hunt can begin. In order for this to work, you will have to plan ahead. A friend of ours did this with her daughter. She gift-wrapped a little flashlight and had her look for it in the house. She was thrilled with it. From then on, she used the flashlight to help her find other little gifts her mom stashed away. Separation anxiety? What separation anxiety? Bribery? Sure, but fun and helpful to all concerned.

CHOKING

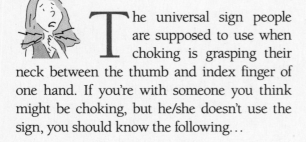

The universal sign people are supposed to use when choking is grasping their neck between the thumb and index finger of one hand. If you're with someone you think might be choking, but he/she doesn't use the sign, you should know the following...

Signs Someone Is Choking

- **The person suddenly cannot speak, breathe or cough.**
- **The person may frantically toss his head and, in a panic, get up quickly from the table.**
- **The person may turn blue and/or collapse.**

Heimlich Remedy for Helping Someone Who's Choking

➤ **Heimlich Maneuver.** If the person cannot speak, breathe or cough, have someone call 911 immediately, while you...

Step 1: Stand behind the person and wrap your arms around his waist. Allow the person's head and upper body to hang forward.

Step 2: Make a fist with one hand. Grasp the fist with your other hand, placing the thumb side of the clenched fist against the person's abdomen—slightly above the navel and below the rib cage.

 CAUTION: Make sure your fist is below the rib cage or you can add to the person's problems by cracking his ribs.

Step 3: With a quick inward and upward thrust, press your fist into the person's abdomen. The lodged piece of food should pop right out. If not, repeat this action a second time.

➤ **Self-Help Heimlich.** If you're alone, and food gets lodged in your throat...

Step 1: Make a fist with one hand and place the thumb side against your abdomen.

Step 2: With the other hand, grab your fist and press your fist in and upward in sharp, thrusting moves.

Another method is to press your abdomen forcefully against the back of a chair or a railing, forcing air out of your lungs and the object to be expelled.

More on Choking

➤ **Self-Help for a Fish Bone That Is Stuck.** If you're at home alone, and a fish bone gets stuck in your throat, don't panic. (That's easy for us to say.) Rush to the kitchen, take a raw egg and swallow it. Now's not the time to worry about cholesterol, especially since the egg will slide the fish bone down. It's also not the time to worry about the safety of eating a raw egg. One out of every 30,000 eggs is said to have the *salmonella* bacteria that can cause a food-borne illness. Chances are, you won't be consuming that one in 30,000. Swallow the egg and get rid of the fish bone!

 CAUTION: Some fish bones lodged in the esophagus require medical attention.

➤ **Choking Prevention.** Cut meat into small, bite-sized pieces. Do not laugh or talk while you have food in your mouth. Alcohol dulls the reflexes, so if you're going to drink and eat, drink *after* you have eaten.

Try this: When you are eating at home alone, eat as though you're out on a first date with the person of your dreams, or you're the star of a reality TV show and the camera is on you. In other words, eat slowly and thoroughly chew each mouthful before swallowing. It's a healthy way to eat in terms of digestion and weight control, and it will minimize your risk of choking.

CHOLESTEROL

People get cholesterol in two ways. The body, primarily the liver, produces varying amounts—typically about 1,000 milligrams (mg) a day—and you also get cholesterol from eating foods from animals (meat, poultry, shellfish, dairy products and eggs).

FYI: Foods from plants (fruits, vegetables, grains, nuts and seeds) do not contain cholesterol.

The American Heart Association recommends that you limit your average daily cholesterol intake to less than 300 mg. If you have heart problems, limit your daily intake to less than 200 mg.

Since cholesterol is in all foods from animal sources, be diligent about portion size, and if you're going to eat meat, make sure it's lean. If you're going to eat poultry, remove the skin. If you're going to eat dairy products, select the fat-free or low-fat varieties. Also consider substituting animal sources of protein with vegetable sources (beans) and soy (tofu) products.

Lowering Bad (LDL) Cholesterol

➤ **Olive Oil.** Olive oil can actually lower the bad LDL (bad) cholesterol. That's not to say you're to guzzle it down. The keyword is mod-

eration. The one that's thought to have the most heart-protecting chemicals is extra virgin olive oil (EVOO).

To earn the "extra virgin" title, the olives must be first cold-processed through a mechanical process extracting the oil from the olives. There must be no chemical solvents or other techniques of extraction to produce the oil.

➤ **Cabbage Family.** Several times per week, eat Brussels sprouts and other members of the cabbage family.

➤ **If You Don't Know from Beans,** it's time you start learning. One or more servings of beans a day can do a lot to lower cholesterol. And what a variety from which to choose—black beans, black-eyed peas, chickpeas, fava beans, kidney beans, lentils, lima beans, navy beans, pinto beans, split peas, white beans and even canned baked beans.

SOMETHING SPECIAL

Amy to the Rescue!

Food may be your all-important key to lowering your cholesterol levels. Okay, so you don't want to spend your day preparing meals. We can relate to that. And even if you don't mind spending time in the kitchen, chances are, the foods that you know how to prepare are the foods responsible for your high cholesterol levels.

Take the easy way out and let Rachel and Andy Berliner and their family business, "Amy's Kitchen," do the cholesterol-free cooking for you.

More information: See the "Weight Control" section, page 220, or visit *www. amys.com* to get more information about these wonderful prepared foods that may be as close as your supermarket shelf.

Portions for the above should be determined by you and your health professional, depending on your cholesterol levels, size and dietary needs.

➤ **Onions** are rich in potassium and vitamin A as well as *calcium pectate*—all LDL fighters. Add them to your daily diet.

➤ **Oatmeal.** A portion of oat bran or oatmeal is a great way to start the day. The beta-glucan in oats helps lower cholesterol.

➤ **Eat Soybeans and Soybean Products** several times a week…at least. Don't make a face! There are delicious meat-like soy foods that can do you a world of good, especially when you consider that you'd be eating them in place of meat. Be adventurous and explore your options at your local health food store.

Lecithin, derived from soybeans, comes in different forms—granules, capsules and liquid. The granules have an interesting taste and texture. As we said before, be adventurous.

➤ **Eating Eggplant** is said to rid the body of cholesterol before it can actually be absorbed by the body. Time to whip up some ratatouille?

➤ **Eat Grapefruit Like an Orange.** Peel it, separate it into sections and enjoy. Come to think of it, eat oranges, too. The white skin covering these fruits and the membrane that separates the sections have pectin, a cholesterol-lowering ingredient.

 CAUTION: Grapefruit, Seville oranges and pomelos (citrus fruit from Southeast Asia) may have serious interactions with several medications. If you are on medication, check with your health professional or your pharmacist for any drug interaction. The Mayo Clinic (*www.mayoclinic.com*) has a sampling of drugs known to have negative interactions with those citrus fruits.

➤ **An Apple or Two a Day.** The apple peel has pectin, so be sure to thoroughly clean the fruit before eating. (See "Healthful Hints," page 283, for cleaning methods.)

➤ **An Avocado a Day.** According to two studies, eating an avocado on a daily basis can lower cholesterol levels as much as some drugs do. If you're concerned about their high fat content, don't be. Avocados have the same type of good fat found in olive oil. So, bring out the guacamole!

➤ **Red Yeast Rice.** Statins (or *HMG-CoA reductase inhibitors*) are a group of cholesterol-lowering drugs whose generic names all end in "statin." This group includes *lovastatin* (Mevacor), *pravastatin* (Pravachol), *simvastatin* (Zocor), *atorvastatin* (Lipitor) and *rosuvastatin* (Crestor).

Statins can cause debilitating side effects, which explains why an estimated 40% of statin-takers stop taking them within a year after starting.

Enter: **Red yeast rice (RYR).** For more than 4,000 years, RYR—rice that has been fermented by the fungus, *Monascus purpureus*—has been used as a traditional medicine in China to improve circulation and reduce blood lipids (fatty substances).

In 1977, a Tokyo researcher discovered a natural substance in RYR—*monacolin K*—that inhibits cholesterol synthesis in the liver. Further research determined that RYR naturally contains at least eight related monacolins, all inhibitors of HMG-CoA reductase, the enzyme that controls cholesterol production in the liver.

In the past, we heard and read about RYR as an effective cholesterol-lowering alternative for people who stopped taking statins or who didn't want to start taking them.

We also heard and read about RYR that was contaminated because of improper growing conditions, and about the Food and Drug Administration (or FDA) going after specific brands of RYR, which were eventually taken off the market because the supplement manufacturers were lacing their products with pharmaceutical compounds. All of that bad press made us want to steer clear of red yeast rice.

And then we learned about Sylvan Bio. The company spent several years doing research and development and is now able to grow, produce and package a 100% natural RYR supplement. Sylvan controls the entire process, combining the purest ingredients with the highest production standards. They then sell their RYR to supplement companies who want to market a product that can be trusted.

We were impressed to know that Sylvan's RYR was selected by cardiologists Dr. David Becker and Dr. Ram Gordon to be used in their clinical study, reported in the June 2009 issue of *Annals of Internal Medicine.*

Over the past 30 years, the results of much research and several studies (including the Becker/Gordon study mentioned above) support the effectiveness of RYR to help lower total and LDL (bad) cholesterol and help reduce rates of heart attacks.

After speaking with Gary Walker, the president of Sylvan Bio, and hearing that they are the only domestic producers of RYR with the USDA Certificate of Organic Operation (and the Star-K Kosher Certification, too), we felt confident enough to write about red yeast rice, knowing that Sylvan's RYR is available to consumers.

The typical recommended dosage is 2,400 mg daily. When you select a brand of RYR, check the label to be sure the product has the words "Certified Organic" alongside the "Quality Assurance International" logo. If it does, chances are the label will also say "Manufactured by Sylvan Bio, Inc.—Produced and Bottled in the USA."

Possible Bonus: Recent research, according to Sylvan, indicates that RYR may provide other benefits, such as restoring bone loss and slowing the onset of osteoporosis.

Suggestion: Take a copy of this page to your doctor and after he/she reads it, ask for his blessing and recommended dosage.

 CAUTION: Do NOT use red yeast rice (RYR) if you are pregnant, may become pregnant or are nursing, have undergone an organ transplant or had major surgery within the last six weeks, are younger than 20 years old, currently have liver disease or a history of liver disease, consume more than two alcoholic drinks per day or are currently taking statin drugs. Have your liver enzymes checked two months after starting RYR as it can cause liver stress.

Also, when taking RYR, avoid grapefruit and grapefruit juice. And, due to RYR's statin-like effect, it may deplete the body's naturally occurring coenzyme Q10 (CoQ10). It would be wise to take a daily CoQ10 supplement of 100 mg to 200 mg when using RYR.

Raising Good (HDL) Cholesterol

➤ **Eat Garlic—lots of it.** Raw is best; supplements are good, too.

➤ **Eat Onions—lots of them.**

➤ **Take Vitamin B-6 (100 mg daily).** B-6 is extremely beneficial to smokers who have low HDLs.

 CAUTION: Do NOT take more than 150 mg of vitamin B-6 a day, as it can be toxic.

Raising HDL and Lowering LDL

Drinking a glass of kale juice every morning can do wonders for raising your HDL and lowering your LDL, according to the findings of a study, reported in *Dr. Frank Shallenberger's Second Opinion* Newsletter (*www.secondopinion newsletter.com*).

At the end of the 12-week study, kale juice increased HDL cholesterol by 27%, improved the HDL:LDL ratio by 52% and decreased LDL by 10%. The *atherogenic index* (a measure of vascular risk) dropped by 24%.

Dr. Shallenberger says that kale is one of his favorite health foods. "It's loaded with wonderful bioflavonoids that can protect your eyes and circulation. It's rich in vitamins A, C, calcium and iron. And now we know it lowers cholesterol."

COLD SORES (FEVER BLISTERS)

Just let's get this straight. We're talking about cold sores here, not canker sores.

This unsightly sore is caused by the *herpes simplex* virus that bursts into bloom when resistance is low because of a cold, the flu, pregnancy, sunburn, stress or other metabolism-altering factors, or it can be transmitted from kissing or some other kind of close personal contact with a person who has a cold sore.

It usually takes about two weeks to clear up. *But we have some suggestions that may speed up the healing process and prevent cold sores from recurring...*

At the First Sign

There's a peculiar tingling feeling the second a cold sore is on its way. People who get cold sores will know exactly what we mean.

➤ **Get Out the Nail Polish.** The second you feel it starting, take colorless nail polish and paint the area where the cold sore is about to emerge. The nail polish prevents the sore from blossoming. The polish peels off within a short time.

Our friend who told us about this cure said that she used it a long time ago and has not had a recurrence of cold sores since. Incidentally, our friend got the remedy from her dermatologist.

Once It's In Bloom

➤ **Freeze It Away.** Dry up the cold sore by applying ice to it. Place an ice cube in a white handkerchief and hold it on the sore for five minutes every hour. Okay, you'd rather do it for a half-hour three times a day or 10 minutes 10 times a day? That's fine. Just keep the ice cube on as long as you can, as often as you can. Reports from those who have used this treatment say that the sore dries up in about two days.

➤ **Dry It Out.** Apply yogurt or buttermilk to the sore to help dry it out. If, after the first application, it seems to be helping, then put on more yogurt a few hours later.

If walking around with yogurt on your face isn't practical, dry out the cold sore with witch hazel. Dab it with a cotton swab that's been dipped in witch hazel. Repeat the dabbing a half-dozen times throughout the day and night.

➤ **Take Away the Pain.** Puncture a vitamin E 400 international units (IU) softgel, squeeze out the oil and cover the sore with it.

Do it three times a day. By the third application, the pain should be gone. By the next day—the sixth application—the cold sore should be getting noticeably smaller. Keep up the treatment until the sore is all gone. If the vitamin E treatment is not for you, use aloe vera instead to help heal the sore. If you don't have an aloe plant, you can buy aloe vera gel in a health food store.

➤ **Red Wine.** If you have an open bottle of red wine, place a teaspoon of it in a saucer and leave it there for a few hours. Then scrape up the solidified remains of the wine and spread it on the cold sore. It may not be easy on the eyes, but the pain should be gone in seconds. The cold sore will take longer to disappear...probably longer than the rest of the bottle of wine!

Cure and/or Prevention

➤ **Acidophilus.** Daily doses of acidophilus can help heal and, better yet, prevent cold sores. You can take acidophilus in pill form (follow dosage on the label); and there's also acidophilus milk. If you can find it in your supermarket or health food store, take at least two tablespoons daily. Yogurt with probiotics (such as Stonyfield Farm, Activia and Yo-Plus) and buttermilk also offer the friendly bacteria to do battle with the herpes virus. For prevention, eat yogurt and drink buttermilk.

The herpes virus thrives on arginine, which is an amino acid. Stay away from these arginine-rich foods—chicken soup, chocolate, cola, nuts, gelatin, grain cereals, peas and beer.

➤ **L-lysine** is one amino acid that can *inhibit* the growth of the herpes virus. So include in your daily diet these foods that are rich in L-lysine—baked potatoes, brewer's yeast and steamed flounder. Wouldn't you know, this list is not as appetizing as the no-no list.

Supplementing your diet with L-lysine tablets can be extremely effective in preventing cold sores or, at least, making them disappear quickly. Dosage ranges from 500 mg to 4,500 mg a day. Please check with a health professional (a nutritionist would be helpful if your doctor isn't) to determine dosage.

 CAUTION: If you're pregnant or are nursing, L-lysine may NOT be for you. Check with your obstetrician.

➤ **Commonsense Prevention.** As cold sores can be quite contagious, do not hug, kiss or shake hands with someone who has a cold sore. If you have the cold sore, be kind, but not affectionate.

And remember: The herpes virus thrives where there's lots of moisture. A perfect spot is the bathroom. Their favorite hangout in the bathroom is your toothbrush. They can live there for days and then reinfect you. You may want to keep your toothbrush in a room that's less humid than the bathroom.

The second you think you're getting a cold sore, throw away the toothbrush you've been using and use a new one. If you didn't catch it in time and the boo-boo blossoms, wait until it heals, then be sure to start using a new toothbrush again. It's important.

It's also important to keep the lip of your toothpaste tube away from your toothbrush so that you don't transmit the virus to the tube and infect your newest toothbrush.

Clean your toothbrush before using it. Mix one teaspoon of 3% hydrogen peroxide in one cup of water and swish your brush around in the mixture. Then rinse the brush with water, and you're ready to brush with a clean toothbrush.

After reading all of this, you may want to consider investing in a toothbrush sanitizer.

AFFIRMATION

Repeat this affirmation at least 15 times, first thing in the morning, last thing at night and every time you look in the mirror…

I am strong. I am free. I radiate good health.

COLDS/FLU

During a one-year period in the US, it is estimated that people catch one billion colds. Most children have about six to 10 colds a year, primarily because of contact with other children in day care and at school. Generally speaking, the average adult has about two to four colds a year…women ages 20 to 30 have more colds than men, probably because of their closer contact with children…and people over 60 have fewest colds, one every other year.

People seem to get more colds in cold weather. My mother led us to believe that if we weren't dressed like Nanook of the North, we would go out in cold weather and "catch a cold." Not true. People get more colds in cold weather because they spend more time *indoors*, where viruses can spread more easily from person to person. Also, during the colder months of the year, the humidity is low, and that's when the most common cold-causing viruses survive best…in low humidity. Ever observe that the lining of your nasal passages are drier in cold weather? That makes you more vulnerable to viral infection taking hold.

Fighting the personal cold battle costs Americans billions of dollars a year in doctor appointments and medications. Want to save some money and feel better fast? Consider some of our suggestions using ingredients you may already have in your home.

Cold/Flu Prevention

➤ **Immune System Strengthener.** Olive leaf extract taken daily can help your immune system fight off colds and the flu. Read all about it in the "It Does a Body Good" chapter, page 257.

➤ **Avoid Catching Colds.** Tests were conducted between people with upper respiratory infections (colds) and people without colds. The tests consisted of kissing. The results suggested that the mouth and saliva are not the number one way colds are spread. Colds are most often transferred by nose-to-nose contact. So, when you or your mate has a cold, kissing is fine…just keep your nose out of it!

Also, when you are around people who are sick, and you're touching the things they've touched—desks, computers, telephones, light switches, doorknobs, silverware, glasses—do not touch your nose or your eyes, and wash your hands often and thoroughly.

At the Onset of a Cold

➤ **Gingerroot.** Peel and grate about a half-ounce of fresh gingerroot or four slices the size of a quarter, and boil in water. Simmer for 15 to 20 minutes. Strain and drink a cup every couple of hours. If you like *hot and strong* tea, then add an eighth-teaspoon of cayenne pepper to the ginger tea. If you like sweet tea, add a tablespoon of raw honey to the ginger tea. If you like tart tea, add the juice of half a small lemon to the ginger tea.

CAUTION: Ginger acts as a blood thinner, so check with your doctor before using it if you are taking a prescription blood thinner. Also, stop using ginger three days before any surgery.

Cold/Flu Remedies

➤ **Universal Cure-Alls.** Every country has its own version of garlic and/or onion cold/flu remedies. *Here are a few of the least complicated/most effective ones...*

• **Eat a raw or a roasted Spanish onion before bedtime.** In the morning, no cold.

• **Peel a clove of garlic, keep it in your cheek,** and every so often, bite into it to release the potent juice. Change the clove every few hours. It is said that the cold will be gone within 24 hours. And, the smell of the garlic should keep people away from you, so you won't be giving anyone else your cold.

• **Take garlic and/or onion softgels** (available at health food stores). Follow the dosage on the label.

 CAUTION: Having garlic on an empty stomach can cause nausea. Be sure to have some food in your stomach before eating garlic or taking capsules. And, be cautious with garlic if you have gastritis.

➤ **A Before-Bed Drink.** We wrote about this in our previous book, *Bottom Line's Secret Food Cures*, but think it's worth repeating here.

When we were growing up, Bubby, our grandmother, would mix up a groan-provoking concoction whenever someone in the family had a cold. The dreaded drink was called a guggle-muggle. We thought it was a cute name that Bubby made up. Now it sounds like something out of the Harry Potter books.

It turns out that many Jewish families have their own guggle-muggle recipes...some more palatable than others.

One day, during the late Edward Koch's last term in office as mayor of the Big Apple, he was on a local TV show with us and said he had a cold. *He then proceeded to share his family's recipe for an adults-only guggle-muggle...*

At bedtime, combine the juice of one grapefruit, one lemon and one orange, preferably a Temple orange (we're not sure if it's because of its taste or because of its name). Add one tablespoon of honey. Pour the mixture into a saucepan and bring it to a boil while stirring. Then add one ounce of your favorite liquor (Ed Koch uses brandy).

As with most guggle-muggles, you drink it down, dress warmly, and get under the covers to sweat it out during a good night's sleep. Next morning, you may awaken without a cold.

➤ **An Anti-Everything for Colds and Flu.** Bee propolis, the sticky sap of trees that's gathered and processed by bees, is an antihistamine, an antibiotic, an antiviris, antifungus and also a decongestant. No kidding, it's amazing stuff! Bee propolis comes in tablets, capsules and liquid form. Follow the recommended dosage on the label.

 CAUTION: If you have a suspected sensitivity to bee products, forget this and go on to another remedy.

➤ **Prevent Dehydration.** You know how they always say, "Drink lots of liquids"? *They are right.* When you have a cold or the flu, and especially if you're running a fever, your body is throwing off water by means of evaporation, sweating and breathing. We don't want to scare you by telling you how harmful dehydration can be, but we do want to impress upon you the need to keep replenishing that lost water. Keep drinking!

➤ **Chest Congestion.** After breakfast or lunch, add a half-teaspoon of Red Hot sauce to a glass of tepid water and drink it. This remedy is so strong, you can almost feel congestion breaking up as the liquid goes down.

 CAUTION: Do NOT use this Red Hot sauce remedy if you have heartburn, gastritis, ulcers or esophagitis.

➤ **Sneezing.** Do it! It's better to expel viruses and bacteria through sneezing than to stifle the sneezes, allowing the enemies to fester in your sinuses. The best way to sneeze is with your mouth open and covered with a tissue.

➤ **Stuffed Nose.** Upper body exercise can act as a natural nasal decongestant. Put on spirited music that arouses your passion and, pencil or chopstick in hand, conduct the band or orchestra that's playing the music. It can be vigorous exercise, so you may not want to overdo your debut as a guest conductor. Stop doing it when your nose unstuffs, or you feel you need to rest...whichever comes first.

➤ **Runny Nose.** Does your nose run? And do your feet smell? Then you're built upside down. But seriously—if you do have a runny nose, put three or four drops of Tabasco sauce in a glass of water and drink it down. Relief should be no more than five minutes away.

 CAUTION: Do NOT use this Tabasco remedy if you have heartburn, gastritis, ulcers or esophagitis.

➤ **Color Therapy.** Clairvoyant and author Barbara Stabiner says to wear a red scarf around your neck to help speed the healing process. It's worth a try.

➤ **Aromatherapy.** The minute that you start feeling flu-ish, prepare a warm bath with a half-dozen drops of eucalyptus oil. Relax in the bath for 15 minutes. Be careful getting out of the tub...the oil will make it slippery. Then, throughout the day, dab a little cinnamon oil on your temples.

When your head is feeling stuffed up, fill the sink (or a bowl if you prefer) with hot water and put a couple of drops of eucalyptus oil in it. Then place a towel over your head, and then lean your head over the sink or bowl, and inhale the cinnamon vapors for two or three minutes.

➤ **Visualization.** "The River of Life" is a visualization by Dr. Gerald Epstein, psychiatrist and director of the American Institute for Mental Imagery (*www.drjerryepstein.org*). Anyone can use it to help get over a common cold. Read it through, then either have someone read it to you as you do it, or tape-record yourself reading it, judging the timing as best as you can.

1. **Once you're seated in a comfortable place,** close your eyes.

2. **Breathe out three times to relax yourself.**

3. **See your eyes becoming clear and very bright.** Then see them turning inward, becoming two rivers flowing down from the sinuses into the nasal cavity and throat, their currents taking away all the waste products, soreness and stuffiness.

4. **The rivers are flowing through your chest and abdomen,** into your legs, and coming out as black or gray strands that you see being buried deep in the earth.

5. **See your breath coming out as black air** and see your waste products emerging from below.

6. **Sense these rivers pulsating rhythmically through the body** and see light coming from above, filling up the sinuses, nose and throat, all the tissues becoming pink and healthy.

7. **When you sense both the rhythmic flow and the light filling these cavities,** breathe out and open your eyes.

Do this visualization exercise every three hours for three to five minutes each time, until the cold clears up.

AFFIRMATION

Repeat this affirmation five times. Each time you say it, think of how meaningful the words are and how they relate to you and your life…

My mind, my body, my work and my relationships are clearly defined. I am in control. I am getting better and better. I am productive and I am loved.

CONSTIPATION

Considering the selection of natural laxatives that are available, it seems to us that no one should have to resort to commercial products that can ultimately, with constant use, *cause* constipation.

First off, if you have constipation, you might want to limit your intake of the following foods that have been known to cause it. These foods include milk, cheese, ice cream, unripe bananas, heavily salted and spiced foods, chocolate, alcoholic beverages and products made with white flour. Sure, all of your favorites. No wonder you're reading this chapter.

Our job is to provide nonchemical remedies that can help you become *regular*; your job is to try them—one at a time—using com-

mon sense and, ideally, with your doctor's approval. We suggest dosages. *More* is not always better. Always take into account your size and system. Start with a moderate amount of whatever appeals to you and experiment by gradually increasing the portion until you find what works best.

➤ **Foods to Start Your Day With.** (Select one of the following and start your day with it, unless otherwise instructed by a health care professional.)

● **Mix a tablespoon of cornmeal in a glass of water and drink it.**

● **Eat a few figs or a very ripe banana.** Both would serve you well in a bowl of high-fiber cereal.

● **Take one tablespoon of aloe vera juice** (available at health food stores) and another tablespoon before bed.

● **Drink a glass of fresh carrot juice.**

● **Drink a glass of warm water with the juice of a lemon.** Add some honey to make it delicious.

● **Put a half-dozen cloves in a mug and add a half-cup of just-boiled water** and let it steep overnight. Then, first thing in the morning, strain out the cloves and drink the clove water.

● **Drink a glass of freshly juiced vegetable juice.** Use any palatable combination of tomato, cucumber, white radish, celery, cabbage, beet or carrot. Chances are, if you are into juicing, you will not need these constipation remedies.

● **Bake and eat an apple for breakfast and another before bed.** Eat raw apples after meals. Be sure to wash off the pesticides (for instructions, see "Healthful Hints," page 283) and eat the peel.

43

➤ **Foods That Will Promote Regularity Throughout the Day.**

• **Eat a ripe avocado**—mash it with a little chopped onion, a teaspoon of lemon and spices (curry or cumin) to taste. Or cut it up into a salad. It's extremely beneficial in many ways, including as an internal lubricant.

• **Sprinkle one tablespoon or two of ground flaxseed or oat bran into food**—soup, salad or stew—on a daily basis.

• **Have a few white or black mustard seeds daily.** Swallow the seeds whole, without chewing them.

• **Drink a couple of cups of bayberry tea every day.**

• **Eat a salad.**

• **Peel and boil a sweet potato in water until it's soft.** Eat it for dessert.

• **As an afternoon snack, eat a cup of cooked cabbage.** It's a low-calorie, anticancer, fiber-filled food that can help conquer constipation.

• **For men only:** Chew a tablespoon of raw pumpkin seeds daily. It's also wonderful for prostate health.

 NOTE: Also see "Salba" in the "It Does a Body Good" chapter, page 268.

➤ **Compress.** Take a white towel and carefully pour just-boiled water on it. When it's cool enough to touch, wring it out and put it on your stomach. To keep in the heat, place another towel over it. Now lay down and relax that way for a half-hour. This can be done in conjunction with some of the other suggestions above.

➤ **Exercise—Long-Term Help.** There are so many reasons to exercise on a regular basis, and one of them is to help prevent constipa-

■ Recipe ■

Candy-to-Go

This recipe is a treat and a treatment for constipation. Eat one or two pieces daily.

• **Process or finely chop ½ pound of prunes,** ½ pound of raisins, ½ pound of figs and ¼ pound of apricots.

• **Combine all of the above ingredients with ½ cup of unprocessed oat or wheat bran.** Thoroughly mix the ingredients together.

• **In an 8-inch square cake pan,** evenly distribute the mixture.

• **Cut up into bite-sized squares,** wrap each square in plastic wrap.

• **Refrigerate the entire batch.**

 NOTE: If you do not want to prepare your own "candy," read all about Gnu Bars in the "Constipation" section of the "Childhood Ailments" section, page 32.

tion. Walk 10 to 15 minutes a day, twice a day.

Also consider taking a tai chi or yoga class, and do some stretching—all of this movement decreases the time it takes for food to pass through the large intestine. And that's a good thing because it limits the amount of water absorbed from the stool into your body. (Hard, dry stools are hard to eliminate.)

Aerobic exercise—brisk walking, jogging, swimming or cycling—accelerates your breathing and heart rate, which helps stimulate the wavelike contractions of intestinal muscles that help move stools onward and outward. (This is probably more than you want to know.) Start exercising and chances are, you will be able to flush away this uncomfortable and unhealthy problem.

➤ **Colon Cleansing Regimen.** You may want to help cleanse your colon on a regular basis by going on a fruit fast once a week or once a month—you set the schedule according to your needs and after checking with your health professional.

Be sure to include ripe pineapple, papaya and/or mango. Also, in compliance with food combining, melons (cantaloupe, honeydew, watermelon, casaba, etc.) should be eaten by themselves to avoid gas buildup.

Or take advantage of psyllium, the beneficial fiber used in some commercial laxatives, without having the unnecessary commercial additives. Ask for powdered psyllium seed husks at health food stores and follow the directions on the label.

 CAUTION: You must have water with the psyllium and then have more water right after you ingest it. Psyllium is mucilaginous (it absorbs water and gets clumpy). It can *cause* blockage if you don't wash it down with a generous supply of water.

➤ **Laugh Away the Problem.** Really. Having a big laugh—a belly laugh—massages the intestines. It also relieves stress, a common cause of constipation. Rent a funny DVD, talk to a funny friend or read jokes on the Internet. You may want to start at *www.ahajokes.com*, *www.jokesclean.com* and *www.danggoodjokes. com*. Also, see page 247 for more on the health benefits of laughter.

COUGHS

 Coughing is simply your body's way of ridding itself of a substance somewhere along the respiratory tract. Most coughs are symptoms of respiratory ailments such as a cold or the flu. *Here are remedies to help you deal with a cough...*

➤ **At the Start of a Cough.** Prepare dill tea (available at health food stores) by adding one teaspoon of dill to a cup of just-boiled water. Let it steep for about seven minutes, strain, if you need it sweetened, sweeten with honey, and drink three cups a day. All it may take to get rid of the cough are just those three cups for just that one day.

➤ **Cough Syrups.** The classic folk remedies for coughs all seem to have honey as one of the main ingredients. *These are no exception...*

● **Roast a big, juicy lemon until it splits open.** Take a teaspoon of the lemon juice with a half teaspoon of raw honey every half hour until there's no more juice in the lemon. By then, the cough should be under control.

● **Prepare garlic syrup by peeling and mincing six to eight cloves of garlic.** Put them in a jar with a cup of raw honey. Let this stand for two hours. Then, when your cough acts up, swallow a teaspoon of the syrup-and-garlic bits. If you swallow it without chewing the bits, the garlic will not stay on your breath.

 CAUTION: Having garlic on an empty stomach can cause nausea. Be sure to have some food in your stomach before eating garlic or taking capsules. And, be cautious with garlic if you have gastritis.

➤ **Decongestants.** Having spicy foods can help you cough up mucus and clear your lungs, sinuses and nose. Get out the chili, horseradish, mustard and garlic.

Garlic can be made into a tea to help clear up a cough. Add a quarter-teaspoon of garlic powder to a cup of just-boiled water. Or peel and mince three medium cloves of garlic and steep them in a cup of just-boiled water for 10 minutes. Strain and drink the garlic tea—three or four cups a day—and add the minced garlic bits to soup or a salad.

 CAUTION: Drinking garlic tea on an empty stomach can cause nausea. Be sure to have some food in your stomach before drinking it. And, be cautious with garlic if you have gastritis.

➤ **Mucus and Cough Chaser.** If you've reached the point where you feel your cough will never go away, fenugreek tea to the rescue! Fenugreek is a powerful medicinal herb that can soften and wash away masses of mucus and clear up your cough in the process.

Start by drinking a cup of the tea every hour or two. After that first day, cut down to four cups each day.

➤ **Bronchial Cough and Chest Congestion.** A bay leaf poultice can work wonders to stop the cough and clear up the congestion. Add 20 bay leaves to a cup of just-boiled water, cover the cup with a dish, and let it steep for 15 minutes. Then, with a strainer, separate the leaves from the liquid. Wrap the leaves in cheesecloth and moisten the cheesecloth by dipping it in the bay leaves liquid. Place this wet bay leaf poultice on your bare chest and cover it with a towel. Relax that way for an hour, and then reheat the liquid and re-dip the poultice

and, making sure it's not too hot, reapply it to your chest for another hour.

■ Recipe ■

Cough Drops

This is the most complex recipe in the book. It was given to us by Ron Hamilton of Great American Natural Products (727-521-4372 or visit *www.greatamerican.biz*) and it's for those of you who are ready for the experience of making your own, natural, super-effective cough drops.

Ingredients

- **¼ cup of dried horehound** (available at health food and herb stores)
- **2 cups of water**
- **2 cups of honey**
- **1 cup of blackstrap molasses**

Instructions

Bring the water to a boil and add in the horehound. Let it simmer for 10 minutes. Strain and put the strained horehound water in a large, heavy pot along with the honey and the blackstrap molasses. The mixture foams a lot, so be sure to use a large pot to avoid a messy range.

Cook the concoction for about an hour-and-a-half and then start testing for readiness. When a drop of the mixture is dropped into cold water and becomes a hard ball, it is ready.

Carefully pour the mixture onto a very lightly buttered cookie sheet. Score this with a knife into cough-drop–sized squares. When they cool, you will have very potent cough drops.

If this remedy calmed down the cough and helped clear up some congestion, do it again next time you feel a bronchial attack coming on.

➤ **Aromatherapy for Bronchitis.** Before bedtime, take a relaxing therapeutic bath. Scent the bath water with four drops of pine oil. If you find the forest fragrance soothing, place a few drops of the oil on a cotton ball and rub it on the back and undersides of wooden furniture, where the aroma can help alleviate bronchitis flare-ups throughout the day.

➤ **Cough with Phlegm.** The owner of a Chinese restaurant shared this powerful, time-tested phlegm-ridding remedy with us. At bedtime, grate a half-ounce of fresh gingerroot. Add these pieces to water and bring to a boil. Then simmer for about 15 to 20 minutes and strain and drink. As you drink the tea, swallow the grated ginger and eat three walnuts. Then go to bed and wake up in the morning phlegm-free and without the cough.

 CAUTION: Ginger acts as a blood thinner, so check with your doctor before using it if you are taking a prescription blood thinner. Also, stop using ginger three days before any surgery.

➤ **Choking Cough.** This is the kind of cough where you are not actually choking on something—you're just coughing like that. All you have to do is raise your hands as high as you can and the choking cough will stop.

➤ **Morning Cough.** If your morning routine consistently consists of coughing, it is time to do something about it. Consider giving up mucus-making foods, especially dairy products…all dairy products. And instead of that cup of coffee, start the day with a cup of thyme tea. With thyme, within no time, you should have coughless mornings.

➤ **Postnasal Drip Cough.** This is not a remedy for postnasal drip; it's a suggestion for quelling a postnasal drip cough and for getting some good ZZZZZZs. Simply sleep on your stomach! Now why didn't you think of that?

➤ **Nervous Cough.** Drink an ounce of aloe vera juice (available at health food stores) first thing in the morning and right after dinner for one week.

➤ **Smoker's Cough.** First—needless to say—stop smoking! Did we lose you or are you still with us? Remove the peel, core and seeds of six apples. Slice the apples in small pieces and put them in a pot with two cups of honey. Cook it on a low flame until it has a syrupy consistency, then put it in a jar and keep refrigerated. Take two teaspoons of the honey-apple syrup between meals and whenever the cough acts up. Now turn to the "Stop Smoking" section, page 188.

AFFIRMATION

Repeat at least 12 times a day, first thing in the morning, after each meal and at bedtime…

I am relaxed and surrounded by positive energy as my body heals itself.

CUTS AND WOUNDS

If a cut or wound is bleeding profusely, put direct pressure on it with a sterile dressing, or the cleanest washcloth available—and get professional medical help immediately.

If you have a minor cut, first rinse it with water, clean it with hydrogen peroxide, and then stop the bleeding by applying any of these…

Remedies for Cuts and Wounds

➤ **Cayenne Pepper**—yes, it will sting, but it will also stop the bleeding.

➤ **Moist Tea Leaves or Tea Bag.**

➤ **Aloe Vera Leaf Gel.**

➤ **Papaya Pulp.**

➤ **Crushed Geranium Plant Leaves.**

➤ **When Help Isn't Close By.** Our Massachusetts friend, Selwyn P. Miles, told us about a young lad who was chopping kindling on a farm. The axe slipped and caught him in the foot between his big and second toes. His dad scooped up a handful of honey from a crock in the kitchen, and smeared it all over the boy's foot. The bleeding stopped instantly and complete healing followed in a short amount of time with hardly any scarring. Yahoo…for the healing power of the enzymes in the raw honey.

Scarless Healing

➤ **Egg on Your Face.** Carefully crack open a raw egg and remove the skin that's inside the shell. Put the wet side of the skin on the cut for a speedy healing without a scar.

➤ **Vitamin E Softgel.** Once the wound closes, puncture a vitamin E softgel and squeeze out the oil on the scarred area every morning, at bedtime, and more often if possible. Be patient. It may take a while for the scar to fade.

➤ **A Special Lemon Paste.** During a visit to Mexico, talented artist Barbara Wasserman was sent flying through a car's windshield. Her face was cut in several places. Considering all the stitches needed to close the cuts, Barbara was sure she'd be scarred for life. Luckily, while convalescing in Mexico, she had a local housekeeper who had been raised with folk remedies. The housekeeper took a big, beautiful abalone shell, put the juice of a lemon in it, and left it outside overnight in the moonlight. By morning, there was a paste formed by the lemon juice mixing with the pearlized part of the shell.

The housekeeper gently applied the paste on the wounds. That night, she added more lemon juice on the shell, once again left it out overnight, then applied the resulting paste on the cuts. This procedure was repeated daily. Every couple of weeks, when the pearlized portion of the shell was used up, a new shell replaced it, until the wounds were completely healed and there was absolutely no trace of a facial scar.

When Barbara talked to us, she had just helped a friend who had had open-heart surgery. After one month of putting the abalone/lemon juice paste on his incision, just a faint hairline scar remained. "And that would completely disappear," Barbara said, "if my friend wasn't lazy about doing this for himself."

Barbara also said that you don't have to put the shell outside under the moonlight. A dark closet overnight is adequate.

We experimented with shells and juice and found that it may take two nights for the juice to eat through the top layer of shell and form a usable paste.

 CAUTION: If you have a fresh scar-producing incision and want to use this remedy, we urge you to check with your health professional and take every precaution against an infection.

DEPRESSION

 Depression is sometimes referred to as the common cold of mental illness. In a given year, depressive disorders affect an estimated 14.8 million American adults. Now that's depressing!

Depression doesn't discriminate. It affects the rich and famous as well as the poor and unknown. In 1841, when Abraham Lincoln was the floor leader of the Whig party, he was quoted as saying, "If what I feel were equally distributed to the whole human family, there would not be one cheerful face on earth." Yes, Mr. Lincoln was going through a depression. He eventually conquered it and went on to become the 16th president of the US.

Another case in point—Winston Churchill. Sir Winston took up painting to help get himself through his bouts of depression.

If an artist's palette isn't palatable to you, you might want to consider the following suggestions to help get you through a depressing time...

 CAUTION: For long-term and severe bouts of depression, it's important to seek professional help.

➤ **A Drink.** Myrrh, which has been around since biblical times, is said to chase the blues away. Put a half teaspoon of powdered myrrh (available at health food stores) in a cup of just-boiled water. Let it cool, and drink a cup twice a day.

Many psychic practitioners believe that burning myrrh incense chases away negative energy.

➤ **Move It! Okay, everyone on your feet, two, three, four.** Yes, exercise can take the place of antidepressant drugs and have the same effect on the chemicals of your brain (those endorphins) that give you a feeling of well-being... and without any of the drugs' side effects. And, as an added bonus, you'll get into great shape.

Some suggestions: Take a good, brisk walk daily, tracking your own personal best records. Rent or buy an exercise video—make sure it's at your own workout level—and start working out. Join a gym or health club and make a commitment to yourself to work out on a daily basis. Exercise can almost immediately make you feel better about yourself and about life in general.

➤ **Get Down and Dirty.** Get out of a mild depression by getting out and doing some gardening. Indoor gardening is good, too. According to the American Horticultural Therapy Association (*www.ahta.org*), the therapeutic benefits of peaceful garden environments have been understood since ancient times. In the 19th century, Dr. Benjamin Rush, a signer of the Declaration of Independence and considered to be the "Father of American Psychiatry," reported that garden settings held curative effects for people with mental illness. If Dr. Rush is right, then think of how beneficial a garden can be when going through a depression. Growing plants and seeing flowers bloom can give you a new appreciation for life and a chance to bury your unhappiness. If you don't have your own garden, find a community garden in your neck-of-the-woods.

➤ **Popping Pills.** For some people who are in a depressed state, vitamin B-6 may be the answer. Magnesium is needed for the most effective absorption of vitamin B-6. Magnesium along with calcium can calm the nervous system and help relieve depression. If you're interested in this remedy, please pay close attention

49

to details. The dosage for an average-sized person is 75 milligrams (mg) of B-6, 100 mg of magnesium and 200 mg of calcium—all twice a day.

 CAUTION: Check with your doctor before you try this remedy and make sure the dosages are right for you. Do NOT take more than 150 mg of vitamin B-6 a day, as it can be toxic.

 NOTE TO WOMEN ON THE PILL: The estrogen in the Pill can stop the absorption of vitamin B-6, along with several other vitamins and minerals. That malabsorption may be the cause of your depression. You might want to consider another means for birth control. Check with your doctor for all of your options.

➤ **After a Loss.** Native Americans used borage to help comfort the bereaved "when the heart weeps with sorrow." Prepare a tea by steeping one heaping teaspoon of borage (available at health food stores) in a cup of just-boiled water for 10 minutes, then strain and drink. Expect a cucumber kind of taste. Drink three cups of this tea throughout the day to help ease emotional pain and grief.

➤ **After a Loss or Any Other Major Trauma.** If you do not seek professional help, get into your own therapy by buying a special notebook to use as an "emotional diary." At least once a day, write down your innermost feelings. Don't censor yourself; let it all out on paper. The purging of your thoughts and emotions can help speed the healing process, assist in the management of your grief and help prevent you from suppressing all that you need to release. When you've completed the process and are feeling a lot better, you may find the process valuable enough to continue.

➤ **Are You a SAD-ist?** SAD (Seasonal Affective Disorder) is a type of winter depression that affects millions of people between September and April, mostly during December, January and February.

Here are symptoms as reported by The National Organization for Seasonal Affective Disorder...

● **A desire to oversleep and difficulty staying awake,** but in some cases, disturbed sleep and early morning wakening.

● **Fatigue and inability to carry out normal routines.**

● **The craving of carbohydrates and sweet foods,** usually resulting in weight gain.

● **Feelings of misery,** guilt and loss of self-esteem. And sometimes hopelessness, despair, apathy and loss of feelings.

● **Irritability and desire to avoid social contact.**

● **Tension and inability to tolerate any type of stress.**

● **Decreased interest in sex and physical contact.**

● **And in some sufferers, extremes of mood** and short periods of hypomania (overactivity) in spring and autumn.

If you've looked at the above symptoms, and think that SAD—a biochemical imbalance in the hypothalamus due to the shortening of daylight hours and the lack of sunlight in winter—may be your problem, seek professional help to determine the severity of the problem and your course of action. For mild cases, the recommended treatment is that you spend more time outdoors in winter. (Sitting indoors, near a window, doesn't do it.) For severe cases, SAD sufferers need phototherapy—full-spectrum lights that can be used in your home. If that's the case, visit the Circadian Lighting International Association (*www.circadianlighting.org*) for guidance in choosing the right light therapy product.

SOMETHING SPECIAL

Leaf Them Laughing

Going through a sad, depressing time can make you supersensitive, which does nothing to help cheer you up. We know something that may—the TickleMe Plant, whose birth name is *mimosa pudica*, and is also known as the "Sensitive Plant."

Tickle this sensitive plant and it moves ...really moves. The leaves close up and the branches dip down. You can't help but smile watching this amazing little plant in action.

These seeds can sprout in three to seven days at 70 degrees (air-conditioned rooms, or cold windowsills are no-nos for the plant). A few weeks after they sprout, they will move when tickled. The plant should grow a foot or more in height in a year. Adult plants can even grow pretty pink flowers (but not all

do). These plants can be grown indoors year-round in a warm room.

If you're thinking it's mostly for young children, yes, they love them...and so will that dear, sweet child in you...the one you probably should be reconnecting with at this time.

The Chipkin brothers—Larry and Mark—grew up around these plants that never stopped entertaining them and their friends.

Mark became a science teacher, and for 30 years, continued sharing the joy of raising TickleMe Plants with his students. And now, the Chipkins are tickled pink to be selling TickleMe Plants.

More information: Visit *www.tickleme plant.com* for a selection of seed packets, kits, greenhouses and more, including experiments and growing tips, or call 845-350-4800.

➤ **Visualization.** Dr. Gerald Epstein, a psychiatrist and director of the American Institute for Mental Imagery (at *www.drjerry epstein.org*), has developed the visualization called "Blowing Away the Dark Clouds" for people who have a general feeling of blueness. *See below...*

1. **Sit on a comfortable, hard-back chair and relax.** Take up to a minute for this process.

2. **Close your eyes and see dark clouds above you.** As you stand under these clouds, see yourself blowing them away to the left by blowing out three breaths (in imagery, not physically). Then look up in the sky to the upper right and watch the sun enter the sky above you. When finished, know that the blues have gone.

3. **Slowly count from one to three.** Open your eyes, stretch, and feel refreshed and happier.

➤ **Gem Therapy.** Clairvoyant Barbara Stabiner says that the sapphire contributes to mental clarity, aids in perception and discernment, is used for protection and can act as an antidepressant.

AFFIRMATION

This affirmation from parapsychologist Jose Silva is based on the words of Émile Coué, a French psychologist who introduced a method of psychotherapy and self-improvement based on optimistic autosuggestion. Repeat it first thing in the morning, each time you catch yourself thinking a negative thought and last thing at night...

Every day in every way I'm better, better and better.

Eat Your Way to a Better Mood

Food can put you in a good mood. When you eat, the nutrients in the food are quickly absorbed into your bloodstream. One organ that's affected by those nutrients is your brain—which is why your mood, mental energy, focus and memory are all directly affected by the foods you eat. When you feel down or sluggish, think about what you have eaten. When you eat junk, you feel like junk.

My favorite good-mood foods, in order of importance...

➤ **Fat-Free Milk** is a lovely combination of carbohydrate and protein in one easy package. Milk is naturally high in *tryptophan* and is a great dietary source of vitamin D, another nutrient that increases *serotonin*. I recommend three eight-ounce servings of milk daily.

For those who can't drink milk: Try soy milk fortified with calcium and vitamin D, although it doesn't contain as much tryptophan as milk. If you have trouble digesting lactose, the sugar found in milk, try using isolated whey protein powder, which contains a protein that is separated from milk and has little or no lactose or fat, but is a rich source of tryptophan. Whey protein powder is available in health food stores. Mix into juice, smoothies or yogurt.

➤ **Fish** is another feel-great food. Cold-water fish, such as salmon and mackerel, have the most omega-3 fatty acids and are known to raise mood. (The most healthful cooking methods are baked and broiled, not fried.) Sole, flounder and cod also contain omega-3 fatty acids and can lift mood. In my work with world-class athletes, I have them eat fish five times a week to improve their mood and concentration.

If you're not a fish eater at all, try eating one serving of fish weekly. Then work up to more fish meals over the week. And try a fish oil supplement. Even my clients who eat fish also take a daily supplement of fish oil—one that combines about 500 mg total of *eicosapentaenoic acid* (EPA) and *docosahexaenoic acid* (DHA).

➤ **Eggs** (with the yolks) are a perfect source of protein and other nutrients, including vitamin D. Yolks are full of *choline*, a B vitamin that's essential for making *acetylcholine*, one of the most abundant neurotransmitters in your body. You need acetylcholine to send messages along your nerves and to keep your memory strong, among other things. I recommend an egg a day (or up to seven a week but no more than one yolk daily). Don't worry about eggs raising your cholesterol. Studies show that one egg a day has no effect on the cholesterol levels of healthy people.

➤ **Cocoa** sends your brain a nice mix of carbohydrates, protein and tryptophan that can help raise your mood and relax you for a good night's sleep. (Don't worry about the caffeine in cocoa. There are only about seven mg in a tablespoon of cocoa powder.) I suggest that you use your third milk serving of the day to make the cocoa.

Best: Make it with alkaline-free or natural cocoa powder, which should be noted on the label. This designation refers to a processing technique for cocoa beans that leaves more of the antioxidants called *flavonols* in the cocoa. Add fat-free milk and a sweetener. Sugar is OK if it doesn't disturb your sleep and you're not trying to lose weight. Agave syrup is a good alternative because it doesn't raise blood sugar levels. If you want a noncaloric sweetener, stevia and Splenda are sound choices.

Susan Kleiner, PhD, RD, author of *The Good Mood Diet: Feel Great While You Lose Weight* (Springboard) and *Power Eating* (Human Kinetics). Based on Mercer Island, Washington, she is a nutritionist who has worked with athletes, professional sports teams and executives, *http://drskleiner.com*.

DIABETES

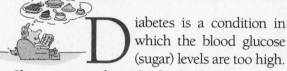

Diabetes is a condition in which the blood glucose (sugar) levels are too high. Glucose comes from the foods you eat and the beverages you drink. Insulin is a hormone that helps the glucose from your blood get into your cells to give them energy.

The two most common types of diabetes are type 1 (insulin-dependent) diabetes mellitus when the body does not make any insulin and type 2 (non-insulin-dependent) diabetes mellitus when the body does not make enough insulin or doesn't use insulin well.

Without enough insulin being properly used, the glucose stays in the blood. Having too much glucose in the blood is what can cause serious problems, often referred to as complications from diabetes.

Who Can Get Diabetes

Anyone can get any type of diabetes at any age. It is for that reason the American Diabetes Association (ADA) (*www.diabetes.org*) changed the name from "juvenile onset" to "type 1," and from "adult onset" to "type 2."

According to the International Diabetes Federation (*www.diabetesatlas.org*), some 371 million people worldwide currently live with diabetes. Included in that staggering figure are more than 29 million children and adults in the US, and one in four doesn't know he or she has it. The numbers keep growing and the ages keep lowering. It's no wonder, since here in America, one in six overweight adolescents (aged 12 to 19) have prediabetes (that's when blood glucose levels are higher than normal but not high enough to be diagnosed as diabetes…yet).

Having diabetes but not realizing it means not taking appropriate and proper care. Those people are at risk for dreaded diabetes complications affecting vital organs and every other part of the body.

 CAUTION: If diabetes runs in your family, or if you have one or more of these symptoms—unusual thirst, frequent urination, blurred vision, unexplainable weight loss, constant fatigue—make an appointment to be tested. All it takes for you to determine whether or not you have diabetes is a simple blood test in your doctor's office.

Management Basics from Joan

Through the years, since I was diagnosed with type 2 diabetes, I have done so much reading, researching, interviewing, experimenting and participating in diabetes groups, desperately wanting to eliminate or at least completely control this condition. No one said it was going to be easy. And it isn't! But each new day brings new ways to make diabetes more manageable.

Managing diabetes means a food plan, weight control, exercise and possibly prescribed medicine. Your doctor can write a prescription, but you need to do just about everything else. *Here are some approaches to help you find the everything else…*

➤ **Consult Experts.** Have your doctor/endocrinologist recommend a diabetes-educator and/or a dietician/nutritionist in order to learn about eating plans. Also check with your insurance company about coverage for a diabetes-educator and/or a nutritionist and for referrals in your area.

➤ **Look for Books.** Go to your local library or bookstore and browse through the books in the Health/Diabetes section for a diet regimen that appeals to you. To give you a head start, see the "Book List" at the very end of this section.

➤ **Find an Exercise Program** that you will stick with. If you're a senior, check out free exercise, dance and movement classes at centers in your area. Take yoga, tai chi, or the Alexander Technique. Look into exercise videotapes or DVDs that you can do in the comfort of your home, in front of your TV.

One of the best, easiest and most beneficial exercises is walking. Just plain walking. Get good walking shoes and a walking buddy for safety reasons…besides, it's more fun to walk with someone. Make sure your walking partner knows you have diabetes and that you both have glucose tablets in case your blood sugar drops too low. To avoid a big drop in blood sugar, the best time to walk is after you've eaten. Results of a small study at Old Dominion University in Virginia found that walkers' postmeal blood glucose readings were lower when they took a 20-minute stroll *after* dinner than when they walked before eating.

Whenever you walk, for best results, walk for at least 10 minutes at a time.

Also consider lifting weights. New studies indicate that a weight-lifting program can dramatically lower blood sugar levels. Since we lose muscle with age, we can rebuild it with weight training. Find a gym or senior center with professional trainers to supervise you. Meanwhile, start walking!

➤ **Keep Careful Records of Your Daily Diet,** blood sugar numbers (with the help of a glucometer*—available through your health insurance company and at pharmacies), and exercise routine, and have your health care provider monitor your results on a regular basis (about every three months), and together, make the necessary adjustments to fine-tune it all. (As a fine-tuning tool, see "Know Your A1C" next.)

Know Your A1C

The tests you do at home with your glucometer and strips show your blood sugar level at that moment. The A1C test (also known as *HbA1c, glycated* hemoglobin or *glycosylated* hemoglobin) shows your average blood sugar level over the past two or three months. It's the best way to see how well your type 2 diabetes is controlled.

According to a study conducted in the US and published in *The Diabetes Educator,* only 24% of diabetic patients knew their last A1C test result. The patients who knew their last A1C level were said to have better assessment of their blood sugar control than those who did not.

Approximately half of the score comes from the last 30 days. If your A1C is high, you and your doctor may need to make changes

---

*Blood Testing Tips: The traditional method of testing your blood sugar involves pricking your fingertip with a small, sharp needle (a lancet). The resulting drop of blood is transferred to a test strip which is then placed into a glucometer. A few seconds later your blood sugar level is displayed.

While newer meters allow you to use alternative testing sites—upper arm, thigh, base of the thumb—blood sugar levels in the fingertip area show changes more quickly than other sites, especially when your blood sugar is changing quickly, like after a meal or after exercise.

To give your fingertips some relief, prick the sides of the fingers. Use your thumb to press your finger pad so that both sides of your finger puff out a little, then prick with the lancet.

To bring enough blood to the surface for testing, wash your hands in warm water and rub them dry to improve circulation. If you're not near running water, get the circulation going by shaking your hands up and down.

in your diet, exercise and medications to help reduce it, which could help reduce your risks of dreaded diabetic complications. In fact, it's been shown that a 1% reduction in A1C (for instance, from 8% to 7%) lowers the risk of diabetic complications by about 40%.

The American Diabetes Association (ADA) recommends an A1C target of 7% or less. The American Association of Clinical Endocrinologists (AACE) recommends an A1C level of 6.5% or lower. The lower the better!

The diabetic with fairly stable daily blood sugar numbers should have his/her A1C tested every three months. If medication, diet or any kind of treatment has been changed, an A1C test is recommended after one month to monitor the new program's effect on blood sugar.

The A1C is usually taken by your doctor during a routine visit. All it requires is a drop of blood. The blood can be taken any time. There's no need to fast. Food eaten that day before the test will not affect the A1C outcome.

The Basics of Foot Care

Every piece of literature about managing diabetes stresses foot care. *Follow simple precautions, such as…*

➤ **Never Walk Barefoot.**

➤ **Dry Off.** After showering or bathing, dry your feet thoroughly, particularly in between your toes.

➤ **Inspect Your Feet Daily** (in the morning and/or at night). If you have a cut, bruise or infection of any kind, check with a podiatrist immediately.

➤ **Have Diabetic Podiatric Examinations at least three times a year.**

➤ **Jimmy Choo? Foo!**…for diabetic feet. Wear shoes that will help protect your feet.

Make comfort and safety your priority, not fashion. Check to see if your health insurance company covers diabetic shoes and prescription orthotics. Some do.

➤ **The Right Type of Socks.** Wear socks that don't create too much friction, and that allow moisture to ventilate properly. Researchers at the University of Missouri found that 100% cotton socks were the worst in terms of causing friction and trapping humidity. Socks made from nylon and other synthetic material were generally found to be best.

➤ **Stubbed Toe Prevention.** Prevent a stubbed toe by keeping a flashlight on your night table and using it if you need to go to the

SOMETHING SPECIAL

A1C for Yourself

If you have to wait a long time for the next doctor's appointment and/or you made changes in your diabetic management program, you can take an A1C test at home.

Bayer's A1CNow SELFCHECK two-test kit is easy (visit *www.bayercontourusbmeter.com* for a step-by-step instruction video) and takes only five minutes for the lab-accurate result.

While this should not take the place of your quarterly doctor visit, it is a wonderful tool for monitoring your progress between visits.

More information: You can find the A1CNow SELFCHECK at Walmart, Walgreens and CVS. For other outlets and questions about the A1CNow tests call Bayer's customer support services at 914-366-1800.

SOMETHING SPECIAL

It's a Croc!

The footwear company Crocs has a medical division, Crocs Rx—an affordable line of shoes designed for specific medical and therapeutic podiatric considerations, the kinds of considerations associated with diabetes, as well as other foot challenges.

The Crocs Rx line of shoes are made from Croslite material that provides a super grip on wet surfaces and does not absorb moisture, so it stays odor-free, and inhibits the growth of bacteria and fungi. All of the shoes have side air portals to keep feet cool and dry (just don't walk through puddles). *Here are three examples from the Crocs Rx line...*

● **Cloud** is specifically designed with diabetic feet in mind. These shoes feature a super-soft footbed, and roomy toe bed, which allows for wearing heavy socks without creating any tightness or pressure points on the foot. The protective front toe cap and elevated heel rim protect the foot from stubbing and bruising. These shoes also accommodate podiatrist-prescribed orthotics.

● **Silver Cloud** contains all of the benefits of the Cloud, plus an infusion of silver ions that's ideal for anyone susceptible to skin breakdown, ulcers, foot fungus and infections.

● **Relief** is designed with an ultrasoft shock-absorbing sole and wide toes. These shoes provide therapeutic relief for plantar fasciitis, bunions, heel pain and arthritis.

While you're at it, try Crocs' Orthocloud socks. They have a double cushion sole—extra padding that protects toes, heel and the entire bottom of the foot. Also, there's no irritating toe seam, and their moisture-wicking fibers keep feet cool and dry.

The Crocs Rx shoes and socks are available online and through podiatrists.

More information: Go to *www.crocs.com*, or call 877-238-4404.

bathroom during the night. Shine the flashlight on the floor in front of you as you walk to the bathroom and then back to bed.

Neuropathy

Diabetic neuropathy is nerve damage that affects approximately 50% to 70% of people with diabetes. This nasty condition usually impacts the limbs—hands and arms as well as feet and legs. The most common symptoms are tingling, loss of feeling or sensation, muscular weakness, discomfort, pain, immobility and the unhappiness that accompanies any one of these symptoms.

If your doctor is like the typical diabetes doctor, his goal for treating diabetic neuropathy is to prevent progression by advising you to be sure to keep your blood sugar numbers down. If you complain about pain, you may be given a prescription for a painkiller, or told to buy an over-the-counter painkiller, both of which have long lists of possible side effects.

FYI: Pain medications work by suppressing the nerve signals, and can actually make your neuropathy worse over time (not to mention what the possible side effects can do).

Yes, we're painting a bleak, but realistic, picture of most health care providers' approach to diabetic neuropathy. If you can identify with this, then it's time to take charge.

Stop Needless Amputations

According to the American Diabetes Association, amputations, especially from diabetes, are on the rise. Perry A~, as she goes by, believes there is a simple, safe and inexpensive solution that could reduce the number of amputations by 50% or more.

So what is this simple solution? Perry A~ explains, "It is a topical treatment with calcium bentonite clay, a clay strong enough to pull infections, gangrene and diseased tissue from the body and stimulate blood flow and oxygen to the area for the rebuilding of healthy tissue.

"During millions of years volcanic ash evolved into veins of clay with supercharged electromagnetic negative ionic charged particles with an alkaline pH. In the rock or powder form clay is dormant...it's a sleeping giant with great healing properties and benefits. But, when clay absorbs water it takes on a life force energy. This electromagnetic energy stimulates circulation and blood flow thereby revitalizing dormant cell energy and speeding up the healing process."

To gain more insight about the use of clay therapy, read about it in the "It Does a Body Good" chapter, page 238.

For information about amputation prevention, read *Reversing Diabetes* by Julian Whitaker, MD (Grand Central Publishing), or visit Dr. Whitaker's Wellness Institute Web site at *www.whitakerwellness.com*, or call 800-488-1500.

SOMETHING SPECIAL

A Stimulus Plan

Thanks to inventor Dr. David Phillips for the ReBuilder 300 Neuropathy Treatment System (*www.rebuildermedical.com*), a treatment that can help relieve pain, numbness and discoloration, and may actually restore the feeling in feet and hands, restore balance and mobility and reduce or eliminate the need for pain medication.

Since first writing about this in our previous book, *Bottom Line's Healing Remedies*, we're thrilled to pass along the good news that the Food and Drug Administration (FDA) approved ReBuilder, and it is now covered by Medicare. For more information, see the "It Does a Body Good" chapter, page 267.

Diabetes-Smart Supplements

The object of this entry is to make you aware of supplements—herbs and minerals—known to help decrease blood sugar levels. Your mission, should you decide to accept it, is to talk to your diabetes team—doctor, diabetes educator, nutritionist (you should have at least two of the three)—for their feedback and dosage recommendations. If you decide to add one or more supplements to help control your glucose readings, track results very carefully. If the supplement works well, and your blood sugar numbers come down consistently, you may need to reduce the dosage of your medication. It is *vital* that you tell your doctor what supplements you are taking and how they affect you, so that medication adjustments can be made.

➤ **Alpha Lipoic Acid.** This potent antioxidant helps with glucose utilization, and peripheral nerve support.

➤ **Chromium Picolinate or Polynicolinate.** This trace mineral makes insulin work more efficiently, and facilitates the assimilation of glucose into the cells.

While you can get chromium from foods such as broccoli, black pepper, dried beans and whole grains, you may also want to take a supplement of chromium.

➤ **B Vitamins.** According to Dr. Susan Lark, "Many of the B vitamins are major players in the regulation of insulin, sugars and fats in the bloodstream, as well as in protecting the organ systems." Dr. Lark recommends taking a good B complex that contains 50 milligrams (mg) to 100 mg of B-1, B-2, B-3 and B-6; 500 mg to 1,000 mg of B-5; 500 micrograms (mcg) to 1,000 mcg of B-12; 300 mcg of biotin; and 800 mcg to 1,000 mcg of folic acid.

Another piece of advice from Dr. Lark is to take B vitamins during the day, rather than at night, as they can be too stimulating and may interfere with your sleep.

 CAUTION: Do NOT take more than 150 mg of vitamin B-6 a day, as it can be toxic.

➤ **Magnesium.** An adequate amount of magnesium (begin with 150 mg two to three times a day with meals and build up to 300 to 400 mg two or three times daily if it's well tolerated) can improve insulin resistance and blood sugar control. According to one study, magnesium citrate is well absorbed. Supplement your supplement by eating magnesium-rich foods such as green leafy vegetables, legumes, nuts and whole grains.

 CAUTION: Magnesium can cause diarrhea. Cut down on the dosage if you experience this effect. Also, some people do better with magnesium oxide if they have trouble with magnesium.

➤ **Gymnema Sylvestre.** This plant from India has been credited with blocking the absorption of simple sugars; helping prevent elevated glucose levels and regenerating insulin-producing pancreatic tissues.

➤ **Banaba Leaf.** This Asian plant contains *corosolic acid*, said to help fine-tune the damaged insulin receptor which is the cause of insulin-resistance diabetes. The corosolic acid in the banaba leaf activates glucose transport into the cells, which results in blood sugar reduction.

➤ **Bitter Melon.** According to Herbal Provider, *www.herbalprovider.com*, bitter melon is an herb that helps regulate blood sugar levels and keeps body functions operating normally. It contains *gurmarin,* a polypeptide considered to be similar to bovine insulin, which has been shown in experimental studies to produce a sugar-regulating effect.

➤ **Milk Thistle.** Generally linked to the treatment of liver problems, this flowering herb seems to be blossoming into a remedy for diabetes. The herb's active component, *silymarin*, may be helpful in lowering blood sugar levels, and reducing the amount of sugar bound to the hemoglobin in a diabetic's blood.

➤ **Sage.** This common herb has been reported to be beneficial in the same way as the popular diabetic medication *glucophage* (Metformin). Sage is also used for liver problems. If you have type 2 diabetes and want to see if sage works for you, keep taking your meds, and whenever you drink a cup of sage tea (up to three cups a day), check your blood sugar number. If your numbers seem to be going down consistently and significantly, work with your health care provider to reduce your medication dosage.

To prepare sage tea for the day, put three tablespoons of sage leaves in a pitcher and pour three cups of just-boiled water in it. Let it steep for 10 minutes. Strain and drink a cup during or after meals. If you use sage tea bags (instead of loose leaves), use two tea bags for each cup.

 CAUTION: Sage can cause seizures in epileptics. Steer clear of sage if you have a history of any kind of seizure.

➤ **Cinnamon.** This spice contains a bioactive component that scientists believe has the potential to help type 2 diabetics. As of this writing, the jury is still out as to whether or not cinnamon significantly decreases blood glucose levels. If you want to see if it works for you, take one-quarter teaspoon of cinnamon, two to three times a day, in tea, food or capsules. It may take up to 40 days to see results.

➤ **Vitamin D.** According to research in Italy, published in the journal, *Diabetes Care*, approximately 61% of type 2 diabetics suffer from chronic vitamin D deficiency. The *New England Journal of Medicine* (July 2007) reported that studies showed 40% of children and nearly 100% of the elderly in the US and Europe were deficient in vitamin D. The lack of vitamin D impairs a person's immunity and ability to produce and respond to insulin.

 NOTE: It is very important to have your doctor test your vitamin D level.

In his newsletter on the topic, Ray D. Strand, MD (*www.raystrand.com*), refers to vitamin D as "the truly essential nutrient." He writes, "Clinical research of vitamin D has now reached a point that we can predictably state that several hundred thousand American lives could be saved each year if people supplemented their diets with 1,000 international units (IU) of vitamin D. Begin taking at least 1,000 IU of vitamin D today. Your body will love you for it.

"This is what nutritional medicine is all about. It emphasizes the true health benefits of supplementing a healthy diet with these optimal or advanced levels of nutrients—not recommended daily allowance (RDA) levels."

But, DO NOT do it alone. Work with a savvy health care professional who can test and monitor you. If you need such a person, ask for recommendations at your local health food store, diabetes support group and health insurance company. Keep looking until you find the right person for you.

Food Awareness

With regard to the following, we're not telling you to buy bread or drink coffee, but if you do, we're suggesting a blood-sugar-wise way to do it.

Incidentally, you may want to prepare a supermarket shopping list as you read through the next few pages.

➤ **Bread.** Look for dense-loaf bread… the coarse-grain kind where you can see kernels. It should feel heavy for its size. A 100% whole wheat loaf that's finely ground and has the texture of white bread will be digested almost as quickly as white bread and have a similar effect on your blood sugar. Dense bread will take longer to digest and will elevate blood sugar more slowly. Also look for bread that has fiber added, making it lower in carbs.

➤ **Fiber Fact.** Consuming 25 grams (g) of fiber a day helps lower cholesterol and control blood sugar levels.

➤ **Coffee.** Laboratory tests have shown that *chlorogenic acid*, a compound in coffee (both caffeinated and decaffeinated), decreases blood sugar. *Quinides*, other compounds found in coffee, help make the body more sensitive to insulin.

When you reach for a cup of coffee, be sure it's *decaf*. After a small study of patients, Duke University researcher James D. Lane, PhD, reported, "Caffeine increases blood glucose by as much as oral diabetes medications decrease it. It seems the detrimental effects of caffeine are as bad as the beneficial effects of oral diabetes drugs are good."

For people with diabetes, drinking coffee or consuming caffeine in other beverages can cause spikes in blood sugar by raising stress hormones that stimulate the release of stored glucose from the liver.

➤ **Fish and Seafood.** *The American Journal of Kidney Diseases* published the results of a study of 22,000 English people. After they ate fish at least twice a week, the abnormally high levels of protein in their urine were lowered. (Elevated protein levels are a sign of kidney disease.) This led to the conclusion that people with diabetes who eat fish twice a week are 75% less likely to develop kidney problems. Eating *quality* fish can benefit *everyone* in many ways.

According to the Environmental Defense Fund's Seafood Selector and the Monterey Bay Aquarium's Seafood Watch programs,

the following are the healthiest fish—high in omega-3s, low in contaminants and produced in a way that is friendly to the environment…

● **Wild salmon from Alaska**—fresh, frozen or canned.

● **Arctic char**—wild if you can get it, if not, farmed is fine.

● **Atlantic mackerel.**

● **Sardines**—canned, in olive oil.

● **Sablefish/black cod**—caught off Alaska and British Columbia.

● **Anchovies.**

● **Oysters**—farmed.

● **Rainbow trout**—farmed (because of moderate PCB contamination, limit kids' consumption to two to three meals a month).

● **Albacore tuna**—caught from US or Canadian fisheries. (Kids up to age 6 should limit consumption to three meals a month because of moderate mercury contamination.)

● **Mussels**—farmed.

● **Pacific or Alaskan halibut**—wild-caught in the Pacific.

➤ **Fruit.** Steve Hertzler, PhD, RD (registered dietician), conducted a study at Ohio State University and discovered that eating fruit an hour before a meal can help keep blood sugar in check. According to Dr. Hertzler, "Once absorbed by the liver, the fructose in the fruit activates an enzyme called *glucokinase*, which helps pull additional sugar from the blood, keeping the blood sugar level stable."

If you are going to try this, start with a little apple or pear or seven to 10 bing cherries. Keep the portion small.

➤ **Garlic.** We wrote an entire book on the *stinking rose* (that's the nickname of garlic), so you can imagine how passionate we are about garlic as nature's super healer. With regard to diabetes, scientific studies say that garlic may increase insulin secretion, which lowers blood sugar. Also, each clove of garlic is filled with antioxidants that help prevent diabetic complications.

 CAUTION: Having garlic on an empty stomach can cause nausea. Be sure to have some food in your stomach before eating garlic or taking capsules. And, be cautious with garlic if you have gastritis.

➤ **Mustard.** Depending on the go-with food, opt for mustard instead of ketchup. Mustard has no sugar, no carbs and is lower in sodium. Always check labels for nutrition details to make sure you're not buying mustard with unwanted additives and unnecessary carbs.

➤ **Nuts.** We've written extensively about the health benefits of nuts, and are now going to add a couple of lines about their value with regard to diabetes. They are a great easy-to-take-with-you snack, giving you protein and healthy fat. Plus they can energize you out of that four o'clock post-lunch slump.

We buy nuts at Whole Foods and Trader Joe's...raw walnuts (a good daily portion is about 14 halves, which equal an ounce), raw cashews, pistachios, peanuts and raw almonds (all unsalted).

Almonds are filled with vitamin E, which is an antioxidant that may protect against kidney, eye and nerve complications.

We also buy no-junk-added peanut butter and almond butter. If your natural foods market has a nut-butter machine, ask for a taste of the freshly ground peanut butter. You'll see that it only needs one ingredient. If you can't get it ground in the store, look for a brand that lists "peanuts" as its only ingredient. Go nuts!

➤ **Oatmeal.** A bowl of oatmeal is a good way to start the day. Its glycemic index* is on the low side and so it takes longer to get absorbed by the blood stream. It is fairly high in fiber and keeps you feeling full until your next snack or meal.

Instant oatmeal is not as beneficial as traditional rolled oats that are cooked slowly. Even better than that, with a lower glycemic index, are steel cut oats (these are whole grain oats from the inner portion of the oat kernel). They take a little longer to cook, but it may be worth the wait because this morning meal may help keep your blood sugar levels under control for the rest of the day...providing you continue to eat low-carb, fiber-rich foods.

Make the oatmeal tastier and healthier by adding cinnamon, flaxseed, walnuts, sugar-free maple syrup and/or even a clove of minced garlic.

➤ **Olive Oil.** Olive oil is your friend. Extra virgin olive oil (EVOO) is your best friend. EVOO comes from the first pressing of olives, making it the purest, least acidic and best tasting.

In *The World's Healthiest Foods* (*www. whfoods.com*), George Mateljan maintains that diets rich in olive oil help prevent dangerous belly fat accumulation, insulin resistance and a drop in *adiponectin* (a hormone produced by

---

*Glycemic Index (GI) is a system for classifying carbohydrate-containing foods, according to how fast they raise blood glucose levels in the body. A food with a higher glycemic value raises blood glucose faster and is less beneficial to blood sugar control than a food that scores lower.

The glycemic index consists of a scale from 1 to 100. The glycemic index separates carb-containing foods into three general categories: (1) high glycemic index foods (GI 70+), causing a rapid rise in blood-glucose levels; (2) intermediate glycemeic index foods (GI 55-69), causing a medium rise in blood glucose; (3) low glycemic index food (GI 54 or less), causing a lower rise in blood sugar.

For more glycemic index information and a free GI database that includes GI food values and carbohydrate counts, visit *www.glycemicindex.com*.

fat cells that promotes sensitivity to insulin). You want to keep up the blood level of *adiponectin* because it helps regulate sugar and fat metabolism, improves insulin sensitivity and has anti-inflammatory effects on the cells lining the blood vessel walls. Too much information? The bottom line is that a Mediterranean-type diet rich in monounsaturated fat from EVOO (and nuts) will improve your sensitivity to insulin, lower your blood sugar and help prevent fat from collecting around your middle.

George Mateljan's EVOO-eating tips...

● **Set your table with a small condiment bowl filled with EVOO** as a butter replacement for use on bread, vegetables, etc.

● **For even more flavor, try adding a few drops of balsamic vinegar** or a sprinkling of your favorite spices to the olive oil.

● **Add olive oil to foods immediately after cooking** to get the most health benefit and flavor from your olive oil.

➤ **Sweet as Sugar.** You probably know about stevia, a nutritional supplement that is made from an intensely sweet extract of natural stevia leaves, said to be 30 times sweeter than sugar. It has no chemicals, zero calories, zero carbohydrates and a zero glycemic index. If you haven't used the little packets to sweeten your drinks, or as a sugar replacement in cooking, then chances are you've had store-bought, stevia-sweetened products. Move over stevia, there's a new kid on the block...xylitol.

America is starting to catch up with Europeans in terms of the use of xylitol, a diabetes-friendly sugar substitute that's said to be absorbed slowly without increasing blood sugar.

Xylitol also has some unique and beneficial side effects. In Finland, where xylitol was discovered in the 19th century, studies have shown that its use dramatically reduces cavities. That's because its sugar-alcohol structure cannot be used by cavity-causing bacteria in the mouth. As a result, all Finnish chewing gum and some American sugar-free gum is now made with xylitol. Another intriguing quality of xylitol is that it seems to inhibit growth of bacteria that cause ear infections. Xylitol is also being researched and tested as a treatment for osteoporosis. One group of Finnish researchers has reported that dietary xylitol may prevent weakening of bones and actually improve bone density.

Look for xylitol at health food stores and natural foods markets.

 CAUTION: Xylitol can cause gas and diarrhea if consumed in excess amounts. Also, it is very harmful for dogs. NEVER allow your pooch to have any food that has xylitol in it.

➤ **Sugar Fact.** On food labels, under "Carbohydrates" there will be a listing for "Sugars." The amount of sugar, per serving, is listed in grams. Every four g is equivalent to a teaspoon of sugar. This knowledge may help you rethink some of your supermarket purchases.

Food Favorites

When it comes to food, we keep it simple. Fresh and raw is best; organic whenever possible and affordable. The foods we prepare are usually low in carbohydrates and high in fiber. We use good fat—olive oil or coconut oil. We season food with garlic, curry, pepper and on rare occasions when we need to add salt to a dish, we use Himalayan Crystal Salt (available at health food stores, natural food markets and at *www.himalayancrystalsalt.com*).

If you were to go food shopping with us, you'd have to have patience. We read every label, paying particular attention to the carb, fiber, fat and sodium counts, as well as the list of ingredients. You should, too. To know exactly what you're eating, you have to know exactly what you're buying.

Here are some foods that pass our label-scrutiny and please our palates...

➤ **Roll Out the Roll-Ups...and Pita Bread, Too.** In 1930 Ed Mafoud's grandfather introduced hearth-baked Syrian pita bread in his bakery in Brooklyn, New York. As word spread, demand increased, and now, 80 years and three generations later, Damascus Bakeries, home of "America's Original Pita," has national distribution, and is a dream-come-true for people with diabetes.

They have a whole wheat pita that has 10 net carbs (17 carbs; seven fiber). It has a low glycemic index, is low fat and is absolutely delicious. One entire whole wheat pita for only 10 net carbs. I knoooooow! Enjoy it with guacamole, egg salad, tuna salad or any low-carb filling.

As great as the pitas are, my favorites are the Damascus Roll-Ups. Heaven! They are flatbread rectangles (wraps), in a selection of flavors including all natural golden flax, red pepper, onion, rye and focaccia. Their carb, fiber and fat counts are extraordinary. At 6 net carbs for a sizable Flax Roll-up, you can use it to prepare a delicious and different wrap every day of the week.

Check your supermarket or natural foods market and if they don't have Damascus Bakeries' products, ask the store manager to order them, or call 800-FOR-PITA (367-7482) for a store in your area that carries them.

An unsolicited testimonial: "It's not often I (Joan) find a diabetes-friendly food that makes meal planning and preparation simple and convenient, while inspiring me to be creative in the

kitchen. Damascus Roll-ups and Pitas do that for me."

To see Damascus Bakeries' complete line, visit *www.damascusbakery.com*.

➤ **Salba Chia—The Just-About-Perfect Food (and Supplement).** Salba is an ancient whole grain, rediscovered by Dr. Vladimir Vuksan, professor of endocrinology and nutritional sciences, faculty of medicine at the University of Toronto. *Total Health Magazine* reports that Dr. Vuksan's studies were irrefutable evidence that consumption of salba results in a simultaneous reduction of blood pressure, body inflammation and blood clotting, while balancing after-meal blood sugar. (For more salba information, see the "It Does a Body Good" chapter, page 268, and visit *www.salbasmart.com* or phone 303-999-3996.)

➤ **Healthy Fast Food.** Gardein (Garden Protein) founder and chef, Yves Potvin, has a lifelong passion and pleasure—bringing people healthy, innovative and convenient plant-based meat-like foods.

Gardein provides two lines: Fresh, found in refrigerated-food sections, and frozen, found in (you guessed it) frozen-food sections.

These meal makers are high in vegetable protein and ridiculously low in carbohydrates, easy to digest and free of cholesterol, animal products and dairy. Most are also a good source of fiber and are low in fat...oh yes, and they're very tasty.

Check your supermarket and natural foods market for Gardein, in some areas it's called, "It's All Good," or go to *www.gardein.com* and click on "where to buy," or call 877-305-6777.

➤ **GG Scandinavian Bran Crispbread—A Good Go-With.** From the slow-baking ovens of Norway comes the highest bran-content product available, GG Scandinavian Bran Crispbread. It is low-carb, high-fiber, fat-free and appropriately known as "The Appetite Control Cracker."

Endorsed by many diabetes experts, each slice of crispbread has three g of carbohydrates, which is cancelled out by its three g of fiber, and only 16 calories. It's wonderful for a snack—dip it in hummus, eat with a salad, spread or melt cheese on it.

Now the product line has expanded to include crushed crackers called GG Bran Crispbread Sprinkles. These sprinkles can add fiber and crunch to food, and can be used in recipes as a high-fiber/low-carb replacement for bread crumbs, meal or flour, as in the recipe below.

■ Recipe ■

GG Bran Crusted Salmon

By Rebecca Brown, corporate development, GG Scandinavian Bran Crispbread

Ingredients

4 salmon filets
Pepper to taste
Cracked red pepper to taste (optional)
3 teaspoons dried tarragon
2 tablespoons Dijon mustard
1 teaspoon balsamic vinegar
3 teaspoons honey
½ cup of GG crackers, crushed, or GG Sprinkles
¼ cup parmesan cheese, grated
3 tablespoons plain yogurt (fat free is best or 2% fat)
1 egg white
2 tablespoons sunflower or olive oil

Instructions

1. Rinse the salmon in cold water, pat dry with a paper towel, cover with plastic wrap and set the filets aside in the refrigerator.
2. In a medium-sized mixing bowl, add all wet ingredients and herbs, briefly whisking until blended.
3. Add the salmon to the mixing bowl and thoroughly coat all of the pieces with the mixture. Cover the bowl and chill in the refrigerator for at least 2 hours. (Ideally, the salmon should be chilled in the mixture 4 hours or more.)
4. In a small bowl stir the parmesan and crushed GG crackers or Sprinkles. Spread the dry mixture onto a plate evenly. Roll the chilled salmon in the Sprinkles mixture until well crusted.
5. In a skillet large enough to hold the filets, heat 2 tablespoons of sunflower or olive oil on medium heat. Add in the crusted salmon filets and sauté until the crust is crisp. It takes about five minutes. With a spatula, carefully flip the salmon filets over for crisping on the other side for another few minutes.
6. Gently place the crispy-crusted filets onto a cookie sheet that's lined with aluminum foil or parchment, and bake in the oven at 325°F for 15 to 25 minutes, or until completely cooked.

 NOTE: Instead of salmon filets, this recipe can also be made using skinless, boneless, chicken filets or white-fish filets.

Look for GG Scandinavian Bran Crisp-bread at your supermarket, health food store or natural foods market. For a selection of recipes or to order online visit *www.brancrispbread.com*.

➤ **Pasta Possibilities.** In general, pasta is a no-no for carb counters, although pasta made from durum wheat (whole wheat pasta) is supposed to have only a moderate effect on blood sugar levels. The only way you'll know if it works for you is by trying a small portion. While you're at it, there are two low-carb pastas that may satisfy a craving for pasta without sending blood sugar numbers soaring…if eaten in moderation, of course. They both have great taste and texture. Try each of them and test your blood sugar two hours after eating to see which one (or both) works for you.

● **FiberGourmet Light Pasta**—At Fiber-Gourmet technology replaces ingredients like flour with 0-calorie fiber, resulting in a 40% calorie reduction. Normally that would make the food taste fibrous and not so good, but they manage to add all that fiber without ruining the taste and texture, thanks to a fiber called *resistant starch*, which the FDA classifies as a fiber. It's the best of both worlds—it tastes like starch, but works like fiber. Your body is also able to tolerate resistant starch much better than other fibers. While most cellulose-based fibers produce gas and bloating, resistant starch in all of the FiberGourmet products are gentle to your stomach. A portion size is filling and satis-fying…always a plus, especially if you want to lose weight.

Check your local health food store or natural foods market for FiberGourmet, or go to *www.fibergourmet.com* to view the variety of shapes and flavors and to order, or call 786-348-0081.

● **Dreamfields Pasta** has five g of digest-ible carbohydrates per serving (two ounces dry or about one to 1.5 cups cooked). It also has twice the fiber and a 65% lower glycemic in-dex than traditional white pasta. This all trans-lates into a lower blood glucose rise after eating Dreamfields, compared with eating the same amount of traditional white pasta.

Check in your supermarket and natural foods market for Dreamfields, or go to *www. dreamfieldsfoods.com* or call 800-250-1917.

➤ **Chocolate.** People with diabetes do not have to miss out on the many benefits of dark chocolate, including reduction of bad (LDL) cholesterol and blood pressure and prevention of blood clots. In addition to the *serotonin* in dark chocolate being a natural mood-boosting antidepressant, let's not forget the production of pleasure-inducing endorphins, or the great taste of chocolate. The key is—all together now—*moderation*. Be sure the dark chocolate you eat has a minimum of 70% cocoa.

● **YC Chocolate sells a line of sugar-free dark chocolate (70% cocoa),** developed by a daughter whose diabetic dad has a sweet tooth. They have a wonderful selection of bars, including our favorites, a dark chocolate bar with whole roasted almonds and a dark choco-late bar with real bits of orange. They also have wonderful gifts. For more information, go to *www.ycchocolate.com* or call 800-433-2462.

● **Found in most sections where candy bars are sold,** including supermarkets, you'll find Lindt Excellence Extra Dark (70% to 85% cocoa) bars. They are not sugar-free, but the carb count is fairly low and the taste is good. Opt for the 85% cocoa and limit the amount you eat at any one time.

➤ **An Emergency Meal.** For all those nights you aren't able to get to the supermarket, and you get home later than you thought and are famished, always have at least one meal that you can take out of the freezer, pop in the microwave and eat dinner in minutes.

Our desperation dish is Tandoor Chef's Kofta Curry (*www.tandoorchef.com/entrees.php# koftacurry*)—an Indian meal that takes five minutes to prepare and is available at some supermarkets and natural foods markets. These vegetable dumplings simmered in a spicy sauce are low in carbs, and go great on top of cauliflower (also in our freezer) instead of rice or mashed potatoes.

If you prefer your own home-cooked meal, next time you prepare one, make extra and freeze a portion or two as your emergency meal.

Dr. Mao's Home Remedies

Doctor of Chinese medicine, Taoist antiaging expert (*www.taoofwellness.com*) and cofounder of Yo San University in Los Angeles, Dr. Mao Shing Ni (known as Dr. Mao—*www.askdrmao. com*) graciously agreed to share some eating tips that are good for diabetics. They are from his book, *Secrets of Self-Healing* (Avery)...

➤ **Baked Pumpkin.** Eat a slice of baked pumpkin topped with olive oil and rosemary every day.

➤ **Soup.** Boil one-half medium head of chopped cabbage, one diced yam and one-third cup lentils in eight cups of water for 30 to 45 minutes. Season lightly with herbs and spices and eat as a soup for dinner. Have this dish two to three times a week for a month.

➤ **Juice.** Juice one daikon radish, three stalks of celery, one cucumber and one bunch of spinach. Drink two glasses a day.

Gem Therapy

In *Gifts of the Gemstone Guardians* (Golden Age Institute), author and leading authority on therapeutic gemstones. Michael Katz reports on energy medicine. This new field uses the energy emanated by gemstones to heal, nourish and illuminate all aspects of our lives.

According to Michael Katz, the gems for diabetes support are...

- **Carnelian**
- **Citrine**
- **Dark green aventurine**
- **Light green aventurine**
- **Emerald**

There is a lot more to this than carrying around a chunk of the appropriate stone. Gemisphere, founded in 1988 by Michael Katz, is regarded a world-class provider of therapeutic quality gemstones. Visit their Web site (*www. gemisphere.com*) for a lot of helpful information on how to choose and use gemstones, or call 800-727-8877 to get a free gemstone advisor consultation.

Worthwhile Web Sites for Diabetics

➤ **Nutrition Data** (*nutritiondata.self. com*) can help you analyze your diet, develop recipes and plan meals according to your specific way of eating. This site will help you calculate everything having to do with food. For example, you can generate a list of low-carbohydrate foods. There is also a special diabetes section with tips and tools for better blood sugar control.

➤ **Carbs Information** (*www.carbs-infor mation.com*) is quite extraordinary and then some. When you go to the site, be prepared to spend time exploring all that it provides. It covers carbs, low-carb diets, carb intake, blood sugar control, dietary fiber and everything else carb related.

➤ **Join the Conversation!** Become part of an online diabetes community. The Joslin Diabetes Center's Diabetes Discussion Boards (*http://forums.joslin.org*) offer you an opportunity to communicate with other diabetics and their families and with Joslin clinical staff as well.

➤ **The Partnership for Prescription Assistance** (*www.pparx.org*) helps qualifying patients without prescription drug coverage get the medicines they need for free or nearly free. Their mission is to increase awareness of patient assistance programs and boost enrollment of those who are eligible.

➤ *DiabetesHealth* (*www.diabeteshealth. com*) is a magazine whose motto is "Investigate, inform, inspire." Check it out.

➤ **Diabetes Action: Research and Education Foundation** (*www.diabetesaction.org*). Have a question? Ask their "Diabetes Educator."

➤ **dLife for Your Diabetes Life!** (*www. dlife.com*) is the Web site for the *dLife* TV show. Find lots of good information, thousands of diabetes-friendly recipes, resources and more.

➤ **DiabetesMonitor** (*www.diabetesmonitor. com*) provides information, advice, resources and support for people with diabetes and their families, as well as for diabetes educators and other health care professionals.

➤ **Children with Diabetes** (*www.child renwithdiabetes.com*) is an award-winning site that helps diabetic kids and their families learn about every aspect of the disease. It includes essays by young people with diabetes and "Ask the Diabetes Team," which lets users pose questions to experts and receive personal replies.

➤ **The American Diabetes Association** (*www.diabetes.org*) has a variety of information to educate the diabetic and the parents of diabetic children. They offer free information packets for recently diagnosed diabetics and free boxes of educational tools for newly diagnosed children. To request a packet, call 800-DIABETES (342-2383).

 ALERT FOR DIABETES PATIENTS: There have been reports of insulin-delivery pumps and glucose-monitoring devices being potentially damaged after passing through full-body or X-ray scanners used by airport security.

If you use one of these devices for diabetes care: Get a letter from your doctor that will allow you to bypass the scanners and be hand-screened instead.

H. Peter Chase, MD, professor of pediatrics, University of Colorado, Aurora.

Recommended Reading

Check out the books listed here to get an idea of the range of information, programs and guidance available for you...

➤ *Reversing Diabetes—Reduce or Even Eliminate Your Dependence on Insulin or Oral Drugs* by Julian Whitaker, MD (Grand Central Publishing). Dr. Whitaker (*www.whitakerwellness. com*) helps you make lifestyle choices with a step-by-step, easy-to-follow type 2 plan that will also help you lose weight and lower cholesterol, blood pressure and heart attack risk.

➤ *Diabetes Survival Guide—Understanding the Facts About Diagnosis, Treatment, and Prevention* by Stanley Mirsky, MD, and Joan Rattner Heilman (Ballantine Books). This book can answer many of your questions, and give you sensible, easy-to-follow suggestions about what, when and how much to eat—included are delicious choices.

➤ *Beat Diabetes Naturally—The Best Foods, Herbs, Supplements and Lifestyle Strategies to Optimize Your Diabetes Care* by Michael Murray, ND, and Michael Lyon, MD (Storey). The goal of this book is to help you balance your blood sugar, drop extra pounds, enhance the effectiveness of medications and reduce your risk of complications.

➤ *The 30-Day Diabetes Cure* by Jim Healthy and Roy Heilbron, MD (Bottom Line Books). A patient-proven diabetes-reversing program that's twice as effective as the leading type-2 drug. Easy and inexpensive, many people have lost weight and gotten off medication with this book.

➤ *The Complete Idiot's Guide to Diabetes* (second edition) by Mayer B. Davidson, MD, and Debra L. Gordon (Alpha Books). Hate the title; love the book. It is a complete guide for people with prediabetes and diabetes.

➤ *Dr. Bernstein's Diabetes Solution* (revised and updated) by Richard K. Bernstein, MD (Little Brown and Company). As a type 1 diabetic for more than 60 years, Dr. Bernstein is living proof that his simple program, based on good nutrition, healthy exercise and (where necessary) small doses of medication, can stop roller-coaster blood sugar swings and promote good health.

➤ *The 30-Day Diabetes Miracle* by Franklin House, MD, Stuart A. Seale, MD, and Ian Blake Newman (Perigee Books). The book is based on the Lifestyle Center of America's program (*www.fullplateliving.org*) to stop diabetes, restore health and build natural vitality. The authors say there's no better treatment than lifestyle modification.

DIARRHEA

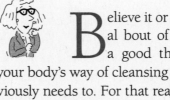

Believe it or not, an occasional bout of diarrhea can be a good thing. Diarrhea is your body's way of cleansing itself when it obviously needs to. For that reason, some health practitioners feel that you should wait six to eight hours before doing anything to stop the condition. (That's easy for them to say!)

Diarrhea can be caused by mild food poisoning, lactose intolerance (an allergic reaction to milk), a minor bacterial infection, fatigue, stress, overeating or eating while upset or very nervous.

Whatever the reason for the condition, it causes depletion and dehydration. During a bout of diarrhea, you lose fluid that contains electrolytes—valuable minerals including potassium, chloride, sodium, magnesium and calcium. It is a good idea to buy one of the sports beverages or bottled water containing electrolytes, to replace those lost minerals and restore your nutrient balance quickly. Check labels in the bottled water section of your supermarket.

Also, be sure to consume plenty of water throughout the bout and afterward, too. Eat foods rich in the lost nutrients—whole grains, potatoes with the skin, ripe bananas and dark green leafy vegetables lightly cooked.

Give your system a chance to get back to itself by not taxing it with fatty, oily foods, sugar and sugar products, white flour products, milk and other dairy products.

Now that you have an understanding of the problem, here is a selection of remedies to help solve the problem.

CAUTION: If you still have diarrhea after two full days of remedy-taking, check with your health professional to make sure it isn't a symptom of something else that requires additional attention.

➤ **Bacteria Destroyer.** If you think that diarrhea is caused by harmful bacteria, drink a tablespoon of apple cider vinegar in a glass of room-temperature water before each meal. Also, make an appointment with your doctor.

➤ **Classic Folk Remedy.** Just about any form of blackberry is the main ingredient of a diarrhea remedy that dates back to biblical times. Every four hours have one dose of either six ounces of blackberry juice, or two ounces of blackberry wine, or one heaping teaspoon of blackberry jam, or two tablespoons of blackberry brandy.

➤ **Pack in Pectin.** Apples are wonderful for stopping diarrhea. Clean an apple according to the instructions in the "Healthful Hints" chapter, page 283. Then grate the apple and let it stand until it turns brown. In other words, you're letting the pectin in the fruit oxidize, duplicating the basic ingredient in some popular over-the-counter diarrhea drugs. Once the grated apple turns brown, eat it.

Cinnamon is also a helpful diarrhea stopper, and it tastes good, too. Sprinkle a quarter of a teaspoon of cinnamon powder on the grated apple.

Wait a few hours, then eat another grated apple with or without cinnamon.

➤ **Carob.** Insoluble fiber in one's diet helps create larger, softer and bulkier stools. Carob (often used as an alternative to chocolate, and as a replacement for cocoa in baking) is an insoluble fiber. It's effective in the treatment of diarrhea because carob tannins bind and inactivate toxins and inhibit the grown of bacteria, both of which may cause diarrhea.

Mix a rounded tablespoon of carob powder (available at health food stores) in a big glass of warm water and drink it before each meal. For carob to do its job, it's important to have it with lots of water it.

➤ **Acupressure.** Lie down, relax and take the heel of your palm and place it on your navel. Press in and, in a circular motion, massage the area for a few minutes. It should help you feel better.

Traveler's Diarrhea

➤ **Traveler's Diarrhea Prevention.** In foreign countries, whenever possible, drink carbonated bottled water instead of plain bottled water. Carbonation helps kill infection-causing microbes that can cause diarrhea or worse. Also, it's a good idea to take probiotics while traveling to prevent diarrhea.

➤ **A remedy from Worldwide Health Agencies and US Health Services** for when you're traveling out of the country and you get diarrhea. You need two glasses. In one glass pour eight ounces of distilled water and add a quarter-teaspoon of baking soda; in the other glass pour eight ounces of orange juice, or any fruit juice, and add a half-teaspoon of honey and a pinch of salt. Drink a mouthful from one glass, then from the other. Keep going back and forth until you finish the contents of both glasses, knowing relief is on its way.

AFFIRMATION

Repeat this every time you go to the bathroom and right before you make a phone call...

I accept myself for the perfect person I am. My mind and body are in harmony with the universe.

DRINKING PROBLEMS

Alcoholism

If you have a drinking problem and do not already know the government and private agencies that offer counseling, see page 73 for contact information. Meanwhile, we offer suggestions to help curb the craving, along with our best wishes for your recovery.

Craving Stoppers

➤ **Herbal Tea.** Angelica root or angelica leaves (available at health food stores) have *glutamine*, an amino acid that's said to inhibit the urge for alcohol. Make tea of the herb by pouring a cup of just-boiled water over one teaspoon of angelica. Let it steep for 10 minutes. Strain and add honey and lemon to taste. Drink three cups a day.

➤ **Herbal Capsule.** Chaparral is a very healing herb, originally used by Native Americans, and is available at health food stores in capsule form. Take one capsule after every meal. It can help detoxify the liver as well as curb the craving.

➤ **Food Power.** Changes in your daily diet can increase your power to resist taking a drink. Let fruit, vegetables and whole grains take the place of white flour, sugar and all sugar products. Enhance food with B-complex vitamins by adding wheat germ and brewer's yeast to soups, stews and cereals.

➤ **Suck on a Clove.** Keep a whole clove (the kind used when preparing ham) in your mouth, mixing it with your saliva, to get rid of the urge to take a drink. It's not a pleasant thing to do, but it has been known to work, and it

70

may be a lot more pleasant than having too much to drink.

AFFIRMATION

Whenever the thought of a drink enters your mind, repeat the following sentences over and over...

I am strong. I am brave and I have control. I am getting better and better.

Social Drinking

Preventing Drunkenness

➤ **From the Philosophers.** In the (translated) words of Greek philosopher Aristotle, "Dine well on cabbage just before starting out for a big evening." In case the Romans demand equal time, here's a quote from Cato, who said, "If you wish to drink much at a banquet, before dinner dip cabbage in vinegar and eat as much as you wish. When you have dined, cut five leaves. The cabbage will make you as fit as if you had had nothing and you can drink as much as you will."

What it all seems to mean is, eat cole slaw, or cabbage in some form, before you imbibe and you won't get drunk. Our advice is to eat cabbage instead of drinking and, for sure you won't get drunk.

➤ **Nuts.** Eat a handful of raw almonds on an empty stomach and they will—supposedly—keep you from an inebriated state.

Sober Up

➤ **Great Grapefruit.** Slowly eating one small grapefruit should help you sober up.

➤ **Sobering Juice.** Juice fresh radishes and slowly drink half a glass of the radish juice.

Hangovers

If you're foolish enough to drink enough to get a hangover, here we arm you with imbibing information and guidelines, prevention methods and symptom soothers…

► **Double Trouble.** Cigarettes and booze contain the same hangover-causing ingredient, *acetaldehyde*. So when you drink and smoke at the same time, you can expect the hangover from hell!

► **When to Drink.** If you're going to drink, be sure to eat first. Drinking on a full stomach slows down the body's absorption of alcohol; the slower the absorption, the less amount of alcohol reaches the brain.

► **Drink While Drinking.** Huh? Let us explain. Drink twice the volume of nonalcoholic beverages as alcoholic beverages to help avoid dehydration of your body cells. Also, the more you fill up on nonalcoholic drinks, the less room you'll have for the hard stuff.

► **Bad Booze.** If we thought you were interested in technical data, we'd tell you about the manufacturing by-products called *congeners* that cause all those nasty side effects from drinking. Instead, we'll tell it to ya' straight…

These are the *worst* drinks in terms of hangovers—bourbon, brandy, rum, scotch, rye, cognac, whiskey, red wine and champagne. Speaking of champagne, any bubbly alcoholic beverage, or even booze that's mixed with a carbonated drink (e.g. gin and tonic), will get into the bloodstream much faster because of the bubbles.

These are less bad than the worst drinks in terms of hangovers—vodka, gin (without the tonic) and white wine.

► **Slow Down.** The average body burns alcohol at the rate of about an ounce an hour. If you pace yourself by nursing your drinks, you won't feel as though you need a nurse in the morning.

► **Do the Right Thing.** Considering that the body burns alcohol at the rate of about an ounce an hour, for each ounce of alcohol you consume, it will take at least an hour before you have full driving faculties. So, if you have had four ounces of alcohol by 8 pm, you should not dare to get behind the wheel of a car until—the earliest—midnight. Let's face it, chances are you're not going to stop drinking at eight. Be smart. Be respectful of your life and the lives of everyone out there. At the *start* of the partying, assign a non-drinking designated driver.

► **Forget Beer and Peer Pressure.** Don't keep up with a friend drink for drink. Your friend may be twice your size and can drink twice as much without facing the consequences. Use your head more than your mouth.

► **For Women Only.** If you drink right before you menstruate, when the estrogen level is low, you will get drunk faster and have more severe hangovers than during any other time of your cycle.

Incidentally, according to researchers at the Mount Sinai Medical Center, women absorb about one-third more alcohol into their blood than men. They get drunk faster and stay that way longer.

► **Hangover Minimizer.** Take a B-complex tablet (50 milligrams [mg]) before you start drinking and another one *while* you're drinking. Alcohol depletes the body of B vitamins, and by replenishing them, you can almost make a hangover not happen.

► **Hangover Prevention.** When you've finished drinking and are ready for bed, stir a tablespoon of sugar into a glass of orange juice and drink it down.

This remedy came to us from a woman who took care of an alcoholic for years. She said that it prevented him from ever having a "morning after" hangover.

The fructose in the drink helps the body burn alcohol quickly.

➤ **"Morning After" Symptom Soother.** Take a quarter of a lemon and rub the juicy side on each armpit. Revolting as this seems, we've been told that it does ease the symptoms of a hangover.

 NOTE: This might sting if you've recently shaved under your arms.

We recommended this remedy in a previous book. When we handed in the manuscript for the book, the publisher gave the pages to an MD. He reviewed all the remedies to make sure they were safe. In the margins of each chapter, he wrote comments like "this is outrageous" and "they must be joking." Obviously, the doctor wasn't into folk remedies. That is, until he came to "lemon on the armpit for hangovers." In the margin, next to this remedy he wrote, "It's the greatest! It helped get me through medical school." This was our very first doctor-endorsed folk remedy.

➤ **Hangover Helpers.** Dehydration is one of the side effects of drinking. It's important to replenish the water lost the night before. You also need to replace the electrolytes (essential nutrients like potassium) that were *flushed* away.

Drink as much water as possible before you go to bed. In the morning, eat or drink any one, two, or three of the following...

• **Tomato juice** (high in fructose, which speeds the body's alcohol-burning process).

• **Tangerine juice** (also helps relieves dry throat).

• **The liquid from banana peel that was boiled in water** (also eat the banana as a source of potassium).

• **Watermelon.**

• **Ten strawberries** (relieves a hangover headache).

• **An apple or two** (relieves a hangover headache).

• **Gingerroot tea** (put four quarter-sized pieces of fresh gingerroot in water and bring to a boil. Simmer for 15 to 20 minutes, then strain and drink. This tea is especially good for an upset stomach caused by drinking).

 CAUTION: Ginger acts as a blood thinner, so check with your doctor before using it if you are taking a prescription blood thinner. Also, stop using ginger three days before any surgery.

• **Sauerkraut juice** (it tastes better than it sounds).

• **Cabbage soup.**

• **Chicken soup.**

• **Beet soup (borscht).**

• **Tripe soup** (if you're not familiar with it and have to ask for the recipe, then believe me, you wouldn't want to have it...with or without a hangover).

• **Clove soup** (boil a dozen cloves in a pint of water).

• **Gazpacho** (for *summer* hangovers).

• **A tablespoon of honey** (a great source of fructose).

➤ **Symptom Soother.** Add one-half teaspoon of salt to eight ounces of club soda. With a straw between your teeth—horizontally, from cheek to cheek—drink the mixture. Do not sip the salted club soda through the straw; the liquid should pass by it on the way to being swallowed. (Don't ask why; we do not know the answer, but the person who told it to us swore it has worked for him.)

▶ **Hair of the Bow-Wow.** If alcoholic beverages cause a hangover, it's hard to believe that more of the same will relieve it. But we'd be remiss if we didn't include one of the best-known and classic "hair of the dog" remedies...

Drink one or two ounces of Fernet Branca, neat. (Not being drinkers, when we first saw the remedy written that way, we thought "neat" was instructing the tipsy reader not to dribble on himself. Most people know "neat" means "undiluted.")

While the internationally acclaimed Fernet Branca has an alcoholic proof of about 80% (and is available where alcoholic beverages are sold, such as liquor stores and bars), it also contains various wonderful extracts such as aloe, gentian, rhubarb, angelica, myrrh, chamomile, cardamom, saffron and peppermint, with a base of grape distilled spirits and colored with caramel coloring.

The Fernet Branca label says it's a "bitter stimulant to the appetite." We've been told it is bitter and that first-timers may want to just belt down the ounce or two...or not.

More Information

▶ **Substance Abuse and Mental Health Services Administration (SAMHSA).** This government agency is devoted to reducing the impact of substance abuse on America's communities. Information specialists can recommend appropriate publications, posters and videocassettes; conduct customized searches for you; and refer you to appropriate organizations. They are available 24 hours, seven days a week to take your calls at 800-662-HELP (4357). All calls are confidential. Visit their Web site at *www.samhsa.gov*.

▶ **Alcoholics Anonymous (AA).** This is a fellowship of men and women who share their experience, strength and hope with each other so they may solve their common problem and help others to recover from alcoholism. The only requirement for membership is a desire to stop drinking. There are no dues or fees for AA membership. AA is not allied with any sect, denomination, politics, organization or institution. Their primary purpose is to stay sober and help other alcoholics to achieve sobriety.

If you're interesting in checking it out, visit *www.aa.org* or call the A.A. World Services office in New York City at 212-870-3400.

▶ **Journey Healing Centers.** In addition to providing treatment and rehabilitation for overcoming alcohol and drug addictions, they have a confidential helpline with a crisis-trained counselor who can guide you to the treatment, program or facility that may be appropriate for you. The toll-free, 24-hour phone number is 844-756-2654. For a directory of recovery resources, visit *www.journeycenters.com*.

A Word from the Wise...

Does Someone You Know Drink Too Much? Warning Signs...and What to Do

Is someone you know drinking too much or too dependent on drugs, legal or illegal? Or maybe you wonder if you yourself have a problem. About 15% of the population develops a substance-abuse problem at some point in their lives, and even people who do not have a serious issue may find that stress tips them into consuming more than is healthy. Whether they reach for alcohol, prescription narcotics or street drugs, substance abuse can become a coping strategy.

One key to recovery is to learn other coping strategies. *The warning signs and what to do next...*

Questions to Ask

Has the following happened more than once in the last 12 months...

1. **Has drinking or drug use caused you to fail to meet an obligation,** such as a deadline at work or picking up a child from school?
2. **Have you been under the influence of alcohol or drugs when driving** or in any other circumstance where you need to be fully alert? *Examples:* While operating machinery, riding a bike or when alone in an unfamiliar place.
3. **Has your drinking or drug use hurt your relationships?** *Examples:* Losing a friendship or triggering arguments with your spouse.
4. **Has drinking or drug use caused you a legal problem,** such as an arrest for drinking and driving?

Answering "yes" to one or more of these indicates substance abuse.

Substance abuse can lead into dependence—a more severe problem. You may be dependent if you answer "yes" to three or more of the following...

1. **Are you using the substance more often** or in greater amounts?
2. **Are you spending more and more time thinking about the substance,** obtaining it and using it?
3. **Do you have physical symptoms when you stop,** such as feeling "hung over" or agitated?
4. **Does it take more of the substance than before to give you the desired effect,** so if you stick to the previous amounts, you feel dissatisfied?
5. **Do you wish you could cut back or stop,** or have you tried and failed?
6. **Have you dropped or cut back on "good" activities,** such as exercise or making an extra effort at work?
7. **Have you continued with the substance even though it is hurting your health,** such as aggravating depression or causing stomach problems?

Heavy Drinking

People often are surprised to realize that they drink more than is safe. "Low-risk" drinking is no more than seven drinks a week (no more than three on any given day) for most women, and no more than 14 a week (no more than four on any day) for men. Also, most people find it surprising that "one drink" is smaller than they think—five ounces of wine, 1.5 ounces of 80-proof liquor or 12 ounces of beer. For some people, such as those with a family history of alcoholism, the only safe limit is no drinking.

About 30% of Americans drink more than the low-risk limits and are considered "at risk." This means that they are likely to develop a substance-abuse problem or may already have one. Heavy drinking also increases the risk for many health problems, including liver disease and cancer, as well as car accidents.

Quitting

If you think you have a problem, there are several ways of reducing your use or quitting. Some people quit all at once...others cut down gradually. However, if you suspect that you have a severe substance-abuse problem, it is important to see a medical doctor before stopping. Quitting can be dangerous. *Example:* If you are dependent on alcohol, within a few hours after your last drink, you may experience shakes, sweats, nausea and headaches. After six to eight hours, you may experience hallucinations, as well as convulsions, which can trigger a fatal heart attack or stroke. A doctor may recommend that you enter a hospital. Go to *www.samhsa.gov* for a government listing of facilities, or call 800-662-4357.

New Ways to Cope

Once you have decided to address a substance-abuse problem, adopt new coping methods...

► **Notice All of Your "Substance-Use Thoughts," and Plan Your Rebuttal.** What is going through your mind before you down the extra martini or take one more pill than prescribed? Come up with an effective counterresponse. *Examples:* Instead of, "I can do what I want," tell yourself, "My drinking hurts the people in my life." Instead of, "This feeling will never go away unless I have a drink," tell yourself, "It'll pass." Instead of, "I don't care about the future," ask yourself, "How will I feel later?"

► **Practice Grounding,** the technique of focusing outward when you are hit by strong emotions or cravings. This minimizes the pull of your inner state, keeping you from feeling overwhelmed and helpless. Grounding can be mental or physical. Experiment with different strategies until you find those that work for you. Try reading aloud, counting to 10 or repeating a phrase to yourself. Run cold water over your hands, or clench and release your fists. If you need physical grounding in public situations, carry an object, such as a piece of yarn or a stone, in your pocket and touch it when you're stressed. Soothe yourself by recalling a peaceful place or thinking of favorite things.

► **Talk to Yourself Compassionately.** Many people are harshly critical of themselves. Strive to coach yourself through challenges with kindness and understanding. *Example:* Say to yourself, "I didn't do well on that job interview, because I need to practice interviewing." Don't say, "You idiot, you'll never get a job."

You might also write down some compassionate statements and read them regularly. *Examples:* "You have suffered a lot and have overcome many challenges." "Even when you were drinking heavily, you always showed your children that you loved them."

► **Be Honest.** Secrecy and lies are part of the problem. Honesty can be liberating. Choose the truth—within yourself and to people you can trust. Be aware that sometimes honesty can get a negative reaction. *Example:* A drinking buddy feels you've deserted him because you no longer go to bars. But being honest helps you form supportive new relationships.

► **Ask for Help.** Some people take on too much, adding to their stress. Make reasonable requests of friends and family, staying specific and tailoring requests to their abilities. The help can be either emotional or practical. *Examples:* Ask a friend to call or visit. Ask a family member to babysit once a week. Asking for help makes you stronger. It increases your resources and allows you to address your needs.

Lisa M. Najavits, PhD, professor of psychiatry at Boston University School of Medicine and lecturer at Harvard Medical School, Boston. She is president-elect of the Division on Addictions of the American Psychological Association and author of *Seeking Safety: A Treatment Manual for PTSD and Substance Abuse* (Guilford) and *A Woman's Addiction Workbook* (New Harbinger). For more, see *www.treatment-innovations.org.*

EAR CONDITIONS

 rench Enlightenment writer Voltaire described ears as "the roads to the heart." Moses Ibn Ezra, philosopher, linguist and poet, referred to ears as "the gates to the mind." And poet, physician Abraham Coles called them "bony labyrinthian caves."

Roads, gates or caves, here are suggestions for their well-being, so lend us your ears.

 CAUTION: NEVER put anything *inside of the ear* if the eardrum is perforated. If you suspect a perforated eardrum, see your doctor.

Earaches

➤ **Heat to Soothe Earaches.**

● **Place a white washcloth in a microwaveable container of water and zap it in the microwave** for about 45 seconds. While it's warm, *but cool enough to touch*, wring out the cloth and place it over your ear.

● **Park your car in a sunny area.** Position your ear so that you feel the warm rays of the sun on it. Stay that way until the earache is gone.

● **Set your hair dryer on warm,** hold it a foot and a half from your head, and direct the air into your ear for about a minute.

● **In a frying pan, warm a cup of kosher (coarse) salt,** then funnel it into a white sock and, making sure it's not too hot, cover your ear with it.

● **If you get an earache as you're making breakfast,** or while you're at an IHOP, put a warm pancake on your ear...without the butter and syrup.

➤ **Garlic Cure.** Puncture a garlic softgel and squeeze out the contents into your ear. Gently plug the ear with a cotton ball and leave it there until you feel relief from the pain.

➤ **Reflexology.** If your ears ache due to being out in cold, windy weather, for instant relief, vigorously massage the tips of your fourth toes, the ones next to the pinkies.

If the earaches have something to do with sinus congestion, try massaging the roof of your mouth. Be sure to wash your hand first.

➤ **Ear Problem Prone.** If your ears are your Achilles heel, then you are built awfully funny. But seriously...if you seem to have ear infections more often than once in a blue moon, the irritants in cigarette smoke may be a contributing factor. Do not smoke! Don't even go near people who are smoking. And don't go to places that allow smoking.

➤ **Gem Therapy for Inner Ear Problems.** According to Barbara Stabiner, clairvoyant and author, amber is the stone for inner ear problems. Wear a piece of amber around your neck, or tape it to your ear, or hold it in your hand.

Swimmer's Ear

➤ **Prevention.** Swimmer's ear is an infection of the skin covering the outer ear canal, usually due to bacteria. It's mostly caused by water collecting in the ear canal and being trapped by wax (see Earwax Removal below). The skin becomes soggy and then serves as an appealing culture media for bacteria. Yuk!

Try an ounce of prevention...make that a few drops of prevention. Right before you go swimming, put a few drops of either jojoba oil or mineral oil (both available at health food stores) in each ear. That should put an end to your recurring swimmer's ear.

➤ **Remedy.** If you did not follow the preventive measure above and you have swimmer's ear, you might want to try this...

Tip your head to the side and, using a medicine dropper, fill the ear with a solution of equal amounts of distilled white vinegar and rubbing alcohol. Grab hold of your lobe and rotate it in a circular motion to make sure the liquid reaches the bottom of the ear canal. Then, tip your head the other way, allowing the liquid to empty out.

Removing Something from Your Ear

➤ **Earwax Removal.** If earwax buildup is bad enough to interfere with your hearing, it's time to do something about it. Mix two teaspoons of tepid water with one-quarter teaspoon of baking soda. Lie down on your bed, on your side, with one ear on your pillow, and use a small spoon or an eyedropper and trickle the liquid mixture into your ear. If you have someone in your home who could do that for you, call on that person and make it easier on yourself. Once the liquid is in your ear, stay that way for an hour. When the hour is up, use a bulb syringe (available at drugstores) and warm water to gently flush out the dissolved earwax. According to Walter C. Johnson, MD and specialist in internal and emergency medicine at DeWitt Army Community Hospital in Virginia, this safe treatment is one of the best for bothersome earwax.

➤ **A Bug in Your Ear.** It can happen... fortunately, not very often. If it happens in the dark, shine a flashlight in your ear. The insect should move or fly to the light. If it happens in daylight, a piece of fruit—an apple or peach —should be held at the ear. This should whet the insect's appetite, especially if the insect is a fruit fly.

Itchy Ears

➤ **Fizzy Fix.** Tilt your head with the itchy ear side up. With a medicine dropper, fill the ear with apple cider vinegar or 3% hydrogen peroxide. Leave it there for 30 seconds, then tilt your head to the other side and let the liquid empty out into a tissue.

 NOTE: When the vinegar or peroxide goes into your ear, expect to notice an unusual sensation—cold and fizzy.

Ringing in the Ears (Tinnitus)

More than 20 million Americans have chronic tinnitus. Since it's actually a symptom rather than an ailment, the thing to do is to find out what is causing the symptom.

Attending a rock concert, standing or sitting near those powerful speakers and being exposed to noise above 115 decibels for a couple of hours can cause tinnitus. Yes, just one concert can cause tinnitus, or even permanent hearing loss.

In addition, more than 200 medicines, including *salycilates* (the active ingredient in aspirin) can cause tinnitus. Check with your doctor or pharmacist about medications you're taking to see if they are one or more of the 200 culprits that cause tinnitus. Other possible causes are mental trauma, hypertension, Ménière's disease, allergies and jaw and neck problems. Find the cause, find the cure.

If it isn't as simple as discovering that a medicine you're taking is causing the ringing, you may need help from an otolaryngologist (ear, nose, throat, head and neck specialist).

During the days you are waiting for the appointment with the doctor, you might want to try the following…

➤ **Fenugreek Tea.** Drink three cups of fenugreek seed tea daily. Prepare the tea by adding a teaspoon of fenugreek seeds (available at health food stores and herb shops) to boiling water and letting it simmer for 15 to 20 minutes. Strain and drink a cup in the morning, another in the afternoon and again at bedtime. Give it a couple of weeks to see results—uh, to *hear* results.

➤ **Ginkgo Capsules** (yep…available in health food stores) can also help stop the ringing. Before taking fenugreek seed tea and/or ginkgo, ask your doctor if these herbs are safe for you, especially if you're on medication. If you get his/her approval, take 40 milligrams [mg]) of ginkgo three times a day for at least two weeks.

Ears and Air Travel

In a plane, before you adjust to the difference in air pressure, your ears can be greatly affected… it can be a real pain in the ascent, as well as the descent, of course.

The act of *swallowing* will open the eustachian tube, which allows the pressure to equalize. To feel comfortable, many air passengers simply chew gum, suck candy or yawn during the plane's takeoff and landing.

For those of you who need something more, try the procedure recommended by the American Council of Otolaryngology…

➤ **Equalize.** As soon as the plane takes off, hold both nostrils closed with your thumb and index finger, then take a mouthful of air. Using your cheek and throat muscles, force air into the back of your nose, as though you were

trying to blow your fingers off your nostrils. While you're doing that, you should hear a pop in your ears. That means that equalization has been accomplished. That is a good thing. Another good thing is that you will amuse anyone who is watching you do it.

 CAUTION: Be sure to do this gently, otherwise it could blow out the eardrums.

AFFIRMATION

Repeat this affirmation first thing in the morning, after each meal, and throughout the day, whenever you think to do it. The more often, the better.

I hear healing words of wisdom and love. I listen and learn.

EYE PROBLEMS

 Eyes are the windows of the soul…the heart's letter…silent tongues of love…the spectacles of the brain…organs through which intelligence shines…the contractors of cataracts …the blinkers that get bloodshot…the sources of sties.

Here are some suggestions that may help you…in the twinkling of an eye.

Sties

➤ **A Classic Sty Remedy.** Take a gold wedding ring and rub the blossoming sty with it. Some people believe it works better if you rub the ring on cloth until it's warm and then rub the sty with it. This treatment was in our first folk remedy book, and we've received a lot of feedback about it. Letters usually start with,

"We thought you were crazy but..." and then the writers go on to tell of their instant pain relief with the ring and the disappearance of the sty soon after.

 CAUTION: Be sure to sterilize the ring before rubbing on the sty.

➤ **A Little Dab'll Do Ya.** Carefully dab a little aloe vera gel on the sty about four or five times throughout the day.

Bloodshot Eyes and Eyestrain

➤ **Eyebright.** What better name than *eyebright* for an herb that can soothe sore eyes, alleviate eyestrain and clear up bloodshot eyes. Mix one ounce of eyebright—the whole dried herb, available at health food and herb shops—into a pint of just-boiled water. Let it steep for 10 minutes, then strain through a superfine strainer. Drink a cup of the tea. Use the other cup of tepid tea for dipping cotton pads and placing them on your closed eyes. Leave the damp cotton pads on your eyes for about 15 minutes.

➤ **Ginger Paste.** Take two tablespoons of ginger powder and add enough water to make a runny paste. Smear it on the soles of your feet, put socks on top and sleep that way. (To protect your linens, you may want to put plastic on the sheet under your feet.) In the morning, your eyes should look and feel fine.

➤ **Potato Poultice.** Make a poultice by wrapping grated apple or potato in a clean fabric—cheesecloth, white cotton or unbleached muslin—and put the moist poultice over your eyes for 20 minutes. The poultice will repair, nourish and strengthen the eyes; relaxing for 20 minutes will take care of the rest of you.

➤ **Prevention of Computer Eyestrain.** The National Institute of Occupational Safety and Health (*www.cdc.gov/NIOSH*) recommends that you take a 15-minute break every hour when working at a computer. Also, position the screen at eye level about 22 to 26 inches away. The two tips can prevent or at least minimize eyestrain. (Learn more of the Institute's recommendations for healthy computer use in "Healthful Hints," page 278.)

➤ **Gem Therapy.** Azurite, a beautiful blue stone, is said to be beneficial for sight as well as for insight. It's used to ease eyestrain, to improve vision and enhance visionary powers.

To use azurite, put a stone on the inner corner of each eye—lids closed, of course. Stay that way for 20 minutes.

➤ **Eyestrain Remedy and Prevention.** Check the "Tooth, Gum and Mouth Issues" section under "Bad Breath: Yoga—Simhasana (Lion Pose)" for this body and mind exercise that may help your eyes (page 204).

Dry Eye

This is an irritating syndrome that affects many people who wear contact lenses, are elderly or are constantly exposed to first or secondhand cigarette smoke, use cold or allergy medications often, sit for long periods of time in front of the TV or computer screen, have blowing air from an air conditioner and furnace or have specific eye conditions such as ptosis, exophthalmos or Sjogren's syndrome. Also, dry eye is a condition that's common to residents of very dry and/or windy environments. *The US cities named as dry-eye hot spots are...*

1. Las Vegas, Nevada
2. Lubbock, Texas and El Paso, Texas (tied for 2nd place)

3. Midland/Odessa, Texas
4. Dallas/Fort Worth, Texas
5. Atlanta, Georgia
6. Salt Lake City, Utah
7. Phoenix, Arizona
8. **Amarillo, Texas**
9. Honolulu, Hawaii
10. Oklahoma City, Oklahoma
11. Albuquerque, New Mexico
12. Tucson, Arizona
13. Norfolk, Virginia
14. Newark, New Jersey
15. Boston, Massachusetts
16. Denver, Colorado
17. Pittsburgh, Pennsylvania
18. Bakersfield, California and Wichita, Kansas (tied for 18th place)

These suggestions can help to prevent or even reverse this uncomfortable condition...

➤ **Supplements.** Vitamins B-6, B-12 and folic acid have been known to help to eliminate the discomfort of dry eyes, in particular if it's caused by wearing contact lenses. Ask your health professional or nutritionist to recommend the appropriate dosage for you.

 CAUTION: Do NOT take more than 150 milligrams (mg) of vitamin B-6 a day, as it can be toxic.

In addition to these vitamins, along with the suggestions below, you will be doing your eyes a favor by wearing contact lenses a lot less often than you do now.

➤ **Omega-3s.** In addition to Harvard studies, the findings of a study led by Biljana Miljanovic, MD, of the Divisions of Preventive Medicine and Aging at Brigham and Women's

SOMETHING SPECIAL

Relief in the Blink of an Eye

Artificial tears can give temporary relief of dry-eye symptoms such as irritation, scratching, burning and inflammation.

When looking for an over-the-counter solution, be sure to seek out the products that clearly state they are "preservative free." Bausch & Lomb Soothe is a preservative-free, long-lasting product that is so worth checking out. It's especially appropriate for those with aqueous-deficient dry eye symptoms caused by mucin layer deficiency.

You'll also want to know that Soothe drops work by building and retaining a unique scaffolding system throughout the aqueous and mucin layers to restore the tear film. Also, hydrophilic polymers hold water and soothing demulcents on the eye's surface.

Hospital, determined that "a high intake of omega-3 fatty acids, commonly found in fish and walnuts, is associated with a protective effect. Conversely, a higher ratio of omega-6, a fat found in many cooking and salad oils and animal meats, compared to omega-3 in the diet, may increase the risk of dry eye syndrome."

Learn more about the benefits of omega-3 in the chapter, "It Does a Body Good," page 260.

➤ **Humidifier.** If you have indoor heating during cold weather, use a humidifier. During warm weather, use air conditioning only if you absolutely must and also consider using the humidifier at the same time. Wear wrap-around sun glasses in windy weather.

➤ **Don't Smoke!** And do not stay near people who smoke!

Also, see the instructions for a Dry Eye Bath on page 82.

A Word from the Wise...

Help for Watery Eyes

Common causes of watery eyes—and what to do...

● **Age-related changes of the surface of the eye can cause tears to pool** in the corners of your eyes. Artificial tears or resurfacing surgery may help—see an ophthalmologist.

● **A blocked tear duct can cause eyes to water.** An in-office procedure or topical steroid drugs can often relieve the problem.

● **Eye irritation or infection can cause constant watering,** which will clear up when the irritation or infection goes away.

● **Excessively dry eyes, caused by allergies or other factors, can cause reflex tearing**—the underlying cause needs to be treated.

● **Some medical conditions, such as a thyroid disorder, can cause eyes to water**—ask your doctor.

Steven L. Maskin, MD, Dry Eye and Cornea Treatment Center, Tampa, *www.drmaskin.com.*

Eyesight Strengtheners

➤ **Ginger.** Many Asian herbalists believe that chewing a very small piece of ginger after each meal can help improve one's eyesight. It will also help digestion and dispel gas.

 CAUTION: Ginger acts as a blood thinner, so check with your doctor before using it if you are taking a prescription blood thinner. Also, stop using ginger three days before any surgery.

➤ **Improve Night Vision.** If you have a problem seeing at night, bilberry and zinc may help improve your vision. Both are available at health food stores. Take 80 mg of bilberry twice a day. Men should also take 50 mg of zinc daily; women should take 25 mg of zinc daily.

 CAUTION: Take zinc with food to prevent stomach upset and nausea. Prolonged use of zinc can cause a copper deficiency. This remedy should be taken for a limited time only. If it's going to help, chances are you will see results within a month.

➤ **Men with Blurred Vision.** If you wear a tie or collar that's too tight, it can actually inhibit the flow of blood to the brain and, in turn, blur your vision. Test it. If you cannot slip your finger between your neck and your shirt collar, then it's too tight. Time to buy a new shirt.

CAUTION: Blurred vision could be a symptom of diabetes, autoimmune diseases, macular degeneration, glaucoma, cataracts, etc., so be sure to check with your doctor if you have this symptom.

Hairspray Tip

➤ **Hairspray Caution.** Do not use hair spray while you're wearing contact lenses or eyeglasses. The spray can coat the lenses with a hard-to-remove film. If you are spraying the front of your hair, be sure to keep your eyes closed tightly, or use a hairspray shield (available in drugstores).

Free Eye Care for Seniors

Do not neglect vision problems because of low or fixed income or inadequate insurance. Check out the Seniors EyeCare Program, previously known as National Eye Care Project (NECP). Under this program, if you are a US citizen or

■ Recipe ■

Dry Eye Bath

You may be able to wash away the chronic sensation of sand in the eyes by bathing the eyes in a solution of pure water and Himalayan Crystal Salt (HCS). The combination of the HCS and pure water is called sole (pronounced "so-lay"), which is super-saturated salty water. To make the eye bath, you first have to prepare a 1% solution of sole, which is similar to the natural salt concentration in the body.

Ingredients

Himalayan Crystal Salt stones (available at health food stores, or visit *www. himalayancrystalsalt.com*).

Distilled or spring water.

Eyewash cup (available at drugstores).

Instructions for Preparing Sole

- **Place about one-inch of Himalayan Crystal Salt stones in a small glass jar that has a lid.**
- **Completely cover the stones with good quality water.**
- **Leave overnight.**
- **The next morning, if you see that all the salt crystals have dissolved, add a** few more to the water. When the water becomes fully saturated (which is the goal), the salt will no longer dissolve (the salt crystals will just sit on the bottom of the jar) and the sole will be ready to use. When not in use, keep the jar covered so that the water doesn't evaporate. Do not refrigerate.

Instructions for the Eyewash

- **Remove any makeup before bathing eyes.**
- **Pour one and a half teaspoons of sole in the eyewash cup** and place over the eye so that no liquid can escape.
- **Gently tip your head back, washing the sole over the eye.** Open and close your eye repeatedly so the sole can thoroughly saturate it.
- **Repeat the last two eyewash steps on your other eye.**

Do this treatment for a few days in a row, and if it clears up the gritty feeling in your eyes, keep doing it.

 CAUTION: Do NOT add any other kind of salt to water and think that you're making sole. There's a HUGE difference between Himalayan Crystal Salt and all other salt, including and especially table salt.

legal resident age 65 and older, have not seen an ophthalmologist in the last three years or more and do not belong to an HMO or have veterans' vision care, you can get the name of a volunteer ophthalmologist in your area. For more information, visit *www.aao.org*, and click on "Find an Eye M.D.," or call 415-447-0386.

Volunteer ophthalmologists will accept Medicare or other insurance as full payment, with no additional payment from you. But, if you do not have any insurance, the eye care is free of charge.

If you think you are a candidate for this program, or if you know a senior who is, call the toll-free helpline today.

AFFIRMATION

For any kind of eye problem, repeat this affirmation first thing in the morning, each time you see your favorite color and last thing at night.

While you're at it, if it's logistically practical, rub your hands together until you feel the warmth you've created. Then cup your hands over your eyes, keeping them there as you say the affirmation…

I see everything in my life happening for my greatest good and I'm finding joy in each day.

A Word from the Wise…

Reading in Dim Light Hurts Your Vision and Other Common Eye Myths

Almost one-quarter of all American adults are nearsighted, and everyone over age 40 will have increasing difficulty reading fine print or seeing clearly in dim light.

Most people understand that age is the main reason for declines in eye health and vision, but there's still a lot of confusion about other factors that help or hurt the eyes. *Common myths…*

Myth: **Sitting too close to the TV hurts the eyes.**

Reality: For generations, mothers have scolded their children for sitting too close to the television. This might have made sense in the 1940s, when TVs emitted fairly high levels of radiation, but it isn't a factor anymore.

But today you could sit with your nose pressed against the screen, and it wouldn't hurt your eyes. If you do watch TV up close, you might experience eyestrain because the eyes aren't designed for prolonged, short-distance viewing. This may result in a headache,

but apart from this, there aren't any risks associated with up-close TV watching.

Myth: **You'll damage your eyes if you read in dim light.**

Reality: Using your eyes, even under difficult viewing conditions, doesn't hurt them. You won't damage your vision by reading in dim light any more than you could hurt your ears by listening to quiet music, but you may develop eyestrain.

Myth: **Computer monitors cause eye damage.**

Reality: Computer monitors are no more likely than TVs to damage the eyes. However, people who spend a lot of time in front of the computer might experience an increase in eye dryness. People don't blink normally when they're engaged in prolonged, up-close focusing. When you're working on the computer, you might blink less than once every 10 seconds. That's not enough to lubricate the eyes. Infrequent blinking causes additional problems in older adults because their tear film is effective for only about seven or eight seconds between blinks—about half as long as in younger adults.

Recommended: During computer sessions, take an "eye break" at least once an hour. Shift your vision to something farther away, and consciously blink every few seconds. Use an over-the-counter natural teardrop to remoisturize your eyes. Good brands include Systane, Optive, Soothe XP and Refresh.

Myth: **Using stronger reading glasses than you need weakens vision.**

Reality: No, it is not true that using a stronger power than you need makes your eyes come to need that power. You can wear any power reading glasses that you want. You need to choose reading glasses based on the distance at which you work. You may want a stronger power for reading the newspaper than for working on the computer.

Myth: *Redness means infection.*

Reality: Eye infections are relatively infrequent compared with the cases of red eyes from noninfectious causes. Viral infections (which do not respond to antibiotics) occur somewhat more often but also are relatively uncommon.

Eye redness usually is due to simple irritation of the surface of the eye—from allergies or from dryness, for example, or from *blepharitis*, an inflammation of the eyelid, which also can cause dry eyes.

Self-test: The eye will be very red if you have an infection (bacterial or viral). With a bacterial infection, you might notice a thick yellow-white discharge. A viral infection is likely to have a clear, continuous watery discharge. Viral *conjunctivitis* (commonly called "pink eye") results in a very irritated, very red eye, which often spreads to the other eye in one to three days. Typically, people with pink eye have had a cold recently or have been exposed to someone with pink eye.

Pink eye is very contagious and can quickly spread to family members and coworkers. To reduce the spread of infection, limit your contact with other people and wash hands frequently. Unlike bacterial conjunctivitis, which is treated with antibiotic eyedrops, there is no treatment for viral pink eye except lubricating eyedrops to reduce discomfort.

Myth: **Extended-wear contacts are safe to keep in when you sleep.**

Reality: The Food and Drug Administration (or FDA) has approved extended-wear contact lenses that you can keep in when you sleep, but I see a lot of patients with eye inflammation caused by these lenses.

The *cornea*, the transparent front of the eye, takes in oxygen all the time. Wearing a contact lens for extended periods decreases oxygen at the eye surface. Silicone hydrogen lenses allow much more oxygen to get to the cornea, but even they can cause irritation and infection when worn too long.

Always follow your doctor's instructions. If your contact lenses are designed to be worn for two or four weeks, then change them at the recommended frequency. If you are wearing your contacts overnight and your eyes become irritated or red, stop wearing them and see your eye doctor. Generally, if you take your contacts out each night, there's less risk for infection and irritation.

Irritation sometimes can be triggered by multipurpose or cleaning solutions. Multipurpose solutions (Opti-Free, ReNu) include chemicals designed to kill bacteria, and some people become sensitive to these products. I recommend a product called Clear Care. The active ingredient, hydrogen peroxide, kills bacteria and other germs. Then, after six hours of soaking, the solution turns into saline.

For people who have difficulty wearing contacts, one-day disposable lenses are another possibility. They are more expensive than the extended-wear lenses but don't require disinfectant solutions.

Brett Levinson, MD, an ophthalmologist who trained at the prestigious Wills Eye Institute, Philadelphia. He is director of the Cornea and Anterior Segment at Specialized Eye Care in Baltimore and a clinical instructor in ophthalmology at University of Maryland School of Medicine.

FATIGUE

We receive complaints from so many people that they're constantly tired...that they lack energy...that they have no get-up-and-go. For the most part, their days start early in the morning and end late at night, with all kinds of responsibilities, pressures, obligations and tension in between. For you people who fit the description above, it may be time to rethink the life you've created for yourself and make some changes.

While you're taking a good, close look at your lifestyle, and contemplating be-kinder-to-yourself changes, we have some fatigue fighters in the form of instant revivers, energy boosters and drowsiness-enders.

► **Instant Reviver.** When you're sitting at a meeting and you're afraid you're going to nod off when you need to be alert and responsive, press your elbows against your sides, or press your knees together, exerting a lot of pressure for just a few seconds. Your blood circulation will be increased, making you feel more with it.

► **The Amazing Kreskin's Amazing Energy Tonic.** If you've ever seen mentalist Amazing Kreskin perform, you've witnessed his tremendous level of energy. The man is a dynamo! *When we asked Kreskin the secret of his stamina, he generously shared his recipe with us...*

Combine six ounces unsweetened cranberry juice and two ounces orange juice. Top it off with a slice of fresh lime, add ice, stir and drink.

Kreskin consumes about a quart of his energy drink daily. That seems a little excessive for the average person who doesn't have Kreskin's hectic show biz schedule, or immediate access to a Porta-Potty. One eight-ounce drink a day sounds like a good picker-upper.

► **An Ounce of Prevention.** Many is the afternoon I've almost dozed off over my computer keyboard, until I discovered the secret of staying awake. Eat a light lunch. Hamburger and fries?—No! Salad?—Yes! Also, when weather permits, a short walk after lunch will go a long way in helping keep you wide-awake and alert the rest of the day.

► **Breathing "Right."** In keeping with many who believe that positive energy is inhaled through the right nostril, put a piece of cotton in your left nostril and breathe through your right nostril for an hour. If you can be by yourself in a quiet space for that hour, so much the better in terms of your revitalization.

► **Energy Boosters**

• **Sunflower seeds.** Instead of a coffee break, eat a handful of raw, unsalted sunflower seeds (available at health food stores). This high-powered protein nosh will do wonders for your energy level throughout the day.

• **Bee pollen.** The more research we do on bee pollen, the more convinced we are that it's a miracle food. It can give you energy and stamina. In fact, many athletes are now using pollen in place of steroids or other dangerous supplements.

 CAUTION: Some people are allergic to bee pollen. Start very slowly—with a couple of granules the first day or two. Then if you have no allergic reaction, work your way up gradually until you take one teaspoon or more a day—up to one tablespoon depending on how you feel. Asthmatics should NOT use bee pollen.

■ Recipe ■

Dr. Kim's Energy Boosters

Ingredients

   Dates (pits removed)—about 10
   Raw pecans—about 1 cup
   Cocoa powder—heaping teaspoon (optional ingredient and/or topping)
   Shredded coconut (optional topping)
   Cashews (optional topping)

Instructions

1. Count out about 10 dates and place them in a bowl.
2. Soak the dates in water. If you think to do this an hour or more in advance, it's fine to use room temperature water. If you're pressed for time and only have a few minutes for soaking, use hot water. The idea is to soften the dates so that they are easily blended into a soft paste.
3. Measure out a cup of raw pecans and put them in a food processor. A strong blender might also work, but for this recipe, a food processor works best.

 NOTE: If you have trouble digesting nuts, soak them in water overnight, strain and dry with a towel before proceeding.

4. Process pecans on low or use a pulse setting until they're nicely ground. You don't want to make pecan butter here, so don't overdo it—you're looking for nicely ground pecans.
5. Add a heaping teaspoon of quality cocoa powder. If you don't enjoy chocolate, it's fine to skip this step.

6. Blend or pulse for another few seconds to bring ground nuts and cocoa powder together.
7. Add six soaked and mildly crushed dates to the mix. It's best to add a little water to create the proper texture. A good way to add just enough, but not too much, water is to lightly shake the dates as you get them out of their bowl of water, then give them a gentle mush with fingers, and add them—slightly wet—to the ground pecans.
8. Process on low or use the pulse setting until the dates and pecans come together into a texture that's like firm cookie dough, enabling you to pinch off teaspoon-sized chunks and roll them up in your palms into bite-sized balls. If need be, add another mashed-up date or two, but always be conservative when adding extra dates. You don't want the mixture to get too moist. It's difficult to fix by adding more nuts.

   Once you're able to pinch off small amounts and roll them up into balls that remain intact, you know that you have the right texture.
9. Once you've rolled out all of the balls, use your taste and creativity to decorate them. Top them off by rolling them in shredded coconut, or sprinkle raw cocoa on them. Keep in mind that because you may have already added cocoa powder to the pecans, adding an extra coat of cocoa powder gives these energy balls quite a rich, dark chocolate-like flavor. If that's what you want, then go for it!

   You can gently press your favorite nuts and/or dried fruits into the tops of the energy balls to provide an endless variety. A whole raw cashew, or half of a walnut is great on each of them.

If you have a few dates, nuts and other ingredients left over, bring them together in the food processor and see what turns up. We've discovered some of our favorite combinations doing just this with leftovers. A good example of such a mish-mash is dates, almonds, coconut shreds and dried tart cherries.

Please note that for different types of nuts, you'll have to adjust the number of dates you use to create a cookie-dough texture that can be rolled up into these energy balls. For example, almonds release less natural oils than pecans, so for almond-date energy balls, you will need to use about nine or 10 small soaked dates for each cup of raw almonds.

Once you've made a batch of energy balls, you and your family or friends can enjoy them right away. If they're all for you, take one or two and refrigerate the rest in a covered container. They'll stay fresh for at least a few days.

You can get bee pollen at your local health food store, or check "Sources," page 310, for our mail-order recommendation.

- **Acupressure.** Energy lines directly connected to internal organs and body functions run through your earlobes. That being the case, use your thumbs and index fingers to rub your earlobes for about 15 seconds. It should wake up your entire nervous system.

➤ **Healthy, Decadent, Nutrient-Dense Energy Balls.** Dr. Ben Kim, editor of *www.drbenkim.com*, a Web site that's dedicated to providing articles, recipes and other resources that promote optimal health, shared his recipe with us. See the recipe starting on the previous page.

Because these energy balls are made out of fiber-rich whole foods, eating just one or two can be surprisingly filling—quite the contrast when you consider that most folks have no trouble eating half a dozen or more mini-donuts in one sitting.

➤ **Winter Fatigue.** If you notice that you feel particularly tired only during the winter months, it may be due to Seasonal Affective Disorder (SAD). See the "Depression" section, page 50, for an explanation and solution.

➤ **Chronic Fatigue.** Many believe that chronic tiredness may be caused by vitamin deficiencies due to an unbalanced diet. Eat foods rich in the B-complex vitamins—whole grain cereal, brewer's yeast and yogurt—and supplement your diet with a B-complex vitamin.

And eat foods rich in vitamin C—citrus fruits, leafy green vegetables, cabbage—and supplement your diet with 500 milligrams (mg) to 1,000 mg of vitamin C spaced throughout the day.

Also, add foods rich in magnesium, such as whole grains, beans, dark green vegetables, soy products and nuts, to your diet.

➤ **Visualization for Drowsiness.** Sit back, close your eyes, and let all the air out of your lungs. Imagine a bright blue-white energizing light entering and filling your entire body as you inhale slowly through your nostrils. Open your eyes and feel refreshed.

➤ **Aromatherapy for Drowsiness.**

- **Put a drop of allspice or cinnamon oil on the inside of your wrist** and take a whiff every time your eyelids start feeling heavy.

- **If you have a real bad case of the drowsies,** puncture a garlic softgel and take a few deep whiffs. That ought to wake you up.

● **If you're at home and need to get your second wind for the evening,** add six drops of lemon, peppermint or thyme oil to your bath water. Relax in the bath for 15 minutes. Always be careful getting out of the tub, especially when using even a small amount of oil.

 CAUTION: If there is any chance you'll fall asleep in the tub, forget this remedy. Try another.

AFFIRMATION

Repeat this affirmation a dozen times whenever you feel yourself dragging (putting on spirited music and repeating the affirmation while listening to the music is even more effective)…

I'm happy, healthy, awake, inspired and raring to go.

A Word from the Wise…

Boost Your Energy in Eight Minutes or Less

When you become drowsy or droop with fatigue, every task seems monumental and even fun activities feel like work.

Helpful: Take a double-pronged approach to invigoration—including on-the-spot techniques for an immediate energy burst…plus simple strategies that take just minutes to do, yet give you long-lasting stamina day after day.

Pump Up Your Energy…

➤ **Wake Up the Nose**—and the rest of you will follow. Aromatherapy stimulates the brain's olfactory center and heightens awareness of your surroundings. Dab on a drop of therapeutic-grade rosemary essential oil (sold at health food stores) on the pulse points behind both ears, as you would perfume…or dampen a

cloth with cool water, sprinkle it with four drops of therapeutic-grade lemon essential oil, then place it on your forehead or the back of your neck for five minutes. Do not dab full-strength essential oil directly under your nose—it could be too strong.

➤ **Belt Out a Few Bars.** As you sing, you inhale deeply, bringing more energizing oxygen into your lungs and increasing circulation throughout your body…and exhale through your mouth, efficiently expelling the waste product carbon dioxide.

Bonus: Choosing a favorite cheerful song lifts your mood.

➤ **Give Yourself a Big Stretch.** Stretching opens the chest, straightens the spine, expands the lungs and relieves energy-sapping tension in neck and shoulder muscles. *Try…*

Seated stretch. Sit in a sturdy chair, feet flat on the floor, hands clasped in front of you. As you inhale, straighten arms and gradually raise them over your head, turning your wrists so palms face the ceiling. Gently press arms as far back as possible, holding for a count of five. Slowly exhale, lowering arms to the starting position. Repeat three times.

Doorway stretch. Stand in a doorway, a few inches behind the threshold, with feet about six inches apart. Raise arms out to your sides and bend elbows to a 90-degree angle, placing hands and forearms on either side of the doorjamb. Keeping your back straight, lean forward slightly to feel a stretch across your chest. Hold for 15 seconds. Repeat three times.

Illustrations by Shawn Banner.

➤ **Take 800 Steps.** A moderately brisk walk—at a pace of about 100 steps per minute—is an excellent way to get blood flowing to your heart and brain. Exercise also triggers the release of *endorphins*, brain chemicals that make you feel alert and energetic. If possible, walk outdoors—the sun's rays activate the synthesis of mood-enhancing vitamin D.

➤ **Just Breathe.** The beauty of this is that you can do it anytime, anywhere, and instantly feel more alert.

A good deep-breathing technique: Inhale deeply through your nose, filling your lungs for a count of four...hold your breath for a count of seven...slowly and deliberately exhale through pursed lips (to regulate the release of air) to a count of eight. Take three normal breaths, then repeat the deep-breathing exercise twice more.

Rationale: This technique pulls the diaphragm downward and creates a negative pressure that draws more blood into your heart. As the heart pumps this blood around your body, all your tissues receive extra energizing oxygen.

Evangeline Lausier, MD, director of clinical services at Duke Integrative Medicine and assistant clinical professor of medicine at Duke University School of Medicine, both in Durham, North Carolina. She's an internist specializing in women's health and complex multisystem illnesses, with an emphasis on preventive lifestyle.

FINGERNAIL ISSUES

Fungus Among Us

➤ **Zinc.** Take zinc tablets, 15 milligrams (mg), three a day, to help get rid of fingernail fungus. And, eat foods rich in zinc such as raw pumpkin seeds, sunflower seeds, mushrooms and whole grains. Zinc is also known to make white spots on fingernails disappear.

 CAUTION: Take zinc with food to prevent stomach upset and nausea. Prolonged use of zinc can cause a copper deficiency. This remedy should be taken for a limited time only. Consult with your health professional for guidance.

➤ **Vitamin E.** Vitamin E is also effective for clearing up fungus on fingernails, as well as dry, rough, itchy skin around fingernails. Puncture a vitamin E capsule and squeeze out the oil on the problem area. Do it at least twice a day. Also, take one 400 international units (IU) capsule of vitamin E daily.

 CAUTION: Due to the possible interactions between vitamin E and various drugs and supplements, as well as other safety considerations, be sure to consult your doctor before taking vitamin E.

Healthier Nails

➤ **Brittle or Damaged Nails.** Cut a piece of onion and rub it on your fingernails. Do it after every meal. It has nothing to do with eating, it's just that you should do this three times a day, and by assigning specific times, chances are you'll do it consistently.

➤ **More on Brittle Nails.** Since brittle nails may be caused by iron deficiency (especially in women), add iron-rich foods such as leafy green vegetables, raisins, whole grains and fruit to your daily diet.

➤ **Nail Softener.** Taking two evening primrose oil capsules (500 mg) per day can soften your nails and do wonderful things for your skin and hair, too. EPO has GLA (*gamma-linoleic acid*), a beneficial fatty acid that most of us hardly get in our normal diet. When taking EPO, be patient. It may take a month or two to get results. It's available in health food stores.

➤ **Splitting Fingernails.** Eat a half-dozen raw almonds daily. They're a good source of protein, vitamins and nutrients, plus linoleic acid which helps prevent nails from splitting. As with most nail remedies, it takes a while before you see improvement.

➤ **Nail Strengthener.** Steep one tablespoon of horsetail (available at herb and health food stores) in a cup of just-boiled water. When it's cool enough to the touch, strain it and dunk your fingers in the liquid for 15 minutes. Do this every day and give it a month or two to see an improvement.

➤ **When You Hammer the Wrong Nail.** If part of the finger is dangling, or bone is jutting out, call 9-1-1 for emergency help.

If it's just a nasty, painful slam, use CPR. No, not Cardiopulmonary Resuscitation. Our CPR stands for **C**old, **P**ressure and **R**aise it. As soon as possible after the slam, dunk the digit into ice or ice-cold water. If it is bleeding, this should stop it. Keep the finger there until the *cold* becomes painful—not much longer than half-a-minute. Then, for 30 seconds put *pressure* on the finger by squeezing it, also to help stop the bleeding, but not tight enough to stop all circulation. While you're squeezing the injured finger, *raise* it above your head to slow the flow of blood. Repeat the entire one-minute procedure over and over—two, three, four dozen times. It may save you from pain, swelling and a black fingernail.

A Word from the Wise...

What Your Fingernails Tell About Your Health

Since the time of Hippocrates, most doctors have examined patients' fingernails during routine physical exams. That's because the fingernail is an important window through which an astute physician can see signs of some diseases and even clues about a person's nutritional status, lifestyle and emotional health.

The fingernails should be strong, with a light pink color to the nail bed (the skin on which the nail rests). A few white spots and/or lines are usually due to injury to the nail bed and are harmless. However, if you have any of the conditions described below, see your physician for an evaluation and treatment, such as the use of medication and/or supplements. *What to look for...*

● **Brittle, dry, splitting nails,** with deep longitudinal (from the cuticle to the fingernail tip) ridges, can indicate thyroid disease, usually hypothyroidism (an underactive thyroid). It also can be a sign of a mineral deficiency, particularly calcium or zinc.

● **Nails loosening or separating from the nail bed** can indicate hyperthyroidism (an overactive thyroid). This condition also can be a sign of psoriasis (a chronic skin disease) or a reaction to synthetic nails or a nail injury.

● **Nail pitting** (deep depressions) can indicate psoriasis, psoriatic arthritis (a condition with symptoms of both arthritis and psoriasis) or chronic dermatitis (skin rash). Nail pitting also can be seen in people with *alopecia areata*, an autoimmune disease that causes sudden patchy hair loss, usually in the scalp or beard.

● **Nails curved around enlarged fingertips** (known as clubbing) can be a harmless condition that runs in families, or it can be a sign of low oxygen in the blood, a common marker for chronic lung disease.

● **Hollowed or dipped nails** (known as spoon nails) are often associated with an iron deficiency. A three-year-old boy I recently saw had 10 tiny scooped-out fingernails that could have each contained a drop of water.

• **Opaque (white) nails** with a dark band at the fingertip (known as Terry's nails) can be a harmless sign of aging, or it can indicate cardiac disease, particularly congestive heart failure.

• **Yellow nails** can be due to nicotine stains, bacterial infection, fungus in the nail and nail bed, chronic bronchitis or lymphedema (swelling and congestion of the lymph system).

• **Bitten nails** can indicate anxiety, severe stress or compulsive behavior.

The best way to keep your nails healthy is to keep them clean, trim and warm. Don't pick at hangnails. Clip them. Limit nail polish remover use to twice a month (it dries nails and makes them more brittle). Protect your nails from harsh chemicals by wearing gloves and avoiding the use of synthetic nails. With normal growth, an injured nail will be replaced in four to six months.

Jamison Starbuck, ND, a naturopathic physician in family practice in Missoula, Montana. She is past president of the American Association of Naturopathic Physicians and a contributing editor to *The Alternative Advisor: The Complete Guide to Natural Therapies and Alternative Treatments* (Time Life).

Manicures

➤ **For a Longer-Lasting Manicure.** Before polishing your fingernails, wipe your unpolished nails with distilled white vinegar, *then* polish. Priming with vinegar should make your manicure last longer.

➤ **Nail Polish Remover Improver.** Acetone nail polish remover can dry out your nails. To help prevent this from happening, add about a half-dozen drops of castor oil to the bottle of nail polish remover. It will still take off your unwanted nail polish, but will be somewhat kinder to your nails.

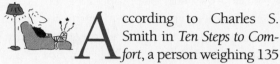

FOOT CONDITIONS

According to Charles S. Smith in *Ten Steps to Comfort*, a person weighing 135 pounds takes close to 19,000 steps during an average day, absorbing a cumulative pressure of more than 2.5 million pounds. No wonder we have problems with our feet. *Here are some solutions...*

Athlete's Foot

Athlete's foot is a fungal infection whose siblings are jock itch and ringworm. What a family! The fungus thrives in a dark, warm, moist place. With athlete's foot, that place is your shoe.

It takes at least a full day for shoes to dry thoroughly after being worn. No wonder, since the average pair of feet give off a half-pint of perspiration daily. Keeping that in mind, don't wear the same pair of shoes two days in a row.

Avoid reinfecting your feet by wiping the insides of your shoes with distilled white vinegar. To be on the safe side, you might also rinse your socks with vinegar and give the bathtub, shower and bathroom floors a quick vinegar wash.

Here are some remedies to consider...

➤ **Vinegar Soak.** Before bedtime, soak the infected foot in apple cider vinegar for 10 minutes. It will sting, but only for a few seconds. Then, moisten gauze with the cider vinegar and put it on the infection, binding it in place with a white handkerchief or Ace bandage and covering it with a sock. Keep it that way overnight and repeat the process the following morning, if possible. If not, wear clean socks during the day and repeat the process every evening until the infection clears up. It may take as long as two weeks.

➤ **Aloe Vera Gel.** Apply aloe vera gel or juice to the foot once in the morning and again at night. You can buy aloe vera gel or juice in health food stores, or if you have an aloe plant, squeeze out the natural gel from a cut leaf. We've been told that consistent applications of aloe have cleared up cases of chronic athlete's foot.

➤ **Pineapple Soak.** Set aside an hour a day to dip your foot with fungus in pineapple juice. When the timer goes off, thoroughly dry the foot and spread baking soda on the affected area.

➤ **Urine Cure.** The external use of urine for medicinal purposes goes back hundreds of years. Did we just lose you, or are you still with us? When our body is under attack, it fights back by manufacturing antibodies and sending them to do battle. These antibodies can be found in our urine. We can take advantage of that fact by using the urine externally to clear up athlete's foot.

Collect a specimen in a bowl and dip your foot in it for 10 minutes. Do it in the morning and in the evening. Yes, you can wash your foot with water afterward. It costs less than the pineapple juice (above) and it almost looks the same!

 CAUTION: If there is any broken skin on your foot, do NOT use this urine remedy.

➤ **Acupressure.** Yes, there's an acupressure point that can help clear up this condition. The point is between the little piggy that had no roast beef and the one that went all the way home. In case you're not into nursery rhymes,

the acupressure point is where the fourth toe and the little toe meet on the front of your foot. First thing in the morning, press that spot for 10 seconds, then another 10 seconds and a third 10 seconds. At night, press that spot again for 10 seconds, three times in a row. It's hard to believe that it could help. It can, and as long as it won't hurt the condition, it's worth a try, along with one of the other remedies above.

Toenail Problems

➤ **Toenail Fungus.** Puncture a vitamin E capsule (400 international units [IU]) and squeeze out the oil onto the nail. Keep it uncovered as much as possible and reapply the oil often. You can also soak infected toenails for 15 minutes a day in a combination of one part distilled white vinegar to two parts water. Or, see the "urine" remedy above.

➤ **Toenail Fungus Prevention.** Raw garlic is a powerful fungus fighter. Eat one or two cloves a day and you may never have athlete's foot or toenail fungus.

 CAUTION: Having garlic on an empty stomach can cause nausea. Be sure to have some food in your stomach before eating garlic or taking capsules. And, be cautious with garlic if you have gastritis.

➤ **Ingrown Toenail.** At bedtime, put a slim wedge of lemon on the problem toenail, keeping it in place with a Band-Aid and covering it with a sock. Sleep that way, and by morning the lemon should have softened the nail enough to ease it away from the skin so you can trim it. The proper way to trim the nail is to cut it straight across, not down at the sides, and not shorter than the toe.

When Your Dogs Are Barking

➤ **Tired, Aching Feet.** Put up a pot of barley or millet—two cups of the grain to eight cups of water. As soon as it's thick-soup consistency, take it off the stove. When it's cool enough to handle, divide the mush into plastic shoeboxes, or a pan or basin large enough for your feet, and put your feet in.

Let the warm mush embrace your barking dogs for at least a half hour, then rinse with cold water and wipe dry with a rough towel. You and your feet should feel rejuvenated.

Incidentally, you can reheat the barley or millet and use it again the next day and the next...only for your feet, of course.

➤ **Hot, Tired, Aching Feet.** Take a basin that's large enough for both of your feet and fill it with one layer of ice cubes—the melon-ball kind are the best for this. If you don't have a large enough basin, use two plastic shoeboxes with a layer of ice cubes in each one. Sit down and rub your feet over the ice cubes. Stop when this massage has your feet feeling completely revitalized, or the ice melts—whichever comes first. Dry your feet with a rough towel. Ready to run the marathon?

Foot Pain

➤ **Shooting, Spasmodic Foot Pain.** If you get shooting pains and muscle spasms in your feet on a regular basis, add wheat germ oil to your daily diet. It can help the blood flow more easily throughout your body, improving circulation. You can use the oil as salad dressing or on yogurt, or you can take wheat germ capsules. Start with 500 milligrams (mg) a day and gradually work your way up to twice that amount. By the end of two weeks, you should feel some relief from the pain.

➤ **Heel Spurs.** When gemologist Joyce Kaessinger had a heel spur (it's an abnormal growth of the heel bone), she could hardly walk and was in constant excruciating pain. Everything she read in medical articles or was told by a podiatrist agreed that "heel spurs are forever."

Joyce believes that whatever comes can also go and started working with crystals. The crystals she used were green tourmaline, black tourmaline, smoky quartz, aventurine and hematite. (All are inexpensive stones that are available at crystal shops. Check "Sources," page 311, for an Internet store.)

At night, following her intuition, she would select a few stones and tape them to the bottom of her foot and sleep that way. During the day, she would lie on the floor and have those stones pointed at her heel while she meditated.

She also said an affirmation: "*I can walk comfortably for as long and as far as I desire.*"

About two weeks later there was a big difference. Joyce was able to walk. And not long after that, the spur completely disappeared.

Joyce feels it's important to continue using the stones and affirmation to some degree, even after you're all better.

A Word from the Wise...

No More Foot Pain!

Many people downplay the significance of foot problems. But that's a mistake.

What a foot problem may really mean: You could have an undetected medical condition. For example, numb or painful feet can be a red flag for the damaged blood vessels and nerves that can occur with diabetes or peripheral arterial disease (a circulatory problem that causes reduced blood flow to the limbs). Foot problems also may be associated with seemingly unrelated ailments, such as hip or back pain.

An effective way to identify the root cause of foot pain is to take a whole-body (holistic) approach that often can replace conventional treatments. *Holistic approaches to everyday foot problems...*

➤ **Go Barefoot.** After spending day after day confined in tight or ill-fitting shoes, the muscles of the foot can weaken—the same way an arm loses muscle tone when encased in a cast. Going barefoot in your home allows your

feet to stretch, strengthen and find their natural alignment.

 CAUTION: People who have diabetes should NEVER go barefoot, as this medical condition commonly causes nerve damage in the feet, which makes it very hard to feel cuts or other injuries. Also, do not walk barefoot on marble or other potentially slippery floors or if you have balance or vision problems. In all of these cases, wear sturdy slippers or similar footwear that protect your feet and provide good traction.

➤ **"Open" Your Toes.** This gentle form of stretching can improve flexibility of the tendons, release tension and stimulate blood flow to the feet and the rest of the body.

It can help prevent foot ailments, such as hammertoe (in which the end of a toe curls downward) and Morton's neuroma (inflammation of a nerve between the toes that causes pain in the ball of the foot), and is useful for people suffering from painful foot conditions such as *plantar fasciitis* (described below).

What to do: Lace your fingers between each toe (imagine holding hands with your foot)...or use physical separators, such as pedicure toe dividers (available at drugstores) or gel-filled YogaToes (available at YogaPro, 877-964-2776, *www.yogapro.com*). Open your toes for five to 30 minutes at least five days per week.

 CAUTION: People with rigid bunions should NOT use YogaToes—they may strain the ligaments and cause additional pain.

For Common Foot Problems

If your suffer from frequent foot pain, you may have one of these common foot problems...

➤ **Bunion.** No one knows exactly what causes this swollen, painful outgrowth of bone at the base of the big toe. Heredity plays a role, but podiatrists also suspect excess body weight and ill-fitting shoes.

Conventional treatment: Store-bought or custom-fitted orthotic shoe inserts to help reduce pressure on the bunion…and/or surgery to correct the position of the toe.

Holistic therapy: To relieve inflammation, massage the foot with peppermint, lemongrass, wintergreen or lavender oil. To make your own massage oil, start with a half teaspoon of a "carrier," such as almond oil or vitamin E oil, and add two to three drops of the healing oil. Warm the oil mixture in the palm of your hand before massaging your feet for five to 10 minutes daily.

➤ **Plantar Fasciitis.** This condition is inflammation of the thick band of tissue that connects the heel to the base of the toes. The pain—often excruciating—is most pronounced under the heel.

Anything that stresses the bottom of the foot can cause plantar fasciitis, including being overweight, suddenly increasing the amount of exercise you do or wearing shoes without arch support.

Conventional treatment: Cortisone injections to relieve inflammation…and/or custom-fitted orthotic shoe inserts to more evenly distribute pressure on the foot.

Holistic therapy: Massage the arch of the foot by rolling a squash ball (a tennis ball is too large) on the floor from heel to toes. Use pressure that is firm enough to move the tissues without causing pain.

This massage reduces inflammation by moving accumulated acids out of tissues. Perform it daily until symptoms resolve. *For plantar fasciitis, also perform this stretch twice daily on a regular basis…*

What to do: Take one large step forward and bend your forward knee. Press the heel of the back leg onto the floor. Hold for 10 to 30 seconds, then switch leg positions. For added stretch, bend the back knee, as well.

Important: If your foot problems affect your ability to walk or don't heal or improve *after two weeks* of home care, see a podiatrist.

Illustration by Shawn Banner.

Sherri Greene, DPM (doctor of podiatric medicine). She has practiced conventional and holistic podiatric medicine in New York City for the past 12 years. Her treatment modalities include reflexology, herbal medicine and essential oils.

Softening/Toughening Feet

➤ **Softening Tough Feet.** The soles of the feet have the body's thickest skin. To help soften and soothe this rough, tough area, get a big, juicy lemon and cut it in half the long way. Take two plastic shoeboxes and divide the squeezed juice of the lemon into them. (See the "Healthful Hints" chapter, page 281, for how to get the most juice out of a lemon.) Cup each half of lemon on each of your heels. Put your feet into the boxes that way and add enough warm water to cover your feet. Stay like that for 15 minutes, then rinse your feet in warm water and dry them thoroughly. You should notice a difference immediately.

➤ **Toughening Tender Feet.** Our out-of-town friends are used to driving everywhere. When they visit New York, we schlep them around town by foot, and by the end of the day they're begging for mercy. *We finally found a remedy to help toughen up soles…*

Get two plastic shoeboxes and in each put one tablespoon of alum (available at drugstores and in some supermarket spice sections) and one-half gallon of cold water. Soak your feet in this solution for 15 minutes after breakfast, after dinner and right before bed.

Continue doing it for as many days as it takes to walk without pain from those tender soles.

 NOTE: This remedy is also said to eliminate foot odor.

➤ **Cracked Heels.** See the "Urine Cure" remedy on page 92 for "Athlete's Foot."

Cold Feet

➤ **Weather-Related Cold Feet.** To keep your feet warm in freezing weather, sprinkle a little cayenne pepper in your socks. It's an old skier's trick, but you don't have to be an old skier to use it.

 CAUTION: The cayenne pepper will make your socks turn red, and it won't wash out completely. Cayenne will also make your feet red, but that should wash off completely, or watch our faces turn red.

➤ **Circulation-Related Cold Feet.**
• **Asian remedy.** For this remarkable remedy you'll need gingerroot, mustard powder, a grater, food processor or juicer, cheesecloth and plastic wrap.

Make ginger juice by grating or food processing one ounce of fresh gingerroot. Spoon the ground pulp into cheesecloth and squeeze out the juice into a little saucer, or put the ginger root through a juicer. Next, mix the juice with two teaspoons of mustard powder. Smear the soles of your cold feet with the mixture and then wrap the plastic wrap around each foot. Stay that way for 15 minutes. Your feet should

feel toasty warm. After you repeat the treatment for a week—seven days in a row—cold feet may soon be just a memory.

 CAUTION: Ginger acts as a blood thinner, so check with your doctor before using it if you are taking a prescription blood thinner. Also, stop using ginger three days before any surgery.

• **Salt paste.** Take a half cup of kosher (coarse) salt and add enough olive oil to make it into a paste consistency. For 10 minutes vigorously rub your feet with the mixture, making sure you give equal time to all the parts of your feet. In the bathtub, rinse your feet with warm water and then with cool water. Dry them with a rough towel. Your feet should feel charged and your circulation should be stimulated.

Toe-Tingling and Numbness

Check "Neuropathy" in the "Diabetes" section, page 56.

Corn Remedies

Q. What's the difference between an oak tree and a tight shoe?
A. An oak tree makes acorns; a tight shoe makes corns ache.

Not funny? Neither are corns. *Here are some remedies...*

➤ **Oil Rub.** Before bedtime, rub the corn with either castor oil, wheat germ oil, the oil from a vitamin E capsule or a vitamin A capsule. After a few minutes of this, let the oil sink in for the next few minutes. Finally, put a sock on the foot and go to sleep. Do this every night for a couple of weeks and you should get rid of the corn.

➤ **Lemon.** At bedtime, cut a dime-sized piece of peel from the top of a small, slim lemon, and insert the toe that has the corn. Put a sock on top of it and keep it on overnight. If the entire lemon on your toe is ungainly, use a wedge of lemon, or just the peel—the white side against the corn. Use a Band-Aid to keep peel in place. Do this every night until you're cornless.

➤ **Onion.** In the morning, put a small onion in distilled white vinegar. At bedtime, cut a piece of the vinegar-soaked onion and put it on the corn, keeping it in place with a Band-Aid. Leave it on overnight. In the morning the corn may be ripe enough to remove.

Yes, this remedy has been known to work after only one application. If it doesn't, repeat the procedure the following day and night.

 NOTE: If none of these remedies makes the corn disappear, it may be time to visit a podiatrist for professional help.

Sweaty, Smelly Feet

➤ **Tea Soak.** Steep four black or green tea bags in a quart of just-boiled water and let them steep for 15 minutes. Then divide the strong tea into two plastic shoeboxes and add enough cool water to make it possible to put your feet in without burning them. Soak your feet for a half hour. Do this twice a day for at least a week, and you should notice a difference, thanks to "tannin," a drying substance in tea.

➤ **Alum Soak.** Get out the two plastic shoeboxes again and mix one-half teaspoon of alum (available at drugstores and in some supermarket spice sections) with one gallon of tepid water in each shoe box. Soak your feet for 30 minutes, then rinse and dry. Doing this once a month should eliminate the problem.

The "Toughening Tender Feet" remedy (on page 95) also works for sweaty feet.

AFFIRMATION

For all of the above foot problems, you can use Joyce Kaessinger's affirmation in the "Heel Spur" remedy above, or you can repeat the following affirmation at least 20 times, any time you feel pain in your feet…

I walk through life with ease and comfort. I advance and grow and keep step with the world.

GALLBLADDER PROBLEMS

The liver produces bile. The gallbladder, the liver's downstairs neighbor, stores the bile and releases it to digest fats. If you have sharp pains—like severe gas pains—under your right rib cage, it could mean that you have gallstones or another gallstone problem.

CAUTION: If you suspect gallstones or any other gallbladder problem, have your condition *medically diagnosed*. While you're deciding on your plan of action, you might want to try one of these remedies. But all of these remedies should be used only with your doctor's approval and close supervision. These gallstone "flushers" can mobilize the gallstones, but also may cause the stones to get stuck in the bile duct, a medical emergency.

Gallstone Removers

➤ **Extra Virgin Olive Oil (EVOO).** The common ingredient in almost all the gallstone remedies we've collected is olive oil. Olive oil seems to open the bile ducts, encouraging the stones to move along and out. Listen to your inner voice (and to your doctor) to guide you to the method that will work best for you.

● **Lie down on the floor and slowly sip half a cup of warm EVOO.** If necessary, do it again in another eight hours. During this process, you might want to tape a piece of the gem, sugilite, to the painful area. According to gemologist Joyce Kaessinger, sugilite is the gem that will help you let go of what's *galling* you.

● **Every day, before breakfast, take two tablespoons of EVOO in a half-cup of grapefruit juice,** or take the EVOO and then drink the juice. Gradually increase the amount of oil

and juice until you're up to a quarter of a cup of olive oil in a glass of grapefruit juice. You should get results within a month.

NOTE: Before beginning the above regimen, if you are taking any prescription medicine, check with your doctor or pharmacist to make sure there is no negative interaction between your medicine and the grapefruit juice.

● **Drink one quart of apple juice every day for five days,** while eating light, sensible meals. On the sixth day, drink a quart of apple juice throughout the day, omit the evening meal, and at 6 pm, take one tablespoon of Epsom salts with a half-cup of water. At 8 pm, take another tablespoon of Epsom salts with a half-cup of water. Then at 10 pm combine four ounces of EVOO with four ounces of fresh lemon juice and drink it down. Within the next 24 hours, stay close to a bathroom for when you get rid of the gallstones. If you do all this, you *deserve* to get rid of the gallstones.

➤ **Native American Style.** "Take a teaspoon of fiddle rosin, put it in a tablespoon, and add jelly or syrup to fill up the tablespoon. That'll make the rosin edible. Swallow it down and, before you can say 'Geronimo,' your gallstone will high-tail it out of there."

Those are the words of a woman who called in to share this remedy with us when we were on a radio show. She told us she was brought up with Cherokee Indians and learned this remedy and others from them. Incidentally, she knows for sure that this remedy works...at least it worked for her.

Rosin is made of resin derived from the sap of various pine trees. You can buy it at music stores that sell string instruments.

Sluggish Gallbladder

➤ **Calming Chamomile.** If your doctor's diagnosis is "sluggish gallbladder," clean out that slothful gallbladder by drinking at least seven cups of chamomile tea each day for seven days. Prepare it by steeping one teaspoon of chamomile in a cup of just-boiled water. After 10 minutes, strain, add the juice of half a lemon and slowly drink it down. The vitamin C from the lemon seems to add to and intensify the cleansing power of the chamomile.

 NOTE: Be sure to get your doctor's approval before starting this cleansing treatment.

Gallbladder Problems Prevention

➤ **Do Not Eat Fatty Foods**—that means foods that are fried, rich desserts, fatty meats and high-fat dairy products.

➤ **Drink Lots of Water and Pure Juices.** Also, eat whole grains, fruits, vegetables, and if you must eat meat make sure it's lean. Boil, broil and steam foods that you can't eat raw.

AFFIRMATION

While we've refrained from reporting the psychological reasons for physical manifestations, we're making an exception here, since the English language has done it for us.

Take a look at your life and recognize all the things that are going on that gall you and acknowledge all the people you have to deal with who gall you. Your anger is probably stopping you from enjoying the everyday things in your life.

Once you acknowledge that no one but you has the power to rob you of enjoying your day, you'll be ready to use your power for your own good.

This affirmation can help.

Repeat the following affirmation at least 15 times, first thing in the morning, last thing at night and every time you walk through a doorway...

My life is a happy challenge. I find real pleasure in everything I do.

GENITAL HERPES

 According to the Centers for Disease Control and Prevention (*www.cdc.gov*), results of a nationally representative study show that nationwide, at least 45 million people ages 12 and older, or one out of five adolescents and adults, have had a genital Herpes infection. It's a sexually transmitted viral infection that's painful and unpredictably recurrent.

Conservatively speaking, one out of every five sexually active adults has it. So, you are not alone. Then again, if you were alone, maybe you wouldn't have it.

Here are, not remedies, but treatments to make you more comfortable, to do away with the symptoms and to help prevent them from returning.

Relieve the Itching

➤ **Goldenseal.** An herbal gift from the Cherokee Indians, goldenseal can help relieve itching and dry up the lesions. Buy goldenseal at a health food store, in powder form, add enough water to make a paste, and gently smear it on the sores.

Hasten the Healing

To let the air help heal the sores and blisters, wear loose-fitting cotton underwear. *Then try any of the following tips...*

99

➤ **Aloe Vera.** Break off a leaf from the aloe vera plant, squeeze out the gel and apply it directly on the sores.

➤ **Vitamin E.** Squeeze out the oil from a vitamin E capsule and put it on the sores. We were told that if you use the oil the second you feel the symptoms coming on, it may actually prevent them from blossoming.

➤ **Arginine.** This amino acid is said to promote the growth of this nasty virus. Eliminate foods that are rich in arginine like chocolate, peas, chicken soup, veal, lamb, beef, bran, buckwheat, nuts, seeds, gelatin, grain cereals, cola and beer.

➤ **L-lysine.** Another amino acid, L-lysine seems to discourage the virus from taking hold. Flounder is loaded with L-lysine. Eating steamed flounder—a half-pound, twice in one day, may rid you of symptoms.

Other foods rich in L-lysine are avocado, pumpernickel, lima beans, lentils, potatoes, cottage cheese and shrimp. You can supplement your diet with L-lysine tablets—500 milligrams (mg) before lunch and 500 mg before dinner. If pregnant or nursing, check with your doctor.

➤ **Lots of Vitamin C.** Big doses of vitamin C have also been proven effective in quickly clearing up herpes symptoms and, in some cases, making them go bye-bye forever. Take 1,000 mg of vitamin C every hour, 10 hours a day, for 10 days. Well, we did say "big doses"! Be consistent with the 10,000 mg a day for the 10 days. If you notice any unpleasant side effects from the vitamin C, stop taking it.

 CAUTION: Be sure to check with your doctor for approval *before* taking megadoses of *anything!* If you get diarrhea from the vitamin C, you know you've taken too much.

➤ **Gem Therapy.** Choose either sodalite or sugilite. Both stones are said to help release guilt, clear the mind of emotional confusion and help one get in touch with one's inner strength. Think about it. *Really* think about it. Is it possible that guilt, emotional confusion and lack of inner strength are being manifested by herpes flare-ups? The sodalite or sugilite may help. See "Sources," page 311, for gem companies.

More information: Visit the American Sexual Health Association (*www.ashastd.org*) for reliable information on sexually transmitted diseases, including herpes. If you don't have access to the Internet, call 919-361-8488 to speak with a health communications specialist

---

AFFIRMATION

Repeat the affirmation at least 10 times, first thing in the morning, last thing at night and throughout the day, right after you have a lustful thought. (It may happen more often than you realize, so be prepared to say the affirmation a whole lot.)

I am a special person. Part of my specialness is my sexuality. My body gives me pleasure without guilt.

GOUT

 Were it not for gout, there might not have been an American Revolution. Instead of attending critical sessions of the British Parliament, William Pitt was home with gout. As a result of his absence, the *Stamp Act* and tea tax, which led to the Boston Tea Party, were passed by Parliament. And the rest is history. The rest really is history.

Throughout history there have been noted gout sufferers: Benjamin Franklin, Sir Francis

Bacon, Michelangelo, Dr. Samuel Johnson, Charles Darwin, Sir Isaac Newton, Kublai Khan, King Henry VIII, Charlemagne, Martin Luther, Oliver Cromwell, Galileo Galilei, Karl Marx, John Milton, Joseph Conrad and Theodore Roosevelt.

Notice that all the gout getters mentioned above are men? Ninety percent of people with gout are men over 40. The 7% of women with the problem get it after menopause.

Okay, so we know who has had it and who gets it. Now what is it? Gout is a metabolic malady, caused by the inadequate processing of *purines* that break down, producing *uric acid* as a by-product. It's the uric acid that causes the problem and the pain. Eliminate foods high in purine and you may eliminate this painful condition.

Foods to Avoid

- **Meat**—most types of meat have high amounts of uric acid, especially turkey, veal, bacon and venison. Beef, and chicken and duck (both without the skin) have moderate amounts of purine. All organ meats—liver, sweetbreads, kidneys, heart, brain.

- **Fish**—anchovies, herring, haddock, sardines, trout (even though they're recommended for people with other forms of arthritis, they aren't good for people with gout).

- **Caviar.**

- **Shellfish**—especially clams, scallops and mussels.

- **Fried foods.**

- **Rich foods**—desserts with white flour and sugar.

- **Baker's and brewer's yeast.**

- **Alcoholic beverages**, especially beer (it has brewer's yeast).

- **Consommé, bouillon, broth and gravies**—all high in purine.

- **Eggs.** While eggs are low in purine, they cause the body to produce uric acid, so we put them on the "Avoid" list.

Foods to Eat

➤ **Your New Menu.** You may be wondering what you should eat. Stick with grains, especially brown rice, nuts and seeds, fresh fruits and most raw vegetables. Try tofu as a source of protein. It's not a forever diet. Once the condition is cleared up, you can introduce some of your favorite foods (in moderation) back into your daily meals.

➤ **A Bowl of Cherries.** The classic gout remedy is cherries. They have an enzyme that helps neutralize uric acid. Eat about four ounces of fresh bing cherries every day between meals. If it's not cherry season, you can drink bottled cherry juice (without added sugar), or buy cherry juice concentrate (available at health food stores), and have one tablespoon three times a day. You can also eat frozen, canned or jarred cherries. People have reported good results from all forms of cherries, including cherry extract and cherry powder.

 NOTE: Be sure to check out "Cherries" in the chapter "It Does a Body Good," page 236, to learn about tart cherries.

While you're at it, add strawberries to your shopping list. They, too, are excellent uric acid neutralizers.

Gout Remedies

➤ **Corny Remedy.** Cut off the kernels from three fresh ears of corn. Place the stripped corncobs in a pot and add water—twice the

101

height of the cobs. Simmer for an hour, then pour the liquid into a bottle and keep it refrigerated. Daily, drink a cup of corncob tea after each meal, until the gout is gone.

➤ **Neutralizing Tea.** Yarrow tea, celery seed tea and dandelion tea can neutralize uric acid and help flush it out of your system. Throughout each day, drink three or four cups of any one or a combination of two or three of these teas.

 NOTE: Yarrow tea has an unusual taste, so you may want to add honey.

➤ **Water Works.** Drink at least eight glasses of water daily. Water intake throughout the day will help dilute the uric acid concentration of urine.

➤ **Exercise Control.** Vigorous exercise will increase uric acid production, and that's not a good thing when you have the gout. Until the condition is gone, exercise in moderation.

A Word from the Wise...

Skip the Soft Drinks

Gout is an inflammatory arthritic disease. High-fructose corn syrup, used to sweeten soft drinks, increases uric acid levels, which are linked to gout. Drinking two sugary soft drinks a day increases risk for gout by a whopping 85%!

Self-defense: Anyone who has a personal or family history of gout should avoid sugar-sweetened soft drinks. Diet soft drinks do not increase risk. Fructose-rich fruits, such as apples and oranges, and fruit juices also may increase risk.

Gary C. Cuhran, MD, ScD, associate professor, department of medicine and epidemiology, Channing Laboratory/Brigham and Women's Hospital, Boston, and senior author of a study of 46,983 men, published in *British Medical Journal.*

HAIR CARE

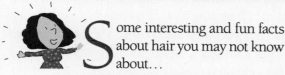

Some interesting and fun facts about hair you may not know about…

● **About 65% of us have straight hair,** while 25% have wavy hair, leaving only 10% with hair that's curly.

● **On the average, hair grows half an inch each month**—a little less in February, of course. Your hair grows fastest when you're in love, probably because your hormones are jumping for joy.

● **Cutting your hair does not influence its growth.**

● **At any given time, 90% of your scalp hairs are growing,** while 10% are resting.

● **The average person loses about 70 to 100 hairs a day**—more if you are sick, anemic, malnourished or the love of your life leaves you. Frequent washing does not increase hair loss.

● **By the time women reach menopause,** 40% will have female pattern (hereditary) hair loss.

● **Talk about losing your hair…**one out of every five men will not lose their hair, while one out of every five men will start to lose their hair at a rapid pace in their 20s. The remaining three out of the five will get bald slowly.

● **It is said that the more hair a man has on his chest when he is 30,** the less hair he'll have on his head by the time he reaches 40. The hormones that are responsible for chest hair also cause male pattern baldness.

Statistics are interesting, but they aren't going to help you take care of your hair. These suggestions may…

Dandruff Chasers

➤ **Gingerroot.** Grate one ounce of fresh gingerroot and take an ounce of chamomile flowers (available at health food stores) and tie them into a piece of cheesecloth. Put the cheesecloth pouch in a gallon of spring water and boil it for 10 minutes. When the liquid cools, pour it into bottles. Label and seal them. To use, after shampooing, massage one-half to one ounce of the liquid into your hair. No need to rinse.

➤ **Aloe Vera.** If you have dandruff, get an aloe vera plant or buy a large individual aloe vera leaf. You may be able to find it at a store that sells organic fruits and vegetables such as Whole Foods. The night before you're going to shampoo your hair, snip off a piece of the lowest leaf of the aloe plant. Peel off the skin of the leaf and squeeze the gel on your hair and massage it into your scalp. Wrap your head in a bandanna and sleep that way. Next morning when you wash your hair, don't use shampoo. Foam up the aloe gel. It's good for your hair and can get rid of your dandruff quickly.

If you don't have the aloe vera plant leaf, buy aloe vera gel at a health food store. Be sure it's 100% organic. A quickie version of the remedy above is to distribute the gel all over your hair, and massage it into your scalp. Leave it that way for 15 minutes, then rinse the gel out of your hair. Repeat this procedure for the next few days, and when you stop, hopefully your dandruff will stop too.

➤ **Apple Cider Vinegar.** Heat up some apple cider vinegar—enough to saturate your hair and scalp with it. Once you've done that, cover your head with a shower cap and stay that way for an hour. Then rinse your hair with plain water. Do this twice a week until the dandruff is gone.

➤ **Peanut Oil.** Warm an ounce of peanut oil, or however much you need to massage it into your scalp. Then follow that with fresh lemon juice. After keeping the oil and lemon on your head for 15 minutes, shampoo it out. Since the strong chemicals in shampoo can cause dandruff, read labels and buy a mild shampoo. Ask your local health food store manager for a recommendation.

For Healthy Hair

➤ **Seaweed.** Include seaweed in your daily diet. It can make a major difference in your energy level, sexual desire, nervous system, digestive system, mental stress, sensory receptiveness, memory, aches and pains and oh yes, it can help give you healthy hair.

Try different kinds of seaweed—dulse, kelp, hijiki, arame, wakame, nori—to find the ones you like best. Find a macrobiotic restaurant in your area, or get a good cookbook and experiment.

If you just can't develop a taste for seaweed, you can always take it in capsule form.

For a Shinier and Fuller Head of Hair

➤ **Bee Pollen.** Take a daily dose of bee pollen (available at most health food stores or check "Sources," page 310).

 CAUTION: Some people are allergic to bee pollen. Start very slowly—with a couple of granules the first day or two. Then if you have no allergic reaction, work your way up gradually until you take one teaspoon or more a day—up to one tablespoon depending on how you feel. Asthmatics should NOT use bee pollen.

➤ **Yoga.** At least once a day, do a headstand. You may need a trusted friend to help you. When you first start this yoga exercise, do it for 15 seconds each time. Then add another 15 seconds each week, until you work your way up to a three-minute headstand.

This asana (posture) is known as "King of Asanas" because you can derive so many benefits from it. In addition to promoting hair growth and shinier hair, headstands can improve brain function because of increased circulation to the brain and give relief from nervousness, tension, sleeplessness, fatigue. It's also said to stimulate four of the most important endocrine glands (the pituitary, pineal, thyroid and parathyroid) that are responsible for our existence.

 CAUTION: This yoga remedy is NOT for everyone. It's only for those who know they can do it safely, carefully and painlessly. Also, do NOT do this exercise if you have high or low blood pressure.

➤ **To Give Dark Hair a Shine.** Prepare strong rosemary tea using a heaping tablespoon of rosemary (available at herb and health food stores) in a pint of just-boiled water. Cover and let it steep for 15 minutes. Strain and take the liquid with you into the shower. Shampoo your hair, rinse it with plain water and then rinse it again with the rosemary tea. (This should not be used on light or gray hair that you want to keep that color.)

To Soften Coarse Hair

➤ **Plain Yogurt.** Shampoo and towel-dry your hair. Then take a pint of plain yogurt and glop it on your hair, making sure it gets evenly distributed. Stay that way for 15 minutes before rinsing out the yogurt with tepid water.

To Condition Hair

➤ **Good Old Mayo.** Spread mayonnaise on your hair and scalp, wrap your head in a towel and let it stay that way for a half-hour. Then wash it out.

➤ **Banana/Avocado Mash.** If you have an overripe banana hanging around and/or a squishy old avocado, mix the meats together and spread it on your hair and scalp. To avoid being attacked by fruit flies, wrap your head in a towel and stay that way for a half hour. Then shampoo your hair clean. Be sure to take precaution not to clog up the drain in the bathtub, shower or sink. Use a "hair catcher," which is inexpensive and available at hardware and discount stores.

For Split and Broken Ends

➤ **Castor Oil.** Gently comb a half-cup of warm castor oil or olive oil through your hair, making sure the oil reaches the ends. With the oil in place, wrap your head in a hot, wet (wrung out) towel and stay that way for a half hour. Then add one egg yolk to your shampoo and wash your hair. Add a half-cup of apple cider vinegar to a gallon of water and make that your final rinse.

Prepare Your Own Hair Products

Most commercial hair gels provide UV protection against the harsh UV rays of the sun. That's the good news. The not-so-good news is those gels are loaded with chemicals that may not be all that great for you and your hair. If you want to prepare your own gel, here are two easy recipes:

➤ **Quick and Simple Gel.** Dissolve about one teaspoon of gelatin in one cup of warm water. That's it. Because it has no preservatives, keep it in the refrigerator. It should last about a week.

➤ **Healthy-Ingredients Gel.** This scentless, gentle-hold gel is particularly effective for taming curly-hair frizzies.

In a small saucepan, bring one cup of water to a boil. Stir in two tablespoons of whole flaxseeds and simmer until it thickens (it takes about 10 minutes). Stir it the entire time.

Once it's thick, remove the seeds by pouring the mixture through a fine strainer into a jar. Allow it to cool.

When it's cool, add one part aloe vera gel to three parts flaxseed gel and stir the mixture thoroughly. The aloe vera will prevent the gel from drying out your hair.

Cover the jar and refrigerate it. It should keep for about a week. Use it as you would store-bought gel.

➤ **Natural Hair Spray.** Take a large lemon or two small ones, cut them into small chunks, and put the chunks in a glass or enamel saucepan. Add two cups of water and bring it to a boil. As soon as it starts to boil, lower the flame and cook until the liquid cooks down to about half the amount—it should take 15 to 20 minutes. Next, strain out the liquid. You may want to press down on the lemon chunks to make sure all the juice is out of them. Put the lemon hair spray in a spray container and refrigerate it. If you don't use it often, put one ounce of vodka in it as a preservative.

 NOTE: Experiment with the do-it-yourself hair spray and all of the other tips in this chapter when you're not going to a special event and want to look outstanding…in a good way.

➤ **Hair-Setting Lotion.** This Bud's for you—if it's gone flat and you need a setting lotion. Just comb any gone-flat beer through your hair and you're set…well, almost. The beer smell should disappear by the time you finish setting your hair.

Curly Hair

You curly-haired kids always wanted straight hair, right? By now, we are hoping you know how wonderful it is to have curls. These tips should make for a *mane* celebration…

➤ **Drying Hair.** Replace the terry cloth towel with paper towels and blot out the excess water to minimize or eliminate frizz. Air dry your hair, or if you must use a blow-dryer, only use one with a diffuser attached to get tame, silky curls.

➤ **Gel Application.** To keep your curls beautifully bouncy, do not apply gel to the ends of your hair because it will weigh them down.

If you have a real frizz challenge, smear gel on a paper towel and plop it on the top of your head. Let it sit there for a few minutes, until you feel your hair has absorbed the gel, then distribute the gel throughout your hair. It should help.

 NOTE: Check out "Quick and Simple Gel" on the previous page.

➤ **Cutting Your Curls.** When you are ready for a haircut, ask to have your hair cut when dry. Yes, dry. Think about it. To have your hair cut exactly the way you want to wear it, your hair should be the way it is when you wear it…dry!

Hair Loss Prevention

If your hair is thinning, and you are sure you are not among the 90% who can attribute it to hereditary factors, these suggestions may help…

➤ **Sulfur** is a mineral that nourishes scalp follicles. Eat foods rich in sulfur—cabbage, brussels sprouts, kale, watercress, turnips, cauliflower, parsnips, raspberries and cranberries. It's best to eat the fruits and vegetables raw; second best is steamed.

Also take a B-complex vitamin. The combination of the two (sulfur-filled foods and B vitamins) should make for healthier hair and more of it.

➤ **An Asian Remedy.** This remedy calls for boiling one pound of snails in water (available at gourmet and Asian fish markets). Once the water cools, wash your hair with it. It's supposed to prevent hair loss. Well, maybe you still lose your hair, but at a snail's pace.

➤ **Drink Barley Water on a Daily Basis.** To prepare it, put two ounces of barley in a pot with six cups of water. Boil it down to half the amount of water. Strain and drink. (Add honey only if you need to make it more palatable.)

If the thinning of your hair has given you an ulcer, the barley water will take care of that, too!

➤ **A Sage Wash.** You might want to try washing your head with sage tea every day. Prepare the tea by using two tablespoons of sage in a pint of just-boiled water. Strain the mixture and drench your scalp with the liquid. They say it may stop your hair from falling out. (Please don't ask us who "they" are!)

Grow Hair Back

There are two versions of this Chinese remedy. Each of them includes fresh gingerroot, and each should be done on a daily basis.

➤ **Version #1.** Finely grate a chunk of ginger and warm it just a little. Then spread it on the bald area and cover it with a shower cap for a half-hour before washing it off.

➤ **Version #2.** Juice ginger (grate it or put it through a food processor and squeeze it through cheesecloth) and add rubbing alcohol—one part ginger to 10 parts alcohol. Dip a cotton ball in the solution and massage the bald area with it. After a half hour, rinse the head with tepid water.

HAY FEVER AND OTHER ALLERGIES

What we have come to know as "hay fever" is, in most cases, an allergy to pollen and mold spores in the air. In the spring there's pollen from trees and grass; starting in mid-August, there's pollen from ragweed and other weeds, along with mold spores from barley, wheat and corn (especially in the Midwest).

The pollen count is highest from sunrise to 10 am, so stay indoors during those hours as much as possible.

If you have a lawn, keep your grass very short—no more than an inch high. It will limit your exposure to grass pollen.

Protection and Prevention

➤ **Use a Mask.** Wear a mask over your mouth and nose when you do gardening to avoid tons of pollen. Indoors, wear the mask whenever you vacuum, to avoid inhaling the dust that gets churned up. Masks are available at hardware stores.

Preseason Immunization

➤ **Bee Pollen.** Four months before hay fever season starts, build an immunity to airborne pollen by taking bee pollen. If you don't have a local beekeeper, you can get bee pollen at health food stores or check "Sources," page 310, for our recommendation.

You can put the bee pollen in anything—juice, water, yogurt, cereal—or just dissolve it in your mouth and/or swallow it.

It's an amazingly effective remedy. Then again, bee pollen is one of nature's perfect foods, containing all the necessary nutrients to sustain life. It's also one of the few things that cannot be duplicated in a laboratory.

CAUTION: Some people are allergic to bee pollen. Start very slowly—with a couple of granules the first day or two. Then if you have no allergic reaction, work your way up gradually until you take one teaspoon or more a day—up to one tablespoon depending on how you feel. Asthmatics should NOT use bee pollen.

➤ **Fenugreek Seed Tea.** A daily cup of fenugreek seed tea (available at health food stores), starting three months before the hay fever season, can desensitize you. The name "fenugreek" means "Greek hay." Coincidence? We don't think so.

➤ **Brewer's Yeast.** Two months before hay fever season rolls around, take brewer's yeast tablets. Read the label for the recommended dosage.

Immunity Boosters

➤ **Red Clover Blossoms.** Available at health food stores, these were a favorite of medieval herbalists and are now gaining popularity again. It's no wonder. Three or four cups of red clover tea a day can help build an immunity to allergies.

➤ **Garlic and Horseradish.** Daily doses of garlic and horseradish can also help build your resistance to allergies. Finely mince a clove of garlic and put it in orange juice or some water and drink it down. Add a quarter-teaspoon of horseradish to vegetable juice or mix it in a salad. Both are strong and may take getting used to. If they help you breathe easier, minimize your allergy symptoms, and maybe even immunize you against allergies, it pays to start getting used to them!

 CAUTION: Having garlic on an empty stomach can cause nausea. Be sure to have some food in your stomach before eating garlic or taking capsules. And, be cautious with garlic if you have gastritis.

Instant Relief

➤ **Honeycomb Cure from Lydia.** I have gotten instant relief from a hay fever attack by chewing a one-inch square of honeycomb (available at health food stores). It's delicious. Swallow the honey and continue chewing the waxy gum for about 10 minutes. Be sure that the honeycomb is from your area of the country—the closer the better.

 CAUTION: If you have a suspected sensitivity to bee products, do NOT chew on honeycomb. Also, asthmatics should NOT have honeycomb.

➤ **Nettle.** A common plant, the stinging nettle, seems to act as a natural antihistamine and offers quick relief from a hay fever attack. According to numerous naturopaths, a freeze-dried extract of the leaves taken in capsules is

best. To control hay fever symptoms, take one or two capsules every two to four hours.

More Hay Fever Relief

➤ **Sleeping with Allergies.** Slice an onion right before you eat dinner and let it sit in a glass of water. When you're ready for bed, drink the onion water. It should help you fall asleep and breathe easier while you sleep.

➤ **Stuffed Nose.** When your nose is stuffed, rub your ears vigorously until they feel as though they're burning. For some odd reason, it should clear up the allergy-caused stuffiness in your nose.

➤ **Aromatherapy.** Hyssop, lavender or chamomile oils are all said to relieve hay fever symptoms. When you have a runny nose, teary eyes and that stuffed-up feeling, put a drop or two of any of the above oils on the inside of your wrist or on a handkerchief, and take a whiff every few minutes.

➤ **Chihuahua Cure.** We received a letter from a woman who informed us about three different cases that she knew of where Chihuahuas somehow rid their owners of severe allergies. The most dramatic of the three stories was about a young girl who had been suffering with hay fever for several years and had tried everything. As a last resort, her uncle bought her a Chihuahua. The family thought he was loco, but it was an adorable little pet and his niece was happy to have this new friend. The bottom line is, the last hay fever attack the young girl ever experienced was the day before she got the dog.

Food Allergy Info

➤ **Biggest Culprits.** The foods that most often cause allergic reactions are—eggs, corn, cow's milk, wheat, gluten, citrus fruit, tomatoes, cane sugar, seafood, nuts and chocolate.

➤ **Chocolate.** If you're allergic to chocolate and really want to continue eating it, try white chocolate. It doesn't have *theobromine*, which may be the substance in dark chocolate that causes your allergic reaction.

Carob is a popular substitute for chocolate. Some people learn to love it as much or more than they loved chocolate.

➤ **Ragweed Allergy Symptoms.** If your hay fever is due to ragweed, you may experience the identical misery-making symptoms after eating cantaloupe, watermelon, honeydew, zucchini or cucumber. These fruits and vegetables have allergy-producing proteins that are extraordinarily similar to those in ragweed, so be aware. If you eat any of these foods and have a reaction, you will know to avoid them in the future.

➤ **Shrimp Alert.** If you are allergic to shrimp, of course, you know not to eat them. What you may not know is that you shouldn't even go into the kitchen when they're being prepared. Breathing in the steam that filters out into the air while shrimp are boiling can be enough to trigger an allergic reaction.

➤ **Gluten Allergy.** Check "Celiac Disease," page 26.

Other Allergies

➤ **Pesticides and Preservatives.** If your allergies are caused by pesticides or preservatives on fruits and vegetables, try to eat organic foods. Also, eat foods rich in selenium such as bran, broccoli, onions, tuna in water, tomatoes and Brazil nuts. (See "Healthful Hints," page 283, for the best ways to clean produce.) And, supplement your diet using selenium tablets

(available at health food stores) following recommended dosage on the bottle. Selenium may also help protect you from pollution in the air.

➤ **Jewelry Allergy.** An allergy to *nickel* is the most common contact allergy among women. The metal pins worn for the first three to six weeks after ears are pierced contain minute quantities of nickel.

People who have their ears pierced with more than one hole in each ear have twice as many allergies. Visit *www.simplywhispers.com* for hypoallergenic earrings.

Incidentally, nickel is found in high-quality gold, silver and platinum as well as in the cheaper costume varieties. This nickel can make you vulnerable to an allergic reaction when you wear any kind of jewelry or even metal buttons, snaps, eyeglass frames, wristwatches and zippers.

In the Nickel Solution Kit, one bottle tests for the presence of nickel, the other bottle gives temporary protection when you wear the jewelry that contains nickel. To find out more about the kit, visit the National Allergy Web site at *www.natlallergy.com* and type "Nickel Solution Kit" into the "Site Search" box on the right-hand side or call 800-522-1448.

➤ **Cell Phone, Yes, Cell Phone Allergy.** If you spend a lot of time on your cell phone, and you have a rash on your cheek or ear, or if you do lots of texting and have a rash on your fingers, you may have what the British Association of Dermatologists are calling "Mobile Phone Dermatitis."

Some, not all, cell phones contain nickel in them. In general, the models that do have nickel are the more fashionable ones with metallic accents, rather than the less stylish looking cells. How do you know which have it and which don't? Test for nickel so that your skin doesn't have to. To learn about and order a nickel test, see the contact information under "Jewelry Allergy" above.

➤ **Fabric Allergy.** If you get a sneaking suspicion that you're allergic to a fabric type, take a piece of that fabric—a swatch will do—put it in a jar with the lid on, and leave it in the sun for five hours. Then open the jar and inhale the air in the jar. If you sneeze, wheeze, turn red, perspire or manifest any allergic reaction, guess what…you're allergic to that fabric.

 CAUTION: If you have asthma, do NOT try this.

More information: For lots more information, and to help find a support group in your area, get in touch with the Asthma and Allergy Foundation of America (*www.aafa.org*) or call their national hotline at 800-7-ASTHMA (278462).

AFFIRMATION

Repeat this affirmation at least 10 times, starting first thing in the morning, every time you leave a place, including your home, and every time you enter a new place, including your car or public transportation, your office, a supermarket—wherever. Then, repeat it another 10 times last thing at night.

Everything is happening for my good. I am safe and I am free to enjoy life.

A Word from the Wise…

Cure Allergies the Natural Way: Three Simple Steps

Seasonal allergies are most commonly associated with springtime. But the flare-ups that occur in the summer can be just as bad—if not worse—due to the added discomfort caused by heat and humidity.

Interesting new fact: Allergy symptoms could be lasting even longer due to extended pollen seasons brought on by climate change, according to a recent analysis.

That's why it's more important than ever for the 40 million Americans who suffer from seasonal allergies to use the most effective therapies—with the fewest side effects.

Good news: You don't have to fill your medicine cabinet with various powerful drugs that can simply temporarily relieve your allergy symptoms and potentially lead to side effects ranging from headache and drowsiness to difficulty breathing. Instead, you can get relief from the natural remedies here.

The Root of the Problem

Most doctors treat allergies with a regimen that includes oral antihistamines, such as *loratadine* (Claritin) or *cetirizine* (Zyrtec), to block the release of histamine so that runny noses and itchy eyes will be reduced…and/or inhaled steroids, such as *triamcinolone acetonide* (Nasacort) or *flunisolide* (Nasalide), to reduce inflammation, mucus production and nasal congestion.

Problem: Aside from the side effects these drugs can cause, many allergy sufferers experience a "rebound effect"—when the drug wears off, the histamine that has been suppressed explodes, causing an even bigger allergic reaction.

Important: To transition from medication to the natural regimen here, first take the natural remedy with the medication, then slowly wean off the medication over several weeks.

Three simple natural approaches…

 CAUTION: Consult a doctor before trying this regimen if you are pregnant or have a medical condition.

110

Step 1: Supplements

Mother Nature has tools that work with your body to stop allergy symptoms. The following naturally occurring substances have few side effects and often are just as effective as over-the-counter and prescription allergy medications.

My advice: Try quercetin, then add fish oil in severe cases.

➤ **Quercetin** is a *bioflavonoid* that inhibits histamine-producing cells. It's in citrus fruits, apples and onions but not in sufficient amounts to relieve allergy symptoms. For optimal relief, try quercetin tablets.

A typical dose: Up to 600 milligrams (mg) daily depending on the severity of your symptoms.

Quercetin also can be taken as a preventive during allergy season. Discuss the dose with your doctor. Quercetin is generally safe. Rare side effects may include headache and upset stomach. People with kidney disease should not take quercetin—it may worsen the condition.

Good brands: Quercetin 300, 800-545-9960, *www.allergyresearchgroup.com*…or Quercetone, 800-228-1966, *www.thorne.com*.

➤ **Fish Oil.** The same potent source of omega-3 fatty acids that is so popular for preventing the inflammation that leads to heart disease also helps with allergies. Look for the words "pharmaceutical grade" and "purified" or "mercury-free" on the label. Choose a brand that provides at least 500 mg of *eicosapentaenoic acid* (EPA) and 250 mg of *docosahexaenoic acid* (DHA) per capsule.

Typical dose: 2,000 mg of fish oil a day. Consult your doctor if you take a blood thinner.

Good brands: Nordic Naturals Arctic Omega, 800-662-2544, *www.nordicnaturals.com*…or Vital Choice fish oils, 800-608-4825, *www.vitalchoice.com*.

Step 2: Nasal Cleansing

Inflammation in the nasal passages due to allergies prevents the sinuses from draining and can lead to sinus infection.

Self-defense: Nasal cleansing once daily during allergy season reduces the amount of pollen exposure and can prevent the allergic reaction in the first place.

 CAUTION: Nasal cleansing may be irritating for some people. If you experience any irritation, discontinue it immediately.

One option: Flush your nasal passages with a neti pot. A neti pot looks like a miniature teapot with an elongated spout (available at drugstores for $8 to $30). Add one tablespoon of aloe vera gel and a pinch of salt to the warm distilled water you place in the pot.

What to do: While standing over a sink, tilt your head horizontally, left ear to ceiling, and gently insert the spout into your left nostril. As you slowly pour the mixture into the nostril, it will circulate through the nasal passages and out the right nostril. Continue for 10 seconds, breathing through your mouth, then let the excess water drain. Repeat on the other nostril. Be sure to disinfect your neti pot with soap and hot water after every use.

Alternative: If using a neti pot feels uncomfortable, try using a syringe bulb…or cup warm water (mixed with salt and aloe) in your hand and breathe it in slowly or use a nasal irrigator.

Recommended: The Grossan Hydro Pulse nasal irrigator, developed by ENT doctor Murray Grossan, 800-560-9007, *www.hydromedonline.com*, $78…or SinuPulse Elite Advanced Nasal Irrigation System, 800-305-4095, *www.sinupulse.com*, $80.

111

Step 3: Acupressure or Acupuncture

Acupuncture and acupressure can relieve allergies by stimulating certain pressure points to encourage blood flow, reduce inflammation and release natural painkilling chemical compounds known as *endorphins*.

➤ **Acupressure.** For 30 to 60 seconds, push (with enough pressure to hold your head on your thumbs) each thumb into the area where each brow meets the nose. Then, press your thumbs just below your eyebrows and slide along the ridges. Finally, press beneath both cheekbones, moving outward with both thumbs toward the ears. Do this sequence three times daily.

➤ **Acupuncture.** While acupressure can help relieve allergy symptoms, acupuncture is generally more effective. We recommend six to 10 sessions during allergy season.

Other Remedies

➤ **Allergy Shots and Drops.** These traditional approaches are in many ways quite natural. Small amounts of an allergen extract are injected. After a number of treatments, you build up a natural resistance to the allergen. Allergy drops (placed under the tongue) are an alternative to allergy shots and work in much the same way.

➤ **Speleotherapy and Halotherapy.** Used for centuries in Europe, these treatments are gaining popularity in the US. With *speleotherapy*, patients spend time in salt caves. *Halotherapy* uses man-made salt rooms that simulate caves. The salt ions combined with unpolluted air seem to improve lung function in those with respiratory and sinus ailments as well as allergies.

Salt mines and salt rooms are not always easy to find. Search online under "salt therapy."

Recommended: In allergy season, four to 12 speleotherapy or halotherapy sessions may be helpful. A 45- to 60-minute session typically costs $10 to $20.

Richard Firshein, DO, director of the New York City–based Firshein Center for Comprehensive Medicine, *www.firsheincenter.com.* He is the author of *Reversing Asthma* (Grand Central) and *The Vitamin Prescription* (Xlibris).

HEADACHES

A headache happens when small blood vessels within the skull dilate and cause increased pressure. That pressure is responsible for the pain we know as a headache.

There are tension headaches, sinus headaches, hangover headaches, do-not-want-to-have-sex headaches, headaches caused from overeating, constipation, cold or flu, eyestrain, allergies, and everything else you can think of. Ice cream!—yes, some people even get headaches when they eat very cold ice cream. That's an easy headache to prevent. Don't eat very cold ice cream. Another no-no—refrain from chewing on chewing gum. The constant movement can stress muscles, which in turn can cause a tension headache.

Headache Remedies

Thanks to the following remedies, you may be able to get rid of a headache by the time you can say, "acetylsalicylic acid."

➤ **Get Sexy!** If you don't want to have sex because you really do have a headache, here's the irony…having orgasmic sex releases *endorphins* that can make headache pain disappear completely.

➤ **Start by Drinking a Glass of Water.** Dehydration is a leading cause of headaches. Water is necessary for delivering vitamins, minerals, sugars, hormones, enzymes and other important substances to where they are needed in your body. If you don't get enough water, it can cause an imbalance because your delivery system isn't able to do its job efficiently, and that can lead to headaches, along with fatigue and overall achiness.

Don't be one of the 75% of Americans who are chronically dehydrated. Make it a point to drink a glass of water every couple of hours. That way, oxygen and essential nutrients will travel more easily throughout your system, and eliminate toxins and wastes more easily—and a headache may never happen again.

➤ **Horseradish Poultice.** Make a poultice of fresh grated horseradish in cheesecloth and put the poultice on the back of your neck. While you're at it, put two smaller horseradish poultices in each bend of your elbows. Keep the poultices on for at least 30 minutes or until the headache disappears.

➤ **Get in the Swing of Things.** Li Shou is Chinese for "hand swinging." Hand swinging redirects blood flow away from your head, relieving the pressure on artery walls that have contracted with tension. The exercise also releases lots of endorphins—the body's own natural morphine—helping ease pain.

According to psychologist Dr. Edward Chang, this is how to perform Li Shou…

• Sit down, rub your palms together for a few seconds until they feel warm. Stroke your face from forehead to chin about 30 times—always in the same direction.

• Stand up, relax and smile. Your feet should be shoulder-width apart, toes pointing forward. Your arms should be hanging naturally at your sides. Let your eyes almost close as you mentally focus down toward your toes.

• Now extend both arms until they're at waist level. Relax and let your arms swing naturally back behind you. Keep swinging your hands back and forth like this in an easy pendulum-like rhythm at least 100 times.

• Keep your mind focused on what you're doing. Don't let your attention wander until the exercise is completed.

Bonus: This exercise is also a great stress reducer.

➤ **Make It Mint.** Massage two drops of peppermint oil (available at health food stores) on your temples. If you have extremely sensitive skin do not use the oil directly on your skin. Instead, put the oil on the top layer of a big folded (man's) handkerchief and tie that around your head. Also, if possible, relax in a hot bath while drinking a cup of peppermint tea.

➤ **Clothespin Cure.** If you have a headache over one eye, take a clothespin and clip it on the lobe of the ear that's on the same side of the headache. We've gotten reports that this clothespin remedy works fast—and that isn't just a line!

➤ **Massage.** The University of California's headache specialists believe that tension headaches are caused by improper blood supply to the brain from tension at the base of the neck and shoulders. Their treatment of choice is massage to relax the tense muscles. That's what friends are for.

➤ **Bubby's Cure.** Every time we visited our grandmother, she was wearing a headband. It was my grandfather's white handkerchief, dipped in distilled white vinegar, wrung out, rolled up and tied around her forehead. Lydia was 10 years old before she realized that Bubby wasn't a Native American...or Willie Nelson in drag. Our grandmother used to get headaches and the vinegar headband worked like magic for her.

Koreans use a similar remedy. They tie a bandanna (without vinegar) tightly around their heads, right over the eyebrows.

➤ **Apple Cider Vinegar and Honey.** Mix two teaspoons of apple cider vinegar and two teaspoons of honey in a glass of water. Drink it slowly, and get results within a half-hour.

More Headache Remedies

➤ **Acupressure.** Place your third finger an inch above the bridge of your nose in the center of your forehead. Without lifting your finger, massage the area in a circular motion. Do it for seven to 10 minutes. If it doesn't drive the headache out by the end of 10 minutes, try something else.

➤ **Gem Therapy.** Amethysts are the tranquilizer of the mineral world. When you have a tension headache, lie down and gently rub the smooth side of an amethyst on your forehead. Rubbing a stone activates its healing vibration. Once it's activated, let it remain on your forehead while you relax. You may also want to repeat the affirmation at the end of this chapter.

➤ **Visualization.** According to Dr. Gerald Epstein, psychiatrist and director of the American Institute for Mental Imagery (*www. drjerryepstein.org*), headaches are characteristically related to one's emotional state. Tension headaches involve worry, and mirror the tension you feel in your life.

The remedy? Turn off the phone, put a "do not disturb" sign on your door and sit in a comfortable chair. Then follow these instructions for what Dr. Epstein calls the "Lake of the Brain" exercise to visualize away your tension headache. Do the exercise as needed, every five to 10 minutes, for up to three minutes each time.

Close your eyes and breathe out three times. Imagine you are looking down at the top of your head. Lift off the top of your skull as if you were removing the top of the shell of a soft-boiled egg. Look inside. Observe the fluid of your brain and the moving nerve fibers that look like water plants underneath. See the fluid draining out of your head completely and feel the tension relieved at the base of your skull and the back of your neck, as you notice the fluid moving down the spinal column to the base. See fresh fluid moving up the spinal column, through the neck, and filling your skull, looking through the clean, clear liquid to the nerve fibers below. Feel the flow of fresh blood through your neck and down into the rest of your body. Put on the top of your skull, breathe out once and open your eyes.

➤ **Morning Headaches.** If you wake up with a headache, it may be that your bedroom has stale air. The room should always have circulating air at night, so crack the window open.

➤ **Weekend Headaches.** If you're a coffee drinker who goes to work during the week and gets headaches at home on the weekend, listen up.

Chances are, you have your first cup of coffee before you leave for work in the morning. Then you probably have your second cup an hour or so after arriving at work. When you're at home over the weekend and don't have to get up as early as you do for work, you may have your first cup of coffee later than usual. The difference of those few hours can cause caffeine withdrawal and the dilation of the blood vessels that increase pressure in the skull—and poof!—a headache.

Either wean yourself off of coffee completely, or on the weekend, have your first cup at the same time as when you go to work.

Temporal Headaches

The temporal headache is experienced as a "pounding in your head" where there is great pressure felt at both sides of the head in the region of the temporal bones (your temples). It can arise when you do not allow yourself to say what you feel.

According to Dr. Gerald Epstein, psychiatrist and director of the American Institute for Mental Imagery (*www.drjerryepstein.org*), the emotional state that's characteristically related to temporal headaches involves rage. Dr. Epstein's visualization for temporal headaches is called "The Silver Band."

Find a comfortable chair where you will not be disturbed and do this exercise every five to 10 minutes, for one to two minutes, until the headache disappears.

Close your eyes. Breathe out three times and imagine a silver band stretched tightly across your skull from temporal bone to temporal bone and flaring out slightly at the ends as it lies on the bones.

See and sense the band tightening around your skull, with the ends pressing against the temporal bones and then quickly releasing; the band and ends squeeze once again and then release quickly; and again a third time. Then open your eyes, knowing that the pain has gone.

Migraine Headaches

According to neurologist Dr. Lawrence C. Newman of the Headache Institute at St. Luke's-Roosevelt Hospital in New York, half of all migraines are caused by food allergies. Any food can be the culprit, but most common are aged cheeses, chocolate, citrus fruit and red wine. Sodium nitrates (found in hot dogs, ham, bacon, lunch meats) and other food additives such as MSG are also responsible for many migraines. Consult with a health professional to determine whether or not you have a food allergy that's causing your migraines.

Interesting Migraine Facts

● **Allergies and migraines are more prevalent among left-handed people.**

● **"Migraine" comes from a Latin word that means "pain in half the head,"** although a migraine can occur in more or less than half the head.

● **Twenty-eight million Americans live with migraine headache pain.** Twenty-five percent of the female population and 8% of the male population are affected by migraines.

● **Famous Migraineurs**...Edgar Allan Poe, Virginia Woolfe, Rudyard Kipling, Leo Tolstoy, Lewis Carroll, Frederic Chopin, Peter Tchaikovsky, Sigmund Freud, Charles Darwin, Julius Caesar, Peter the Great, Thomas Jefferson, Ulysses S. Grant, Robert E. Lee, Karl Marx, Elvis Presley, Woody Allen, Whoopi Goldberg, Kareem Abdul Jabbar, Elle Macpherson, Carly Simon, Loretta Lynn, Elizabeth Taylor and Lisa Kudrow.

Since misery likes company, we thought that prestigious list would make you feel better. To make you feel a whole lot better, you might want to try...

Migraine Remedies

➤ **Hot Water.** Put your feet in a basin of hot water and an ice pack on the back of your neck. This remedy came to us from a California screenwriter, and screenwriters know from headaches.

➤ **Ice Packs** on the head and neck without the feet in hot water (see above) seem to help some migraine sufferers.

➤ **Watermelon.** Take a slice of watermelon, eat the meat and bind the rind! Make sure the rind stretches across your forehead to your temples and hold it in place with a handkerchief or Ace bandage. While waiting for the watermelon rind to draw out the pain, you might want to repeat the "Tension Headache" affirmation given at the end of this chapter.

➤ **Eat a Handful of Raw Almonds.** Chew them thoroughly before swallowing. If you happen to have almond oil, smear an eighth-teaspoon of the oil on a slice of bread and eat it slowly, again chewing it thoroughly.

➤ **Caffeine** seems to constrict the blood vessels in the skull. That generally stops the jagged edges or other tricks your eyes are playing on you at the start of a migraine. Caffeine may also reduce the pain of the headache. Prepare a very strong cup of Chinese black tea or coffee, or drink caffeinated soda, sipping slowly for fast relief.

➤ **Visualization.** Dr. Gerald Epstein claims migraine headaches most often involve anger. His visualization exercise for migraines is called "Open Eyes." Relax in a comfortable chair in a quiet place, and do the exercise as needed when a headache occurs, for two to three minutes at a time.

With your eyes open, look up and out to the side of the headache for two to three minutes steadily. Then return to your normal gaze.

Migraine Prevention

➤ **Feverfew.** The herb feverfew has a centuries-old reputation as a remarkable migraine headache remedy. It's available in capsule form at health food stores. Follow the dosage on the label.

➤ **Yarrow Tea.** Drink a cup of yarrow tea daily. If you buy the loose herb (available at health food stores) rather than teabags, use a heaping teaspoon in a cup of just-boiled water. Strain and drink slowly.

NOTE: Yarrow tea has an unusual taste, so you may want to add honey.

➤ **For women only.** Get pregnant. For some unknown reason, women don't have migraines while they're pregnant.

AFFIRMATION
Repeat this affirmation first thing in the morning, last thing at night and at the first sign of tension...
I am wonderful! I love and appreciate myself.

HEART HEALTH

The late Dr. Willis Potts (1895–1968), who was surgeon-in-chief at the Children's Memorial Hospital and a professor of surgery at Northwestern University Medical School, both in Chicago, Illinois, said, "The heart is a tough organ. A marvelous mechanism that, mostly without repairs, will give valiant services up to a hundred years."

These suggestions may help rack up the hundred years...

 CAUTION: Please check with your health professional before trying any of these self-help remedies, whether or not you have a history of heart problems.

 NOTE: Be sure to read the "It Does a Body Good" chapter, page 239, for lots of heart-saving and -strengthening information, including and especially those sections on donating blood and omega-3s.

➤ **Atherosclerosis Prevention.** Avoid animal fats. If you do eat fatty food—especially fatty meat—have raw garlic and onion, too. Or take a couple of garlic/onion pills daily. No matter how much garlic and onion you have, you still have to cut down your animal-fat intake significantly to help prevent atherosclerosis, which is specifically related to fatty deposits in the arteries.

 CAUTION: Having garlic on an empty stomach can cause nausea. Be sure to have some food in your stomach before taking garlic capsules. And, be cautious with garlic if you have gastritis.

In parts of Asia, walnuts have been used for medicinal purposes for a long time. A Chinese herbalist told us that eating a handful of walnuts a day can help prevent atherosclerosis. Eat the walnuts along with a sensible, heart-safe diet and get regular exercise.

➤ **Heart Disease Prevention.** If you like hot and spicy, this is for you. Eat two teaspoons of jalapeño pepper every day. Pepper can stimulate the body function that dissolves blood clots, thus helping to prevent heart disease. Also add

raw garlic to your daily diet. Crush or mince a clove and add it to food after it has been cooked and right before you're going to eat it.

 CAUTION: Do NOT use this pepper or garlic remedy if you have heartburn, gastritis, ulcers or esophagitis.

➤ **Palpitations.** If you are having heart pain or palpitations, see your doctor immediately! If you have had a very recent examination and told your doctor about occasional palpitations, and he/she assured you that it's nothing much to worry about, then you may want to try these...

• **Tea.** Prepare a cup of rosemary tea or wild cherry bark tea (both of these are available at health food stores). Drink three cups every day for prevention; and a cup whenever the palpitations start to act up.

The wild cherry bark tea has the power to calm you down quickly. The rosemary tea helps strengthen the heart. It's a good idea to take turns drinking each of the herbal teas.

• **Aromatherapy.** Relax away the palpitations in a warm bath to which you've added six drops of orange blossom oil, also called neroli (available at most health food stores).

➤ **Heart Strengthening Exercise.** So you want to lead a band? Good!—it's great exercise for the heart. A study concluded that orchestra conductors live seven-and-a-half years longer than the average person. It's no wonder. Conducting is a real workout that helps strengthen the heart muscle and tone the circulatory system.

Get a baton at a music shop, or use a pencil or chopstick. Select music that lights your fire. Tap the music stand—you're ready to begin.

You may need to start slowly and work your way up to 10 minutes a day, or 20 minutes three times a week. Check with your doctor before you make your debut. It really is fun and strenuous exercise.

➤ **After a Heart Attack.** Get a pet! Studies show that the majority of people who have had heart attacks and who have pets have a speedier recuperation period and a longer survival rate than people without pets.

➤ **Angina—Night Attack Prevention.** Raise the head of your bed a few inches. Put wooden blocks under the legs at the head end of your bed. According to a noted cardiologist, sleeping propped up like that can help stop the nighttime angina attacks.

➤ **Herb for a Healthier Heart.** Hawthorn berries won our hearts. According to John B. Lust, naturopath, herbalist and author, hawthorn can help regulate heart action and normalize blood pressure. It also is good for heart muscle weakened by age, inflammation of the heart muscle, atherosclerosis and nervous heart problems.

You can drink hawthorn berry tea, take hawthorn (freeze-dried extract) capsules or hawthorn tincture. Dosage depends on your condition and the medication you may or may not be taking. Talk it over with your health professional (doctor and/or nutritionist) and take it with his/her supervision. You should be monitored, especially if you're on medication, because as the hawthorn improves your condition, you might be able to cut down on your medication.

➤ **Vitamin for a Healthier Heart.** According to recent research, vitamin C can profoundly help prevent arterial damage which, in turn, leads to heart attacks and strokes.

Eat foods rich in vitamin C—citrus fruit and leafy green vegetables—and supplement your diet daily with at least 250 milligrams (mg) of vitamin C.

➤ **Prayer for a Healthier Heart.** There was a study conducted of two groups of people born into the same religion. One group of people had a firm belief in God, and practiced the traditions of their religion on a daily basis; the other was a nonpracticing group. The observant group had fewer heart attacks than the nonobservant group.

In analyzing these results, the researchers said, "The strong belief in a Supreme Being and the role of prayer may in themselves be protective."

Recommended Reading

➤ *The New Heart Disease Handbook: Everything You Need to Know to Effectively Reverse and Manage Heart Disease* by Christopher P. Cannon, MD, and Elizabeth Vierck (Fair Winds Press). This book by cardiologist Dr. Christopher Cannon will help you develop a heart-healthy lifestyle. Drawing on his experience, research and the results of clinical studies, Dr. Cannon covers every aspect of heart health—care, treatment, prevention, reducing risks, heart-friendly foods, tests, surgical procedures and how to make the most of consultations with your doctors.

AFFIRMATION

Repeat this affirmation 12 times, starting first thing in the morning, every time you sigh, every time you shake your head "no" and last thing at night...

I choose to love myself and my life. I find goodness and beauty all around me.

HEMORRHOIDS

 Hemorrhoids are varicose veins in or around the rectum.

As you might imagine, sitting on a horse when you have hemorrhoids is a real pain. And so it was for Napoleon, who had such a bad case of hemorrhoids, he was unable to sit on his horse to survey the battlefield and plan his next move. That's when he let his next-in-command do the planning from atop his steed. Generally speaking, the next-in-command was not as clever a military strategist as Napoleon, and it didn't take long before Napoleon was defeated at Waterloo...and all because of his hemorrhoids.

The whole course of history could be different if Bonaparte had known about the following...

Hemorrhoid Remedies

➤ **You Choose.** With a cotton swab, apply any one of the following several times during the day. Then, right before bed, dampen a cotton ball with one of the liquids from the list below and place it against your rectum, keeping it in place with paper tape (available at drugstores) or a large Band-Aid...

- **The oil squeezed out of a vitamin E softgel or wheat germ oil.**
- **Fresh lemon juice** (yes, it may sting).
- **Diluted witch hazel,** especially when there's bleeding (and yes, it may sting).
- **Papaya juice** (pure and additive-free). Papaya pills also have papain, papaya's healing enzyme. They're inexpensive and taste like candy. Take four orally after every meal.

- **Aloe vera gel or juice** (available at health food stores). Also take one teaspoon of the aloe orally after every meal.
- **Make a poultice of white bread that's been dipped in egg white** and place it against the rectum.
- ➤ **Reflexology.** The back of the leg, an inch or two up from the ankle bone, is the reflex area that relates to the rectum. Gently massage that sensitive area and you may get hemorrhoidal relief.

AFFIRMATION

Repeat this affirmation at least 12 times, first thing in the morning, last thing at night, and throughout the day every time you sit down...

I set myself free of anger and resentment, leaving room for all the good things coming to me now.

HERPES

See "Genital Herpes," page 99.

HICCUPS

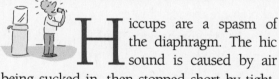 Hiccups are a spasm of the diaphragm. The hic sound is caused by air being sucked in, then stopped short by tightened vocal cords. It's the least serious ailment, for which we have the most remedies.

Classic Remedies You Probably Already Know About

➤ **Drink Sugar and Water.** Or take a teaspoon of sugar.

➤ **Hold Your Breath.** Joan's favorite is to hold her breath and think of 10 bald men.

➤ **Drink Water from the Far Side of the Glass.**

➤ **Silverware in Water.** Place a piece of silverware in a glass of water and drink the water with the handle of the silverware resting or pressing against your temple.

➤ **Sip Water Through a Hanky.** Position a handkerchief over a glass of water and sip.

➤ **Another Way to Drink.** Put your index fingers in your ears while someone holds a glass of water for you to drink.

Soon-to-Be-Classic Remedies That Just May Cure Your Next Case of Hiccups

➤ **A Toe Hold.** Place a penny between any two toes of one foot and transfer the penny to any two toes of the other foot, being careful not to let the coin touch the floor.

➤ **The Eye Press.** Follow your pinkies straight down to the end of your palm till you come to those last tufts right before your wrists. Use those tufts to gently press on your eyeballs for no more than a minute.

➤ **Aromatherapy.** Take long and deep whiffs of sandalwood oil.

➤ **Tea.** The verdict is in. Dill seed tea is the most effective tea for hiccups. Boil one teaspoon of dill seeds in water. Simmer for 15 to 20 minutes. Don't dilly-dally—strain and drink as soon as it's cool enough.

➤ **Pucker Up.** A favorite among bartenders is a wedge of lemon with Worcestershire sauce sprinkled on it. Bill Tull, NBC prop master, recommends Angostura bitters on lemon.

➤ **A Cool Cure.** Some say place an ice bag right below the rib cage; others say the ice bag should go on the pit of the stomach. Wherever, keep it there for three to five minutes.

➤ **The Ol' Paper Bag.** Remember the old hiccup remedy where you breathe in a brown paper bag a few times? We have an update on it, with specific instructions that make it a sure cure.

Scrunch the neck of a brown paper bag and form a circle around your mouth, allowing no air to escape. Now, taking short, strong, hard breaths, inhale and exhale 10 times—no more, no less. When you're finished, don't be surprised if your face is flushed. Do be surprised if you still have the hiccups.

➤ **Acupressure.** Massage your feet for five to 10 minutes. The middle of the bottoms of your feet, right below the balls of your feet are the pressure points for the diaphragm. This deep massage can stop hiccups and also make you feel rested. Think of how rested you would feel if you have someone else massage your feet. Hey, what are friends for?

Hiccup Prevention

➤ **Nutmeg.** It is said that if you wear a nutmeg around your neck, you will not get the hiccups. But then again, think of all the fun you'd be missing by not trying out some of these remedies.

INDIGESTION

According to Mindfully.org, a nonprofit research site, Americans eat 815 billion calories of food each day—that's roughly 200 billion more than needed. No wonder we have indigestion. *Here are remedies to remedy that awful feeling…*

▶ **Take Tea.** See how fast any one of the following can settle your stomach—peppermint tea, chamomile, ginger, raspberry, sage, fennel, caraway, anise, dill, parsley or blackberry, all available at health food stores. If you buy tea loose rather than in bags, use a heaping teaspoon in a cup of just-boiled water. Let it steep seven to 10 minutes, strain and drink slowly.

▶ **Tropical Treat.** Papaya, pineapple, mango and kiwi all have healing enzymes. If you can get the fresh ripe fruit, eat a portion as dessert.

If the fruit isn't available, drink papaya and/or pineapple juice. Make sure the juice is additive-free. If you don't have juice, take four papaya pills after a meal. The fruit, juice and pills are the best-tasting medicine around.

▶ **Great Grapefruit Grating.** Wash, dry, then grate the peel of a grapefruit. Spread out the tiny grated crumbs to dry on paper towels. Then put them in a jar with a lid, label it and put it in your medicine cabinet (it keeps for quite a while). Whenever you have an upset stomach, take up to a teaspoon of the grapefruit crumbs. Chew them, making sure you saturate them with your saliva. Good-bye Tums. Hello crumbs!

▶ **Get Back-on-Track Diet.** Ahhh, the glamour of show business…traveling to exotic places to shoot a movie…eating the traditional food of the area. California producer Jill Alman shared her on-location upset stomach remedy with us. It's the BRAT diet. For two or three days she eats only Bananas, Rice, Apples and Toast.

▶ **Reflexology.** Vigorously massage the instep of each foot. Start in the center, right below the ball of the foot, and work your way toward the outer edge. There should be a particularly sensitive spot on each foot. Those spots correspond directly with the stomach. Once you've found them, dig in with your thumb and knuckles as you continue the deep massage for seven minutes or more, if you have the stamina to continue.

▶ **Gem Therapy.** Peridot is a yellow-green stone that is said to help release emotional tension when placed on the solar plexus (the pit of the stomach). That emotional tension can be the cause of indigestion and the stone can help be the cure. Another stone suggested by gemologists is citrine. It's golden in color and good for cleansing the digestive system.

AFFIRMATION

At the first sign of indigestion, relax and repeat at least a dozen times…

I let go of my fears and I am left with my gifts. I am now willing to share my gifts with the world, and the world is willing to accept them.

Gas

An on-in-years neighbor loves to say, "When I was young, life was a gas. Now, gas is my life!"

This may fall into the category of TMI (too much information), but for those of you just a tad curious about this unpleasant and embarrassing bodily function, Dr. Billy Goldberg of

MSNBC's *The Body Odd*, posted this list of fascinating flatulence facts…

- **Most people pass gas about 14 times a day.**

- **Women pass gas as much as men.**

- **A person produces about a half a liter of gas a day.**

- **On average, a fart is composed of about 59% nitrogen, 21% hydrogen, 9% carbon dioxide, 7% methane and 4% oxygen.** Less than 1% of their makeup is what makes farts smell bad.

- **The gas that makes flatulence reek is hydrogen sulfide.** The more sulfur rich your diet, the more your gas will stink. Some foods that cause really smelly gas include beans, cabbage, cheese, soda and eggs.

- **The temperature of a fart at time of creation is 98.6°F.**

- **Flatulence has been clocked at a speed of 10 feet per second.**

Generally, gas is caused by air that's swallowed when you eat—especially if you eat fast, and eat foods that cause gas. Loose-fitting dentures can cause intestinal gas; so does drinking through a straw, drinking carbonated beverages, sucking on candy, chewing gum, smoking and constipation.

Gas Remedies

Here are some more simple remedies to help relieve this uncomfortable condition…

➤ **Ginger Tea.** Cut three or four quarter-sized slices of fresh gingerroot. Or keep gingerroot in the freezer and grate a chunk. Bring ginger and water to a boil, then simmer for 15 to 20 minutes. Strain and drink right after a gas-causing meal or any time you have gas pains.

 CAUTION: Ginger acts as a blood thinner, so check with your doctor before using it if you are taking a prescription blood thinner. Also, stop using ginger three days before any surgery.

➤ **Aloe Vera Gel.** Take a tablespoon of aloe vera gel after every meal or whenever you feel trapped air bubbles in your stomach.

➤ **For Those Who Do Yoga.** Do a headstand (if you are used to doing them). Stay upside down for just a minute. This temporary, drastic position change can help relieve blocked gas.

➤ **Vitamin B-5.** Pantothenic acid (vitamin B-5) is reputed to help maintain a healthy digestive tract. A daily dose of 250 milligrams (mg) has also been known to clear up cases of gastritis.

➤ **Herbal Tea.** After eating, drink a cup of one of the following herb teas—peppermint, chamomile, yarrow or sage.

➤ **Popping Pills.** The enzymes in papaya pills can help you digest food and eliminate gas. Chew four of the candylike pills after every meal. They're perfect to carry with you when you eat out, so don't leave home without 'em.

➤ **Extra Virgin Olive Oil (or EVOO).** Drink an ounce of warm EVOO and take a walk, but not too far from a bathroom.

➤ **Beans—Repercussion Prevention.** When you're cooking beans, throw in a few pieces of potatoes. When the beans are ready, take out the potato pieces and the gas should go out with them.

If you do eat beans that weren't prepared this way, eat a piece of watermelon right after the beans, and you should experience fewer repercussions.

➤ **Acupressure.** Massage the insteps of the bottom of your feet for about 10 minutes. It should help release trapped gas.

➤ **Aromatherapy.** At the first sign of a gas pain, put a couple of drops of essential geranium oil on your wrist and take a few deep whiffs.

Gas Prevention

➤ **A Simple Solution.** In order to digest proteins, you need a lot of *hydrochloric acid*, a powerful acid in stomach juices that helps the body break down food. Salads require no hydrochloric acid. When you eat a salad before your main (protein) course is served, the hydrochloric acid in your stomach is wasted on the salad. When you then have your protein—meat, fish, chicken, cheese, soy, beans—there's not enough hydrochloric acid to properly digest the food. As a result, you have gas and other indigestion problems.

The simple solution is to eat your salad with your main course, or right *after* you finish eating the protein portion of your meal, but not *before*.

➤ **Mustard Seeds.** Put a half-level-teaspoon of yellow mustard seeds in a half-cup of water and drink it down without chewing the seeds. Do this a half hour before lunch and a half hour before dinner. It can make a tremendous difference.

AFFIRMATION

At the first sign of a gas pain, or a bloated feeling, relax and repeat at least seven times...

I let confidence push fears out of my body and I am blessed with well-being.

A Word from the Wise...

Gas Be Gone!

Though the average person expels gas about 14 times a day, sometimes gas gets trapped in the body, causing uncomfortable bloating. *What you should know...*

● **Flatulence** occurs when bacteria ferment undigested carbohydrates in the colon. The telltale noise is caused by vibration of the anal opening. The odor depends on the foods eaten and types of bacteria present. Flatulence producers include asparagus, beans, bran, broccoli, brussels sprouts, cabbage, corn, onions, pasta, peas, potatoes, prunes and wheat. Dairy foods cause gas in people who lack the enzyme *lactase* needed to digest the milk sugar *lactose*. Called *lactose intolerance*, this gets more common with age.

Over-the-counter remedies: Charcoal tablets or *simethicone* (Gas-X) may help by breaking up big gas bubbles. Beano contains an enzyme that breaks down cellulose, a carbohydrate in legumes and cruciferous vegetables—take it just before eating. To help prevent gas, take a daily supplement that contains the probiotic *Bifidobacterium infantis*, such as the brand Align. For lactose intolerance, avoid dairy foods or try Lactaid supplements, which contain lactase.

● **Belching happens after you swallow air.** Avoid fizzy drinks, gum, eating too fast, gulping, using a straw, smoking. Another culprit is anxiety, which makes people breathe rapidly and swallow more often.

Calming: Inhale for five seconds...hold five seconds...exhale for five seconds...hold five seconds...repeat.

123

See your doctor: If you are troubled by excess flatulence or belching, your doctor can examine you for any underlying gastrointestinal problems.

Douglas A. Drossman, MD, adjunct professor of medicine and psychiatry, and former codirector of the Center for Functional Gastrointestinal and Motility Disorders at University of North Carolina, Chapel Hill, School of Medicine. He has published two books and more than 400 articles on gastrointestinal disorders.

Heartburn

Heartburn does not affect the heart. It's an irritation caused by too much acid backing up (of refluxing) from the stomach into the esophagus.

It's unpleasant and generally caused by smoking, having caffeine (coffee, caffeinated tea, chocolate, aspirin or cola), drinking alcohol, eating animal fats, fried and spicy foods, tomato products and other acid-producing food and falling asleep soon after you've eaten. One other major factor is stress—known in our family as "aggravation."

When you think of all the things you eat or drink that can cause heartburn, isn't it amazing that you don't get it more often?

Heartburn Remedies

➤ **Magic Herbal Tonic.** Slippery elm bark (available at health food stores) neutralizes acid, absorbs gas and helps digestion too. Put one level teaspoon of slippery elm powder in a cup of just-boiled water and let it steep for five minutes. Strain and drink slowly. It can make a big difference in a little amount of time.

➤ **Get Grounded.** Take a pinch of coffee grounds, let your saliva mix with them for a minute or two, and spit them out.

We would think it causes heartburn rather than cures it, but the woman who gave us the remedy told us to try it. Actually, we had friends try it (our mother didn't raise stupid children), and they said it works.

➤ **Lettuce Blend.** Put two iceberg lettuce leaves (about four ounces) along with six ounces of cold water in a blender and push "purée." Pour the thickish greenish liquid into a glass, and drink slowly.

Heartburn Prevention

➤ **Don't Lie Down Right After You've Eaten.** In fact, wait two to three hours before you assume a prone position, or be prepared to assume the risk of heartburn.

➤ **Gum.** British researchers fed half of their test subjects a fatty-foods meal that would be a typical acid reflux trigger, and then gave them sugarless gum to chew for a half hour. The other half of their test subjects had the same meal, but didn't chew sugarless gum after eating. The gum-chewing group had much milder heartburn symptoms or none at all, compared with the non-chewers.

According to Zach Rosen, MD, medical director of the Montefiore Family Health Center in the Bronx, New York City, "Chewing gum stimulates the flow of saliva, which neutralizes stomach acids. It also makes you swallow more often, which triggers *peristalsis*—the muscle contractions that help move food down your digestive tract."

➤ **Raise the Bed.** Chronic heartburn sufferers might consider raising the head of the bed by placing six-inch blocks under the legs. Be sure it's done by a carpenter or someone who knows how to properly secure the blocks in place.

Nausea

In order to deal most effectively with nausea, you should figure out the reason for it.

Are you "sick to your stomach" about some situation or relationship in your life? If that's why you're feeling awful, then confront whatever it is and work it out. A good cry may also relieve tension and nausea.

Are you taking any medication? It can cause nausea. Check with your doctor or nutritionist or pharmacist.

If you're nauseous because you've had too much alcohol, you're in the wrong section of the book. You want "Hangovers" under "Drinking Problems," page 71.

Are you pregnant? Check "Morning Sickness" under "Pregnancy Concerns," page 155.

Are you feeling nauseous in a plane, train or car? Turn to the section on "Motion Sickness," page 140.

Did you overeat or eat foods that didn't agree with you? This is the right place!

➤ **Ginger.** The classic remedy for nausea is ginger ale. Sip it slowly. Or, even more effective is to dissolve a half-teaspoon of ginger powder in a cup of warm water and drink it down. If you prefer the real thing, put four quarter-sized slices of gingerroot in water and bring to a boil. Simmer for 15 to 20 minutes, then strain and drink. Or grate a chunk of frozen gingerroot, boil in water, then simmer and drink slowly, with the little bits of grated ginger.

 CAUTION: Ginger acts as a blood thinner, so check with your doctor before using it if you are taking a prescription blood thinner. Also, stop using ginger three days before any surgery.

➤ **Peppermint.** A strong cup of peppermint tea is calming to the system and settling to the stomach. If you have fresh peppermint leaves, crush them and put them on your stomach, touching your bare skin, of course. Bind them in place and stay seated, rather than lying down.

➤ **Barley.** If you're not on a low-carb diet, eat a small bowl of barley, even if you're not hungry. It's a soothing food, particularly effective for digestive disorders that cause nausea. Make the barley more palatable by adding low-sodium soy sauce.

➤ **Cucumber.** If you just cannot push down a bowl of barley, eat half of a peeled cucumber. It should have a calming, cooling effect on your digestive system.

➤ **Traditional New England Remedy.** Using a nutmeg grater, grate a nutmeg down to half its size. Flat side up, put the solid half-piece of nutmeg under the broiler until oil seeps out of it. As soon as the broiled nutmeg is cool enough to touch, tape it, flat side down, to the pit of your stomach. Once all the heat has gone out of it, reheat it and put it back in place, unless the nausea is gone by then. Keep the grated nutmeg in a closed container for use in cooking.

➤ **At a Hotel.** If you don't want to get more nauseous when you get the room service bill for a bottle of ginger ale, then get a free bucket of ice from the ice machine in the hall. Sucking on ice chips can cure nausea. Don't chew the ice chips; it can cause teeth problems.

➤ **Outdoors.** We always carry a couple of Ricola Natural Herb Cough Drops with us. When we're outside, and one of us feels nauseous—not that it happens often—we unwrap a Ricola and pop the drop in our mouth. The peppermint in it is fairly strong and relieves nausea and upset stomach within no time. It also works indoors as well.

➤ **Reflexology.** Dig your thumbs into the area between the second and third toes of each foot (the big toe is the first toe) and massage deeply for at least five minutes. Rest, then start again. If, after 10 minutes of massage, you no longer feel nauseous, it worked.

AFFIRMATION

At the first wave of nausea, relax and repeat over and over…

I am free of fear. I now know that I am in the right place, at the right time, and I am doing the right thing.

Stomach Rumbling

Those embarrassing rumbling sounds that are loudest during a job interview and at what otherwise would have been a romantic moment are caused by intestinal wall contractions and the movement of gas and liquid.

If you're on *Jeopardy*, and you're asked for the medical term for the rumbling sounds, the answer is *"borborygmus."*

If you're asked what to do to prevent it, here are some suggestions…

➤ **Change Eating Patterns.** Instead of having three meals a day, have more than three but eat a lot less at each meal.

➤ **Change Air-Swallowing Patterns.**

● **Don't gulp down food.** Eat slowly.

● **Don't drink very hot beverages.** They cause you to swallow air in an attempt to cool the drink.

● **When you drink, keep your upper lip in the liquid.** That way, air won't be gulped down or sipped in.

● **Avoid aerated foods**—things that are put through a blender or whipped in some way.

● **If all these rules make you sigh, don't!** Sighing also causes you to swallow air.

➤ **For Special Occasions.** If you have to give a presentation or sit through a long meeting at work, you don't want your stomach rumbling to be heard by your audience or co-workers. A television producer told us that she shares this remedy with all of her guests—"To prevent stomach rumbling, eat a banana right before show time and drink some water." Don't forget to bring a banana with you.

➤ **Acupressure.** If you don't have a banana, and you haven't had a chance to eat, and you don't want your stomach rumbling to be heard in front of other people, have your thumb draw tiny circles, massaging the area halfway between your breast bone and navel. Do it for about 15 seconds. The spot that you are stimulating is a direct link to the brain's appetite control center (the hypothalamus). It should give you a feeling of fullness, stopping the rumbling before anyone could hear it.

INSECT BITES AND STINGS AND SNAKEBITES

Insects

Bee and Yellow Jacket Stings

➤ **Stinger Strategies.** If the stinger remains in your skin, do not pull it out with tweezers. The tweezers will squeeze the venom out of the stinger and into you. Just flick the stinger off with your fingers, or scrape it off with a knife or credit card.

➤ **Stinger Treatment.** Chances are you will be stung outdoors and will not have some of the ingredients for some of the remedies. Treat the sting with whatever *is* available. *Here are some suggestions…*

• **Slit open a cigarette,** moisten the tobacco, and pack it on the sting.

• **Mix a tablespoon of baking soda with enough water to make a paste,** and put it on the sting.

• **Do you already know about the healing properties of meat tenderizer on a sting?** Well, you will now. *Papain* is the enzyme in meat tenderizer that breaks down the protein in bee venom. The general rule is one part tenderizer to four parts water, applied to the stung area. Some people wet the area and sprinkle on the tenderizer. With both methods, do not leave it on for more than a half-hour because it can start to irritate the skin.

• **Rub on apple cider vinegar.**

• **Put a slice of raw onion or a peeled, sliced clove of garlic on the sting,** wrap a bandage around it, and leave it there for at least two hours.

• **Several drops of one of the following oils**—castor oil, cinnamon oil, vitamin E oil or wheat germ oil—placed on a cotton ball and applied directly on the sting should stop the pain and hold down the swelling.

• **Put an ice pack on it** if it's already swollen.

Mosquitoes

➤ **Stop Mosquitoes (and Vampires) in Their Tracks.** If you dread mosquito bites more than you mind smelling of garlic, then we've got a remedy for you. Rub garlic over all your exposed body parts before reaching a mosquito-infested area. Mosquitoes will not come near you. They hate garlic. Garlic is to mosquitoes what kryptonite is to Superman. One university biologist tested garlic extract on five species of mosquitoes. The garlic got 'em. Not one mosquito survived.

➤ **Mosquito Bite Itch Prevention.** You have about three minutes after you've been bitten to neutralize the element in the mosquito's saliva that causes the itch. Quick!—reach for the baking soda. Pour a little in your palm and make a paste of it by adding some water. Then smear it on the bite. Time's up! You're still looking for the baking soda? Put it where it's handy when needed.

Insect Repellents

➤ **Mosquito and House Fly Repellents.** The following repellents should help keep mosquitoes and other flying pests away from you…

• **Garlic**—eat lots of raw garlic or take garlic pills.

 CAUTION: Having garlic on an empty stomach can cause nausea. Be sure to have some food in your stomach before eating garlic or taking capsules. And, be cautious with garlic if you have gastritis.

• **Onions**—eat a raw onion or two daily and a mosquito won't dare come near you.

• **Parsley**—rub sprigs of it on your exposed areas.

• **Apple cider vinegar**—rub it or spray it on your exposed skin.

• **Be sugar-free and alcohol-free** and you'll be mosquito-free.

• **Brewer's yeast**—take two tablespoons daily with your meals to prevent being mosquitoes' meals.

• **For an extremely effective insect repellent,** mix one part geranium oil with 10 parts soybean oil and bottle it. If you suspect you may have a sensitivity to soybean oil, test a couple of drops on your arm. No reaction? Good. When you're going to an insect-infested area, rub the oily solution on all of your exposed skin, avoiding your eyes, nose and mouth. While outdoors, reapply every couple of hours.

Once you're indoors for the night, be sure to wash the geranium oil off your skin with soap and warm water to prevent the oil from staining your bedding.

The following repellents should help keep mosquitoes and other flying pests away from your home...

● **The smell of citronella** is known to repel insects. You can sprinkle the essential oil concentrate (available at herb shops and some health food stores) where needed. Other oils that are as effective are eucalyptus, rosemary and geranium.

● **Hang bouquets of dried tomato leaves** in each room to repel mosquitoes. This works for flies and spiders as well.

● **In Europe, window boxes abound.** They not only look pretty, they keep houseflies away. You can, too, by having any of these easy-to-grow insect-repelling plants on your window ledges, near doorways and on patios or terraces—sweet basil, tansy, fennel and geranium.

➤ **Gnat Repellent.** If you're going into a gnat-infested area, protect yourself by coating your exposed body parts with a thin layer of baby oil.

➤ **Ant Repellents.** If you have an ant problem, do a thorough clean-up job of the area(s) they frequent, then use one or more of these *ANT*idotes...

● **Dried bay leaves**—good for kitchen cabinets. Bay leaves lose their effectiveness after about a year.

● **Coffee grounds**—good for doors and windows.

● **Petroleum jelly**—fill in the cracks in walls or around the sink.

● **Mint leaves**—plant them near entrances, windows and terraces.

● **Cayenne pepper**—good in cabinets or on counter tops.

● **Fresh lemon juice**—with a medicine dropper, drip the juice in floorboard cracks, window sills and door jambs.

● **Whole cloves**—wedge them into corners of cabinets, drawers or wherever the ants are entering your home.

➤ **Yellow Jacket Repellent.** When you are having a picnic outdoors and don't want any uninvited guests flying in to join you, pour apple cider vinegar in a couple of saucers and place them around your picnic area.

➤ **Lyme Tick Repellent.** Chrysanthemums attract Lyme ticks and have a substance that then kills them. This is interesting information that, unfortunately, won't help when you're romping in the park. In other words, even if you're holding a bouquet of chrysanthemums, you still have to tuck your pants into your socks for protection against those little buggers.

➤ **Moth Repellents.** When you're ready to store your winter woolens, go to an herb shop for either dried lavender or cedar chips. They will repel moths as effectively as camphor mothballs, but with a much more pleasant fragrance.

➤ **Dry-Food Worms Repellent.** When dry food like cereals, beans and flour are stored in your kitchen cupboards for a while, particularly in warm weather, you may find some added protein in there that you didn't pay for...and don't want. Prevent worms, grain beetles and other creepy-crawlies from invading your vittles

128

by putting a couple of dried bay leaves in each box or sack of dry food. If you have room, keep the sack of flour in the refrigerator.

More information: For more information on pesticides and the safest way to get rid of insects, including land management without toxic pesticides, contact the National Coalition Against the Misuse of Pesticides at 202-543-5450 or *www.beyondpesticides.org/.*

Snakebites

A snakebite is serious and, hopefully, will never happen to you. But, if you go camping in deserted, snake-infested areas, you should know about charcoal and always carry it with you, just in case you lose your snakebite kit.

If you're bitten by a snake, get to a doctor immediately! Until you get professional medical attention, begin treatment quickly, before swelling begins. Open several charcoal capsules, collect the contents and add enough water to make it the consistency of a smooth paste. Apply the paste directly on the bite, then spread the rest around that area of your skin. As soon as that's done, swallow 10 charcoal capsules.

Keep track of the time. Ten minutes after the first application of charcoal powder, scrape it off and put on another layer of the charcoal paste.

The charcoal on the bite should help draw out and absorb the snake's venom. If the venom gets into your system, the charcoal capsules can absorb it in the gastrointestinal tract.

If the bitten area starts to swell and the pain increases, apply an ice pack (if possible) and continue to take the charcoal pills until you get professional medical help. Hurry!

IRRITABLE BOWEL SYNDROME

Irritable bowel syndrome (IBS), sometimes called spastic colon, is a common and nasty problem with uncomfortable and unpredictable symptoms—diarrhea or constipation, abdominal pain or cramping, gas and bloating, nausea usually after eating, fatigue, headache, mucus-covered stools, the urge to have another bowel movement after you've just had one and depression or anxiety (well, is it any wonder?).

There doesn't appear to be one specific cause of IBS. Many people who think they have IBS are *lactose intolerant*. Their bodies cannot absorb lactose, an enzyme found in milk and other dairy products. Either ask your doctor to test you for lactose intolerance, or stop eating dairy products for a week and see how you feel.

For many people, IBS flare-ups are due to emotional stress. In which case, make up your mind to find a way to make your life a lot less stressful. Meditate, take tai chi classes, find a biofeedback practitioner...whatever it takes for you to calm down so that you can better handle whatever stresses you emotionally. Makes sense, right?

These dietary suggestions to help prevent IBS symptoms also make sense. You may not like making these changes in your diet, but if it's going to make the quality of your life more comfortable, DO IT! As you gradually make changes meal by meal, pay close attention to what agrees with you and what doesn't. Consider making an appointment with a nutritionist. Meanwhile, you may be able to narrow down your symptom triggers and control or completely eliminate this problem.

129

Dietary Recommendations

➤ **Fiber.** Add nonsoluble fiber to your diet—whole grains, fruit and vegetables. Bran and flaxseed are wonderful, but if either or both have not been part of your meals, add them gradually so that your body can get used to them. Too much too fast can cause gas and the runs.

➤ **Water.** Be sure to drink seven or eight glasses a day, especially if you're adding fiber to your diet. The water will help your bowels perform effortlessly.

➤ **Gas.** Go easy or eliminate foods that are big-time gas causers such as beans, cabbage, cauliflower, Brussels sprouts and onions. Don't drink through a straw and stay away from products that use artificial sweeteners such as sorbitol, mannitol and xylitol (soda, chewing gum, candy).

➤ **Fat.** A low-fat diet may make the difference between feeling good and the misery of colonic contractions. Stay away from fried foods and heavy sauces for starters.

➤ **Coffee.** Coffee seems to be harsh on IBS sufferers. Stay off it for a week, or change to decaffeinated and see if you feel better.

➤ **Spicy Foods.** This is something else to test. Eliminate spicy foods from your diet for a week. If you feel better during that week, get used to bland foods as you slowly introduce some spiciness back into your meals.

➤ **Cigarettes.** Do you smoke? Stop!... But not with anything containing nicotine, like gum. It may be the nicotine that is causing the problem. See the "Stop Smoking" section, page 188, for suggestions to help you quit.

➤ **Alcohol.** If you must imbibe, do not do it with beer because of its complex carbohydrates, or with red wine because of its tannin. Don't blame us, we got it from William J. Snape, Jr., MD, motility specialist at California Pacific Medical Center in San Francisco.

Symptom Relievers

➤ **Peppermint Oil.** Referred to as "the world's oldest medicine," peppermint is an effective digestive aid and also offers *analgesic* (pain-killing) properties. In a study, Italian researchers reported that 75% of the patients who took peppermint oil capsules for four weeks had a major reduction in IBS symptoms.

Take peppermint oil in "enteric coated" capsules. The enteric coating will allow the capsules to reach your intestines before they dissolve. If the capsules are not enteric coated, they will break down in your stomach, doing you less good and may even cause heartburn.

➤ **ALE.** We thought we'd get your attention by using the acronym for artichoke leaf extract. Several studies were conducted with IBS test subjects who were given ALE. One study involved people who had IBS for about three years. They took ALE for about six weeks and the results were quite impressive in terms of the relief of IBS symptoms including constipation, gas, loss of appetite, intestinal cramps and nausea.

Artichoke leaf extract comes in capsules. Be sure the label says that the extract is standardized to contain 15% to 18% *chlorogenic acid* (also called *caffeoylquinic acid*) and/or 2% to 5% *cynarin*.

➤ **Exercise.** While toning up your body, you will tone up your bowel, and get rid of gas. A little workout can also relieve stress. And don't forget that exercise releases *endorphins* to help lessen pain. We're not talking about training for the Olympics. A brisk walk will do. See "Pole Walking" in the "It Does a Body Good" chapter, page 266.

Acupuncture for IBS

In a recent finding, people who received six acupuncture treatments over a three-week period experienced less abdominal pain, bloating, diarrhea, constipation and other IBS symptoms than those who received no treatment. Needles were inserted at various points, including near the stomach, liver, spleen and large intestine. Researchers believe acupuncture may help by balancing hormones and triggering a relaxation response.

More information: To find a board-certified acupuncturist, go to *www.nccaom.org*—the Web site for the National Certification Commission for Acupuncture and Oriental Medicine.

Anthony Lembo, MD, assistant professor of medicine, Harvard Medical School, Boston, and leader of a study of 230 adult IBS patients, published in *The American Journal of Gastroenterology.*

ITCHING

What could cause skin to itch? Dryness, heat, allergies, lotions, ointments, creams, medications and, according to *www.localhealth.com*, a formative provider of online medical health information, 1,354 medical conditions. Most itches come and go before you can figure out the cause.

It's easy for us to say, but try not to scratch an itch, because scratching can cause infection. Also, by resisting the urge to scratch, you will give an itchy patch time to clear up. If it stays red, raw or oozes, and if it gets worse with treatment rather than better, get professional medical help.

Meanwhile, think about anything new you've applied to your skin, foods you've eaten, clothing you've worn or wash detergents you've used. Think about what is going on in your life—emotional highs and lows. *While trying to pinpoint the itch trigger...*

Remedies for Itching Relief

➤ **Dip a White Washcloth in Milk,** wring it out, and place the wet cloth on the itchy area.

➤ **Moisten the Itchy Area with Water.** Then take a pinch of salt (coarse kosher salt is preferable) and rub it on that same area. Stop when the itching stops—probably in a few minutes.

➤ **Eat Foods That Are Rich in Iron**—green leafy vegetables, fish, dried fruits, wheat germ and cherry juice.

➤ **Do Not Wear Loud, Bright, Hot Colors** like red, shocking pink, fuchsia or orange. They seem to encourage itching. Blue, on the other hand (or on any other part of your body), can actually help stop the itching.

Rectal Itching

Irritation of the skin around the anus—the canal that's the outlet for your rectum—often causes itching. Scratching the itch can cause more irritation, soreness and even burning.

While discovering the possible cause and cure, ease the symptoms by using moist pads instead of toilet paper after bowel movements.

Possible Causes of Rectal Itching

➤ **Caffeine.** Cut down considerably on caffeine, or cut it out completely. That means coffee, cola, aspirin and chocolate. If, within two days, the itching stops, chances are you

131

have a sensitivity to caffeine and through trial and error—make that, trial and itching—you'll discover the amount of caffeine your body will tolerate.

➤ **Tomatoes, Citrus Juices and Beer** can also cause rectal itching. It's easy enough to find out. Just eliminate the suspected food or drink from your diet for two or three days. If the itching stops...bingo!

➤ **Yeast Overgrowth** is one common cause of rectal itching. Go on a yeast-free diet—that means reading labels of all the processed foods you eat to look for yeast as an ingredient—and watch for results.

Rectal Itch Remedies

➤ **Instead of Soap, use diluted white vinegar to wash** the rectal area.

➤ **Spread Plain Yogurt on a sanitary napkin and place it on the itchy area.** Change the dressing every couple of hours.

Jock Itch

This fungal infection of the groin is contagious. Don't scratch it—you can spread it to other parts of your body including your scalp (it's then called "ringworm").

➤ **Garlic Oil.** Three times a day, apply the oil from garlic capsules to the fungal patches until it clears up completely. To eliminate the ideal conditions for growing fungus, wear loose-fitting, cotton underwear to keep air in and moisture out.

 CAUTION: Since garlic oil can be very irritating to sensitive skin tissue, do a small test patch before applying to a larger area.

A Word from the Wise...

Three Favorite Natural Treatments for Itching

Natural medicines that gently—yet effectively—treat common causes of itching...

➤ **Chamomile Tea.** For itching due to insect bites, eczema, hives or poison ivy, oak or sumac, use two tea bags per 12 ounces of water and let it steep for six minutes. Soak sterile gauze or clean cotton cloth in the tea, and apply compresses for 15 minutes to the itchy area several times per day.

➤ **Calendula and Comfrey Ointment.** These plants are common ingredients in topical salves that often include vitamins A and E in an olive oil base. This salve works best for dry, scaly rashes that result from contact dermatitis, fungus or eczema. For a moist, itchy rash with oozing clear or yellow fluid, use a tea or tincture preparation of calendula only. Apply the tea in a compress or pour or spray it on the area.

➤ **Oatmeal.** It is best for itching caused by hives or insect bites. Fill a muslin or cotton bag with one cup of raw, rolled oats. Attach the bag to the spout of your bathtub and let the water flow through the bag as you fill a tub with warm (not hot) water. Lie in the oatmeal water for 20 to 30 minutes several times a day until the itch is gone. An oatmeal bath product, such as Aveeno, also can be used. For poison ivy, oak or sumac, use a compress of the oatmeal water.

Jamison Starbuck, ND, a naturopathic physician in family practice in Missoula, Montana. She is past president of the American Association of Naturopathic Physicians and a contributing editor to *The Alternative Advisor: The Complete Guide to Natural Therapies and Alternative Treatments* (Time Life).

MASTITIS

 Mastitis (inflammation of the breast) is a common benign cause of breast mass. It's most often seen in women who breast-feed after childbirth, but it can also develop in women who are not breast-feeding. Women with diabetes, chronic illness, AIDs or an impaired immune system may be more susceptible. It also can occur in women after menopause.

The two common kinds are—*acute mastitis* involving bacterial infection, and *chronic mastitis* with no infection, just tenderness and pain.

This is a condition that you should check out with your health professional. Chances are you will be treated with antibiotics. If you are put on antibiotics, be sure to take acidophilus available at health food stores. Antibiotics have no discretion—they destroy the good as well as the bad bacteria, therefore you'll need acidophilus to replace the beneficial bacteria. Acidophilus capsules should have one to two billion viable acidophilus cells. Read the label carefully.

 NOTE: Take acidophilus right *after* you've eaten and at least two hours *before* or two hours *after* you take an antibiotic. That way you won't diminish the effectiveness of the antibiotic while reaping the benefits of the acidophilus.

Mastitis Remedies

The following remedies have been known to work wonders for many women with mastitis…

➤ **Garlic.** Garlic is a potent natural antibiotic. Finely mince a clove or two of garlic and drink it down in a glass of water. Do this two or three times a day. Also, until the mastitis is gone, take a large dose of vitamin C—3,000 milligrams (mg) to 5,000 mg per day—to help boost your immune system so that your body (and the garlic) can fight the infection.

Dr. Chris Deatherage, naturopathic physician in Missouri, suggests that his patients with mastitis mix a dropperful of echinacea tincture, three cloves of raw garlic and four to six ounces of carrot juice in a blender and drink the mixture every two hours throughout the day. Dr. Deatherage reports many quick, permanent cures.

 CAUTION: Having garlic on an empty stomach can cause nausea. Be sure to have some food in your stomach before eating garlic or taking garlic capsules. And, be cautious with garlic if you have gastritis.

➤ **Dandelion Leaf.** If you have recurrent mastitis, dandelion leaf tea may be the answer once and for all. Have three cups of the tea (available at health food stores) every day. Also, make a poultice of the leaves and put it on your breast once a day for at least 20 minutes. Expect results within a month.

➤ **Vitamins.** One naturopath we know prescribes 250 mg of vitamin B-6 daily and 400 international units (IU) of vitamin E twice a day. Since vitamin B-6 can be toxic, you should not take this dosage for more than a couple of weeks. The typical recommended dose for B-6 is no more than 150 mg a day.

CAUTION: It is important that you check with your doctor before trying any of these self-help treatments.

AFFIRMATION

Repeat this affirmation 10 times, first thing in the morning, each time you comb or brush your hair, and last thing at night…

I accept myself as a healthy and happy woman, blessed with normal and natural bodily functions.

MEMORY LOSS

While doing research for this book, we talked to a lot of people and it seems that everyone—regardless of age—feels as though they're losing their memory. We feel it's due to data overload.

With television, radio, newspapers, magazines, the Internet and all of the social networking (Twitter, Facebook, LinkedIn) going on, we have so much coming at us day and night, it's no wonder we walk into a room and can't remember what we went to get, or the names of the people in the room.

Most of us beat ourselves up when we can't remember someone's name. Here is something to consider...way back when our brains were evolving, let's say some 60,000 years ago, most people lived in little isolated villages. How many names did each person have to remember? A hundred? A hundred and twenty if they were really sociable? We personally have five times that many people in our high-rise apartment building. So what if you don't remember someone's name! Just say, "Please tell me your name once again?" At this point, everyone understands this syndrome because they, too, go through it on a regular basis.

Some reassuring information: As we get older, we do lose brain cells, but our aging brains make up for cell loss and actually increase brain functions.

For instance, our ability to understand and explain heightens as wisdom and judgment deepen. In fact, the ability to speak and write improves after age 50; philosophers don't reach their peak until 70 or 80.

So, now that we've eliminated aging as a reason for memory loss, let's look at three common causes...

1. **Depression.** When you're depressed, you don't pay very much attention to anything, hindering your ability to create and store new memories.

2. **Alcohol abuse** usually results in memory loss.

3. **Medication.** Memory loss can be a side effect of some medications.

If you are having serious memory problems, worrying about it won't help. Consult a doctor as soon as possible. It may be a chemical imbalance that can be easily remedied.

James M. Barrie, the author of *Peter Pan*, described memory as "What God gave us so that we might have roses in December." Read the suggestions in this chapter, follow the ones appropriate for you—and get out the vase for those roses.

 NOTE: You must give the following remedies at least a month, and often two, to get noticeable results.

Ways to Improve Your Memory

➤ **Food.** Eleanor Roosevelt was known to have an exceptionally good memory. How good was it? It was so good, elephants used to consult with her! *But seriously....*

We were told that when Mrs. Roosevelt was quite elderly, she was asked to what she attributed her great memory. Her answer was three cloves of garlic a day. It's been reported that Mrs. Roosevelt dipped the garlic cloves in either honey or chocolate.

The easiest way to eat raw garlic is to finely mince it, put it in water or juice, then just drink it down. If you don't chew the little bits, the smell of garlic won't stay on your breath very long, if at all. Don't have garlic on an empty stomach. And, be cautious if you have stomach problems.

➤ **Mental Exercise.** Watch game shows on TV and shout out answers before the contestants do. Do crossword puzzles and number games like Sudoku. Do jigsaw puzzles. Take an adult education course every semester. Write your memoirs. Take up painting. Learn to play the harmonica or the recorder. There's no limit to the stimulating and fun mental exercises out there for you. Use your creativity to find them!

➤ **Deep Breathing.** Breathe in through your mouth, then breathe out through your nostrils. Keep inhaling through the mouth and exhaling through the nostrils for two minutes, five times throughout the day. This breathing exercise is said to help you turn mental malaise into idea-filled days.

➤ **Herbal Teas.** Throughout your day, drink two to three cups of rosemary and/or sage tea (available at health food stores). Add a cup of just-boiled water to a heaping teaspoon of either herb. Steep, strain and drink.

➤ **Forget Forgetfulness.** The average American spends a full year out of his/her life looking for lost objects. Luckily it's spread over a long period of time, but you can cut down on that amount of time, not to mention the frustration. Write a list of the half-dozen things you misplace most often—keys, eyeglasses, watch.

Simply take a pretend picture every time you put any of the objects down somewhere. Hold one hand over one eye, make a lens-like circle with the other hand, and look through it with the other eye. Blink as though your eye is a camera taking a picture of the object. An hour, a day or even a week later, when you need that object, you'll be able to picture exactly where it is.

If you have a cell phone that has a camera in it, you can actually take a picture of your most-misplaced objects each time you put one down somewhere, unless your cell phone is one of the things you keep misplacing.

➤ **Improving Your Short-Term Memory.** When you have to learn something you'll be needing very soon (short-term memory)—maybe for a test you're taking, or for a meeting you're going to—go over the information in the morning. It could be the morning of the test or meeting, or the morning before. The key word here is reviewing information in the *morning* for improved short-term memory.

➤ **Improving Long-Term Memory.** Your long-term memory powers are at their peak in the afternoon. If you need to learn something you'll have to recall weeks later, study it between noon and 5 pm.

➤ **Gem Therapy.** The stones for improving one's memory are amethyst and amber calcite. Wear or carry either or both with or on you, and your memory should improve. If you remember to get these stones and carry them with you, they're working already.

➤ **Aromatherapy.** Crush caraway seeds, keep them close by, and every once in a while take a whiff. It's said to strengthen the memory. Vary the whiffing with coriander seeds and ground cloves.

➤ **Advice to Consider.** According to a Chinese proverb, "The palest ink lasts longer than the most retentive memory." Write down whatever it is that you really want to remember. The act of writing it will help you remember it, even though you won't have to remember it, since you will have it in writing. This has been very effective both of us.

Recommended Reading

➤ *Brainpower Game Plan: Sharpen Your Memory, Improve Your Concentration and Age-Proof Your Mind in Just 4 Weeks* by Cynthia R. Green, PhD, and the editors of *Prevention* (Rodale Books). Dr. Green founded the renowned Memory Enhancement Program at Mount Sinai School of Medicine in New York City, where she is assistant clinical professor of psychiatry. Teaming up with the editors from *Prevention*, they've created a day-by-day plan to improve your everyday memory up to 78%. It includes body movement to maximize brain cell development and growth; foods with nutrients that help your brain stay vital and games that maximize brainpower.

A Word from the Wise...

What People Still Don't Know About Brain Health

Everybody wants as much brainpower as possible. To achieve that goal, large numbers of Americans have started eating more omega-3-rich fish (or taking fish oil supplements) and begun daily exercise routines, such as walking, biking, swimming or aerobic dancing. But there are other lesser-known strategies that you also can adopt to maximize your brainpower. *What I recommend for my patients in addition to fish consumption and exercise...*

1. **Consider taking ginkgo biloba and bacopa monnieri.** Ginkgo is widely recommended for its brain-boosting effects. However, a lesser-known herb—*bacopa monnieri*—is also an excellent choice. Both herbs support cerebral circulation and mental focus. For my patients who want to maximize their ability to retain

136

new information, I recommend 120 milligrams (mg) of each herb daily.

 CAUTION: If you are pregnant, breast-feeding or take any medication—especially for anxiety, depression, any mental disorder or dementia—consult your doctor before using the supplements described here or adding them to your treatment regimen. Ginkgo, in particular, should not be used with blood thinners, including aspirin.

Also helpful: Phosphatidylserine (or PS). Research has shown that this protein-derived nutrient is helpful in slowing the progression of dementia and improving focus and concentration. A typical dose is 300 mg per day. PS may be taken alone or in addition to the herbs described above.

 CAUTION: People with a soy allergy should NOT take PS—most of the formulas are derived from soy.

2. **Watch out for anxiety.** Many people fail to recognize the degree to which anxiety can interfere with focus and concentration. If you suspect that anxiety may be compromising your brain function, ask your doctor about taking *gamma amino butyric acid* (GABA), an amino acid that is naturally present in our brains. Optimal amounts of GABA allow the mind to both relax and focus, without causing sleepiness or sedation. A typical dose is 100 mg one to three times a day.

3. **Try Kundalini yoga.** All forms of yoga involve stretching and focused breathing, but Kundalini (the word refers to concentrated life force, according to Indian philosophy) is my favorite because it incorporates a variety of deep breathing exercises that simultaneously wake up and calm the brain. I recommend practicing

this form of yoga for 45 minutes at least once weekly. To find a Kundalini yoga teacher near you, consult the International Kundalini Yoga Teachers Association, 505-819-0886, *www. ikyta.com.*

As an alternative, you can improve your brain health by practicing deep breathing. Sit quietly in an erect position with a straight back and breathe in and out through your nose. Inhale as slowly and as deeply as you can, extending your abdomen outward...exhale as fully as possible, trying to push all of the air out of your lungs. Do this for five minutes daily, setting a timer if necessary.

4. Keep your whistle wet. Adequate water intake is crucial for optimal brain health. Drink one-half ounce of water per pound of body weight daily.

Jamison Starbuck, ND, a naturopathic physician in family practice in Missoula, Montana. She is past president of the American Association of Naturopathic Physicians and a contributing editor to *The Alternative Advisor: The Complete Guide to Natural Therapies and Alternative Treatments* (Time Life).

MENOPAUSE

Hot flashes, facial flushes and night sweats are all part of the spectrum of menopausal symptoms. But according to a study done at the University of Alabama at Birmingham Center for Nursing Research, women who are clear about their purpose in life have an easier time going through menopause. They experience fewer emotional and physical menopausal symptoms. So, if you're assertive, independent and authoritative, you can skip these pages and get on with your life's work. The rest of you, read on to learn how to deal with the symptoms.

Hot Flashes

➤ **Breathe Away Hot Flashes.** Do this breathing exercise and exorcise those flashes. Breathe in through the nose to the count of six; breathe out through the mouth to the count of six. Do this 10 times in a row. Do not pause in between breaths.

➤ **What to Wear.** Wear cotton or wool clothing. The natural fibers will provide more ventilation than synthetics offer, allowing you to cool off faster from the hot flashes.

➤ **Instant Revive.** Rush to the refrigerator and open both doors—the refrigerator part and the freezer part—and stand as close to it as possible. If you're in the street, go into the nearest supermarket and hang out in the frozen food section. While you're chillin', discover new foods and read their nutritional labels and ingredients.

➤ **Facial Flushes.** Suck on an ice cube. It will cool the blood in the area of the neck and the flushing will be gone in a flash.

➤ **Night Sweats.** An oatstraw tincture (available at most health food stores) can help prevent night sweats, make you more energetic, and it's good for your skin and hair, too. Take 20 drops in water three times each day, after every meal.

More on Menopause

➤ **Help for Many Menopausal Symptoms.** We've all heard good things about ginseng. Many herbalists believe that ginseng is only for men. The comparable female Chinese medicinal root is dong quai. It is said to have been used in Asia for thousands of years to rejuvenate female glands.

For minimizing the symptoms of menopause, we sing the praises of dong quai...the "Dong Quai Serenade."

Dosage varies depending on the extent of one's symptoms. For average menopausal problems, take one capsule of dong quai (available at health food stores) three times a day. For more severe problems, increase dosage accordingly but not excessively. To determine the dosage appropriate for you, check with your health professional, nutritionist or knowledgeable health food store manager.

The powdered herb has a celery-like taste. You can open the capsule and sprinkle the contents on salads or in soups or stews.

To derive the full benefit of dong quai, many herbalists believe that you should not eat fruit or drink other strong root teas for at least three hours after taking it.

CAUTION: Dong quai may increase sensitivity to ultraviolet rays. People taking dong quai should avoid prolonged exposure to the sun. Also, for women who are still menstruating, dong quai can cause heavier menstrual flow. If you are on medication, check with your doctor or pharmacist about possible negative interactions before taking dong quai.

➤ **Hormone Balancer.** Suma is an herb that comes in capsule form, is available at health food and vitamin stores, and is said to be a hormone balancer. Follow dosage on the label.

➤ **Gem Therapy.** Chrysocolla is the stone for female problems. It symbolizes wholeness and gives one a sense of peace and well-being. Place it over the third eye (on your forehead, between your two eyes) and you will feel a calm that surrounds you.

138

Recommended Reading

➤ *The Wisdom of Menopause—Creating Physical and Emotional Health and Healing During the Change*, Christiane Northrup, MD (Bantam Books). Dr. Northrup writes from her personal experience and as an ob-gyn who has researched and treated many women going through menopause. Dr. Northrup describes the symptoms of menopause, followed by both traditional and alternative treatment options.

You may also want to check out the good doctor's follow-up book, *The Secret Pleasures of Menopause* (Hay House). In this candid guide, Dr. Northrup helps to prove that menopause does *not* decrease libido. She writes about the ease of reaching orgasm and sexual satisfaction with the goal of experiencing life after 50 as the most pleasurable time of your life.

AFFIRMATION

Repeat this affirmation 15 times a day, first thing in the morning, every time you look in the mirror, and last thing at night...

I welcome this change in my life. I marvel at my body. It's all happening for my greatest good.

MENSTRUAL ISSUES

A delicate hormonal balance is responsible for regular menstrual cycles. Therefore, physical or emotional upheaval may be responsible for menstrual irregularities. Keep in mind that some menstrual irregularities can be normal, especially during the early teen years and for several years before menopause. Take a look at your age and at your physical and emotional state, then take a look at the rest of this chapter for help.

Premenstrual Syndrome (PMS)

PMS seems most prevalent in women who are in their 30s and 40s. The wide variety of physical and emotional symptoms of PMS are thought to be related to the high level of hormones in the second half of the menstrual cycle, when the estrogen level is higher.

Here are some suggestions for overcoming the biochemical causes of those PMS—**P**roblematic **M**onthly **S**ymptoms.

➤ **Vitamin B-6.** This vitamin can make a big difference when it comes to that time of month. Take one B-6 (100 milligrams [mg]) daily. You might want to raise the dosage to 150 mg during the week before you get your period.

 CAUTION: Do NOT take more than 150 mg of vitamin B-6 a day, as it can be toxic.

➤ **Dong Quai** is a medicinal root used in China to revitalize female glands. Dosage varies depending on the extent of one's symptoms. For typical PMS symptoms, take one capsule of dong quai (available at health food stores) three times a day. For more severe cases, increase dosage accordingly but not excessively.

 CAUTION: Dong quai may increase sensitivity to ultraviolet rays. People taking dong quai should avoid prolonged exposure to the sun. Also, for women who are still menstruating, dong quai can cause heavier menstrual flow. If you are on medication, check with your doctor or pharmacist about possible negative interactions before taking dong quai.

➤ **Caffeine.** If you eliminate caffeine from your diet (that means coffee, chocolate, aspirin, colas and more), your pre-period symp-

toms and the during-your-period pains may not be nearly as troublesome.

➤ **Yarrow Tea.** This odd-tasting herb may be the answer to your period problems. Each of us has had occasion to drink it. It's amazing. Before I even finished the entire cup of tea, my period pains were gone. We've actually changed friends' lives with this treatment...women who couldn't cope with PMS and others who had to put their lives on hold while they doubled up in pain during the first two days of their period.

Make yarrow tea (yarrow is sold at most health food stores or check "Sources," page 309, for an herb outlet) by steeping a teaspoon of the herb in a cup of just-boiled water for about seven minutes. Strain and drink when needed.

 NOTE: Yarrow tea has an unusual taste, so you may want to add honey.

Menstrual Cramps Prevention

➤ **Cramp Bark.** If you suffer cramps, what should you take? Cramp bark, of course. It's a Native American remedy (available at herb shops and some health food stores) and is also known as squaw bush.

To prevent cramps, drink two cups of cramp bark tea daily, starting a week before you're expecting your period.

Prepare the ground-up cramp bark according to directions on page xviii.

➤ **Vitamin E.** A daily dose of 400 international units (IU) of vitamin E can take the misery out of the menses. Take it in the morning, right after breakfast.

 CAUTION: Due to the possible interactions between vitamin E and various drugs and supplements, as well as other safety considerations, be sure to consult your doctor before taking vitamin E.

More Menstrual Matters

➤ **Slow the Flow.** Raspberry leaf tea—a cup after each meal and one at bedtime—can help decrease your menstrual flow.

Prepare the tea by steeping a teaspoon of the herb in a cup of just-boiled water for about seven minutes. Strain and drink. It can also ease crampiness and the pain of swollen breasts. Raspberry tea is available at health food stores.

➤ **For All Menstrual Problems.** Suma is an herb that comes in capsule form, is available at health food and vitamin stores, and is said to be an *adaptogen*—correcting whatever needs to be corrected. Follow the dosage on the label.

➤ **Gem Therapy.** Chrysocolla, an exquisite rich blue/green opaque stone, definitely has female energy, according to gemologist Connie Barrett. In fact, it's recommended for men who want to get in touch with their feminine side.

Wear chrysocolla around your neck, carry it with you or tape it on the problem area as you meditate, do a visualization or repeat an affirmation.

AFFIRMATION

Repeat this affirmation 10 times, first thing in the morning, each time you comb or brush your hair and last thing at night…

I accept myself as a healthy and happy woman, blessed with normal and natural bodily functions.

MOTION SICKNESS

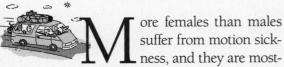

More females than males suffer from motion sickness, and they are mostly between the ages of two and 12. But plenty of adults are troubled with it. In fact, 75% of all astronauts experience some form of motion sickness.

Meanwhile, back on Earth…here are various suggestions for preventing or curbing this unpleasant condition…

Motion Sickness Prevention

➤ **Ginger.** Twenty minutes before you board a plane or any other form of transportation, mix a half teaspoon of ginger powder in a glass of water and drink it. Or, take two capsules of powdered ginger.

Think about the leading over-the-counter motion sickness drug. This ginger remedy has been tested and found more effective than that drug…and without any of the side effects.

 CAUTION: Ginger acts as a blood thinner, so check with your doctor before using it if you are taking a prescription blood thinner. Also, stop using ginger three days before any surgery.

➤ **A Penny.** This falls under the remedy category you-may-think-this-is-crazy-but-it-seems-to-work. Before you start out on your journey, tape a copper penny in your navel. Our friend said she always travels wearing nice underwear in case of unexpected security measures calling for disrobing. Her concern now is how to explain the penny in her navel.

➤ **Ice-Cold Something.** Place a can of ice-cold beer behind your left ear, resting on your neck. Come to think of it, an ice-cold can of soda, juice—anything—will help prevent motion sickness.

➤ **Air Conditioning.** Help stave off motion sickness by putting on airs. On a plane, open the overhead vent; in a car, train, or bus, be sure to open a window; on a boat, stay on deck.

➤ **Use a Newspaper.** Before starting out, drape a black and white newspaper over your shoulders as though it were a beauty parlor cape. The smell of the paper and ink should help whether you're in a car, bus or train.

➤ **Acupressure.** Take the middle three fingers of one hand and put them on the inside of your wrist of the other hand, starting at the crease that separates the hand from the wrist. The top finger will be on the pressure point that can prevent motion sickness. If you press that point while that hand is relaxed, your fingers should curl in. If that happens, you know you have the correct pressure point.

In order for this remedy to work, you have to exert constant pressure on that point. One way to do that is to put a button on the pressure point and a sweatband on your wrist to hold the button in place. For a similar commercial product on the market, check health food stores, boating shops or Magellan's Travel Supplies (see "Sources," page 313, for their listing).

➤ **The Best Place to Sit.** In a plane, sit toward the front or over the wheels. Do not sit in back of the plane. The tail moves more than the middle or front. In any form of transportation, always sit near a window and look out; focus on things far away, not the nearby sights that are whizzing by.

➤ **The Best Time to Travel.** Travel after dark and lower the odds of getting sick. When you fly by night, you can't see the unsettling motion as much as you do during daylight travel.

How to Spell Relief Anywhere

When you're feeling queasy, on a plane or on the ground, relief is just a kitchen, restaurant or bar away.

➤ **Tropical Fruit Juice.** Drink a glass of papaya or pineapple juice.

➤ **Peppered Soup.** Eat a bowl of vegetable soup with a quarter of a teaspoon of cayenne pepper in it—half a teaspoon if you can stand it that hot.

 CAUTION: Do NOT use this cayenne pepper remedy if you have heartburn, gastritis, ulcers or esophagitis.

➤ **Forget the Martini.** Eat two or three olives.

MUSCLE PAINS, SPRAINS, STRAINS AND CRAMPS

Muscle Pains

➤ **Better Carrying.** Maybe you carry a briefcase in the same hand every day? On which side do you carry groceries? A pocketbook? A baby? Once you become aware of your daily toting pattern, you may realize why you have muscle pain in certain parts of your body.

The remedy is obvious: Retrain yourself to keep shifting packages (or a baby) from one side to the other. Or, if possible, balance your load by carrying even amounts on each side. When practical, ask the supermarket packer to divide your purchases into two even shopping bags.

➤ **Capsaicin.** Endorphins are the body's natural painkiller. A substance found in red-hot peppers is said to stimulate and increase the production of endorphins.

Conclusion: Incorporate red-hot peppers into your diet to help you handle pain.

 CAUTION: Do NOT use this capsaicin remedy if you have heartburn, gastritis, ulcers or esophagitis.

A Surprising Cure for Joint and Muscle Aches

When you hear the term "weight lifting," you might think of bodybuilders with bulging muscles. Only in the past few years has it become more widely known that weight lifting—often called strength training—also helps control body weight and increase bone mass.

What most people still don't know: Weight lifting can play a significant role in relieving muscle and joint pain. Even though doctors often overlook muscle weakness as a cause of pain, it is the culprit in an estimated 80% to 90% of my patients, many of whom are ages 60 to 90 and suffer from aching joints and muscles.

Surprisingly, muscle weakness contributes to pain even in people who have been told by a physician that a structural problem, such as a torn ligament or arthritis, is responsible for their symptoms.

Why Do Strong Muscles Fight Pain?

Exercises designed to strengthen muscles improve joint function and overall body mechanics in two important ways. When the muscles of a joint are weak, the bones can move out of position, causing bone surfaces to rub together and leading to irritation and pain at the joint. Also, because muscles work together to produce movement, if one is underdeveloped, other muscles can easily become strained.

The following exercises target areas that are especially prone to pain-causing muscle weakness that often goes undetected.

The exercises require hand weights or ankle weights. Both are available at sporting-goods stores.

142

Typical cost: Hand weights—$10 a pair... ankle weights—$20 a pair.

Helpful: When choosing weights, select ones that you can lift about 10 times without straining. If your muscles are not tired by the time of the last repetition, choose a heavier weight.

For each exercise, perform three sets of 10 repetitions two to three times a week. As you lift the weight, breathe out and count to two... as you lower it, breathe in and count to three.

NOTE: Consult your doctor before starting any new exercise program.

CAUTION: See a doctor if your pain was caused by a traumatic injury, such as a fall...if your discomfort is constant and/or severe... or if you have limited range of motion (less than 50% of your normal range). In these cases, the pain may be due to a problem that cannot be improved with exercise.

Best exercises to relieve...

Shoulder and Elbow Pain

What's targeted: The *rotator-cuff* muscles, which hold the humerus (upper arm) bone in place when you lift your arm. Building the rotator-cuff muscles also alleviates the strain on forearm muscles that leads to elbow pain. Rotator-cuff muscles can be strained during such activities as driving or using a computer for long periods without supporting the arms.

What to do: Sit in a chair placed at the front edge of a table with your left side a few inches from the corner of the table. Hold the weight in your left hand and rest your left elbow on the front edge of the table. Your hand should be about three inches below the table top with your palm facing down.

Raise your forearm, keeping your wrist straight, until your hand is about three inches above the table. Lower the weight to the starting position. Reposition the chair so that your right side is next to the table, and repeat the exercise with the weight in your right hand.

Shoulder Pain

What's targeted: The *posterior-deltoid* muscles located at the back of the shoulders. These muscles tend to be weaker than the front shoulder muscles due to our natural tendency to hold and carry objects in front of our bodies, which makes the chest, front shoulder and bicep muscles work harder. This imbalance can throw off bone alignment in the shoulder joints, causing pain.

What to do: Stand with your feet a little more than shoulder-width apart. Position yourself so that your knees and elbows are slightly bent and your back is slightly arched. Hold a weight in each hand in front of your thighs, palms facing each other. Using your shoulders, extend your arms out to the side until the weights are about six inches from your thighs, stopping the motion before your shoulder blades begin to come together. Return the weights to the starting position.

Elbow Pain

What's targeted: The *wrist-extensor* muscles, which run along the top of the forearm. Building these muscles relieves strains caused by gardening, playing tennis or other activities involving repetitive wrist movement, gripping or squeezing.

What to do: Sit with your feet flat on the floor directly under your knees. While holding a weight in your right hand, rest your right forearm on the top of your right thigh with your wrist about three inches directly in front of your knee and your palm facing down. Place your left hand on your right forearm to keep it steady. Using your wrist muscles, lift the weight until your wrist is fully flexed. Return to the starting position. Repeat the exercise on your left thigh, using your left hand.

Hip, Knee and Heel Pain

What's targeted: The *hip-abductor* muscles, which support your legs when you walk and climb stairs. Strengthening these muscles can relieve muscle strain at the hip joint and prevent the knee and foot from rotating toward the midline of your body when you walk (causing knee pain and heel pain)—instead of staying in line with your hip.

What to do: Lie on your right side on a carpeted floor or a mat with an ankle weight strapped to your left leg. Fold your right arm under your head and bend your right leg. Place your left hand on the floor in front of you for support. Flex your left foot (as if standing on it) and raise your straightened left leg to hip height, keeping it in line with your torso. Lower your leg to the starting position. Lie on your left side and repeat the exercise raising your right leg.

Illustrations by Shawn Banner.

Mitchell Yass, physical therapist and founder and director of PT2 Physical Therapy & Personal Training in Farmingdale, New York, *www.mitchellyass.com.* He is author of *Overpower Pain: The Strength-Training Program That Stops Pain Without Drugs or Surgery* (Sentient).

Sprains and Strains

➤ **RICE.** For most sprains and strains, especially if accompanied by pain and swelling, the word to remember is RICE. With us, this could mean that you prepare brown rice and... but no!

In this case each letter stands for part of the treatment: **R** for rest—keep the injured body part still; **I** for ice—use an ice bag or an ice-cube-filled plastic bag with a towel around it, 10 minutes on/10 minutes off throughout the day; **C** for compression—bind the sore muscle with an Ace bandage; and **E** for elevation—keep the sprained limb raised.

Beyond RICE Remedies

➤ **Paste Massage.** Take an egg white and mix in enough salt to form a thick paste. Gently massage the sore area with the paste. Don't wash it off until you're ready to repeat the procedure in two hours.

 CAUTION: Do NOT use this paste massage remedy if you have lesions on the affected area.

➤ **Dip and Wrap Solution.** Heat up three ounces of water and dissolve a tablespoon of salt in it. Then add three ounces of distilled white vinegar. Dip a white washcloth into the solution, wring it out and wrap it around the sore area. When the cloth starts drying, re-dip it and re-wrap it.

➤ **Bread Wrap.** To relieve the pain of a sprain and reduce the swelling, warm a cup of apple cider vinegar, then soak a piece of bread in it and place the bread on the sore area. Put a piece of plastic over it and a towel over that. Keep it that way for four hours.

➤ **Onion Wrap.** This remedy is useful if pain and swelling accompany a sprained or strained muscle. Grate an onion, or put it through the food processor. Take the gratings, put them on the sore or swollen area and wrap the area with plastic wrap.

➤ **Bay Leaf Bath.** Relax in a bay leaf bath to soothe strained muscles. Put a half-cup of bay leaves in a pint of just-boiled water. Cover and let it steep for 20 minutes. Strain—not you, the bay leaves—and pour the liquid into your nice warm bath. Sit in the tub for at least 15 restful minutes.

➤ **Gem Therapy.** Malachite is an exotic green stone with a pattern of swirls on it and is thought to be able to draw out pain. We were told that this somewhat expensive stone should be the size of the painful spot. If you have muscle pain throughout your body, you don't want to have to buy a malachite boulder, so forget this remedy. If your pain is very localized, place the stone on the exact spot and stay that way for 15 minutes. This may be a good time to say the affirmation on the next page.

Leg Cramps and Other Muscle Spasms

➤ **Water.** Dehydration is one common cause of leg cramps. Electrolytes are minerals —such as calcium, sodium, potassium—that help the cells to function at their best. When you are dehydrated, an electrolyte imbalance can occur and cause muscle cramps. So it's obviously important to keep hydrated. Drink six to eight glasses of water a day.

➤ **Calcium Could Be the Answer,** especially in light of the information above. Calcium is one of the main electrolytes that affects muscle cramping. Take a look at your diet. You may want to add calcium-rich foods, including green leafy vegetables, broccoli, seeds and almonds. Drink fresh carrot juice. It contains calcium lactate that can do you a world of good.

Also, it may be a good idea to take calcium supplements. Since magnesium helps the absorption of calcium, you should consider capsules combining the two minerals. Depending on your size and the severity of your condition, take 800 milligrams (mg) to 1,000 mg of calcium and 400 mg to 500 mg of magnesium daily. It is important to consult your doctor to determine the appropriate dosage for you. While the pain is intense, your doctor may recommend low-dosage capsules at two-hour intervals, adding up to whatever daily dosage is prescribed.

 CAUTION: Magnesium can cause diarrhea. Cut back on the dosage if you experience this effect. Also, some people do better with magnesium oxide if they have trouble with magnesium.

➤ **Nighttime Relief for Leg Cramps.** Take a piece of silverware—a spoon is best and it doesn't have to be silver, stainless steel is fine—and keep it by your bedside. When you awaken with a leg cramp, put the spoon on the cramp and it will uncramp instantly. Also see "Swimmer's Leg Cramps" below.

➤ **Swimmer's Leg Cramps.** When you get a cramp and you're in the water, pinch your *philtrum*. Don't tell me you don't know what a philtrum is. It's the space between the upper lip and the nose. Grab hold of that little fleshy area from side to side and pinch! The leg *will* uncramp.

Of course you can also use this remedy on land, in bed…wherever.

➤ **Leg Cramp Prevention.** Wear socks to bed all year 'round and, we were assured by the person who shared this remedy with us, you'll have fewer, if any, leg cramps. Wearing socks to bed is also said to assure a sounder night's sleep. The socks can be heavy or light—they're all effective.

➤ **Toe Cramps.** When your toes cramp, simply force yourself to point the toes toward your knee. Do it and the toes will uncramp.

AFFIRMATION

Repeat this affirmation 15 times a day, starting first thing in the morning and whenever a song pops into your mind, or when you hear music…

Energy flows through my muscles, making it easy to move to the music I love.

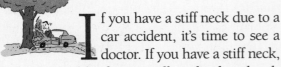

NECK CARE

If you have a stiff neck due to a car accident, it's time to see a doctor. If you have a stiff neck, accompanied by fever, swollen glands, a headache and nausea, it's time to see a doctor. If your stiff neck is accompanied by tingling or sharp pain that shoots down to your fingers, it's time to see a doctor!

But…if you woke up with a stiff neck—no accident, no other symptoms—chances are you slept with your head and neck at a peculiar angle, and these suggestions can help…

➤ **Turn Up the Heat.** Start the day by taking a long, hot shower. Let the warm water cascade down your neck. In the afternoon and again in the evening, put a heating pad on your neck for about 20 minutes each time. If you don't have a heating pad, soak a towel in hot water, wring it out and wrap it around your neck.

 NOTE: To buy a microwaveable corn heating bag, visit *www.corn-bags.com* for a big selection.

 CAUTION: If the stiff neck is the result of a recent injury, do NOT use heat on your neck. It won't help and may even worsen the pain.

➤ **Make Motion Your Lotion.** "Gentle stretching and movement can help restore flexibility to a stiff neck," says Tab Blackburn, physical therapist and vice president of Clemson Sports Medicine and Rehabilitation. "If you can move the neck gently four or five times a day, it's literally like pouring lotion on it." Tab Blackburn recommends carefully turning the head from side to side. Look over your right shoulder

146

for a count of five, then look over your left shoulder for a count of five. Do this side-to-side movement three times. Repeat the complete exercise throughout the day and night, for a total of four or five times.

➤ **Radish Poultice.** To supply moist heat to the painful area, prepare a poultice by putting grated radishes into two thicknesses of cheesecloth or a large white cotton handkerchief. Obviously, we can't tell you how many radishes to use; it depends on the size of the radishes and the size of your neck area. Be sure the poultice—grated radishes wrapped in a cloth—is long enough to go around your neck and wide enough to dip down and rest on your back and shoulders. To keep the radishes' "heat" in once it's on your neck, put plastic wrap around the poultice and let it stay that way for a half hour. During that half hour, you might want to repeat the affirmation (on the next page) over and over.

➤ **Acupressure.** Vigorously massage the area a drop below the base of the back of the little toe. Massage for at least five minutes and you should feel less pain and stiffness in your neck. It's ideal to get someone to massage both feet at the same time. Even though your neck will feel better after the first massage, continue massaging three times a day for a couple of days.

Possible Stiff Neck Prevention

➤ **Baby, It's Cold Outside.** Keep your bedroom window closed if it is cold outside. Do not give yourself reason to cuddle up into a gawky position just to keep warm…and risk waking up with a stiff neck.

SOMETHING SPECIAL

Pillow Power!

Core Products is a company that was born when its founder, Phil Mattison, saw a chiropractor for an aching neck. That visit led to the development of their first orthopedic pillow, over 20 years ago. Core now has a wide range of tested and professional-approved products to help eliminate neck pain, including bed and travel pillows.

Our experience with two Core pillow styles (Tri-Core and Double Core) made us realize what a difference a pillow makes! It's a treat to have a great night's sleep and wake up without a pain in the neck.

Core's orthopedic pillows are hypoallergenic, machine washable and designed to solve or prevent orthopedic problems related to the neck and spine, offering support and comfort for the head and neck while enjoying good ZZZZZZ's.

Their best-seller is the Tri-Core Pillow, which aligns the spine and supports the neck in its natural position, whether you sleep on your back or your side. By supporting and preserving the natural curvature of the neck and spine, the pillow helps correct nerve malfunction, promote healing of injuries and lessen further problems.

The Core people tell us that users experience a positive difference within days of sleeping on the pillow (it did for each of us), and for some people, it helps alleviate airway blockages, which is a major cause of snoring.

More Information: Visit *www.coreproducts.com* and start by looking at their line of orthopedic pillows. If you cannot decide which Core product is appropriate for you, call 877-249-1251 and a representative will help guide you to the item that's best suited to your specific need.

One more thing…Core Products guarantees your satisfaction with every product you buy.

AFFIRMATION

Repeat this affirmation starting first thing in the morning and each time you nod your head and are reminded of the stiffness…

I stir up the gifts within me and use them to face all challenges. I am a real winner.

A Word from the Wise…

No More Back, Neck or Leg Pain: The Easy, Drug-Free Secret

Millions of people suffer from chronic back, neck and leg pain. Doctors are likely to diagnose arthritis or a disk problem—but in many cases, that diagnosis is wrong. In my work as a physical therapist, I have found that much of joint and muscle pain can instead be traced to *muscle imbalances*, created when one muscle group gets overworked and becomes thick and shortened. A muscle must be at optimal length to contract properly, so a disproportioned muscle is not only weak…but it also affects the opposite muscle, which compensates by becoming overly long.

These weak and imbalanced muscles pull nearby joints (and other muscles) out of alignment, and that can lead to painful irritation

147

and inflammation. This commonly occurs with the thigh muscles, affecting the low back and knees, and the shoulder and upper back muscles, affecting the neck. By bringing these muscles back into balance, you can realign these joints and relieve chronic pain.

How to Get Relief

To get help for the most common areas of pain, do either the lower-body or upper-body exercises on the following page two to three times a week, depending on your own area of pain.

Or you can do all four exercises—to ensure that your posture will improve and that you will feel stronger and more agile. These exercises use hand weights and resistance bands, which are available at sporting-goods stores and online. Choose enough resistance so that your muscles feel tired after 10 repetitions.

 NOTE: Always consult your doctor before starting any new exercise program.

Low-Back Pain and/or Knee Pain

Doctors love to blame low-back pain on disk problems, but the real trigger in most cases stems from the fact that we all work our front thigh muscles (quadriceps) much more than the backs of our thighs (hamstrings) and gluteal muscles (buttocks). As a result, the front thigh muscles get bigger and shorter. This pulls the front of the pelvis downward, causing the low back to arch. Over time, this causes the low-back muscles to become short and weak, leaving them susceptible to painful strains and spasms. Shortened quadriceps also lead to chronic knee pain because they pull up on the kneecap, causing friction between bone surfaces and inflammation in the knee joint.

Solution: Stretch out the quadriceps and strengthen your hamstring and gluteal muscles. This will lengthen and strengthen your low-back muscles and take pressure off your knees.

To stretch quadriceps: First, loop a non-stretchy belt (such as one made from leather) around one ankle. Then lie flat on your back along the edge of your bed so that the leg with the belt looped around the ankle hangs off of the bed. The other leg should be bent with the foot flat on the mattress. Pull the belt in toward your buttocks so that your knee bends. Continue pulling until you feel a pleasant stretch in the front of your thigh. Hold for 20 to 30 seconds, release, then repeat the stretch two or three times.

To strengthen the hamstrings and gluteals: Holding a dumbbell in each hand, stand with your feet slightly wider than your shoulders, legs straight. (Practice your form first without the dumbbells. Then when you can do the exercise properly, add in dumbbells heavy enough so that you notice the hamstrings working.) With palms facing your thighs, slowly run the dumbbell down the front of the legs, as far as the knee, the mid-shin or the ankle, until you feel a pleasant tension in your hamstrings. Keep your back straight and your head in line with your back. Slowly return to starting position. Do three sets of 10.

Neck Pain and Headaches

Most neck pain and stiffness occurs because the muscles in the chest, the front of the shoulders and the biceps become overworked and shortened. Meanwhile, their opposing muscles in the upper back and back of your shoulders become overstretched and weak, creating a stooped, "forward-shoulder" posture. This will leave the muscles that support the head too weak to do their job, causing neck pain and headaches.

Solution: Strengthen the muscles between your shoulder blades and your shoulder muscles (posterior deltoids). This will pull your shoulders back, shortening and strengthening the muscles that support your head.

To strengthen the muscles between the shoulder blades: Take a resistance band and make a knot in the middle of it. (Practice the move first without using a band, and then choose a strong enough band.) Place the knot over the top of a door, then shut the door so the knot is trapped on the other side and the ends of the band hang straight down like handles. Place a chair facing the door, close enough so that when sitting, you can take an end of the band in each hand with your arms straight out in front of you. Grab the ends of the band and, keeping your arms at shoulder height, bend your elbows and bring them straight back, so that your shoulder blades squeeze together. Return to starting position. Perform three sets of 10.

To strengthen the posterior deltoids: Stand with your feet a little more than shoulder-width apart, holding a dumbbell in

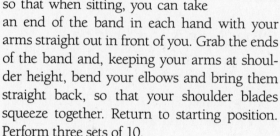

each hand in front of your thighs. Bend both your knees and elbows slightly. Slowly lift both arms out sideways until they are about six inches to the sides of your thighs. Stop at the point just before your shoulder blades start squeezing to-

Illustrations by Shawn Banner.

gether. Return slowly to starting position. Do three sets of 10.

Mitchell Yass, physical therapist and founder and director of PT2 Physical Therapy & Personal Training in Farmingdale, New York, *www.mitchellyass.com.* He is author of *Overpower Pain: The Strength-Training Program That Stops Pain Without Drugs or Surgery* (Sentient).

NEURALGIA

An inflammation of a nerve is *neuritis.* When the condition is accompanied by pain, it's called *neuralgia.* Most common is *trigeminal neuralgia* or *tic douloureu,* an inflammation of the fifth cranial nerve that causes severe pain on one side of the face.

Neuralgia can be caused by dental problems. If you've been diagnosed by a doctor and checked out by a dentist, and neuralgic pain persists, you may want to try these tips...

➤ **Lemon Juice.** Gently rub fresh lemon juice on the painful area and immediately follow up by placing a hot, wet, white washcloth on the same area. Leave it until the cloth is cool. If it helped ease the pain, repeat the process two hours later.

➤ **Hops.** Part of the hemp family, hops are used primarily to flavor beer. A poultice of hops (available at health food stores) can help bring quick relief from pain. Put a half cup of hops in cheesecloth. Leaving room for the hops to expand, tie the cheesecloth securely so that none of the hops can hop out. Dip the poultice in just-boiled water for two minutes. Shake it until no liquid is dripping, and apply it when it cools off enough to apply without burning the skin. Put it on the neuralgic spot with a dry towel on top to keep the heat in. As soon as it's no longer warm, reheat the poultice by re-dipping it in hot water, and reapply it. Again, not too hot!

➤ **Chamomile Oil.** To help eliminate facial pain, all you may knead is a nine-minute massage. Using a circular motion, gently massage chamomile oil (available at health food stores) on the nape of the neck, the temples and the sinus areas for three minutes each. Notice how just one drop of oil will go a long way.

➤ **Potato.** Bake a potato, cut it in half, and when it's cool enough, place both halves face down on the painful area. To keep the heat in, cover them with a towel. Baked potatoes have been known to draw out neuralgic pain. We've also heard that a mashed potato poultice can do the same thing. No, not one report of relief from French fries.

Neuralgia Prevention

➤ **Old German Folk Medicine.** If you eat a large portion of raw sauerkraut daily, you should not be troubled with neuralgia.

AFFIRMATION

Repeat this affirmation 15 times throughout the day, starting first thing in the morning, whenever you touch anything that's warm and last thing at night...

Love fills me with happiness, harmony and healing energy.

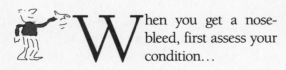

NOSEBLEED

When you get a nosebleed, first assess your condition...

 CAUTION: If blood is flowing from both nostrils or it is persistent or heavy, it may not be a simple nosebleed. You should get professional medical help immediately.

For the average, one-nostril nosebleed, sit up, calm down and...

What to Try First

➤ **Pack and Pinch.** Gently blow your nose to clear out all the blood you can, making it easier to clot. Then pack your nose with a cotton ball. You can use a dry cotton ball, or you can dip it in distilled white vinegar or distilled witch hazel. Once the cotton ball is in the nostril, pinch together the fleshy part of your nose—gently but firmly—and stay that way for six to eight minutes.

 CAUTION: Vinegar could be irritating to the mucous membranes in the nose.

If Your Nose Is Still Bleeding...

Do the pack and pinch process one more time, or try one of the following...

➤ **Garlic.** Take off the outer shell of a bulb of garlic, then crush the bulb to a paste. Sculpt the paste into a pancake the size of a silver dollar. If your right nostril is bleeding, put the garlic pancake on the instep of the bottom of your left foot. If your left nostril is bleeding, put the garlic pancake on the instep of the bottom of your right foot. Keep it in place with a handkerchief or Ace bandage and keep your foot elevated until your nosebleed stops, probably within 10 minutes.

CAUTION: Garlic can irritate the skin. You can dilute garlic with olive oil to minimize this effect. Also, avoid putting garlic on areas where there are cuts.

➤ **Hands.** Submerge your hands in hot water or raise your hands over your head. Or raise the arm that's on the same side as the bleeding nostril. Hold the arm stiff, put your hand against a wall, then lean on the wall.

➤ **Feet.** Make some cayenne tea—one-quarter teaspoon in a big mug of warm water—and drink it while soaking your feet in a basin (or two plastic shoe boxes) filled with hot water.

 CAUTION: Do NOT drink cayenne tea if you have heartburn, gastritis, ulcers or esophagitis.

➤ **Stiff Upper Lip.** If you're outdoors when you get a nosebleed, clean off a leaf and place it under your upper lip. If there are no leaves around, place a dime under your lip or a piece of brown paper bag.

Nosebleed Prevention

➤ **Yarrow.** It is said that a daily cup of yarrow tea (available at health food stores) will keep you free of nosebleeds. Most herbs have more than one name. Yarrow is also known as "soldier's woundwort," "old man's pepper," "knight's milfoil," and—wouldn't-you-know?—"nosebleed."

 NOTE: Yarrow tea has an unusual taste, so you may want to add honey.

A Word from the Wise...

Nosebleed Know-How

Most nosebleeds occur because of colds or minor irritations caused by nose-picking, cold, dry weather and/or forceful nose-blowing. The nose has many small blood vessels that help keep the nasal passages warm and humidify the air you breathe. Although nosebleeds are rarely life threatening, they occasionally are a symptom of other medical conditions, such as bleeding disorders or high blood pressure. If your nose bleeds for more than 15 minutes at a time, ask your doctor for an evaluation.

If you do get a nosebleed, lean forward slightly, and using your thumb and index finger, gently squeeze together your nostrils for at least five minutes. This practice is preferable to tilting your head back during a nosebleed, because it helps prevent blood from trickling down the throat.

Murray Grossan, MD, otolaryngologist, Cedars Sinai Medical Center, Los Angeles.

151

POISON IVY

We live in New York City and poison ivy is one of the few things neither of us ever worries about. However, when speaking to groups across the country and while doing radio and television shows, we're constantly asked for poison ivy remedies.

Urushiol is the heavy oil in poison ivy that causes an allergic reaction. Plants with urushiol grow in every state except Alaska and Hawaii, so it's no wonder that as many as 10 million Americans a year are affected by these plants.

How to Recognize Poison Ivy

Before you venture into areas that are likely to have poison ivy, learn to recognize the three-leafed menace. If you have access to the Internet, visit *http://poisonivy.aesir.com/view/pictures.html*, or go to your local library and find a book that has pictures of poison ivy. Take note of the thin, pale stems with three leaves on each stem.

World gardening authority Elvin McDonald shared with us this poison ivy poem from foliate folklore—"Leaflets three, let it be."

➤ **The White Paper Test.** Always carry a piece of white paper with you. If you think a plant is poison ivy but you're not sure, try the white paper test. Take hold of the plant with the paper and crush the leaves. If it's poison ivy, the juice on the paper will turn black in five minutes.

Getting Rid of the Plant

Never get rid of a patch of poison ivy by burning it. The plant's oil gets in the air and can be inhaled. You don't want poison ivy oil in your lungs. It can be very harmful. *Instead...*

➤ **Dig and Dry.** While wearing gardening gloves, uproot the plants and leave them on the ground to dry out in the sun.

➤ **A Wet Solution.** Prepare a solution of three pounds of salt in a gallon of soapy water. Spray the poison ivy plants over and over to make sure the solution does its job.

 NOTE: Tools that are used for digging up poison ivy plants need to be thoroughly washed with the (above) solution. When you're finished destroying the poison ivy and cleaning your tools, carefully take off your gloves, turning them inside out, and dispose of them. You may need to toss your clothes away as well, since the poison ivy oil may not wash out completely and can stay active for at least a year.

Poison Ivy Remedies

➤ **Nature's Antidote.** The natural antidote is jewelweed (ironically also known as Spotted Touch-Me-Not). Of course, as you must learn to recognize poison ivy, you must also know what jewelweed looks like. Visit *http://altnature.com/jewelweed.htm*, or go to your local library.

Jewelweed almost always grows right near poison ivy. Mother Nature—what a gal! *There are several ways to use the jewelweed plant...*

• **Ball up the whole plant and use it to wipe the poison ivy oil off the skin.**

• **Crush the leaves and stem,** releasing the juices, and apply it to the rash every hour throughout the day.

• **Prepare a solution to keep on hand.** Pick the whole plant and break it into small pieces. Cover it with at least a quart of water and let it boil until the water is dark orange. Strain the liquid into a jar, cover it and refrigerate until needed.

➤ **Cold Water—Quick!** If you realize you just brushed up against poison ivy and you can get to cold water within three minutes, you can wash away the nasty oil. Do not use regular soap. One theory is that the oil from the soap can seal in the poison ivy oil.

If you don't get the exposed area under cold water within minutes, you can still save yourself from the itchy rash by rubbing on dish detergent. Do it for 30 seconds, then rinse it off. If it doesn't prevent the rash, it will at least minimize the inflammation and blistering. According to Dr. Adam Stibich, director of the Dermatology Clinic in Alabama, dish detergent, used full-strength, works within two hours after poison ivy exposure, because it strips your skin of the plant oil that causes the rash.

➤ **Watermelon.** Yes, watermelon—both the rind and the meat of the melon—and glide it over and over the rash-ridden body parts. Let it dry naturally. Within a day, the condition should improve greatly.

➤ **Aloe Vera.** Every home should have an aloe vera plant. To help heal a poison ivy rash, take a small piece of the plant, squeeze out the gel, and apply it to the affected areas.

➤ **Vitamin E.** Puncture a vitamin E softgel, squeeze out the oil and apply it to the rash.

➤ **Extra Virgin Olive Oil (EVOO).** Until you pick up an aloe vera plant or a bottle of vitamin E, apply extra EVOO to the rash.

➤ **Paste to Relieve Itch.** Make a paste of cornstarch and water, baking soda and water or oatmeal and water. Start with the dry ingredient and add enough water to make a paste.

Put it on the rash for temporary relief from the itching.

➤ **Be Prepared Take-Along Tea.** Make a quart of strong mugwort tea. (Mugwort is available at health food stores.) Bottle it and keep it in the refrigerator. The second you realize you have poison ivy, get the mugwort tea and wash the skin. If done quickly enough, you can remove the rash-causing oil from the skin. Never use warm mugwort tea. It will open the pores, allowing the oil to sink in.

➤ **Buttermilk.** Dip white washcloths in one pint of buttermilk, with or without a tablespoon of salt mixed in, and apply the cloths to the affected areas. Keep dunking and reapplying. Then, after the last dunk, let it dry naturally. The buttermilk should help bring down swelling, stop running sores and dry up the rash.

Poison Ivy Prevention

➤ **Whiskey Washcloth.** A woman in the Midwest shared this with us, saying that it works for her and her family. Neither of us has tested this, so you're on your own. Proceed with caution.

Wet a washcloth with whiskey, rub your exposed body parts with it before going into poison ivy–infested regions, and contact with poison ivy will not affect you.

➤ **Resistance-Builder.** Eating romaine lettuce daily for two weeks before being exposed to poison ivy is said to help build one's resistance to it. It's a good reason to eat salads every day.

➤ **Immunization.** First, get a goat. Did we lose you or are you still with us? Have the goat graze where there is poison ivy. It will not harm the goat. After the goat has eaten the poison ivy, put on gloves and, making sure all your body parts are covered, milk the goat. Throw that milk away. The second milking—ah, that's the important one. Drink at least a pint of milk from the second milking and it may immunize you for up to a year…or not.

Poison Oak

Poison oak is to the West Coast what poison ivy is to the eastern part of the country. The consensus of opinion is that the remedies for poison ivy are also effective for poison oak sufferers. So read all of the above.

PREGNANCY CONCERNS

Pregnancy is a very personal experience. What's true for one mother-to-be may not be so for another. For that reason, it's most important to check with your obstetrician before you adopt any of the suggestions here.

While Pregnant

➤ **Avoid the Risk of Miscarriage.** Stop smoking! In women who smoke, it is estimated that miscarriages occur in about 25 out of 100 pregnancies.

➤ **Mercury in Fish and Shellfish.** Women who are nursing, or pregnant or who might become pregnant, should read and heed the report put out by the Environmental Protection Agency (EPA) and Food and Drug Administration (FDA). *Some points of the report are covered below…*

Fish and shellfish are an important part of a healthy diet. They contain high-quality protein and essential nutrients, are very low in saturated fat, and contain the all-important omega-3 essential fatty acids. A well-balanced diet that includes a variety of fish and shellfish can contribute to heart health and children's proper growth and development. So, women and young children in particular should include fish or shellfish in their diets due to the many nutritional benefits.

However, nearly all fish and shellfish contain traces of mercury. For most people, the risk from mercury by eating fish and shellfish is not a health concern. Yet, some fish and shellfish contain higher levels of mercury that may harm an unborn baby or young child's developing nervous system. The risks from mercury in fish and shellfish depend on the amount of fish and shellfish eaten and the levels of mercury in the fish and shellfish. Therefore, the FDA and the EPA are advising women who may become pregnant, pregnant women, nursing mothers and young children to avoid some types of fish and eat fish and shellfish that are lower in mercury.

By following these three recommendations for selecting and eating fish or shellfish, women and young children will receive the benefits of eating fish and shellfish and be confident that they have reduced their exposure to the harmful effects of mercury.

1. **Do not eat shark, swordfish, king mackerel or tilefish** because they contain high levels of mercury.
2. **Eat up to 12 ounces (two average meals) a week of a variety of fish** and shellfish that are lower in mercury.
   - **Five of the most commonly eaten fish that are low in mercury** are shrimp, canned light tuna, salmon, pollock and catfish.
   - **Another commonly eaten fish, albacore ("white") tuna has more mercury than canned light tuna.** So, when choosing your two meals of fish and shellfish, you may eat

up to six ounces (one average meal) of albacore tuna per week.

3. **Check local advisories about the safety of fish caught by family and friends** in your local lakes, rivers and coastal areas. If no advice is available, eat up to six ounces (one average meal) per week of fish you catch from local waters, but don't consume any other fish during that week.

Adhere to these same recommendations when feeding fish and shellfish to your young children, but serve smaller portions.

 CAUTION: Some doctors advise against eating fish during pregnancy and lactation and recommend a fish oil supplement instead. Consult your doctor.

➤ **Prevent Allergies in Baby.** Throughout your pregnancy, do not overload on any one food item. During at least the last three months of pregnancy, do not eat foods to which you're allergic, and you can avoid passing along that allergy to your baby. Even while nursing, stay away from those foods.

➤ **Healthy Sleeping Position.** If you sleep on your left side, you will improve blood flow to the placenta.

➤ **Minimize Stretch Marks.** Get out the sesame oil. Rubbing the oil on your body every day can let the skin stretch at its own pace and help prevent subsequent stretch marks.

➤ **Morning Sickness.** Morning sickness usually starts around the sixth week of pregnancy, peaks during the eighth and/or ninth weeks, and ebbs off after the thirteenth week. *Here's what you can do about it…*

● **Papaya.** Keep papaya juice (without any additives) or papaya concentrate in the re-

frigerator. A glassful of the juice or the diluted concentrate can make you feel better quickly.

● **Ginger.** A lot of testing has been done with ginger powder for motion sickness. The results have been impressive. Ginger powder is more effective than the leading medicines on the market—and with none of the side effects.

Ginger also seems to be very effective for morning sickness. The recommended dosage is two capsules of powdered gingerroot prior to breakfast. Or simply make yourself a cup of tea by boiling four quarter-sized slices of fresh gingerroot in water. Simmer for 15 to 20 minutes.

We keep gingerroot in the freezer and when we want tea, we simply grate a chunk of it to make tea. We don't strain out the little pieces. We drink it all as an after-dinner digestion aid.

 CAUTION: Ginger acts as a blood thinner, so check with your doctor before using it if you are taking a prescription blood thinner. Also, stop using ginger three days before any surgery.

● **Almonds.** If you are having waves of nausea during the day when you are out and about, eat raw almonds. One almond has more protein content than beefsteak, is rich in calcium, potassium, the B vitamins, vitamin E plus other vitamins and minerals. Don't leave home without them. Six to 10 almonds make a healthy snack and can quell the queasiness. They also make heartburn disappear in a heartbeat.

Delivery

➤ **For a Tear-Free Delivery.** To enhance elasticity and lessen the chances of tearing during childbirth, oil the opening to the vagina every day during pregnancy, using sesame oil.

➤ **Tea for Easier Delivery.** Even some obstetricians are now prescribing raspberry leaf tea. The herb has vitamins A, C, B and E, also calcium, phosphorus, iron and more good stuff that can help reduce labor pains and make for an easy, fast delivery.

Preparation also varies considerably. The recipe we like best is used in Chinese medicine. Pour one pint of just-boiled water over two rounded teaspoons of dried raspberry leaves (available at health food stores and in bulk at herb shops). Let it steep for a half hour. Strain and drink the tea throughout the day. In cold weather, you may want to warm it up a little before drinking.

Or try Squawvine. Doesn't the name of this trailing evergreen make you feel as though —once you drink the tea made from the herb— you go out on the prairie, squat and have your baby? Herbalists agree that it can help make childbirth a quick and easy experience.

Preparation and dosage of Squawvine (available at herb shops or check "Sources," page 309) is the same as raspberry leaf tea (above). In fact, you can combine the two herbs, a rounded teaspoon of each in a pint of just-boiled water, to make one extremely beneficial tea.

 CAUTION: Check with your *doctor* to see if either of these teas are right for you. They are ONLY used during the *last four to six weeks* of pregnancy.

➤ **Stamina Booster for a Much Easier Birth.** According to British childbirth writer Sheila Kitzinger, if you eat garlic and onions on a regular basis, starting in your third month, your stamina will increase, and birth will be easier. If you need a scientific reason to justify your antisocial breath, the *linoleic acids* in both garlic

156

and onion help produce *prostaglandins* that help stimulate cervical effacement and dilation.

After Baby's Birth

➤ **Getting in Shape.** Asian tradition says that, after childbirth, eating seaweed— kelp and dulse—one or two small portions a day for a month, helps get the uterus back to its original size.

➤ **Promoting Your Milk Supply.** Alfalfa tea, anise seed tea and dill seed tea (available at health food stores) are all said to help ensure milk supply in breast-feeding moms. To prepare the tea, boil a teaspoon of any of the above in water. Simmer for 15 to 20 minutes, strain and drink before each feeding.

➤ **While Nursing.** See "Mercury in Fish and Shellfish" above under "While Pregnant," page 154. Also see "Mastitis," on page 133.

PROSTATE CONDITIONS

 The prostate is a gland in the male reproductive system. Its job is to make and store a component of semen. Located in the pelvis, under the bladder and in front of the rectum, the prostate surrounds part of the urethra, the tube that empties urine from the bladder. A healthy prostate is about the size of a walnut. If the prostate grows too large, the flow of urine can be slowed or stopped.

See a health professional at the first sign of any of these prostate symptoms...

• **Difficulty urinating.**

• **Having a hard time starting or stopping the flow of urine.**

- **Needing to urinate often, especially at night.**

- **Weak flow of urine.**

- **Pain or burning during urination.**

- **Difficulty having an erection.**

- **Blood in the urine or semen.**

- **Frequent pain in the lower back, hips or upper thighs.**

Before you panic, take comfort from the National Cancer Institute (NCI). They say that although these symptoms can be symptoms of cancer, they are much more likely to be caused by noncancerous conditions. It is important to check with a doctor. The sooner the better!

You will be doing yourself a major favor by having a prostate exam, rather than walking around, fearing what you think is the worst... prostate cancer. As the NCI says, your symptoms are much more likely to be caused by noncancerous conditions.

There are two common prostate problems—*prostatitis*, an inflammation or infection of the prostate that affects men 30-something to middle-age; and *benign prostate hyperplasia* (BPH), or enlargement that usually affects men who are over age 60.

 NOTE: Since medical experts concur that coffee and alcoholic beverages are harmful to anyone who has a hint of a prostate problem, eliminate those stimulants immediately. That includes beer, which can raise *prolactin* levels in the body—elevated levels of this hormone can eventually lead to prostate enlargement.

Once you have had your prostate exam and were told that you have a noncancerous prostate condition, you may want to consider the following...

BPH and Prostatitis

The remedies included here are intended to reduce the size of the prostate and make urinating easier and more regular. If you really want to do the right thing for your prostate, you'll drink about eight glasses of water a day, cut down or eliminate red meat and other unhealthy fats in your diet and incorporate some of the suggestions listed here and in the following section under "Prostate Problem Prevention."

➤ **Think Zinc.** Eat a handful of pumpkin seeds—plain, no salt—every day. These seeds are rich in zinc that will help reduce an enlarged prostate. They also have diuretic properties to help with difficult urination.

If you want to hydrate your system, prepare pumpkin tea by crushing a handful of the fresh seeds. Place them in a one-pint jar or big mug and pour just-boiled water over them. Let it cool to room temperature. Strain and drink the pint of pumpkin seed tea throughout the day.

➤ **Saw Palmetto** can help men maintain a healthy prostate, according to several studies. The dosage for an enlarged prostate, recommended by Pamela W. Smith, MD, director of the Center for Healthy Living & Longevity (*www.cfhll.com*) and speaker on the topic of anti-aging medicine, is 160 milligrams (mg) of saw palmetto twice daily. Dr. Smith also recommends that you speak to your doctor before taking this herb, and ask if it's something you should be doing, given your medical history, and if the dosage is right for you.

➤ **Stinging Nettle.** According to the University of Maryland Medical Center (at *www. umm.edu*) the stinging nettle root is used widely in Europe to treat BPH. Studies in people suggest that stinging nettle, in combination with other herbs (especially saw palmetto), may be effective at relieving symptoms such as reduced urinary flow, incomplete emptying of the bladder, post-urination dripping and the constant urge to urinate. Laboratory studies have shown stinging nettle to be comparable to finasteride (a medication commonly prescribed for BPH) in slowing the growth of certain prostate cells. However, unlike finasteride, the herb does not decrease prostate size.

German medical herbalists recommend two to three teaspoons of stinging nettle extract a day for the treatment of BPH.

➤ **Watermelon** is rich in *lycopene*. Eat the meat of the melon and use the seeds as the Amish do. Place one-eighth of a cup of seeds in a one-pint jar and pour just-boiled water over them. When the tea cools, strain and drink it throughout the day. Do this for 10 days.

Prostate Problem Prevention

➤ **An Annual Exam.** We mentioned this above, but it's worth mentioning again—schedule an annual prostate exam. If there's a problem, catch it early and clear it up before it gets worse.

➤ **Vitamin A.** There seems to be a strong statistical association between low vitamin A status and prostate cancer. Eat foods rich in beta carotene (the precursor to vitamin A) such as broccoli, carrots, cauliflower, Swiss chard, endive, kale, collard greens, mustard greens, dandelion greens, spinach, tomatoes, loose leaf lettuce, cod liver oil, winter squash, sweet potatoes, watercress, turnip greens, beet greens, cantaloupe, peaches, apricots, prunes, cherries and papayas.

 CAUTION: Vitamin A supplements can be toxic. They should be taken only under the supervision of a health professional.

➤ **Pygeum Africanum Extract** comes in capsules of 50 mg each and is available at most health food and vitamin shops. Take two or three a day to help prevent prostate trouble—or to help treat the onset of a prostate problem.

➤ **Cukes.** It is said that cucumbers contain beneficial hormones. Nourish the prostate gland by eating a large cucumber daily.

➤ **Oat Straw.** Prepare the oat straw tea by adding a teaspoon of the dried herb (available at health food stores) to a cup of just-boiled water. Let it steep for 10 minutes. Strain and drink it daily.

➤ **Tomatoes.** At least two servings per week of tomatoes and tomato products—salsa, sauce, tomato juice—contain enough of the antioxidant compound *lycopene* to help decrease risk of prostate cancer by half. Pink grapefruit, guava and watermelon also contain lycopene.

See "BPH and Prostatitis" above for preparing watermelon tea. Also see the "It Does a Body Good" chapter, page 260, for the all-important omega-3 information.

Prostate Resources

If you are diagnosed with prostate cancer, your best line of defense is knowledge of your options. Talk to the men in your circle of family and friends who have gone through this. Ask for their input.

Take responsibility for learning as much as you can. *The following Web pages are loaded with valuable insights...*

• **The National Cancer Institute (NCI) prostate cancer home page** provides resources concerning prevention, screening, treatment, clinical trials and supportive care. This page can be found on the Internet at *www.cancer. gov/cancertopics/types/prostate.*

• **Prostate Cancer Treatment (PDQ)** includes information about prostate cancer treatment. This summary of information from the NCI's comprehensive cancer information database is available at *www.cancer.gov/cancertop ics/pdq/treatment/prostate/patient.*

• *Treatment Choices for Men with Early-Stage Prostate Cancer* describes many treatment choices available to men diagnosed with early-stage prostate cancer and examines the pros and cons of every treatment. This NCI booklet is available from *www.cancer.gov/publica tions/patient-education/understanding-prostate-cancer-treatment.*

AFFIRMATION

Repeat this affirmation nine times a day—starting first thing in the morning, every time you look at your watch, and last thing at night...

I richly deserve all the good things in life—happiness, love and the best of health.

A Word from the Wise...

Protect the Prostate

Lowering cholesterol may protect the prostate as well as the heart.

Recent finding: Long-term statin use—for more than five years—has been shown to help prevent prostate cancer.

Self-defense: Reduce cholesterol by eating more fruits and vegetables, losing weight and taking medication if necessary.

J. Brantley Thrasher, MD, FACS, professor and William L. Valk Chair, department of urology, University of Kansas Medical Center, Kansas City.

RINGWORM

Ringworm is not always ring-shaped and it isn't caused by worms. It is a common fungal infection that can affect the skin, groin, hands or beard. Most common is ringworm of the scalp. It may look like round, bald patches. As the infection spreads outward, the inside of the circle seems to clear up, making it look like a ring. Yes, that's why the name of the condition has a *ring* to it.

Ringworm doesn't always produce a ring pattern. It can look like dandruff or black-dotted stubble. Severe cases have swollen, red, crusty and painful areas with blister-like bumps.

A doctor can diagnose the condition by examining a hair or skin sample under a microscope to check for the ringworm fungus.

Be aware that ringworm is very contagious, which is a good reason you don't want to use anyone else's comb, brush or towel. You can also get ringworm by petting infected dogs and cats. Once you have ringworm, you have to take care not to scratch the sore, scaly area. You can easily spread the parasite to other parts of your body.

Here are some remedies that can help clear up the condition...

➤ **This Makes Cents.** Put a copper penny in vinegar and leave it there until it turns green. Then take the wet penny and rub it on the ringworm. The combination of the vinegar and greened copper is said to make it better. Repeat the procedure at least three times a day.

➤ **Garlic and Oil.** Finely mince two cloves of garlic and mix them together with the oil from three punctured vitamin E (400 international units [IU]) softgels. Spread the mixture on the infected area three times a day to stop the itching and start the healing.

CAUTION: Garlic could be irritating to the skin. Avoid putting garlic on areas where there are cuts.

➤ **Wasabi Paste.** Yes, Japanese horseradish has been known to clear up ringworm. Buy a tube of the prepared paste (available in Asian or gourmet food stores) and rub it on the affected area in the morning and before going to bed. After a few days of this routine, you may be completely ringworm free.

AFFIRMATION

Repeat this affirmation at least 10 times, first thing in the morning, last thing at night, and each time you blame yourself or others for something...

I forgive myself and I forgive others. There's great harmony in my life now.

SCIATICA

 Sciatica is a swelling of, or injury to, the sciatic nerve (or a swelling/injury of the surrounding muscles), causing pain, soreness or tingling. The deep and severe pain can be as extensive as the nerve, which starts at the base of the spine and goes down the buttock and legs to the feet.

Sometimes sciatic pain may be caused by a misalignment in the body. If that's the case, professional help, such as an acupuncturist or Alexander Technique lessons would be needed to properly align your body.

Bed rest and heat in the form of hot baths and heating pads are usually recommended for sciatica, along with warmed castor oil or olive oil packs and massages.

We have additional suggestions for you to try after you first check with your health professional...

➤ **Hops to It.** A poultice of hops can bring fast relief for sciatic pain sufferers. Yes, the same hops used for making beer. In fact, the Spanish name for hops is, *flores de cerveza*, which means "flowers of beer." Be warned, it doesn't smell like flowers and it doesn't smell like beer. Actually, the smell is rather unpleasant. *But if it relieves the pain...*

The poultice you're going to make is to be placed directly on the sore area, so you're going to have to use your judgment as to how much of the herb to use, depending on the extent of your painful area. You might start by steeping three tablespoons of hops in a cup of just-boiled water. After 10 minutes, strain off the liquid, but don't throw it out. Then put the moist hot hops in cheesecloth, wrapping it around to form a poultice. Put it on the painful area and keep it there until it cools off. When that happens, heat up the hops water and pour it over the poultice, remoistening and reheating it. Once again apply the poultice while it's nice and hot—as hot as you can take it without burning your skin. Keep doing this until you feel relief.

➤ **Massage Mixture.** Grate a chunk of gingerroot (it's easier to grate if you keep it in the freezer), or put it through a food processor. Put the pulp in a piece of cheesecloth or fine strainer and squeeze out the juice into a container. Mix an equal amount of sesame oil with the ginger juice, then massage the mixture on the painful areas. There may be a burning sensation from the ginger. If you feel it's too strong, simply add more sesame oil. If it seems to bring relief, repeat the process a few hours later.

➤ **Vitamin E.** Take 400 international units (IU) of vitamin E daily. It has been quite effective for so many people with sciatica. You should notice results within a couple of weeks.

 CAUTION: Due to the possible interactions between vitamin E and various drugs and supplements, as well as other safety considerations, be sure to consult your doctor before taking vitamin E.

➤ **Celery Tea.** Drink a cup of celery tea before each meal and at bedtime. Not only has it been known to relieve pain but, for some people, it actually clears up the condition. Dried celery is available at health food stores. Use a heaping teaspoon in a cup of just-boiled water and let it steep for 10 minutes. Strain and drink.

➤ **Acupressure.** Vigorously massage the little tuft at the base of your pinky, on the same side as the sciatic pain. Keep at it for at least six minutes. It can ease the pain considerably.

We've Got Your Back!

If you carry a thick wallet in your pants pocket, it may be pressing on your sciatic nerve when you sit, and causing back pain. If that's the case, look into the Back Saver Wallet. It is 50% to 60% smaller than a regular wallet, but will hold all your essentials and always folds flat.

The Back Saver Wallet is made from high-quality leather, making it extremely strong and durable.

More information: Visit *www.core products.com* or call 877-249-1251. Also, see page 13.

➤ **Aromatherapy.** Jasmine, considered the symbol of sensuality, is also known to soothe sciatic pain. Mix a half-teaspoon of jasmine oil with two teaspoons of liquid lecithin (both available at health food stores) and massage the painful area. The lecithin increases absorption into the skin.

AFFIRMATION

Repeat this affirmation at least 15 times, before and after each meal and during any kind of treatment—drinking celery tea, massaging the base of the pinky, using a hops poultice, whatever...

I walk through life with joy and ease, safely doing whatever I please.

SEXUALITY

The most sexually active people in the world are supposedly the Mangaians of Polynesia. (Now *there's* a place to open up a motel.) It has been reported that the average 18-year-old couple makes love three times a night, every night. About 10 years later, at age 28, their sex life dwindles down to two times a night, every night. The report stopped there. The reporter was either too busy to do a follow-up, or just too tired.

In any case, we don't have to worry about the Mangaians. And we may not have to worry about you, once you check out some of these suggestions...

Better Sex

➤ **The Best Time for Sex—Day vs. Night.** Research says that sunlight enhances one's sex drive. It has to do with the arousal of the pituitary gland, which regulates the ovaries and testes. And that happens during the brightest part of the day. The lack of daylight is a signal for the brain's pineal gland to produce *melatonin*, a substance that inhibits ovulation, sperm production and hormones that are responsible for sexual desire.

➤ **The Best Months for Sex.** Studies show a direct correlation between men's highest levels of testosterone—the hormone that regulates their sex drive—and the months of optimum sunlight, which are in summer and early fall. When you're planning your vacation, keep in mind the fact that July is the month with the longest and sunniest days of the year. But don't travel to South America in July. It's winter there then and testosterone levels in men are lowest in the winter months.

➤ **Aromatherapy for Sexual Arousal.** Fill the air with the essence of rose, vanilla, jasmine, ginger, pine or ylang-ylang and it will fill your heart with lust. For industrial strength stimulation, dab a drop of any one of the oils right under your nose. It works for both men and women.

Stay away from lavender. It will make you feel like going to bed…for a good night's sleep.

➤ **Gem Therapy for Sexual Energy.** The stone with the most sexual energy is the ruby. You don't have to have an expensive faceted gem. There are rough rubies that are fairly affordable and there are raw ruby crystals that are reasonably priced.

If rubies don't turn you on, you might turn to the orange carnelian with a slight hint of red, also known for its sexual energy.

A Word from the Wise…

Ask for What You Want in Bed

Sexual satisfaction eludes many women—but you don't have to settle for so-so sex.

Solution: Tell your partner what pleases you. *Here's how…*

➤ **Figure Out What Turns You On.** If you are not sure what feels good, spend private time pleasuring yourself…when you and your partner have sex, pay attention to what excites you.

For inspiration: Read *Pleasure* by Hilda Hutcherson, MD (Perigee).

➤ **Recognize That Your Partner Isn't a Mind Reader.** Many women think, "If he loved me, he'd know how to please me"—but most men need to be taught. To avoid hurt feelings, explain, "As my body has changed, so have my desires. Let's experiment to see what feels best now."

➤ **Don't Say *Don't*—Say *Do*.** If I say, "Don't think of a pink elephant," what's the first thing you think of? A pink elephant. Only after-

ward does the brain compute the "don't." The same thing happens when you tell your partner, "Don't squeeze my breasts"—which may lead him to inadvertently keep doing the unwanted behavior.

Better: "It excites me when you kiss my breasts."

➤ **Show and Tell.** Put your hand over his, and show him how to stimulate you. Describe in detail what you want—"Please run your fingers slowly up my thigh"—then respond with enthusiasm.

Judy Kuriansky, PhD, a clinical psychologist and sex therapist on the adjunct faculty of Columbia University Teachers College in New York City. She is author of five books, including *The Complete Idiot's Guide to a Healthy Relationship* (Alpha). Her Web site is *www.drjudy.com.*

For Sexual Stamina and Vitality

➤ **Bee Pollen.** To extol the benefits of bee pollen, the title of Noel Johnson's book says it all: *A Dud at 70…a Stud at 80!* (Plains Corp.).

 CAUTION: Some people are allergic to bee pollen. Start very slowly—with a couple of granules the first day or two. Then if you have no allergic reaction, work your way up gradually until you take one teaspoon or more a day—up to one tablespoon depending on how you feel. Asthmatics should NOT use bee pollen.

➤ **Sweet Treat.** Halvah, candy from the Middle East, dates back to when Cleopatra was dating. It is said to be especially effective for women.

You can buy halvah, but the commercial product does not have the potency of halvah made by loving hands at home.

It's easy to prepare. Grind a cup of sesame seeds. Mix in raw honey until it's the consistency of firm dough. Then break off chunks and roll them into bite-sized pieces and enjoy.

Sesame seeds and raw honey are a powerful combination of magnesium, calcium, potassium, lecithin, phosphorus, bee pollen, aspartic acid and more. Partake of the confection and you'll want to partake of the affection.

Aphrodisiacs

The most effective aphrodisiac is your own passion. The second most effective aphrodisiac is said to be ground rhinoceros horn… or is it a horny rhinoceros on the ground?— whatever. *There's talk that these are the third best aphrodisiacs…*

➤ **Damiana Leaf** (botanical name is *turnera aphrodisiaca*, so that should tell you something). Use damiana extract (available at health food stores) five to eight drops daily.

➤ **Seaweed**—daily portions of dulse or kelp can help.

➤ **Legumes**—most common and popular are peas, beans, lentils, alfalfa and peanuts. Word has it that St. Jerome did not allow nuns to eat beans for fear they would cause the nuns to get into bad habits.

➤ **Hot-Hot-Hot Spices.**

➤ **The Allium Family**—garlic, onion, scallion, shallots, chives. (They may be effective aphrodisiacs, but keep a breath freshener handy.)

 CAUTION: Having garlic on an empty stomach can cause nausea. Be sure to have some food in your stomach before eating garlic or taking capsules. And, be cautious with garlic if you have gastritis.

➤ **Triple A**—asparagus, arugula, artichokes.

➤ **Fruit**—bananas, fresh figs, cherries, peaches.

➤ **Sunflower Seeds**—raw, shelled.

➤ **Foods Rich in B Vitamins**—green leafy vegetables, fish, wheat germ, almonds and peanut butter—the kind you get in health food stores without additives or preservatives.

➤ **Men Who Sweat a Lot** during sex ooze testosterone which is a biological turn-on for women.

Passion Promoters Just for Women

➤ **Dong Quai.** What ginseng does for men, dong quai is said to do for women. This Chinese root comes in several forms including tablets, capsules and extracts—all with recommended daily dosage on the labels. Check out your selection and the dosage with your health professional to make sure it's appropriate for you.

 CAUTION: Dong quai may increase sensitivity to ultraviolet rays. People taking dong quai should avoid prolonged exposure to the sun. Also, for women who are still menstruating, dong quai can cause heavier menstrual flow. If you are on medication, check with your doctor or pharmacist about possible negative interactions before taking dong quai.

➤ **This Spud's for You.** A daily dose of potato juice can get the ol' juices going. Take a medium-sized potato, scrub it clean and grate it or feed it into a food processor. Place the pulp on cheesecloth or in a fine strainer, squeeze out the juice, then bottoms up.

 NOTE: Please do not expect an "instant thaw." It may take a while (or a new mate) for results.

Repeat this affirmation every time you look in the mirror...

I accept my sexuality as part of my healthy, functioning mind and body. I allow myself to experience getting and giving physical pleasure and joy.

Passion Promoters for Men Only

It's important to determine whether the impotence you're experiencing is physical (perhaps a side effect of medication you're taking, or atherosclerosis, or a high-fat diet). There are many tests a doctor can give you to help pinpoint a physical cause. Then again, your impotence may be psychological (bedroom boredom or the fear of failure). An estimated 90% of all cases are psychological and temporary.

Physical or psychological, you may want to try the following suggestions with your doctor's supervision...

➤ **Ginseng** comes in many varieties—tablets, capsules, powder, extract and the fresh whole root. Some herbalists think that eating a small slice of the whole root every day is the most beneficial way to take ginseng. Then again, some herbalists opt for the herb in powder form. Go to a health food store or herb shop and see what's available. Read labels. Ask knowledgeable store personnel for their input. When you know what you want, check out your selection and the dosage with your health professional to make sure it's appropriate for you.

It probably took a while for your problem to manifest itself; it may take a while for you to get results. Be consistent and patient and ask that your partner be patient, too.

➤ **True Unicorn** is an herb in the lily family. The roots of the plant are used for digestion, nervous stomach, gas, menstrual problems and fertility boosts. It's also been known to help reverse impotency. Take five to eight drops in water every day.

➤ **Oat Straw Tea** (available at health food stores) can be prepared by steeping two teaspoons of the herb in one cup of just-boiled water. After five minutes, strain, drink a cup for breakfast and a cup after dinner, daily.

➤ **Pumpkin Seeds**—a handful of raw and unsalted—should be added to your daily diet. While you're at it, also eat raw or roasted sesame seeds—two tablespoons a day. Wash it down with sarsaparilla tea (available at health food stores). The seeds and the tea are said to be sexual stimulants and may also help prevent prostate problems.

➤ **Impotence Prevention.** Some Japanese practitioners advise their male patients to squeeze their testicles on a daily basis, once for each year of their life. A friend in Florida, J. Walter Allen, had just celebrated his 97th birthday. When we told him about this preventive treatment, he said, "There goes my day."

If you have impotence, repeat this affirmation every time you look in the mirror, and again, last thing at night...

I accept my sexuality as part of my healthy, functioning mind and body. I allow myself to experience complete fulfillment, getting and giving pleasure and joy.

Infertility

Throughout an average woman's reproductive years, she has about 400 to 500 eggs that can be fertilized. During one average man's ejaculation, his testes manufacture about 400 million sperm cells. *If all of this is inconceivable, these suggestions may help...*

Fertility Made Easier for Men and Women

➤ **Stop Smoking!** Studies show that cigarette smoking can affect men's fertility by lowering the sperm count and causing the sperm to have less motility. Women smokers may be less fertile because of altered hormone levels. Also, spontaneous miscarriages occur much more often in smokers than in nonsmokers.

➤ **Relax.** Stress in men can promote muscle spasms in the sperm ducts that can interfere with the transmission of semen. Stress in women can cause an enlarged uterus, can prevent ovulation and can cause abnormal cervical secretions that immobilize sperm.

➤ **Eat Seaweed.** Have a portion every day—dulse, kelp, wakame, nori or any of the others. It is especially nourishing for the reproductive systems of both men and women. (Look at the population of the countries where seaweed is a formative industry and eaten regularly—China and Japan. I rest my case.)

➤ **No-Nos!** Eliminate green peas and yams from your diet. They contain estrogenic chemicals that are known to be antifertility agents.

➤ **Zero PFCs.** *Perfluorinated chemicals* (PFCs) are found in many products including food packaging and nonstain carpets. PFCs are also used to manufacture nonstick cookware. A recent study from the University of California, Los Angeles, showed that women with the highest levels of PFCs took twice as long to become pregnant as women with lower levels of the chemicals.

The advice from experts is to hold on to your nonstick pans, but before heating, add oil or butter to the pan, and never leave it on the fire without anything in it. Also, don't use scratched pans that have a nonstick coating. Plus, eat a diet that includes lots of vegetables and not much meat. A study showed that levels of one kind of PFC were highest in women with a meat-heavy and vegetable-light diet.

Feng Shui

Feng shui (pronounced "fung shway") is a Chinese practice, at least 5,000 years old, believed to utilize the laws of both Heaven (astronomy) and Earth (geography). The goal is to balance your environment's energy flow known as Qi or chi (pronounced "chee") so that you may live in harmony with your surroundings and enjoy good health, good luck and well being.

To increase your fertility, you may want to try the following feng shui tips, in addition to whatever else you may be doing, including appropriate medical care.

➤ **Your Bed.** First, de-clutter the area under your bed. Take out all of the shoe bags, or whatever else you have tucked away out of sight. Then, unless you're obsessively, compulsively clean, this feng shui practice should be easy to follow. For the whole period of time you are trying to conceive, and even when you are pregnant, do not sweep, vacuum, dust or clean the space under and around your bed. The plan is to allow the energy to circulate under and around your bed, especially while you are sleeping. Got that? No stuff under the bed, and forget about the dust bunnies.

➤ **Your Home Entrance.** Make sure that nothing, we mean not a thing, is blocking your entranceway—in and around your front door. If an umbrella stand is on the side of the door and an umbrella's handle is leaning over, move it! If a plant's leaves extend to the door, move the plant. Look outside and check for anything blocking the front door. To help increase your fertility, you want to have a clear flow of energy to and through the door leading to your home.

➤ **Poison Arrows.** Look around for any "poison arrows"—sharp edged corners in your home, most likely your furnishings. If you can't get rid of those poison arrows, conceal them with plants, or in some other creative way, so that they won't disturb the power of the atmosphere's good energy.

➤ **Fertility Symbols.** Stack the deck by keeping fertility symbols in your bedroom. The elephant is a popular fertility symbol, as is the rabbit. It's easy to find figurines of those animals.

Kwan Yin is the Goddess of Compassion, known to increase fertility. Keep a statue of her in your bedroom. (Any Chinese gift shop will have these statues, or for a major selection, go to Google and type in "Kwan Yin statues.") You'll also want to have her around once the baby arrives because Kwan Yin guards the souls of children.

Throw in a rose quartz crystal for good luck. (See "Sources," page 311, for a gem outlet.)

See page 290 in "Home Health Hints" for more information on feng shui.

Fertility Helpers for Women

➤ **Smart Lubricant.** If you need to use a lubricant for intercourse, use organic egg white during the days you are fertile. Commercial lubricants may interfere with the sperm's survival and mobility. Since the white of an egg is protein, and the sperm is mostly protein, the egg white will not hinder the sperm's potential. Use room-temperature egg white. It can be applied to the penis or in the vagina.

 CAUTION: The egg whites in this remedy could contain Salmonella.

➤ **Mighty Mineral.** Take dolomite (it's available at health food stores) daily. This combination of calcium and magnesium can promote pregnancy. Follow the dosage on the label.

➤ **No Caffeine.** Unlike the daddy-to-be, the mommy-to-be should stay away from coffee or anything with caffeine, including cola, tea, chocolate, cocoa and aspirin. According to a study, one cup of coffee per day may reduce fertility by 27%.

Researchers in Maryland say that alcohol consumption can reduce a woman's chance of conceiving by more than 50%.

➤ **Pillow Trick.** Right after having intercourse, place a pillow under your bottom and stay that way for a half hour. Let gravity help move the could-be-kiddies along.

Sperm Boosters for Men

➤ **Take Royal Jelly**—up to 1,000 milligrams (mg) a day—to increase your sperm count and make them more aggressive. Most health food stores carry products from the bee, or check "Sources," page 310, for telephone and Internet ordering.

 CAUTION: If you have a suspected sensitivity to bee products, forget this and go on to another remedy.

➤ **Eat Raw Carrots.** They're rich in zinc, which is known to increase the sperm count. Nondomesticated rabbits eat few, if any, carrots and they don't reproduce nearly as frequently as the domesticated carrot-eating rabbits.

➤ **Keep Cool Where It Counts.** High body temperatures have been shown to decrease production of sperm. What that means in practical terms is, stay out of the hot tub or sauna. Opt for vacations in the shade and air-conditioned bedrooms. Since briefs hold the testicles closer to the body, raising the temperature in there, wear boxer shorts.

According to the results of a recent study from the State University of New York, the heat generated when using a laptop on one's lap may significantly elevate the temperature of the scrotum, potentially causing a drop in one's sperm count. Use a desktop!

➤ **A Cold Shower?** A half hour before intercourse, take a cold (yes, cold) shower for five minutes. The cold water might improve sperm motility by stimulating blood flow. Right after the cold shower, warm up with a strong cup of coffee. A cup of java is said to give a boost to the little swimmers.

➤ **Sperm Level Fact.** According to a report in *Fertility and Sterility*, a journal that supports research in the field of reproductive medicine, the frequency of a man's ejaculation influences his sperm count. Sorry to say that the fewer times a man makes love, the higher sperm count rises.

According to researchers, compared with one ejaculation per week, two ejaculations per week caused sperm levels to fall 29%; three ejaculations and the levels fell 41%. Now that you know this, it's up to you and your mate to pace yourselves.

➤ **Orgasm Helps.** Just so you know, the bigger the woman's orgasm the better her chances are of getting pregnant. During an orgasm, contraction of the woman's pelvic muscles help the sperm move up the vaginal canal and fertilize the egg.

168

SHINGLES (HERPES ZOSTER)

The same virus that produces chicken pox in children causes shingles in adults. The infected and inflamed nerve centers are usually accompanied by patches of blisters and intense pain, mostly affecting the chest, abdomen and/or face.

The following suggestions can bring instant relief from pain and itching, and may even clear up the condition completely...

➤ **Apitherapy.** The more we research the benefits of apitherapy—treatment using honeybee products—the more impressed we are with results.

To rid you of the pain of shingles and to help heal these lesions, smear bee propolis in liquid form on the sore area a few times throughout the day. Use a soft pastry brush or a makeup brush. Liquid propolis is available at some health food stores and through the bee products distributor in "Sources," page 310.

Another bee product that is extremely healing is raw honey. Spend a few pennies extra if you have to, and you *will* have to, to get the raw stuff. Just like with the liquid bee propolis, spread the honey on the sore areas a few times throughout the day, and expect pain to disappear and lesions to start healing.

 CAUTION: If you have a suspected sensitivity to bee products, forget this and go on to another remedy.

➤ **Ace It.** If you have shingles on your chest, gently bind the affected area with an Ace bandage, particularly before going to bed.

The small amount of pressure from the bandage can relieve the pain without hindering your breathing.

➤ **Leek.** If you have a juicer or a food processor, prepare fresh leek juice and apply it directly to the blistered areas for immediate relief of the itching.

 CAUTION: Do NOT put leek juice on open lesions, as it could burn or irritate skin tissue.

➤ **Elderflower Tea.** Available at most health food stores, prepare elderflower tea by adding a teaspoon of the dried herb to a cup of just-boiled water. Cover the cup and let it steep for four to six minutes, then strain and drink. Herbalist Ann Warren-Davis says, "Drink it three or four times a day. I've known it to clear up shingles in a day or two."

➤ **Vitamin E Oil.** Throughout the day, puncture vitamin E capsules and squeeze out the oil on the blisters. It stops the itching and, in some case, brings about a complete cure.

➤ **Aloe Vera.** Shingles is one of many problems that can be helped by the gel of the aloe vera plant. When using the plant, start with the bottom leaves first; they're the oldest. Either peel away the top layer of the leaf's skin and spread the gel on your skin, or cut off a piece of leaf and squeeze out the gel. For many, aloe means instant relief.

AFFIRMATION

Repeat this affirmation starting first thing in the morning, right after applying anything to the sore lesions and last thing at night…

I am relaxed and surrounded by positive energy as my body heals itself.

SINUS CONGESTION

Sinus conditions could be caused by weather changes, by air conditioning, an overheated room, allergies, gosh—almost anything, including dust that collects in one's mustache. It's up to you to discover your sinus triggers. It's up to us to give you suggestions that may help alleviate sinus symptoms.

➤ **Honeycomb.** During a sinus attack, chew a one-inch square of honeycomb (available at most health food stores). After you swallow the honey, continue chewing the waxy gum for about 10 minutes. It can help stop the sneezing, clear up the congestion and give you a spurt of energy, too.

 CAUTION: If you have a suspected sensitivity to bee products. do NOT chew on honeycomb. Also, asthmatics should NOT have honeycomb.

➤ **Fenugreek Seed Tea.** One old folk remedy for dissolving mucus is fenugreek seed tea (available at health food stores). When your sinuses need to be drained, prepare the tea by boiling one teaspoon of fenugreek seed in water. Simmer 15 to 20 minutes, then strain.

➤ **Ginkgo Leaves.** In Asia, the leaves of the ginkgo biloba tree have been used as medicine for more than 2,800 years. Now that the hearty ginkgo trees are popular in America, we are discovering the medicinal value of their beautiful fanlike leaves. They can help relieve sinus congestion. Crush a handful of the leaves, boil them and carefully inhale the vapor. If you don't have the fresh leaves, ginkgo can be purchased in capsule form. Check with your doctor before taking ginkgo capsules.

➤ **Ice Is Nice.** According to Dr. Nicholas Murray from the University of Melbourne in Australia, an ice pack applied to the bridge of the nose and across the cheekbones shrinks inflamed tissues.

➤ **"Brace-Yourself" Cocktail.** In a pot, combine one cup of tomato juice, one teaspoon of finely chopped fresh garlic, one-quarter to one-half teaspoon of cayenne pepper (depending on your hot-spice tolerance) and one teaspoon of lemon juice. Heat the mixture until it's warm. Pour into a 10-ounce glass and brace yourself—then drink it. Be careful with garlic and cayenne if you have stomach issues.

➤ **A Salt Water (Saline) Irrigation.** Inhaling salt water is the classic folk remedy for sinus problems. It's been around for hundreds of years simply because it works. Thanks to the Ayurvedic/yoga medical tradition, we have the Neti pot. It's an interesting-shaped ceramic pot that looks like if you rub it, a genie will appear. An easier, more modern version of the self-irrigating saline system is Nasaline. Both the Neti pot and Nasaline can be found at pharmacies and health food stores, and come with instructions. Research affirms that these nasal irrigation practices are an effective way to alleviate sinus symptoms—and may reduce the need for nasal sprays and antibiotics.

If you don't have any of the store-bought irrigation systems, here's a do-it-yourself version of it...

First, dissolve one-quarter teaspoon of salt (some people prefer to use sea salt) in one cup of warm spring or distilled water. (Tap water may include contaminants, such as chlorine, that can further aggravate your sinus condition.)

The object of this is to inhale the salt water solution through your nostrils—one side at a time—have it go down toward your throat, and spit it out of your mouth rather than swallow it. This is not pleasant at first, but you get used it.

You can pour the salt water into your cupped hand, close one nostril, and inhale it through the open nostril, or you can use a medicine dropper or a small cup with a spout designed especially for this purpose and available at health food stores. In any case, you have to tip your head back and then spit the solution out of your mouth. After you've inhaled through both nostrils a few times, gently blow your nose.

You may cough the first few times you do it, but it should get a lot easier with practice. You may even get to the point where you look forward to doing it. For congestion and inflamed tissues, do it once or twice a day.

If you have a sinus infection, use this salt water treatment two to four times a day to speed up the healing.

 CAUTION: Nasal cleansing may be irritating for some people. If you experience any irritation, discontinue it immediately.

➤ **Scallions.** If you can hardly breathe and can hardly stand it anymore and are willing to try this remedy, your stuffed-nose misery level is probably at an all-time high, and you deserve for it to work.

You'll need two scallions (also called green or spring onions). Once you read the rest of this remedy, you'll know the size scallions to buy. Cut off most of the green fronds, leaving an inch or two, and cut the roots off the white bulb. Gently put each bulb in each nostril...just a little way in. (Now you know why the size of the bulb is important.) Within a minute or two, your nose will start to run. Good. Remove the scallions, blow your nose and enjoy breathing again.

➤ **Reflexology.** Use the inside top half of your thumb, or a teaspoon to apply pressure on the roof of your mouth. This reflexology remedy can help make your headache disappear as it breaks up congestion.

➤ **Acupressure for All Sinus Symptoms.** Vigorously massage the back of your three smallest toes at their base. Within minutes, you should feel the sinus passages open. Once that happens, end the treatment by massaging the base of the big toes for two or three minutes.

AFFIRMATION

Repeat this affirmation starting first thing in the morning, every time you pick up a tissue, and last thing at night…

I breathe easy knowing I am surrounded by positive energy, healing feelings, and people who love me.

SKIN CARE

No need to spend hundreds of dollars on an expensive skin care regimen. Check out these all-natural treatments that are just as effective, but cost much less…

Facials

Below are facials that deep clean, nourish, tone and tighten the skin, as well as stimulate circulation. Go through the types, find the one that most appeals to you—considering your skin type—and, with a clean face and neck, go to it!

➤ **Normal Skin Facial.**

• **When honeydews are in season, mash the meat** of the melon and smear it on your face and neck. After 20 minutes, rinse with cool water and pat dry.

• **Take two tablespoons of light cream or plain yogurt,** combine with one teaspoon of raw honey. Smear it on your face using an upward and outward motion. After 15 minutes, wash it off with tepid water and pat dry.

➤ **Sensitive Skin Facial.** Mix one tablespoon of sour cream with one tablespoon of wheat germ flour until it has a creamy consistency. Spread it on your face and neck and relax with it on for 20 minutes. Then rinse off with tepid water and pat dry. Do this at least once a week.

➤ **Dry Skin Facial.** Actress and beauty authority Arlene Dahl shared her favorite facial mask with us.

Beat two egg yolks and apply them to your clean face, forehead and neck, carefully avoiding the sensitive area around your eyes. Leave it on for 20 minutes as you relax on a slant board with your feet about 30 degrees higher than your head. If you don't have a slant board, improvise. Lie on your bed with pillows under your feet. Do not talk while you are relaxing—the egg yolk can crack on your face and you don't want that to happen.

At the end of 20 minutes, gently wash your face with lukewarm water and pat it dry. You should feel just great with your skin tightened and toned. Do this at least once a week.

We met Arlene Dahl years ago at a TV studio. The lights were as bright as could be and we stood right next to her. Not only was Ms. Dahl gracious and lovely, this senior citizen was truly beautiful and had flawless skin. I don't know about you, but we're getting out the egg yolks.

➤ **Oily Skin Facial.** Use the same procedure as for dry skin (above), but use egg whites instead of yolks.

Incidentally, Arlene Dahl told us that both of these facials were used by Cleopatra. Like most women at different stages of their lives, Cleo's skin must have changed from oily to dry.

More Skin Care

➤ **Dead Skin Sloughers.**

• **Abrasive.** Once per week, slough off dead skin particles with an abrasive paste. Take a quarter cup of stone-ground cornmeal and mix in enough water to make a thick paste. Using an upward and outward motion, gently scrub your face (or any area that needs to be sloughed) with the cornmeal. Then wash it off with tepid water and wipe dry with that same upward and outward motion.

• **Enzymes.** Dip cotton pads in fresh pineapple juice and put them on your face. Leave them on for 15 minutes, then rinse your face with tepid water. For this to be an extremely effective dead skin slougher, you must use fresh pineapple juice only because of its enzymes.

• **Makeup cleanser.** Sesame oil or almond oil on a cotton ball will do a thorough job of taking off makeup, including waterproof mascara.

➤ **Moisturizers.** Moisturizers will not nourish the skin with moisture—they cover the skin with a thin film that holds in the skin's moisture. Use a moisturizer after cleansing. *Try the all-natural ones below...*

• **Oil.** Using a plant mister, spray your face thoroughly with spring water or distilled water. Then pat on a thin layer of sunflower or sesame oil. The oil should prevent the water from quickly disappearing and your hungry dry skin will soak up moisture for hours. You may want to add a few drops of light perfume to the oil.

• **Grapes.** The late beauty expert Paul Neinast of the Neinast Salon in Dallas would often recommend green Thompson seedless grapes as a moisturizer. Cut each grape in half and gently crush it on your face and neck. Be sure to let the grape juice get at the corners of your mouth and around your eyes. According to Paul, it's great for getting rid of crow's feet and the tiny cracks around the edges of the mouth.

Leave it on for about 20 minutes and then wash it off with tepid water and pat dry.

➤ **Pore-Closer and Skin Tightener.** In keeping with the grapes in the remedy above, Paul Neinast also recommended using grapes in the form of champagne. Give yourself a champagne skin splash—like a man splashes on an after-shave lotion—to close pores and tighten loose, slightly sagging skin, especially beneath the eyes and around the throat.

➤ **Dry and Aging Skin Refresher.** Peel a peach, remove the pit, then mash the peach meat. Apply it to your freshly washed face and neck. (It's good for hands, too.) Leave it on for 20 minutes, then rinse with cool water. It should restore the acid balance and regenerate tissue of dry, aging skin.

➤ **Good Skin—Good News.** Antioxidants called *flavonols* can smooth the skin and decrease its sensitivity to the sun. Here's where the good news comes in. Dark chocolate, with at least 70% cocoa content, has these all-important flavonols that help the blood flow to your skin, making your skin look more hydrated. If you plan to eat dark chocolate, limit yourself to one or two ounces a day, and be sure the chocolate has at least 70% cocoa content.

➤ **Complexion Perfection.** Think zinc! Eat foods rich in zinc—whole grains, sunflower seeds, pumpkin seeds (get them shelled and raw at health food stores), beans, spinach, mushrooms, brewer's yeast and wheat germ. Of course you can supplement your diet with zinc tablets, but do so with the guidance of a health professional. Prolonged use of zinc can cause a copper deficiency.

➤ **Pimple Prevention...Sorta.** The second you feel or notice a pimple forming, which could be up to a month before it actually forms, put an ice cube on it and keep it there for three to five minutes. Do this a few times throughout the day, until there's no trace of the pimple.

➤ **Blemish Cleanser.** Add two tablespoons of chamomile (available at health food stores) to a pot of water. Bring it to a boil, then remove it from the burner. Take a large towel, put it over your head and put your head over the steaming pot. Be careful. Do not get too close to the hot pot...just close enough for the herbal steam to clean out your pores for about five minutes. After the steaming, let the air dry your skin.

Wrinkles

➤ **Skin Saver.** Approximately 10% to 20% of the wrinkles a person gets are the result of aging, facial expressions and smoking. The other 80% to 90% of lines and wrinkles are caused by exposure to the sun. While you can (and should) stop smoking, you can't stop aging, or turn off your facial expressions, but you can block out the sun's damaging UVA and UVB radiation with sunscreen. To be effective, sunscreen must be used properly. See page 197 for "Sunscreen Savvy."

➤ **Wrinkles Away.** Almond oil (it's sold at health food stores) is said to soften the little lines around the eyes and mouth. Gently massage the oil on the problem areas twice a day.

➤ **Wrinkle Prevention.**

● **Pillow talk.** Sleeping with your face pressed into the pillow causes wrinkles. Train yourself to sleep on your back or on your side with your face off the pillow. (See "Something Special—Pillow Power!" in the "Neck" section, page 147, for pillows that can help you retrain yourself to sleep on your back or side.)

● **Facial regimen.** Give yourself regular wrinkle-prevention facials. Blend equal amounts of plain yogurt and brewer's yeast together until smooth. Spread it on your face and neck and leave it on for 20 minutes. Then rinse off with tepid water and pat dry. Do this twice a week.

➤ **Wrinkle Removers.** Neinast said that if you follow this treatment in the morning and again in the evening, wrinkles should begin to disappear within weeks and your skin can look years younger...

● **In a wooden bowl** (metal or plastic is a no-no), put two slices of lemon. Heat half-and-half (enough to cover the lemon slices), so that it's a little warmer than taking the chill out. If your skin is oily, use four slices of lemon. If you have dry skin, use one slice of lemon and use twice as much half-and-half.

Pour the heated half-and-half over the lemon, cover the bowl and let it sit for three hours. Then strain and gently massage the liquid into your face and neck, with your middle three fingertips, in circular upward and outward motions. Allow it to dry on the skin—give it about 15 minutes—then remove it with a wet washcloth and follow up with a thin layer of olive oil.

• **To prepare for this next treatment,** pin your hair out of the way and wash your face and neck with warm water. Next, with your fingers, spread a thin layer of raw honey on your face and neck. Leave it on for 20 minutes, then rinse with tepid water and pat dry.

Raw honey can do wonders for the skin—everything from clearing up blemishes, holding in moisture and restoring weather-beaten skin to smoothing away wrinkles.

➤ **Say "No" to Skin Spoiler.** If you don't want deep wrinkles around the eyes and lips long before Mother Nature intended them to be there, or if you dread the thought of looking in a mirror and seeing that your skin has a grayish-yellowish pallor and the texture of dry leather, then don't let a cigarette touch your lips. If you're already a smoker, stop right now and turn to the "Stop Smoking," section, page 188, for help. In a matter of weeks after you quit that nasty habit, the quality of your complexion will improve.

Under-Eye Puffiness and Dark Circles

You can only blame a little on genetics. Puffiness and dark circles are mostly caused by stress, caffeine, alcohol, sugar, white flour, food allergies and too little sleep.

Start by cutting down on caffeine, alcohol, sugar and white flour in your diet. *And continue with the following suggestions…*

➤ **Potato Poultice.** Prepare one big poultice or two smaller ones with a grated raw potato in layered cheesecloth. Place the poultice(s) over your closed eyes on your lids and under your eyes. Leave it on for 20 relaxing minutes. Wash with cool water and pat dry. Poof!—no puffiness.

➤ **Sleep.** To lighten the dark circles under your eyes, you have to repeat the above

procedure every day and get sufficient sleep every night. According to Dr. Nicholas Perricone, author of *The Perricone Promise* (Grand Central), "Lack of sleep increases production of *cortisol*, which can cause swelling throughout the body, including around the eyes, and can create dark eye circles."

➤ **Temporary Eye De-puffer.** Wet two green tea bags and put them in the refrigerator for a half hour. Place the chilled tea bags on your eyes for about 10 minutes.

➤ **Alpha Lipoic Acid.** Available at vitamin and health food stores, this powerful antioxidant has strong detoxification properties. Ask your nutritionist for the dosage you should be taking, or follow the suggested dosage on the label.

➤ **Ester-C.** To stimulate collagen production and thicken under-eye skin, take an Ester-C supplement. Ester-C is nonacidic and stomach-friendly and contains natural vitamin C *metabolites*. These help it work differently than ordinary vitamin C, while still providing C's important benefits to your immune system, joints, heart, eyes and skin.

Lip Care

Chapped Lips

Do you have chapped lips even when it's not cold outside? As with all conditions, figuring out the cause is key. *See if any of the following apply to you…*

• **Smoking** (one more of the gazillions of reasons to quit).

• **Frequent lip licking.** It may give you a few seconds of relief, but saliva evaporates quickly and makes the condition worse. Become aware of doing it and make a real effort to stop.

• **Do you use chapstick or lipstick that contains** *propyl gallate*—a chemical that can cause a contact allergy? Call the company that manufactures the chapstick and/or lipstick you use and ask for a list of ingredients or if propyl gallate is one of the ingredients. Be suspicious if they are not forthcoming with information.

Also check on the chemicals in all of your cosmetics and skin care items. Consider changing to nonallergenic products.

• **Vitamin deficiency or vitamin overload can cause peeling and painful chapped lips.** Have your doctor test your vitamin levels, paying special attention to vitamins A, B-1, B-2, B-6, B-12 and C and iron. Once the results are in and analyzed, have a nutritionist help you with a plan that will get you in balance.

• **Dehydration is responsible for many cases of chapped lips.** Hydrate from the inside out. Make a concerted effort to drink several ounces of water every few hours throughout the day.

• **There are some medications, such as those to treat acne, that cause chapped lips.** Check with a pharmacist for side effects of your medication(s).

SOMETHING SPECIAL

A Dream Cream

While you're figuring out the cause of your chapped challenge, and trying any of the above remedies, you probably need to go outdoors and live your life. You also need to protect your lips, especially in cold weather.

We have found that LaROCCA Shield Multi-Active Lip Balm nourishes your lips as it protects them, thanks to their incredible ingredients...

• **Colloidal Gold** is known to promote electron transfer with the metal ions naturally found in the skin, which stimulates cell turnover. Colloidal Gold also has antimicrobial and anti-inflammatory properties.

• **L-arginine** is an important amino acid that is essential during the synthesis of collagen.

• **Mangosteen Extract** has antiaging, antioxidant, antiviral, antibiotic, antifungal and antimicrobial properties.

• **Camu Camu** provides powerful phytochemicals that help strengthen the immune system, maintain healthy gums, eyes and skin and protects against herpes.

• **Cha de burge** is used to help kill viruses.

• **Hyaluronic Acid** brings moisture into the skin.

• **Sea Buckthorn** provides vitamins (C, A, B-1, B-2, B-6, B-9, E, K, P, F) and minerals (calcium, magnesium, potassium, iron).

• **Alpha Lipoic Acid** is a potent antioxidant that helps prevent wrinkling of the skin and other damage from sugar, including accelerated aging.

• **You can apply this soothing lip balm throughout the day,** especially after eating, before going outdoors and while you're out. It makes a difference—your lips feel better and look better.

More information: Access LaROCCA Skincare at *www.laroccaskincare.com* or call 818-748-6114.

- **Breathing through your mouth can dehydrate your lips.**
- **Sensitivity to flavoring agents,** especially red dye found in candy, gum and mouthwash.

Remedies for Chapped Lips

Once you figure out the cause and eliminate it, you will no longer be bothered by chapped lips. Until you do, here are remedies that can help clear up the condition...temporarily.

➤ **Mustard Oil.** Available at Indian groceries—suggested for external use only—mustard oil is aromatic, soothing to the skin and used primarily on stiff, painful joints.

This application is a good, old-fashioned folk remedy that came to us from a woman who grew up in Jammu, India, where they have cold, breezy winters and a lot of chapped lips. Take a cotton puff, dip it in mustard oil and put it in your navel. Keep it in place with a piece of tape. Change the cotton puff daily (after your shower) and, within five days, your lips should be fine.

 CAUTION: If your navel becomes irritated, stop using mustard oil.

➤ **Cucumber.** Peel and slice a piece of cucumber and rub it on your lips. The little pieces of dead skin should come off and your lips should feel less chapped.

➤ **Honey and Oil.** Take advantage of honey's healing and antibacterial properties by smearing a layer of it on your lips. Let it stay that way (even though it's tempting to lick it off) for a minute or two, then seal it in with a light coat of coconut oil. If you don't have coconut oil, use olive oil. Keep it on for about 10 minutes, then gently wipe your lips clean. Repeat this procedure every day, and your lips should be nice and smooth within a week.

176

Hand Care

Chapped Hands

To prevent catching a cold or the flu, you're told to keep washing your hands, especially when you're around other people. While it is a smart thing to do, don't be surprised if you trade that cold for a pair of chapped hands.

Yes, water will dry out your hands. Soap, unless it's very mild and has cold cream in it, will make your hands more chapped and faster.

➤ **Do's and Don'ts.**
- **If you go to a public restroom where they have a hot-air blower, don't use it,** as it can dry out your hands, causing chapping. Opt for paper towels, or if there are none, use toilet tissue.
- **Always wear rubber gloves when you do the dishes.**
- **You probably wash your hands much more often than you realize...for instance, after reading a newspaper.** Wear cotton gloves around the house and you won't have to keep washing your hands. If you do things that require a good grip, wear leather gloves.

➤ **Moisturizers.**
- **Crisco!** Use very little. Rub it on your hands until you can hardly tell it's there. Many doctors who constantly have to scrub up, use Crisco to moisturize their hands.
- **Olive Oil.** Mix a quarter of a teaspoon of oil (olive oil or your favorite bath oil) with a quarter of a teaspoon of glycerin (available at pharmacies). At bedtime, massage a thin layer into your hands. Wait 10 minutes, then mix up another batch and once again, massage it into your hands. For this remedy to be extra-effective, and to protect your bedding, wear cotton gloves overnight.

Easy Does It!

The Easy-Carry Handle cushioned-grip handle absorbs impact and stress, while preventing shopping bag handles from cutting into your palms.

Made primarily for women's hands, the handle distributes the weight of your loaded-up shopping bags—up to 50 pounds—and simply makes your groceries and other packages easier and more comfortable to carry. Put the handle on your dry cleaning hangers, and avoid the pain caused by hangers digging into your hand.

A board-certified ergonomist, Dr. Jay Finkelman praises its ergonomic design and you will too, once you've used it.

More information: Go to *www.senior-friendlyproducts.com,* or call 503-567-8597.

Grimy Hands Cleanser

➤ **Oil Me.** When your hands are downright dirty, use olive oil to clean off the grime, grease and tar. Vigorously massage the olive oil into the hands, then wipe them with paper towels. For hard-to-get-out stains, you may have to oil your hands again, adding some sugar as an abrasive. To get the olive oil off your hands, rinse them with warm water and wipe them with more paper towels.

Sweaty Hands Prevention

➤ **Pinch Trick.** Do your hands sweat a lot right before you have to shake hands with someone? This is a common nervous response, especially when you want to make a great first impression. To preoccupy your brain and not give it time to cause those sweaty palms, when no one's looking, pinch your midriff so that it really hurts. Hold the pinch for about 10 seconds, as close to handshake time as possible.

SKIN CONCERNS

Skin is one of our body's largest and heaviest organs. The average adult's skin measures 19 square feet and weighs about nine pounds. The thinnest sections of skin are on your eyelids; the thickest are on the palms of your hands and the soles of your feet.

The average person sheds about a pound-and-a-half of skin particles each year. By the time you're 70, you will have lost a little over 100 pounds of outer skin. Skin particles that are shed are replaced with another coat of skin about once a month. And you say you have nothing new to wear!

There are close to 1,000 diseases and conditions that can affect our skin. *In this section, we're going to deal with the half dozen or so most common skin problems, starting with…*

Acne

➤ **Bee Acne-Free.** Use a jar with a cover to make this acne solution. Put eight ounces of water in the jar, then add 10 drops of bee propolis extract (available at most health food stores or check "Sources," page 310). Dip a cotton ball into the solution, then dab the acne area with it. Start first thing in the morning and continue throughout the day whenever you can. Be sure to apply the solution after each time you wash your face and at bedtime. Be consistent and do it every day for at least three weeks, unless the acne clears up before then.

➤ **Aloe Vera.** Use aloe vera juice (available at health food stores) to help heal acne. With a cotton ball, dab it on first thing in the morning and last thing at night. If possible, apply it throughout the day, especially after you wash your face. Again, we urge you to be consistent and do it every day for at least three weeks, unless the acne clears up before then.

➤ **Stinging Nettle Tea.** Prepare the tea with a teaspoon of the stinging nettle herb in a cup of just-boiled water. Let it steep for 10 minutes. Strain and drink three to four cups a day. Stinging nettle is known to help heal several skin problems including acne.

Acne Scars

➤ **Dole Out This Remedy.** To diminish acne scars, put pieces of fresh pineapple on the acne scars and leave them there for 15 minutes a day.

➤ **Vitamin E.** Puncture a vitamin E softgel and squeeze out the oil on the acne scars. Do this at least an hour before going to bed, after you've washed your face for the night. Be consistent and patient. It may take quite a while before you see results.

 NOTE: If you want to try both remedies, use the pineapple right after dinner and the vitamin E oil close to bedtime.

Age Spots

The correct medical term for these brown patches we call age spots is *lentigines*. They are caused by changes in pigmentation in sun-exposed areas of skin. They are also (wrongly) referred to as liver spots. The liver has nothing to do with the formation of the spots. *To be spotless...*

➤ **Red Onion.** Rub the patches with a slice of red onion for two or three minutes at a time, at least twice a day. Be consistent and patient for results.

➤ **Enzymes.** The treatment that promises to be the fastest age spot remover is one using fresh pineapple juice. The key word is *fresh*... not canned, jarred, bottled, frozen, powdered or concentrated. If you want the bromelain enzyme to get in there and help dissolve those spots, we're talking FRESH pineapple juice.

Make sure your skin is clean and oil-free or cream-free. Dip a cotton ball in the pineapple juice and place it on the spot. Leave it there for 20 minutes, then rinse with tepid water and pat dry. Do this every day and within a week the spots may start fading.

➤ **Vitamins.** Daily doses of vitamin E along with vitamin C have been known to decrease the accumulation of the pigment that causes the appearance of age spots.

 CAUTION: Due to the possible interactions between vitamin E and various drugs and supplements, as well as other safety considerations, be sure to consult your doctor before taking vitamin E.

Freckles

Forget removing freckles. We think the most you can hope for is making them a bit lighter. *If you're interested in that, there are several remedies from which to choose...*

➤ **Eggplant.** Rub freckles with slices of fresh, raw eggplant every day. That's known to lighten them.

➤ **Cranberries.** Rub fresh, crushed up cranberries on your bespeckled skin. Do this on a daily basis, leaving it on for 15 minutes. Rinse with cool water and pat dry.

➤ **Your Own Solution.** If you're really determined to make *light* of your freckles, collect six ounces of your urine in a jar, add a tablespoon of white vinegar and a pinch of salt. Cover the jar and 24 hours later, with a cotton ball, pat the solution on the freckles. After a half hour, rinse with cool water. Do this every day until the freckles fade, or until you begin to appreciate your charming natural adornment.

 CAUTION: If there is any broken skin on your face, do NOT use this remedy.

➤ **Go Sugar-Free.** It is said that the more refined sugar you eat, the darker your freckles are going to be. This sounds like an old wives' tale. It isn't. It's based on scientific research.

Conclusion: Eliminate refined sugar from your diet and watch your freckles fade.

Boils

A boil is an infection of a gland or a hair follicle, usually filled with pus. There are several foods that can help draw out the infection. Apply one of the following directly on the boil, wrap an Ace bandage or clean white handkerchief around it and let it stay that way for an hour…

➤ **Slice of Tomato** that's been warmed.

➤ **Banana Peel.** The inside of a ripe (brown speckled) banana peel.

➤ **Cabbage Leaves.** Wash a couple of green or white cabbage leaves and boil them for a minute or two. While they're still warm, but cool enough to handle, place them on the boil.

➤ **Red Onion.** Cut a small red onion in half, take out a little center section of one half, and place the centerless half over the boil.

TAKE NOTE

Emollients and Eczema

According to the National Eczema Society (*www.eczema.org*), emollients are noncosmetic moisturizers—creams, ointments, lotions and gels—that keep the skin moist and flexible, so it's more comfortable, less itchy and less prone to cracks.

Creams contain a mixture of fat and water and feel light and cool to the skin. All creams have preservatives which may or may not cause sensitivity.

Ointments do not contain preservatives, and can be quite greasy. They are effective at holding water in the skin and are particularly good for very dry and thickened skin. Do not use ointments on weeping eczema; use a cream or lotion instead.

Lotions contain more water and less fat than creams, and do not moisturize the skin as well. People who have eczema on hairy areas of the body prefer lotions.

The advice from the National Eczema Society is…

➤ **Use an emollient liberally and frequently**—at least three times a day.

➤ **Apply gently in the direction of the hair growth.** Never rub up and down vigorously. It could trigger itching, block hair follicles or create more heat in the skin.

➤ **Continue to use the emollient, even when the eczema has improved.** This will help prevent flare-ups.

➤ **Emollients, if used every day, may be all you need** to keep mild to moderate eczema under control.

> **Once the Boil Opens.** It is a good thing for the boil to open on its own, and have the pus expelled. You'll notice that the pain disappears, but it will leave a hole in the skin. Add two tablespoons of fresh lemon juice to a cup of just-boiled water. Dip a cotton ball in the lemon water and use it to gently clean and disinfect the area. Then put a sterile bandage on it.

Hives

Right now, out of every 1,000 people, 11 men and 14 women have hives. *If you are one of them, here's what to do...*

> **Vinegar/Cornstarch.** Thoroughly blend one ounce of distilled white vinegar with three ounces of cornstarch and dab the hives with the mixture. It's an antiseptic, it stops the itching and it can dry up the hives.

> **Peppermint.** Boil a cup of water, then stir in one rounded teaspoon of dried or fresh peppermint leaves. Let it simmer for 10 minutes. Strain the peppermint tea and refrigerate it. Once the tea is nice and cool, use a cotton pad or cotton puffs to dab the refreshing liquid on the hives. It should stop the itching...temporarily.

Eczema

This inflammation of the skin usually starts with red, dry, itchy skin, and then produces weepy lesions that become encrusted and scaly.

> **External Do Not's and Do's.**
> - **Do not wear tight clothing** or rough, scratchy fabrics including woolens.
> - **Do not use soaps that will remove your skin's natural oil.** Instead use one of the many moisturizing soaps on the market—Eucerin, Aveeno, Dove, etc.
> - **Do not bathe or shower more than once a day.** Remember, you do not want to remove your skin's natural oil.

- **Do not use hot water.**
- **Do not use washcloths, brushes or loofahs.** They will add to the skin's irritation and may cause more itching.
- **Right after the bath or shower, do not rub dry**—pat your skin almost dry. While your skin is still a little wet, gently apply an emollient for extra hydration.

> **External Treatment.** An effective external treatment is to put the contents of two chaparral capsules into a pint of just-boiled water. Cover and let it stand until it's cool—at least 10 minutes. Strain through a superfine strainer or through unbleached muslin. Dip a white washcloth in the chaparral tea and place it on the sore spots. Do it twice a day for 15 minutes at a time.

> **Internal Remedies.**
- **Eat one tablespoon of blackstrap molasses daily.**
- **Eat one raw potato a day.**
- **Eat a few teaspoons of watercress each day.**
- **Have one teaspoon of sesame oil daily,** but only if you check with your health professional first. Cooking with it doesn't count; you must have it straight from the bottle.
- **If you have a juice extractor,** make yourself a daily green drink using green vegetables (i.e., alfalfa sprouts, parsley, spinach, celery, lettuce).
- **Add one-half tablespoon of turmeric to five ounces of water and drink it down.** Do this once in the morning and once in the afternoon.
- **Drink an ounce of aloe vera juice after each meal.** (If you have an aloe vera plant, apply the gel from the leaves to the affected area at least twice a day. If you don't have an

aloe plant for your skin, use the same aloe juice you're drinking.)

Psoriasis

In our books and during most every public appearance, we make mention of the fact that we are reporting, not prescribing. This is no exception. *Here are some reportings that may help clear up this challenging skin condition...*

➤ **Oil of Oregano.** This potent oil should be used internally as well as externally. Take two oil of oregano softgels twice a day. Meanwhile, prepare the external oil by thoroughly cleaning a glass jar or bottle that has a cover. Once it's clean and dry, fill it two-thirds with extra virgin olive oil, and one-third with oil of oregano (both the oil and softgels are available at health food stores). Put the cover on the jar and shake it so that the two oils blend. Use a soft, lint-free, cotton square or round (they come in packages of 80 or 100, and are usually in the makeup section of drugstores) and apply the oil mixture on the psoriasis outbreak. Do this twice a day. And don't forget to take the oil of oregano softgels twice a day. If it seems to be agreeing with you, and you can stand the oregano smell, be patient and give it a chance to work.

➤ **Shark Cartilage.** Dr. I. William Lane, in his book *Sharks Don't Get Cancer* (Avery), reports on the successful use of shark cartilage for psoriasis. "Experience is limited," says Dr. Lane, "but already indicates that the effective dosage level for psoriasis is one gram per 15 pounds of body weight taken for 60 to 90 days.

"Be aware," Dr. Lane cautions, "in this treatment, the itching and scales will be the first symptoms to disappear. Without the scales, the redness of the skin will appear to intensify since the large bed of capillary vessels will be more

apparent. This capillary bed will also slowly disappear."

Look for unadulterated 100% pure shark cartilage such as BeneFin or Cartilade. It's available at most health food stores, vitamin shops and pharmacies, and it's costly, but if it works, it's worth it. And if it doesn't work, you'll know by the end of 90 days.

 CAUTION: The late Dr. Ray Wunderlich, Jr., respected physician and founder of the Wunderlich Center for Nutritional Medicine, thought children, athletes and people with compromised circulation should be wary of prolonged usage of shark cartilage. Be sure to check with your health professional before starting this self-help program.

➤ **Aloe.** Drink an ounce of aloe vera juice after each meal. If you have an aloe vera plant, apply the gel from the leaves to the affected area at least twice a day. If you don't have an aloe plant for your skin, use the same aloe juice you're drinking.

➤ **Omega-3.** Studies show that substituting omega-3 fish oils for other fats in your diet may help heal psoriasis. Check with your health professional to determine the right amount of fish oil for you. Daily doses of flaxseed oil (a great source of omega-3) has also proven effective.

➤ **Burdock Root Tea.** Prepare the tea by bringing four cups of water to a boil. Add a large tablespoon of dried burdock root (available at health food stores), cover and let simmer on a very low flame for a half hour. Strain, then divide the liquid into two portions. Drink each portion on an empty stomach—one portion before breakfast and the other before dinner. Do this daily and watch for results within a few weeks. Burdock root is an effective detoxifier, which may be the reason it has been known to help clear up severe cases of psoriasis.

➤ **Gluten-Free.** There seems to be a connection between psoriasis sufferers and an inability to digest gluten. Gluten is a protein found in grain. Try a gluten-free diet. That means no wheat, oats, barley or rye. It doesn't mean bye-bye bread. Check your health food store for a good selection of gluten-free products including breads, oats, crackers and frozen prepared foods.

Skin Cancer Prevention

➤ **Vitamins A and C.** According to the results of a study at the University of Arizona, eating one teaspoon of orange peel per week reduces the risk of skin cancer by 30%. As a bonus, the orange peel's high vitamin C and A contents helps fight infection, colds and flu. As if that weren't enough, orange peel is easy to digest and is effective in helping digest fatty foods.

SLEEP MATTERS

Sound sleep is one of the foundations of good health. End the day and start your night's sleep with comforting, positive and optimistic thoughts. (See the "Affirmation" at the end of this section.)

A Good Night's Sleep

➤ **A Calming Bedroom.** To ensure a good night's sleep, arrange your bedroom so that it has a calming influence on you...

• **Paint the walls a soft, quiet color—** blue, pink or green. It can make a big difference in your night's sleep, even though your eyes are closed.

• **Make sure that the things you see right before falling asleep do not stimulate your nervous system,** or aggravate you in any way. In other words, you don't want a desk near your bed, reminding you of all the work you have to do. And, you don't want to see the folder with all your unpaid bills calling out, "Pay me! Pay me!"

• **Aside from a good reading light next to or over your bed,** have soft, flattering lighting in the bedroom, making it feel cozy and warm.

• **Media use before bedtime may cause sleep problems,** according to the findings of a study published in the journal *Sleep and Biological Rhythms*. Stay away from the computer, especially if you're a game player, and turn off the television for at least an hour before you intend going to sleep. Instead, relax and read a book or write in a journal.

➤ **Time for Sleep.** How much sleep is enough? According to research done at the Henry Ford Hospital in Detroit, chances are you need more sleep than you're getting. Experiment by going to sleep a half hour earlier than usual each night for a week. If you don't feel more alert and energetic, go to sleep an hour earlier the second week.

Be sure you go to sleep at an earlier hour at night, rather than sleeping an hour later in the morning. Sleeping later in the morning increases body temperature and hormones may be depressed, which can result in sluggishness and lethargy.

Remedies for Occasional Insomnia

➤ **Yawn.** Open your mouth and remember how it feels to yawn. Bring on a yawn...and another one...and another. Yawning makes you feel sleepy, and chances are, you'll be asleep before you can get yourself to stop yawning.

End the day and start your night's sleep with your own comforting, positive and optimistic thoughts. (For some examples, see the "Affirmation" at the end of this section.)

➤ Aromatherapy.

● Onion. Chop a yellow onion in chunks and place the chunks in a jar with a cover. Place the jar on your night table. Once you're in bed and having trouble falling asleep, uncover the jar and take a deep whiff or two of the onion. Recover the jar, lie back and think lovely thoughts. You should be asleep within 15 minutes.

● Pillow stuffer. The classic insomnia folk remedy is a pillow made of hops. Have you ever smelled hops? It's vile. You may fall asleep just to escape the smell.

We found something a lot more pleasant that's said to be just as effective. It's celery seeds. Stuff a little pillow with them and sleep on it.

 NOTE: Go to "Something Special—Pillow Power!" in the "Neck Care" section, page 147, and read about how a pillow can help realign your body, improve your night's sleep and help you to wake up pain-free.

➤ Bedding. Use all-cotton bed sheets. According to consumer advocate Debra Lynn Dadd, who focuses on toxic-free living, polyester-cotton sheets are coated with formaldehyde, a substance that can cause insomnia. While manufacturers do not have to by law list when fabrics are treated with formaldehyde resins, you can spot the ones that are when you read any of these terms on the labels —crease-resistant, permanent-pressed, no-iron, shrink-proof, water-repellant, waterproof, stretch-proof, permanently pleated.

➤ The Kitchen Sink. Having a hard time falling asleep? The answer may be in your kitchen sink. In certain folkloric circles, it is believed that dirty dishes left undone can cause insomnia.

➤ Trick or Treat. Eat pumpkin—as a side dish or as a dessert—and your insomnia may be no more than a dream.

➤ Breathing Kundalini-Yoga-Style. The left nostril is connected to the right hemisphere of the brain. Breathing through the left nostril can activate the *parasympathetic nervous system,* which counteracts stress and helps calm you and put you into a sleep mode.

Lie on your right side, which will help open your left nostril, then use the thumb or index finger of your right hand and close the right nostril. Take long, deep breaths through your left nostril for a couple of minutes, until you fall asleep.

➤ Herbal Tea. Drink a cup of herbal slumber-inspiring tea—chamomile, dill, heather, anise, a nephew (just testing to see if you're asleep yet), peppermint or rosemary.

➤ Melatonin. This hormone is produced by the pineal gland and is involved in regulating sleeping and waking cycles. Bright lights lower melatonin levels, so put away the book, the jigsaw puzzle, the sewing or anything else that requires bright lights at bedtime. Allow at least a half-hour in a dimly lit room before shutting the light completely.

If you try the dimly lit room, and still have trouble falling asleep, you may want to raise your melatonin level. Dr. Russell J. Reiter, professor of neuroendocrinology at the University of Texas Health Science Center in San Antonio, conducted a five-month study and found that tart cherries contain significant amounts of melatonin. For lots more information about tart cherries, including their ability to slow the aging process, and a source for these little tart beauties, see "Cherries," on page 236, in the "It Does a Body Good" chapter.

Meanwhile, if you choose to take a liquid or tablet melatonin supplement (available at health food stores), first check with your health professional and if he/she says it's safe for you to take, start with the lowest dosage.

Nightmares

The average adult has at least one nightmare a year. One in five hundred people has nightmares once a week. About 5% of the adult population has nightmares even more often than once a week.

➤ **A Smelly Sock?** We got this remedy from a reputable radio host in Rhode Island. Take a smelly sock—your smelly sock—wrap the instep of the sock around your throat, and sleep that way. It will not only prevent nightmares, it also helps a sore throat (see page 186).

➤ **Gem Therapy for Occasional Insomnia and Nightmares.** Hold a piece of amethyst in your hand to help you fall asleep. Place a piece of amethyst in your pillowcase to prevent nightmares.

➤ **Talking While Asleep.** Take hold of the big toe of a person who's talking in his sleep and he'll tell you anything you want to know. This remedy came to us from the hills of South Dakota…or was it from a California divorce lawyer?

AFFIRMATION

End the day and start your night's sleep with your own comforting, positive and optimistic thoughts. You may want to say it in the form of a prayer. Studies show that praying helps relax your mind as well as your body. Keep it simple and from your heart, saying what's most important to you. For example…

184

I pray that I fall asleep and have beautiful dreams, and awaken to make the world a better place in some wonderful way. I pray for a restful night's sleep, and that I wake up feeling great and creating a day of productivity and pleasure.

Sleep Apnea

When It's More Than a Snore

Snoring is a loud sound made while asleep. It's caused by any obstruction in the airway. Snoring, while annoying to one's bedmate, is not in itself a harmful condition.

Sleep apnea, on the other hand, is a disorder in which a person stops breathing during sleep, often hundreds of times throughout the night. There is a complete blockage of airways, depriving the sleeper of oxygen, which can have a major impact on health. Most people with sleep apnea do snore, but snoring does not mean you have sleep apnea.

Sleep apnea is a common condition that affects an estimated 12 million American men, women and children, and while it is treatable, it is often undiagnosed, despite the potentially serious consequences.

The American Sleep Apnea Association (ASAA) has developed a sleep quiz. Take it here to help you decide whether or not you may have sleep apnea.

1. **Are you a loud, habitual snorer?**

2. **Do you feel tired and groggy on awakening?**

3. **Are you often sleepy during waking hours** and/or can you fall asleep quickly?

4. **Are you overweight and/or do you have a large neck?**

5. **Have you been observed to choke, gasp or hold your breath during sleep?**

If you answer "yes" to any of the above questions, it doesn't necessarily mean that you have sleep apnea. It does mean that you should discuss your symptoms with your physician or a sleep specialist. Or ask the ASAA for more information on the diagnosis and treatment of sleep apnea. Visit their Web site at *www.sleepapnea.org*, or call 888-293-3650.

Different treatment options exist. The one that is right for you depends upon the severity of your apnea and other aspects of your disorder. Sleep apnea should not be ignored and untreated.

Help for Moderate Obstructive Sleep Apnea Syndrome

The results of a controlled study published by *BMJ* (formerly the *British Medical Journal*) concluded that regular training of the upper airways by playing a didgeridoo reduces snoring in people with moderate obstructive sleep apnea syndrome, allowing them and their partners improved sleep quality, which in turn reduces daytime sleepiness.

The didgeridoo is a rhythm wind folk instrument, so you play *beats* instead of melodic songs. Learning the instrument is intuitive and you don't need any previous musical training. Even though it's a wind instrument, you don't use lung power. The didgeridoo is played with gently vibrating lips, voice and tongue movement.

For more information, visit LA Outback, *www.laoutback.com,* and see their large selection of beautiful, affordable and authentic Aboriginal didgeridoos and instructional CDs and videos. You can also call 760-992-5982, and speak with any of the company's caring and helpful people.

Snore Stoppers That Just Might Work for You

Anthony Burgess, English author, playwright and composer, mused, "Laugh and the world laughs with you, snore and you sleep alone." To prevent that from happening, stop drinking and stop smoking and, chances are, you'll stop snoring. Alcohol and cigarettes cause the swelling of tissues that cause snoring.

➤ **Collar Cure.** Have you ever heard a person with a whiplash injury snore? They don't. Well, not if they sleep with a cervical collar around their neck. The collar prevents the chin from resting on the chest—a position that partially closes the windpipe and causes snoring. When you wear the collar, the chin stays up and the windpipe stays open.

➤ **Clip Clop.** If someone else is snoring, make a clacking noise with your tongue, the noise you make to imitate the clip clop of a horse. It works. It will either make the snorer stop snoring, or it will awaken the snorer, in which case he will stop snoring.

More information: For sleep facts, information and referrals to sleep disorder centers in your area, visit the National Sleep Foundation's Web site at *www.sleepfoundation.org*, or call 703-243-1697.

AFFIRMATION

Repeat this affirmation at bedtime, over and over until you fall asleep...

I let go of all the pressures of the day in exchange for a good night's sleep. I feel in harmony with the universe, and secure with myself.

SORE THROAT

This throat inflammation can lower your resistance and leave you vulnerable to other ailments that attack when resistance is down. Let's just nip this sore throat in the bud...

⚡ **CAUTION:** If your sore throat isn't gone after three days, see a health professional and get tested for strep throat.

Classic Sore Throat Remedies

➤ **Classic Remedy #1.** Honey and lemon was a standard in our house. Mom would squeeze the juice of a lemon into a big mug of just boiled water and add enough honey—one to three tablespoons—to make it delicious.

Or, in another version, mix a tablespoon of honey with the juice of a lemon...no water added. Have it either way every couple of hours.

➤ **Classic Remedy #2.** Mix two teaspoons of apple cider vinegar in a glass of warm water. Take a mouthful, gargle with it and spit it out, then swallow a mouthful. Again, gargle a mouthful, spit it out and swallow a mouthful. Notice a pattern? Do this until there's no liquid left in the glass. Repeat the process once an hour. By the third or fourth hour, the sore throat is usually gone. (This remedy works for us every time.)

➤ **Classic Remedy #3.** Dissolve a heaping teaspoon of salt (kosher salt is preferred, but table salt will do) in a glass of warm water and gargle with it. If it helps, do it again in an hour. If it didn't seem to make your throat feel better, try one of the other remedies.

186

More Sore Throat Remedies

If none of the above classic folk remedies appeals to you, find one of the following that does, use it and make it your own classic sore throat remedy...

➤ **Pineapple Slices.** Eat a few slices of fresh pineapple. A grapefruit can be effective, too, and so is drinking one glass of grapefruit juice.

⚡ **CAUTION:** If you take medication, check in with your doctor or pharmacist to be sure that there is no medicine interaction with grapefruit.

➤ **Horehound Tea.** Throughout the day, drink horehound tea (available at health food stores). Simply steep a teaspoon of the herb in a cup of just-boiled water, and as soon as it's cool, strain and drink.

➤ **The Bartender's Remedy.** Instead of sucking candy to soothe your throat, suck on an olive. Remove the pit and keep the meat of the olive in your mouth until you finally chew it and swallow it. Then take another olive.

➤ **We Get Letters.** Because of limited space, we don't reprint letters from people who graciously share their remedies with us. *Of course there's always an exception and this is it...*

> Ladies,
> Here's a home remedy I used 65 years ago that is as amusing as it is effective. Don't ask me why it works, but it did when I was 10. Later when my daughters were about the same age it worked for them too.
> For a sore throat, when you retire, wrap your neck in a dirty sock. The dirtier the better. I reasoned it was the warmth, but a towel doesn't work; the sock does! No kidding!!
> Yours truly,
> Selwyn P. Miles

NOTE: To everyone who uses this remedy, boil the soiled sock with a few lemon slices and it will get sparkling white again…that is, if it was a white sock when it was new.

➤ **Reinfection Prevention.** Bacteria can live on your toothbrush and reinfect you. While you have the sore throat, dip your toothbrush in just-boiled water before using it. As soon as your sore throat is completely gone, get a new toothbrush.

➤ **Acupressure.** Massage deep into the web-like area between the thumb and the index finger. It can help relieve the rawness of an inflamed throat.

➤ **Aromatherapy.** Essential pine oil has antiseptic properties. Add a couple of drops of the oil to a pot of just-boiled water and carefully inhale the vapor. Throughout the day, reheat the water with the pine oil and inhale.

AFFIRMATION

Whenever you look at a watch or clock, it's "time" to blow your own horn by repeating this affirmation…

I am the best there is! I shout my praises loud and clear.

Strep Throat

Strep throat should not be taken lightly. It can lead to serious illness if not treated properly. A doctor can test for strep in minutes. Pardon the repetition, but…if your sore throat doesn't go away in three days, go to the doctor and be tested.

If you have a dog or cat and you get strep throat more often than once in a blue moon, you may be catching the *streptococci* from the animal. Get the vet to check the pet. When your pet is free of the bacteria, you probably will be, too.

➤ **Strep Throat Remedy.** If you think you have strep throat and absolutely cannot get to the doctor to be tested, then every hour, take three alfalfa tablets and every third hour add 100 mg of vitamin C. Start this regimen in the morning and stop at bedtime. If you're not all better the next morning, do it for another day. Then, no more excuses, get to a doctor!

Laryngitis

Do you cradle the receiver between your shoulder and neck while you talk on the telephone? If that's what you do, you may be straining your larynx in order to produce sounds when your head is tilted. If that's what's causing your laryngitis, hang up the phone and go get yourself a headset.

If your laryngitis is not caused by the tilt of your head as you talk on the telephone, see if you can get your voice back by following one or more of these remedies…

➤ **Drink Lots of Liquids.** But stay away from cold drinks. Cold fluids can make the problem worse. Also stay away from milk and other dairy drinks.

➤ **No Alcohol!** Since you want to keep the larynx moist, alcoholic beverages—even the so-called medicinal mixtures—are a no-no. They just dry out the larynx.

➤ **Stay Away from Mint.** Any kind of mint or mentholated drinks or cough drops. They can dry out your vocal cords.

➤ **Do Not Gargle.** Your vocal cords do not need the stress that gargling causes.

➤ **Do Not Whisper.** Whispering also stresses the vocal cords. In fact, shut up! For a day or two, write instead of talk.

➤ **Drink Slippery Elm Bark Tea** (available at health food stores). Have three or four cups a day for a soothing glaze on the vocal cords and relief from the pain of an abused throat.

➤ **Chew on Chestnuts.** Remove the shells of a few uncooked chestnuts and chew the chestnut meat like you would chew gum. It's said to be helpful in curing laryngitis.

➤ **Drink Sage Tea.** Prepare strong sage tea by using a heaping teaspoon of the herb in a cup of just-boiled water. Let it steep for 10 minutes, strain and drink. Sage will not only help heal the laryngitis, it will also strengthen your voice. Drink three cups a day until your voice is back to normal.

SPLINTERS

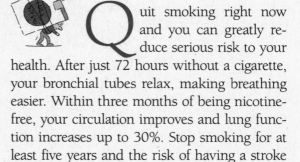

Attempting to remove any splinter using tweezers may make the problem worse. The tweezers may push the splinter deeper into the skin or break off the splinter and leave part of it embedded beneath the skin. *Save the tweezers for your eyebrows, and consider the simple and safer splinter-removing methods below...*

➤ **Easy-to-Remove Splinter.** When the splinter is sticking out, not deeply imbedded, and you don't want to risk breaking it off by pulling it out, take a piece of tape—Scotch or adhesive—and put it on the splinter. It will also work with a thin layer of school-type white glue spread on the splintered area. Try to figure out the direction in which the splinter is facing so that you can yank off the tape or the glob of glue accordingly. If it doesn't work the first time, give it a second or third try.

➤ **Hard-to-Remove Splinter.** Wrap a strip of raw bacon around the area with the splinter and cover the bacon with a piece of cloth. Keep on overnight and in the morning, when you remove the bacon, chances are, you will also remove the splinter.

➤ **Hardest-to-Remove Splinter.** Take a teaspoon of ground fenugreek (available from most health food stores) and add enough water to make a paste of it. Place it on the sore area and wrap gauze around it. Keep it on overnight. In the morning, when you clear away the fenugreek, the splinter should have surfaced and you can scrape it or tape it off. (See above.)

STOP SMOKING

Quit smoking right now and you can greatly reduce serious risk to your health. After just 72 hours without a cigarette, your bronchial tubes relax, making breathing easier. Within three months of being nicotine-free, your circulation improves and lung function increases up to 30%. Stop smoking for at least five years and the risk of having a stroke will drop to just about the same chance as a nonsmoker's.

That's the good news. And if that is not enough incentive to make you determined to quit smoking, here are some of the extremely unpleasant things the approximately 4,000 nasty chemicals in cigarettes may be doing to you each time you light up...

• **Smokers suffer from heartburn** more often than nonsmokers and more indigestion, ulcers and constipation.

• **Smokers suffer from insomnia** more often than nonsmokers.

- **Smokers tend to have cold hands and feet,** since smoking decreases the flow of blood to the extremities.

- **Smokers tend to have dryness in the throat.**

- **A smoker's complexion is generally drier,** more leathery looking and the skin tone is drabber than complexions of nonsmokers.

- **A smoker is more likely to have 10 times more wrinkles**—especially around the eyes and lips—than nonsmokers.

- **If a smoker has a face-lift,** the blood vessels could constrict and affect the healing process.

- **Men who smoke have a lower sperm count,** less sperm motility and more abnormal sperm than nonsmoking men.

- **Women who smoke have a higher percentage of miscarriages** than nonsmoking women.

- **That nasty stale-cigarette smell is a real turnoff.** Action on Smoking and Health (ASH) once had a sticker that said, "Kissing a smoker is like licking an ashtray."

You may not smell it (smoking dulls your senses), but everyone around you smells it on your breath, your hair, your clothes, in your car and in your home, from the carpeting to the curtains, and all of the furniture in between.

Need a little more incentive? Aside from saving your life and the lives of people affected by your secondhand smoke, think of the money you'll save. *Now then...*

Withdrawing from Cigarettes Painlessly

This is an effective process that works if you let it. Take advantage of ALL of the suggestions, to make it easy—yes, easy—to cut down, cut down, cut down, until you cut cigarettes out of your life completely.

➤ **A Special Tonic.** Mix a half-teaspoon of cream of tartar (available in supermarket baking and/or spice sections) into eight ounces of orange juice and drink it before bedtime. The cream of tartar helps clear the nicotine out of your system.

Each cigarette you smoke robs your body of about 25 milligrams (mg) of vitamin C. The orange juice will help replace that vitamin C.

Once you've made up your mind to stop smoking and start this regimen, be consistent! Take the drink every night without fail. Then, the following day, when you reach for a cigarette, you may think twice about it. Ask yourself, "Can I do without this cigarette?" You may decide not to have that cigarette. Throughout this process, keep up an inner dialogue with yourself. It will help prevent resorting to your old habit of mindless smoking, just picking up a cigarette any old time, without thinking about it.

By reducing the number of cigarettes you have each day, you should be able to ebb off them completely (and without torturing yourself) by the end of a month, if not sooner.

Daily Tips

Make it easier *not* to smoke. *Follow these suggestions...*

➤ **Brands.** As you're ebbing off, every time that you buy a pack of cigarettes change brands to ones that are less appealing to you. It will reduce the pleasure of smoking and it can affect your blood chemistry reaction, making you relieved to break the habit.

➤ **Buying Power.** Do not buy cartons of cigarettes. Buy one pack at a time and only after you've finished a pack.

➤ **Your First.** Each day, wait an hour longer than the previous day before lighting your first cigarette.

➤ **Distraction.** When you have a real craving for a cigarette, tell yourself you can have the cigarette in about five minutes. Meanwhile, do something absorbing, something that takes your total concentration to do and that takes longer than five minutes.

➤ **Change Is Good.** Figure out your favorite times and situations for smoking and avoid them. For instance, if you always smoke while you're driving a car, take public transportation until you've kicked the habit.

➤ **More Change.** It's a good idea to hang out in places where smoking is prohibited and to hang out with people who don't smoke and mind if you do.

Cigarette Substitutes

Here are foods you can eat and things you can do to help resist the temptation to smoke...

➤ **Sunflower Seeds.** Instead of reaching for a cigarette, reach for a handful of raw, shelled unsalted sunflower seeds. They provide the same psychological boost you get from cigarettes and the nerve-calming effect of tobacco. Sunflower seeds also help nourish the nervous system. They're a great cigarette substitute!

➤ **Gingerroot.** Take one small piece of fresh gingerroot and chew on it. It's strong and burns. It's that burning quality that makes it a good substitute for cigarettes. Unlike smoking a cigarette, ginger will make your mouth feel clean and refreshed.

 CAUTION: Ginger acts as a blood thinner, so check with your doctor before using it if you are taking a prescription blood thinner. Also, stop using ginger three days before any surgery.

➤ **Radish Juice.** Juice a fresh radish or daikon (Japanese radish available in most supermarket produce sections) by grating it or by putting it in a food processor and then squeezing the grated pulp through cheesecloth. Add honey to taste and drink the juice. You can also toss the grated radish in a salad.

➤ **Clove.** Suck on a clove. It isn't fun to do, but it sort of numbs your mouth and lessens your desire for a cigarette.

➤ **Acupressure.** Quell the urge to light up by pressing the acupressure point in the middle of the breastbone directly between your two nipples. Press it three times in a row, for 12 seconds each time.

➤ **Alkaline.** There is thought to be a strong connection between acidic body chemistry and a craving for nicotine. If you decrease the acidic foods you eat and increase the alkaline foods, you can cut down on your nicotine craving. Some alkalinizing foods are apples, berries, raisins, sweet potatoes, carrots, celery, mushrooms, onions, peas, lima beans and almonds.

➤ **Breathing.** At least once a day, instead of taking a cigarette or any of these substitute foods or drinks, resist the craving by taking 10 slow, deep breaths of air. Don't be surprised if the deep breaths leave you completely satisfied. It's also good for your lungs.

➤ **Herbal Tea.** A few cups of slippery elm bark tea a day can help submerge the urge to smoke. You may want to alternate with oat straw tea, marjoram tea and magnolia bark tea—all available at most health food stores.

➤ **Hold On.** To replace the physicality of a cigarette in your hand, hold a pen, pencil or artificial cigarette. If you really want something to play with, twist a paper clip or buy some Chinese exercise balls (available at some Asian shops, health food stores and through New Age catalogs listed in "Sources," page 311).

➤ **Try a Yo-Yo.** Playing with a yo-yo can help divert your attention and relieve the stress of withdrawal. Alan Amaral, the founder of Yomega, started playing with a yo-yo to help kick his smoking habit, and then founded the Yomega Corporation.

For the Yomega product line, including the Yo-Yo with a Brain, visit *www.yomega.com*. To speak with a customer service rep, call 800-338-8796.

Our Closing Thought on Smoking

We greatly respect you for wanting to stop smoking and we send every good wish for your success.

More information: Action on Smoking and Health (ASH) is a nonprofit tax-exempt legal action antismoking US organization that has been solely devoted to the many problems of smoking for more than 40 years. ASH also serves as an advocate of the nonsmokers' rights movement.

For all kinds of helpful, healthful information and to learn more about ASH's work, visit *www.ash.org* or call 202-659-4310.

AFFIRMATION

Repeat this affirmation starting first thing in the morning, every time you eat, drink or do something instead of smoking a cigarette, and last thing at night…

I'm proud of the choices I make. My reward is good health and joy.

STRESS, ANXIETY AND PANIC ATTACKS

 ome great minds of our time have written about stress, tension and anxiety. When you read what they have to say, it doesn't seem so bad after all. In fact, reading these things actually calmed me down, making me feel a whole lot better.

According to Pulitzer prize-winning journalist, Felix Morley, "From tension…all human progress springs."

"It is well to remind ourselves," says existential psychologist Dr. Rollo May, "anxiety signifies a conflict, and so long as a conflict is going on, a constructive solution is possible."

The late Dr. Stanley J. Sarnoff (1917–1990) of the National Heart Institute said, "The process of living is the process of reacting to stress."

On coping with stress, this is how Dr. Robert S. Eliot, cardiology professor at the University of Nebraska, sums it up: "Rule number one is, don't sweat the small stuff. Rule number two is, it's all small stuff. And if you can't fight and you can't flee, flow."

Stress

Here are some suggestions for reducing stress, tension and anxiety…

➤ **Tranquilizer Teas.**

• **Chamomile.** The classic folk remedy to calm the nerves and help you relax is chamomile tea (available at health food stores). Steep a teaspoon of the herb in a cup of just-boiled water. After five minutes, strain and sip slowly.

191

• **Catnip.** When you need to be more tranquil, prepare a cup of catnip tea (available at health food stores) by steeping a heaping teaspoon of catnip in a cup of just-boiled water. After five minutes, strain and drink. If you have a cat, be sure to put the catnip away in a secure place, or your feline will make a beeline for it.

➤ **Calm-Down Juice.** Let celery juice calm your jittery nerves. If you don't have a juice extractor, find a health food store that has a juice bar and order celery juice either straight or with some carrot juice mixed in. Keep in mind that celery is a natural diuretic.

➤ **Vitamin Therapy.** Experts agree, taking a super B-complex vitamin daily may reduce feelings of tension and anxiety.

➤ **Reach for Sesame.** When something stressful happens suddenly, the blood calcium level can drop, making the situation seem worse. Reach for a handful of sesame seeds, or any other food rich in calcium—hard cheese, cottage cheese, sardines, salmon, anchovies, almonds, tofu, soybeans, rhubarb, spinach, broccoli, kale, collard and mustard greens. The big calcium boost can help you get through an unanticipated emotional upheaval.

➤ **Daily Unwind.** Find a convenient, comfortable place to take a one-hour vacation every single day. When you wake up in the morning, make an appointment with yourself, name a specific time and keep to it. During that hour, do whatever relaxes you. Read, watch TV, do a crossword puzzle, knit, listen to music (more about that a little later)—whatever gives you pleasure.

➤ **Unburden Yourself.** Writer Garson Kanin said, "There are thousands of causes for stress, and one antidote to stress is self-expression. That's what happens to me every day. My thoughts get off my chest, down my sleeves and onto my pad."

Yes, get it off your chest and onto a pad. Keep a diary. You may want to spend 10 minutes of your daily unwind (see remedy above) to let it all out on paper.

➤ **Portable Antistress Machine.** Stress is always with us—during rush-hour traffic, while trying to find your cell phone, being told the computer is down after waiting on line at the bank.

What we really need, according to Stuart F. Crump, Jr., is an antistress machine that's as portable as our problems. And he has one. It's a yo-yo. Actually, Stuart, also known as "Professor Yo-Yo," has 500 of them and has written several books on the subject, including *Amazing Yo-Yo Tricks* (Publications International). He says that yo-yoing is an excellent way to cope with stress throughout the day, wherever you are. Most of us did it as children, and once you know how, you never forget. So start playing with a yo-yo and you can have the world on a string!

Visit the Yomega Corporation's Web site at *www.yomega.com.*

➤ **Music Hath Charms to Soothe.** Let go of tension and anxiety by listening to calming music. There is a big selection of tapes and CDs in most health food stores and book stores. Select instrumentals—no vocalists—and stick with slow, regular rhythms that feature piano and string instruments—harp, guitar, violin and cello. Avoid brass instruments.

➤ **Hot vs. Cold.** Some say that a cold bath or shower is invigorating and can convert your nervous tension into creative energy. Others think a hot bath or shower improves circulation and encourages your body to relax. Whatever works for you. In either case, it may be the negative ions released in the shower that

TAKE NOTE

Dr. Andrew Weil's 4-7-8 (or Relaxing Breath) Exercise

Dr. Andrew Weil, physician and author (*www. drweil.com*), is best known for bringing to light the field of integrative medicine—the happy combination of mainstream medical therapies and complementary and alternative therapies for which there is scientific evidence of safety and effectiveness.

This breathing exercise that Dr. Weil is sharing with us is one that he recommends to help relax and reduce stress…

"This exercise is utterly simple, takes almost no time, requires no equipment and can be done anywhere. Although you can do the exercise in any position, sit with your back straight while learning the exercise. Place the tip of your tongue against the ridge of tissue just behind your upper front teeth, and keep it there through the entire exercise. You will be exhaling through your mouth around your tongue; try pursing your lips slightly if this seems awkward.

- Exhale completely through your mouth, making a whoosh sound.
- Close your mouth and inhale quietly through your nose to a mental count of **four.**
- Hold your breath for a count of **seven.**
- Exhale completely through your mouth, making a whoosh sound to a count of **eight.**
- This is one breath. Now inhale again and repeat the cycle three more times for a total of four breaths.

"Notice that you always inhale quietly through your nose and exhale audibly through your mouth. The tip of your tongue stays in position the whole time. Exhalation takes twice as long as inhalation. The absolute time you spend on each phase is not important; the ratio of 4:7:8 is important. If you have trouble holding your breath, speed the exercise up but keep to the ratio of 4:7:8 for the three phases. With practice you can slow it all down and get used to inhaling and exhaling more and more deeply.

"This exercise is a natural tranquilizer for the nervous system. Unlike tranquilizing drugs, which are often effective when you first take them but then lose their power over time, this exercise is subtle when you first try it but gains in power with repetition and practice. Do it at least twice a day. You cannot do it too frequently. Do not do more than four breaths at one time for the first month of practice. Later, if you wish, you can extend it to eight breaths. If you feel a little lightheaded when you first breathe this way, do not be concerned; it will pass.

"Once you develop this technique by practicing it daily, it will be a very useful tool that you will always have with you. Use it whenever anything upsetting happens—before you react. Use it whenever you are aware of internal tension. Use it to help you fall asleep. This exercise cannot be recommended too highly. Everyone can benefit from it."

If you practice this at least once a day, you'll soon be able to do it quickly and effectively whenever you need to de-stress.

help you feel better. See the next entry for more about those ions.

➤ **Negative Ions.** Practitioners of qigong, the ancient Chinese mind-body therapy, believe in the power of flowing water because it releases negative ions (charged molecules) into the air. Breathing negatively charged air can help you feel tranquil, relaxed and improve your sense of well being.

If you are overcome with stress and worry, get as much fresh air as possible. Good quality negatively ionized air is found in natural outdoor environments, especially around evergreen trees, by waterfalls, at the beach and in the fresh air before, during and after storms. The best ratios of negative to positive ions are around moving water—oceans, rivers, streams, fountains and waterfalls.

If you can't get to a beach or local park, consider getting an air purifier that works by emitting negative ions.

For a quick picker-upper, let the water from your faucet flow over your hands for two or three minutes.

➤ **Shall We Tense.** This easy-to-do exercise will take the stress right out of your body in no time. If possible, lie down on the floor with your eyes closed. If that's impractical, sit with your eyes closed. Make a fist with both hands and tense the muscles in your fingers, wrists and forearms. Stay that way for five seconds, then release the tension, letting it fall away from your fingers, wrists and forearms. Continue the tensing/relaxing process with your shoulders, neck and face, and then your legs, feet and toes. Notice the uncomfortable feeling when you tense up; then fully enjoy the experience of completely relaxing.

➤ **Meditation.** Choose a word that has a calming and uplifting influence on you. If you can think of one that ends with an "m" sound or an "n" sound, do so. Some examples are charm, fun, home, tame, win.

Sit in a comfortable chair, eyes closed and body relaxed. Say that word to yourself over and over each time you exhale. If your mind drifts, the second you realize it, go back to the word, and say it over and over while exhaling. Do this every day for 15 minutes. If you find it a pleasant and beneficial experience, you may want to meditate twice a day.

This form of meditating can make a tremendous difference in your central nervous system. It can also lower your blood pressure and slow down your heart rate.

➤ **Visualization.** When you feel tension building, or if you're already stressed out, take 10 minutes to recondition your transmission with this simple visualization exercise.

Sit in a comfortable chair and close your eyes. Breathe out all the air in your lungs, then slowly breathe in. As you exhale, visualize a huge theater marquee with bright lights flashing the number "3" three times. Take another slow, deep breath, and as you exhale, visualize the number "2" flashing three times. Take one more deep breath, slowly, and when you exhale, see the number "1" flashing three times.

Now that you're relaxed, picture paradise on earth. What is or would be your favorite place in the whole wide world? The beach? A cabin in the mountains? A field of flowers? Imagine yourself being wherever you'd be happiest. Feel free to thoroughly enjoy the visit for a few minutes.

When you're ready to return to the here-and-now, slowly count from one to three. Open your eyes, stretch and notice how refreshed you feel.

That little getaway gives you the chance to let go of stress, allowing the body's healing energy to take over.

Panic Attacks

The second a panic attack starts, say to yourself, "This is a panic attack and it will be over very soon. It will not harm me. Now I'll relax and start my controlled breathing exercise."

To the count of five, take a deep breath in through your nostrils, hold it for another count of five, and breathe out through your mouth to the count of 10. Keep concentrating on the five-five-10 breathing process and, before long, that panicky feeling will be gone.

Have you seen a health professional about your panic attacks? If you haven't, you should. This is one challenge where a psychologist can help you figure out the cause of the panic attacks. Once the cause is determined, the next step is overcoming the cause to effect a cure. We urge you to seek professional help.

If you have been professionally diagnosed, and you're both convinced that the attacks are not caused by a physical problem like hypoglycemia or PMS, but by stress, consider these commonsense, will-do-you-a-world-of-good suggestions...

➤ **Confront Fearful Situations** instead of worrying about them.

➤ **Don't Sit Around Second-Guessing** every possible scenario. Instead, go directly to the source—contact the person who has the answer(s) you need.

➤ **Exercise Daily,** even if it's just taking a brisk walk for a half hour.

➤ **Eat a Well-Balanced Diet**...but that's an old story. Also, stay away from soda, caffeine and anything with sugar. No one said it's going to be easy.

➤ **Be Kind to Your Sensitive Soul.** That means don't read, watch or listen to bad news. When you do watch TV, listen to the radio, go to a movie or read, choose lighthearted things...uppers. Opt for laughs over lumps, funny instead of fatal, joy-inspiring rather than panic-provoking.

Nerve-Wracking Situations

We didn't know what the heading should be for these remedies, but all we had to do was mention some examples—making a speech, asking for a raise, going for a job interview—and we thought of the three words that sum it up best: nerve-wracking situations.

Public speaking is at the top of many people's list of things they dread doing. *Glossophobia* (yes, there's even a word for the fear of public speaking) can be overcome. The secret is to plan, prepare and practice. That's in your control. Do your homework before the event—as we said, plan, prepare and practice—and follow some of our suggestions on the day of your presentation. You may even enjoy the experience and look forward to your next speaking engagement.

➤ **Beverage Advice.** On the day of your event, limit your intake of caffeine and alcoholic beverages for at least 12 hours before you're scheduled to speak. Also, to keep your voice in tip-top condition, do not drink milk or ice cold drinks two hours prior to your performance.

➤ **Aromatherapy.** The effect of scents on the psyche is potent and immediate. So, right before "showtime," take a couple of whiffs of black pepper. No, not ground black pepper. That'll make you sneeze. There are aromatherapy inhalers available at most health food stores and one of them is black pepper. A few whiffs can boost confidence and amplify courage. That confidence and courage, along with planning, preparing and practicing, can make you a star.

➤ **Reflexology.** This reflexology remedy involves your hands. Put your palms together against your chest as though you're praying. Intertwine your fingers and stay that way for about five minutes, until your entire body feels relaxed. Be sure your feet are flat on the floor and your shoulders are down. Closing your eyes may make you feel even more relaxed.

➤ **Gem Therapy.** Rhodochrosite is the stone for relieving stress and anxiety. Wear it, or carry it.

➤ **Anchor Yourself.** Think of a time you did something that was super. Relive the feeling you felt, knowing you were wonderful and appreciated. Remember that feeling and re-create it the second you step into the spotlight.

How Stress Affects Your Immune System: You May Be Surprised!

After 30 years of stress research, psychologists Suzanne Segerstrom at the University of Kentucky and Gregory Miller at the University of British Columbia discovered that modern stresses bring about complex reactions in addition to the simple fight-or-flight response that causes your heart to race and a rise in your blood pressure.

Doctors Segerstrom and Miller organized modern stressful situations into major categories. One of their categories was public speaking, considered by many of us to be extremely stressful.

When test subjects were asked to speak in public or to do mental math, the tasks surprisingly activated their fast-acting immune

response. That is the body's all-purpose defense system for fighting off infections and healing wounds. People participating in these short-term stresses had up to twice as many natural killer cells in their blood ready to fight the early stages of infection.

So next time there's a short-term stress, where there's an end in sight, you can relax, knowing that it's serving your immune system in a *good* way.

Recommended Reading

➤ *The Superstress Solution* by Roberta Lee, MD (Random House). Dr. Lee, a world-renowned integrative physician, has a superstress solution that includes recognizing, rebalancing and protecting against stresses small and large. Her four-week diet and lifestyle program will help you relieve anxiety, sleep well, restore your ability to relax and build resilience against future stress.

A Word from the Wise...

Surprising Stress Relievers

Deep breathing does work—but there are other effective ways to de-stress. *Unique techniques...*

➤ **Create a Personal Stress-Relief Kit** that contains five favorite objects, one for each of the senses—for example, a smooth stone to touch, a sachet to smell, flavorful gum to taste, a beloved photo to look at, a mantra to read aloud. When stress overwhelms, focus on one or more of these objects to help you feel centered, suggests psychotherapist Leila Keen, LCSW, of Durham, North Carolina.

➤ **Keep a Bottle of Bubbles Handy**— blowing bubbles blows off steam.

➤ **Bake Something That Calls for Repetitive Movements** to promote a meditative state of mind—kneading dough, slicing apples.

➤ **Sing *Loudly*** when stuck in traffic.

➤ **Laugh.** Even if you fake it at first, you'll feel calmer.

➤ **Reread the Final Chapter of a Favorite Novel** in which good triumphs.

Tamara Eberlein, former editor, *HealthyWoman from Bottom Line*, an e-letter, Boardroom Inc.

SUNBURN

Do you know that you can actually get very sunburned while swimming under water? You can also get a sunburn from the reflected rays of sand, water, snow and even cement. And it doesn't have to be a sunny day. You can get a severe sunburn on foggy and hazy days.

When you get a sunburn, you shed the top layer of burned skin and the new top layer of skin is then extremely sensitive to the sun. It takes three months for your skin to be the same as it was before the sunburn.

What we're getting at with all this information is that you must take precautions.

Sunburn Prevention and Protection

The best way to prevent sunburn is to stay out of the sun. Not practical? Okay then, since the sun is strongest between 10 am and 4 pm (standard time), schedule your outdoor activity before 9 am or after 5 pm. Still not too practical? A doable solution is sunscreen. Don't leave home without it!

➤ **Sunscreen Savvy.** The point of sunscreen is to block out the harmful ultraviolet

(UVA and UVB) rays of the sun that are damaging to skin...

● **A quality sunscreen that protects against UVA and UVB radiation** should have an SPF (Sun Protection Factor) of at least 15 and contain either *avobenzone, titanium dioxide* or *zinc oxide.*

● **Sunscreen should be the last product applied,** especially on the face, preventing water-based foundations and moisturizers from breaking it down and having it lose its effectiveness.

● **Apply sunscreen liberally to all of your sun-exposed areas.** It's said to take about one fluid ounce to cover an adult's body.

● **It takes 20 to 30 minutes for sunscreen to be absorbed by the skin,** so apply it a half hour before going out into the sun.

● **Reapply sunscreen every couple of hours while in the sun.** But reapply it *right after* swimming, toweling off or sweating profusely.

● **Use lip pomade with an SPF of 30** to protect your lips from getting sunburned. Be diligent about reapplying it after you eat or drink.

● **Wear a hat with a brim,** wear sunglasses and keep applying sunscreen if you want to save your skin—literally.

NOTE: Your shadow can give you an idea as to how much ultraviolet (UV) exposure you are receiving. A shadow that is longer than you are means UV exposure is low; a shadow that is shorter than you are means the UV exposure is high.

If you're careless enough to go out without proper protection, here are some remedies to help heal your sunburned skin...

Sunburn Soothers

➤ **Three-Step Relief.**

• **Quick.** As soon as possible, take a cold shower. You know how you run cold water on pasta to stop the cooking process? Yup! The cold water will stop your skin from continuing to burn.

• **Next.** Mix equal amounts of baking soda and cornstarch, depending on how much skin got sunburned, then add enough water to make a paste. Apply it to the affected areas.

If more than just your face is sunburned, pour cornstarch and baking soda into a cool bath and relax in it for a while. When you get out, forget the towel—just dry off naturally with the cornstarch and baking soda on your skin.

• **Then.** Apply aloe vera gel directly on the sunburned areas. Aloe vera gel is available at health food stores, or if you have an aloe plant, squeeze the gel out of the leaves, starting at the bottom of the plant with the oldest (most beneficial) leaves.

Incidentally, buying an aloe plant is like buying a pharmacy. There are close to 100 medical uses for this easy-to-grow succulent.

➤ **Pain-Relieving Blender Recipe.** Ron Hamilton of Great American Natural Products shared his soothing sunburn remedy with us.

In a blender, put one peeled cucumber, one-half cup of oatmeal, one teaspoon of dried comfrey or slippery elm (either is optional) and one-half cup of yogurt. Blend well, then apply directly on the sunburned areas. It should give you quick relief as it takes out the pain and the redness.

➤ **Sunburned Face Treatment.** At the Neinast Salon in Dallas, Texas, the late beauty expert Paul Neinast treated sunburned faces by soaking slices of tomato in buttermilk for about 10 minutes and applying the slices to the face. This relieves the pain, draws out the heat and closes the pores all at the same time.

➤ **Red to Tan.** Smear the sunburned areas with wheat germ oil, and don't be surprised if the red turns tan as it helps heal the skin.

➤ **Acid Mantle Restorer.** Mix equal amounts of apple cider vinegar and water. Gently sponge the mixture on the sunburned skin. It helps restore the acid mantle (the film on the surface of the skin that acts as a barrier to bacteria, viruses and other contaminants).

➤ **For Peeling Skin.** Mash the meat of a ripe papaya and put it on the peeling skin. Papaya, with all its wonderful enzymes, helps tone the skin while it removes dead cells. Keep on for a half hour, then rinse it off with cool water.

For Sunburned Eyes

➤ **Potato.** Grate a raw potato and wrap it in cheesecloth. Put this potato poultice on your closed eyes and let it stay there, while you relax, for at least a half hour. Oh—and promise yourself that you'll never let this happen again.

➤ **Tea Bags.** Moisten a couple of tea bags with cool water and put them on your eyelids. Let them stay there for at least a half hour. If the tea bags dry up in that time, wet them again and reapply.

AFFIRMATION

While treating the problem with any of the above remedies, repeat this affirmation until the heat is out of the sunburned skin...

I am calm and cool. I have peace of mind. There's happiness in my heart.

TOOTH, GUM AND MOUTH ISSUES

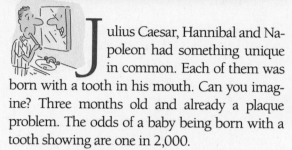

Julius Caesar, Hannibal and Napoleon had something unique in common. Each of them was born with a tooth in his mouth. Can you imagine? Three months old and already a plaque problem. The odds of a baby being born with a tooth showing are one in 2,000.

A full set of teeth consists of 32 teeth. The average working adult has about 24 teeth. And by the time that adult is 65, he/she is down to an average of 14 teeth. More than half of all people over the age of 17 are in the early stages of some type of gum disease. But, these are statistics we have control over with proper tooth and gum care.

 NOTE: Be sure to read about "Oil Pulling" in the chapter "It Does a Body Good," page 254. Don't forget!

Children should have a dental checkup every six months; adults should see their dentist once a year. Meanwhile, here are suggestions until you get to the dentist, including tips on how to care for your teeth and gums (please know that these remedies are not meant to replace the dentist)...

Teeth

Toothache Relief

To ease the pain of a toothache while waiting for the dentist's appointment, you may want to try one of these...

➤ **Lime.** Dip a cotton ball in freshly squeezed lime juice and put it on your aching tooth.

➤ **Cinnamon Oil.** Massage cinnamon oil on the painful area.

➤ **Mustard.** Take a little chunk of peanut butter, put mustard or mustard powder on it and place it, mustard-side down, on the sore tooth. The peanut butter is used to hold the mustard in place.

 CAUTION: Mustard can burn mucous membranes in the mouth.

➤ **Sesame Seeds Mouthwash.** When you have a toothache and swollen gums, crush a half-cup of sesame seeds and put it in a small pot with a cup of water. Boil it until you have about a half-cup of water. Then strain out the seeds and use the liquid as a mouthwash to relieve the pain and swelling.

➤ **Aloe Vera.** Squeeze the gel from the leaf of an aloe vera plant directly on the tooth. Keep doing that until the pain completely disappears, the plant disappears or it's time for your dentist appointment.

➤ **Horseradish or Garlic.** This unusual remedy is said to work with horseradish or garlic. Grate a two-ounce piece of fresh horseradish, wrap each ounce separately in doubled pieces of cheesecloth and put them in the bend of each arm until the toothache goes away. If you prefer garlic, peel and mince two cloves and...you know the rest.

Actually, placing a piece of horseradish or garlic directly on the problem tooth may also relieve the pain.

 CAUTION: Garlic can burn mucous membranes in the mouth.

➤ **Yarrow Poultice.** Steep a heaping teaspoon of yarrow (available at herb stores or see "Sources," page 309) in a few ounces of just-boiled water. After a minute, strain out the liquid and with the remaining moist herb make a tiny poultice in a little piece of cheesecloth to put on your sore tooth.

Minimize Dental-Work Pain and Promote Healing

The bad news is that you need dental work. The good news is, there are several things you can do to help reduce the pain and speed up the healing…

➤ **Before.** Starting a week before the dentist's initial treatment, take 10 milligrams (mg) of vitamin B-1 (thiamine) daily.

➤ **Before and After.** Take 500 mg of bromelain three times a day on an empty stomach. Bromelain, the protein-digesting enzyme in pineapple, is a powerful anti-inflammatory agent and is used to relieve swelling and speed tissue healing.

 CAUTION: Bromelain is NOT recommended for people with a pineapple allergy, or with gastritis or active gastric or duodenal ulcers. Also, people taking anticoagulant drugs such as *warfarin* should consult with their doctor before taking bromelain.

If bromelain is taken with food, it will act more like a digestive enzyme than an anti-inflammatory.

➤ **After.** Once extensive dental work or oral surgery is over, mix one teaspoon of liquid chlorophyll in a half-cup of water and gently swish it around your mouth. Swallow it or spit it out—the choice is yours. Do this three-minute process a half-dozen times a day to ease the discomfort and hurry the healing.

➤ **After.** Massage the gums with peppermint oil, covering the area with the teeth on which the work was done. You may have

200

to do this every few hours until the pain stops recurring.

Tooth Decay Prevention

This information falls into the you're-not-born-knowing-this category…perhaps it's the why-didn't-you-tell-me-sooner category…then again, maybe it's the I-wish-I-didn't-know/ignorance-is-bliss category…

➤ **Beware of Citrus.** Don't suck a lemon, or any other citrus fruit. They can gradually dissolve calcium from your teeth. After eating an orange, grapefruit, lemon or tangerine, or after drinking any kind of citrus drink, rinse your mouth with water…then rinse again.

➤ **Beware of Cola.** Tooth enamel loses minerals and grows softer within five minutes of drinking cola.

➤ **Raisins Worse Than Caramel!** *The Journal of the American Dental Association* published the results of a study that says raisins stick to your teeth and, therefore, cause more cavities than all other standard snacks, and more than caramel, fudge, chocolate and cookies. So, after eating raisins, be sure to brush your teeth to prevent cavities.

➤ **Plaque Formation Prevention.** The bacteria and food particles in your mouth form plaque. Plaque, if not brushed away regularly, builds up and causes cavities, gum problems and bad breath. *Aside from diligent brushing and flossing, here are some plaque repellents to drink and eat after meals…*

• **Eat an apple.**

• **Eat a few strawberries**…not dipped in chocolate!

• **Eat aged cheeses**, especially after eating sugary food or drinking cola. The cheese must be aged—cheddar, Swiss, Monterey Jack are best. Eating a half-ounce is adequate.

• **Drink green tea.** It's a great antioxidant and beneficial in so many ways, including as a plaque repellent.

• **Chew sugarless gum** for at least 10 minutes after you've eaten. It will produce saliva that will counterbalance the acid in the plaque. According to researchers at the Indiana University School of Dentistry, the potential for tooth decay decreased by an average 72% when patients chewed gum after eating.

Teeth Clenching and Grinding (Bruxism)

When the late Kenneth R. Goljan, DDS, started practicing dentistry, teeth clenching and grinding were problems for elderly patients. As the years went on, the patients with the problem became younger and younger. Now, close to 40 years later, clenching and grinding their teeth is a prevalent problem among preteens.

The doctor felt this problem related to today's pressure-packed lifestyle. And, watching the evening news on TV before going to bed feeds our insecurity and compounds our self-generated stress.

In addition to Dr. Goljan, many experts agree that stress may be the key to the cause of bruxism.

Dr. Goljan's "Seven-by-Seven" system can help put an end to the problem. This system has been tested, fine-tuned and used successfully for many years. Follow it exactly as it is written here.

In your own comfortable words, write down the answers to these four questions— keep the answers simple…

1. **What exactly is the problem?** (*Sample answer:* "Clenching and grinding my teeth is bad for me.")

2. **Why is it a problem?** (*Sample answer:* "It causes me pain and makes me unhappy.")

3. **What are you going to do about the problem?** (*Sample answer:* "I will not clench and grind my teeth anymore.")

4. **Why do you want to do something about the problem?** (*Sample answer:* "This will make the pain disappear and I will be happier.")

Study your four phrases; analyze them, and when you're sure there aren't any hidden or double meanings that your subconscious can choose and act on, then memorize them. This is where the "Seven-by-Seven" comes in. You are to say your four answers seven times in a row, seven times a day.

According to Dr. Goljan, the best times to do it are: (1) Breakfast, (2) between breakfast and lunch, (3) lunch, (4) between lunch and dinner, (5) dinner, (6) between dinner and bedtime, (7) bedtime.

The ideal situation is for you to be in a comfortable environment and to say the words out loud, with feeling. If that's not practical, then whisper the words. If that's awkward too, then do the best you can.

Seven-by-Seven works. (Many of Dr. Goljan's patients got positive results in a matter of days.) You shouldn't repeat the four answers fewer than seven times in a row, seven times a day; doing it more than that may make it even more effective.

Once you stop clenching and grinding your teeth, you can stop doing the Seven-by-Seven system. But you have to realize that the bad pattern will always be in your subconscious. If given the opportunity—during stressful conditions, for example—that old pattern may raise its ugly head. It is for that reason, Dr. Goljan wisely suggested, you do a day or two of the Seven-by-Seven every two weeks or maybe once a month to reinforce the new programming.

If Dr. Goljan's Seven-by-Seven works for you, you can apply it to everything in your life that's a problem.

Grind Less, Sleep Better: At bedtime, chew two chewable calcium tablets. Make sure the label specifies "chewable." Be sure to count this calcium as part of your total calcium supplementation for the day.

202

Gums

For the sake of your gums, read about "Oil Pulling" in the chapter "It Does a Body Good," page 254. *Also, check out the remedies below...*

Gingivitis

Thanks to TV commercials, "gingivitis" has become a common word for an even more common condition. If you have gingivitis—red, swollen, bleeding gums—there are treatments that can help. All the herbs, tinctures and vitamins mentioned below are available at health food stores. In order to get positive results, you must keep at it daily—morning, noon (if possible) and night...

➤ **Garlic and Parsley.** There is a combination of garlic and parsley extracts in capsules. Take two every four hours for at least three days.

 CAUTION: Having garlic on an empty stomach can cause nausea. Be sure to have some food in your stomach before eating garlic or taking capsules. And, be cautious with garlic if you have gastritis.

➤ **Calendula.** This is a healing herb, related to arnica, chamomile and yarrow. Add a teaspoon of tincture of calendula to two tablespoons of water. Hold it in your mouth for three minutes, then spit it out. Do it two to three times a day, starting first thing in the morning and last thing at night.

➤ **Bee Propolis.** This miraculous compound is made by bees mixing their saliva and digestive enzymes with balsams and resin collected from certain trees. Use bee propolis as a toothpaste, and/or dissolve five drops of propolis in a half-glass of water and ration out this milky drink throughout the day.

CAUTION: If you have a suspected sensitivity to bee products, forget this remedy and try another.

➤ **Vitamin C.** In addition to any of the above, take vitamin C (500 mg) twice a day.

Tartar Prevention

Plaque, a sticky, colorless film of bacteria, forms on teeth through the natural course of eating. For most people, brushing and flossing teeth regularly removes plaque before it hardens. The hardened material is known as tartar and needs to be removed professionally.

For those of you who take great care of your teeth and gums—always brushing after meals, flossing and gum-massaging, in addition to staying away from sugary foods and eating raw, firm and fibrous vegetables and fruit daily—but still have plaque buildup, here's a helpful tip…

➤ **Papaya Pills.** To help stop the formation of problem-causing tartar, take two papaya pills after every meal. Keep one pill on each side of your mouth and just let it dissolve. It can kill bacteria, rid you of dead gum tissue and help digestion, too.

Denture Wearers

➤ **Sore Gums.** Massage sore gums with myrrh tincture (available at health food stores), or put a half-teaspoon of the myrrh tincture in a cup of warm water and use it as a mouthwash.

➤ **Denture Cleanser.** Keep your dentures clean by soaking them overnight in a cup of distilled white vinegar. Be sure to rinse them well before using.

➤ **Dentures and Gas.** If you have more gas than usual and you can't figure out why, check the fit of your dentures. Bad-fitting dentures can cause you to swallow lots of air, thus the additional gas.

➤ **Keep Dentures Fitting Better Longer.** As the years pass after you've started wearing dentures, your jawbone shrinks. That shrinking process can throw off the proper fit of your dentures. To slow down and minimize jawbone shrinkage, eat foods rich in vitamin D—bone meal, tuna, sardines, salmon, herring, cod, milk and milk products. Also eat foods rich in calcium—steamed leafy green vegetables (collard, dandelion and mustard), sesame seeds, sardines, cheddar cheese, Swiss cheese and seaweed. You can also supplement your diet with vitamin D and calcium capsules or powder. Ask your health professional for the dosage that's appropriate for you.

➤ **Time to Reline.** If dentures do not fit properly, go to the dentist for help. It may be as simple as having the dentures relined. The relining may enable you to comfortably and thoroughly chew whatever you want to eat, which will make your digestion better, and will certainly add to your enjoyment of food.

Mouth

Bad Breath

If you're troubled by occasional bad breath and you know it is not a symptom of indigestion, gum disease or anything other than occasional bad breath, these suggestions may help…

➤ **Parsley and Vinegar.** Dip two sprigs of parsley in distilled white vinegar and chew it, chew it, chew it.

➤ **Peppermint Oil.** Mix three drops of peppermint oil in a glass of warm water. Take a mouthful, swish it around your mouth, and spit it out. Take another mouthful and gargle with

TAKE NOTE

An attorney advertisement in a New York newspaper caught our attention. The headline asked: *Have you suffered injuries from denture cream zinc?*

According to the ad, hundreds of individuals are suing denture cream manufacturers for inadequate warnings of the dangers of zinc overuse.

Intrigued, we quickly got the whole story...one that every denture wearer should know. Many Food and Drug Administration (FDA)–approved denture creams contain zinc. With constant use over a period of time, zinc can lower levels of copper in your body and also rob it of other essential minerals. All of this zinc exposure can cause *neurodegeneration* of the central and peripheral nervous system. Nerve damage symptoms, according to the attorney's advertisement, are tingling in hands, weakness and numbness in arms and legs, difficulty walking and loss of balance and cognitive or memory impairment.

The following simple blood and urine tests may be used by your health care professional to determine if you have high levels of zinc—zinc red blood cell count (RBC), copper RBC, spot urine test for zinc, spot urine test for copper, blood test for ceruloplasmin.

According to a detailed clinical assessment of a study group of patients with some of the symptoms mentioned above due to zinc overexposure, denture cream was the source of the excessive zinc. They all had a history of ill-fitting dentures which required large amounts of denture cream.

The good news is that their zinc and copper levels normalized after they stopped using the denture cream that contained zinc. See "Something Special—Think No Zinc!" on the next page for more information.

it, then spit it out. Keep doing that until you finish the glassful.

➤ **Seeds.** Thoroughly chew a few fennel seeds, dill seeds or anise seeds, then spit them out or swallow them.

➤ **Tongue Brushing.** Every time you brush your teeth, brush the bacteria, minute food particles and toxins off your tongue, too. Use your toothbrush or scrape your tongue with a teaspoon or commercial tongue-scraper sold in drugstores and health food stores. A dozen brushes or scrapes from back to front ought to do it.

➤ **Yoga—Simhasana (Lion Pose).** Yoga is an ancient discipline originating in India and involving mind and body exercise. The physical exercises are called asanas. In Sanskrit, *simha* means lion and you are about to learn the *simhasana*, or "lion pose" yoga exercise.

You will want to do the simhasana in the privacy of your own room. As unattractive as it makes you look, that's how beneficial it is.

Not only is it said to eliminate bad breath, it also relieves tension in the chest and face; helps those who stammer or stutter; strengthens face, throat and eye muscles; reduces eye strain and helps keep the skin of the neck nice and firm. Ready to roar?

Step 1: Kneel on the floor with your knees six to 12 inches apart. If you have sensitive knees, kneel on a blanket or exercise mat. If you have knee problems, sit in a chair and keep your feet flat on the floor under your knees.

Step 2: Kneelers, sit back with your perineum (bottom) resting on top of your heels. Be sure your back and head are upright.

Step 3: Press your palms on your thighs, near your knees and spread your fingers wide.

Step 4: (This is going to seem complicated. It isn't. Do it slowly the first time so that you can coordinate your breathing with your tongue, your eyes and a big roar.) Inhale through your nose, open your mouth wide, stick out your tongue with the tip curling down toward your chin. While you're doing this, open your eyes wide and fix your gaze either on the space between your eyebrows or at the tip of your nose. Then exhale through your mouth, bringing the breath over the back of your throat and letting out a loud "haaaa" sound, like the roar of a lion.

Step 5: Do it three times, then rest for a minute, and if you feel up to it, do it another three times.

We checked with many sources and none agreed as to the amount of times to do the lion pose, or how often to do it throughout the day. Start with two or three times a day. Then let your inner voice guide you. You can't overdose on this yoga exercise.

Dry Mouth

This is an uncomfortable problem for many people. The most common trigger is the use of medications, especially antihistamines, and drugs to treat high blood pressure, depression and heart disease. Read the labels of prescription and nonprescription drugs, and chances are one of the possible side effects is dry mouth. If you are on medication that says dry mouth is one of the possible side effects and are experiencing dry mouth, speak to your doctor. Perhaps your medication can be changed to something as effective as what you're taking, but without this troublesome side effect.

Meanwhile, here are some suggestions for overcoming dry mouth…

➤ **Breathing.** Make a conscious effort to breathe through your nose as much as possible. As you're drifting off to sleep, breathe through your nose and program yourself by saying, "I will sleep with my mouth closed while breathing through my nose."

➤ **Seeds.** To moisten your mouth and help freshen your breath, chew the seeds we mention in "Bad Breath" (fennel, dill and anise).

➤ **Gum.** Chew sugarless gum sweetened with xylitol. The key is the sweetener. Aside from keeping your mouth moist, xylitol can help reduce cavity-causing bacteria.

 CAUTION: Xylitol can cause gas and diarrhea if consumed in excess amounts. Also, it is very harmful for dogs. NEVER allow your pooch to have any food that has xylitol in it.

➤ **Snacking.** Stimulate the saliva glands by munching on celery stalks. They have high water content, good fiber and few calories.

➤ **Produce Saliva.** Gently chew your tongue. Within half a minute, you should be able to manufacture enough saliva to relieve the dryness.

➤ **No-Nos.** Coffee and alcoholic beverages are diuretics and will contribute to dry mouth. Cut down on them or cut them out completely.

➤ **Mouthwash.** Most mouthwashes in stores contain alcohol to help destroy bacteria. Alcohol is a drying agent that can make dry mouth worse. Needless to say, do not use any mouthwash that contains alcohol!

Make your own herbal mouthwash. Boil two and a half cups of water. Combine one teaspoon of dried rosemary, one teaspoon of dried peppermint or spearmint and one teaspoon of anise seeds. Add the herbs to the just-boiled water. Cover and let it steep for 20 minutes. Strain and pour the liquid into a glass jar with a lid. Use as a mouthwash or gargle.

ULCERS

We urge you to try these remedies, but only with your doctor's supervision. Promise. C'mon, promise. I'll be your best friend. Actually, you should be your own best friend and take good care of yourself. That means, having a health care professional oversee your ulcer treatment.

The most prevalent misconception about ulcers are that milk is soothing and that spicy foods can kill you. Wrong! There is controversy about the benefits of milk. Let me put it this way…There are many foods more healing than milk—spicy foods, for instance. Yes, you read that right. *Keep reading and decide which suggestion(s) may be for you…*

➤ **Diet Do-Withouts and Additions.** A Chinese stomach ulcer remedy calls for diet changes. Eliminate fried foods and products that contain flour, including bread. Also, no alcoholic beverages and no smoking.

In addition to the no-nos above, have one teaspoon of olive oil before each meal, and end your day with a tablespoon of powdered alfalfa in a glass of water.

➤ **Catnip Tea.** Catnip is a member of the mint family and, like other mint family members, is soothing and healing for a variety of stomach situations such as intestinal cramps, gas and the reason you're reading this—stomach ulcers.

Drink a cup of catnip tea before each meal. Prepare the tea by steeping two tablespoons of dried catnip leaves (available at herb and health food stores) in a cup of just-boiled water. Place a saucer over the cup and let it stay that way for 15 minutes. Remove the saucer, strain and drink. You may want to sweeten catnip tea with honey.

Bonus: Catnip tea is also used to treat anxiety, insomnia and is said to help prevent nightmares.

 NOTE: Most cats go crazy for catnip and will go to great lengths to get at it. If you have a cat and plan to use this remedy, keep the catnip in a tightly-sealed sturdy container and locked away in a cat-proof cabinet.

➤ **Apple Cider Vinegar.** First thing in the morning, use cotton balls or a pastry brush to paint the soles of your feet with apple cider vinegar. Let them dry naturally before putting on socks or hose. Put on another layer of vinegar right before dinner. Just do it and don't be surprised if it works.

➤ **Aloe Vera Juice.** During the last few years, we've received the same remedy from several people who used to have ulcers. The key words here are, "used to have ulcers." Their remedy consisted of aloe vera juice (available at health food stores), one tablespoon after each meal.

➤ **Barley.** Our friend's mother was diagnosed with an ulcer. She called and asked us which foods were most healing. Out of the few that we mentioned, her mother decided on barley. She made barley and barley water a major part of her daily diet. The results were wonderful. In fact, her doctor was so impressed with the fast healing, he now recommends barley to other ulcer patients.

Boil two ounces of pearl barley in six cups of water. When there's about half of the water left—three cups—take it off the fire. Strain and let the liquid cool. Add buckwheat honey to taste. Buckwheat honey is wonderful for ulcer sufferers. It can help neutralize stomach acid and soothe delicate membranes of the digestive tract. With or without honey, have at least three cups of barley water a day.

You can also eat the barley as a side dish or in soup or stew, but drinking the barley water is most important.

➤ **Bananas.** Eat them! Bananas have compounds called protease that help eliminate bacteria in the stomach that are thought to be the major cause of stomach ulcers. Also, bananas contain substances that help cells in the stomach lining to produced a thicker protective mucus barrier against stomach acids. Two great reasons to include bananas in your daily diet.

➤ **Bee Propolis.** This is a sticky substance collected by bees from the buds of certain trees. Bees use it to help hold their hive together. People can use propolis to help heal ulcers. You can get propolis extract, tablets or capsules at most health food stores or check out "Sources," page 310, for a supplier. Take 500 milligrams (mg) three times a day until the condition clears up completely.

 CAUTION: If you have a suspected sensitivity to bee products, forget this and go on to another remedy.

AFFIRMATION

Repeat this affirmation three times in a row. Each time you say it, start with your fists clenched and up against your chest. When you say "I let go…," thrust your arms and fingers out into the air in front of you. When you say, "I replace it with…," bring your arms back in, hugging yourself. Go through this process first thing in the morning, whenever you walk into a room and no one else is there (doesn't that happen each time you go to the bathroom?), and last thing at night.

I let go of my anxiety and my anger. I replace it with love and harmony.

URINARY AND KIDNEY PROBLEMS

As part of the urinary tract, the average adult bladder holds 24 ounces of urine. When the walls of the bladder are stretched, nerve impulses trigger the urge to urinate. That usually happens when the bladder has 10 to 16 ounces of urine.

The two kidneys, shaped like kidney beans and located in the back of the abdomen, on each side of the spine, are the principal organs of the urinary system. The kidneys filter the blood—all of it—once an hour.

The urinary system is extraordinarily sophisticated and, as with all complex machinery, things can go wrong. Because an accurate diagnosis is all-important, consult a health professional as soon as you suspect a urinary problem. If you plan to use any of these home remedies, check with that health professional first.

Urinary Problems
Frequent Urination

If you have the urge to go every two minutes, long before your bladder could have accumulated the appropriate ounces of urine, try either or both of these remedies…

➤ **String Beans.** Clean and wash a half-pound of string beans, put them in a pot and cover them with water, then add another cup of water. Cover the pot and cook the string beans for 10 minutes.

Once a day, on an empty stomach, eat the string beans and drink the water they were cooked in. Depending on your size and appetite, the half-pound of cooked string beans and water may be too much for you to eat at one time. Use your discretion and comfort level when it comes to portion size.

➤ **Raw Chestnuts.** A Chinese remedy for stopping the frequent urge to urinate is to eat three fresh, uncooked chestnuts before breakfast and three after dinner. (Use a nutcracker to open and peel them.) Take your time chewing them thoroughly.

Painful Urination

➤ **Aloe Vera Juice.** This juice can help heal an inflamed bladder that may cause painful urination. Take a jigger of aloe vera first thing in the morning and right after your evening meal.

Urinary Tract Infection

➤ **Cranberry Juice.** Drink a cup of cranberry juice daily. Get the health food store kind, without added sugar and preservatives.

AFFIRMATION/VISUALIZATION

Be seated in a comfortable chair. After you say this affirmation just once, take seven slow, deep breaths. As you take each one, visualize the air you're inhaling as blue-white healing energy. Feel it flowing through your body, repairing whatever needs to be repaired. Do this affirming/visualizing process first thing in the morning—maybe even before you get out of bed—and do it once at coffee break time in the afternoon, and again before you go to sleep.

I release my anger and I relax. With each breath I take, healing energy enters my body, flows through me, and I am better and better.

Kidney Problems
Kidney and Bladder Infection

 CAUTION: If you think you have a kidney infection, see your doctor. Kidney infections require antibiotics.

➤ **Flaxseed Tea.** Available at the health food store, flaxseed can help fight a kidney infection. Prepare tea by boiling one tablespoon of flaxseed in water. Simmer for 15 to 20 minutes. Strain out the flaxseed (if you're at all constipated, retain the flaxseed and eat it). Most important for the kidney and bladder infection is that you drink two cups of flaxseed tea daily.

Kidney Detoxifier

➤ **Parsnip—A Great Detoxifier.** It can help clean out your kidneys, and might even promote the passing of stones. One serving of parsnip is not going to do the trick. We're talking about eating parsnip at least twice a day for at least a week. Use your size and comfort level when it comes to portion size. Steam it, grill it or bake it, and eat it! It's good, and good for you.

Kidney Stone Dissolvers

Constant sips of liquid are essential for flushing the kidneys and helping dissolve stones. *Ask your doctor which drink(s) are best for you...*

➤ **Juicer Needed.** Fresh parsley juice has been used with success to dissolve kidney stones. To sweeten the strong green taste of the parsley, add fresh carrot juice. Start with two-thirds parsley and one-third carrot and adjust the proportions after tasting.

➤ **Cranberry Juice.** For a little variety, you may want to drink cranberry juice. Not only does it help with most urinary problems, it also can help dissolve kidney stones.

➤ **Watermelon Tea.** Watermelon seed tea is a wonderful diuretic and kidney cleanser. Collect a half cup of watermelon seeds and simmer them in three cups of water until the water starts to turn a color. Take it off the heat, strain out the seeds, let it cool and drink the tea. If you need to sweeten it, add some honey.

Next time it's watermelon season, collect the seeds and freeze them so if you or anyone you know needs a kidney cleanser, you'll have the seeds. Be sure to buy watermelon that has seeds, not the seedless kind.

➤ **Herbal Teas.** These herbal teas have been known to dissolve kidney stones—sometimes within hours. Several cups must be consumed to get results. A health professional can guide you to the right herb and dosage. Teas to consider—chamomile, buchu, cornsilk (fresh or dried) and uva ursi (also called bearberry).

Passing the Kidney Stones

➤ **Collect the Stones.** When you suspect that you might pass a stone or gravel, urinate through unbleached muslin or a linen handkerchief—or into a chamber pot—so you can catch it. It's important to turn the stone over to your doctor. Analysis of it can help you prevent a recurrence of the problem. For instance, the stones may be *calcium oxalate stones*, which means you should stay away from spinach, rhubarb, almonds and cashews. Or the stones may be *uric acid stones* caused by gout. Get to the bottom of it by collecting the stone, and be sure to follow through with the professional medical analysis.

Kidney Stone Prevention

➤ **Rice Bran.** Eating two tablespoons of rice bran can help prevent kidney stones. Sprinkle it on salads, soups and stews. You can also stir it in juice or shakes.

Gem Therapy

➤ **Bloodstone.** Hold it, rub it, wear it, carry it with you or tape it to your body—the area on your back that's closest to your kidneys.

AFFIRMATION

Repeat this 15 times a day, starting first thing in the morning, every time you urinate and last thing at night…

As my fears melt away, I am empowered by the unlimited good that's out there for me.

VAGINITIS

The two most common types of vaginitis are yeast and bacterial infections. While there is quite a selection of home tests available, have your doctor test you to determine the type of infection and its severity. The usual course of action is an antifungal for yeast infections and antibiotics for bacterial infections. But, antibiotics have no discretion—they destroy the good as well as the bad bacteria. Therefore, when taking antibiotics, you must take acidophilus to replace the beneficial bacteria. Available at health food stores, the capsules should have one to two billion viable acidophilus cells.

NOTE: Take acidophilus right *after* you've eaten and at least two hours *before* or two hours *after* you take an antibiotic. That way you won't diminish the effectiveness of the antibiotic while reaping the benefits of the acidophilus.

Once the antibiotic does its job and rids you of the infection, we'd like to help you prevent it from recurring.

Vaginitis Prevention

➤ **Let Some Air Up There.** Wear loose-fitting cotton panties. Cut the crotch out of your panty hose. Stay away from tight-fitting slacks or jeans. Wear skirts. Also, sleep without panties.

➤ **Laundering Instructions.** Launder with unscented detergent. Do not use bleach or fabric softener. They can irritate sensitive skin. After laundering cotton panties, iron them to make sure all bacteria are destroyed.

➤ **In the Bathroom.** When you go to the bathroom, always wipe from front to back.

➤ **Skip the Soap.** Do not wash the vagina with soap. The natural pH balance can be unbalanced by soap, which is usually alkaline, leaving you more susceptible to infection.

➤ **A Natural Antibiotic.** Add garlic to your diet—raw garlic is, by far, best.

 CAUTION: Having garlic on an empty stomach can cause nausea. Be sure to have some food in your stomach before eating garlic or taking capsules. And, be cautious with garlic if you have gastritis.

➤ **Yeast Infection.** If a yeast infection (Candida) is a recurring problem, for starters, immediately eliminate processed sugar from your diet. Then get a book that will guide you through the steps necessary to get rid of the yeast infection. One such book is *The Candida Cure—Yeast, Fungus and Your Health* (Quintessential Healing, Inc.) by Ann Boroch (*www.annboroch.com*), a 90-day program for anyone with yeast-related conditions. This book can help bring your body back into balance and reinstate vibrant health. Included are recipes, recommended foods and two weeks of sample menus. You could also try *The Yeast Connection Cookbook* by William G. Crook, MD, and Marjorie Hurt Jones, RN (Square One).

At the Onset of Vaginitis

➤ **Pau d'arco.** This is an herb that can ease the symptoms or rid you completely of the infection.

Prepare pau d'arco tea by pouring eight ounces of freshly boiled water over a pau d'arco tea bag in a cup. Cover the cup and let it steep for 10 to 15 minutes. Before taking out the tea bag, gently squeeze it to release the last of the herbal extract. Drink two to four cups daily, or

211

as directed by your doctor or nutritionist. If you buy loose tea, follow the preparation instructions on the box.

 CAUTION: Consult your doctor before using pau d'arco, especially if you are taking an anticoagulant medication, or are pregnant or nursing.

Vaginal Itching

➤ **Garlic.** In most instances, garlic will stop the itching. To prepare garlic water, dice six cloves of garlic and put them in a quart of just-boiled water. Cover it and let it steep for 20 minutes. Strain and wash the genital area with the liquid.

 CAUTION: If you have a red or raw yeast rash, this remedy could burn. Try a pau d'arco wash instead.

➤ **Acidophilus.** Break open two or three acidophilus capsules (available at health food stores) and mix with enough vegetable oil to form a runny paste. Gently smear it on the sore, itchy area. It should stop the itching quickly and start healing the irritated skin.

AFFIRMATION

Repeat this affirmation 10 times a day, first thing in the morning, each time you comb or brush your hair, and last thing at night…

I accept myself as a healthy and happy woman, blessed with normal and natural bodily functions.

VARICOSE VEINS

 One of every two women past the age of 40 has varicose veins. As for men in the same age bracket, one out of every four has the problem. For those of you with varicose veins, exercise and elevation of your legs are extremely important in the healing process. Plus, the following remedies can really make a difference.

➤ **Address Constipation.** Constipation is one of the leading causes of varicose veins. If you have this problem, do something about it immediately. Start by turning to the "Constipation" section, page 43, in this book. Get rid of that problem and you may get rid of painful varicose veins and prevent a recurrence.

➤ **Seated Posture.** Do not cross your legs when you sit. *Women:* For a graceful, feminine look, sit with your knees together and your legs slanted to the side.

➤ **Leg Wear.** Do not wear socks, hose or garters that will constrict the blood flow at any point on your legs.

➤ **Exercise.** Walking is wonderful, as is swimming. Do some kind of exercise on a daily basis. See page 214.

➤ **Lift Those Legs.** Elevate your legs for at least a half hour a day. Actually, any time you can sit with your legs elevated, do so.

➤ **Cigarettes.** Do not smoke! Just two cigarettes a day contain enough toxic substances to start destroying cells in the linings of veins.

➤ **Weight.** If you are overweight, make up your mind to lose the extra pounds for the sake of your veins. See the "Weight Control" section, page 217.

➤ **Horse Chestnut.** Horse chestnut is the most popular herbal treatment for varicose veins in Europe. The herb's active component is thought to be aescin (or *escin*), which is said to counteract inflammation, tone and protect veins, scavenge tissue-damaging free radicals and block enzymes that break down supporting tissue.

Horse chestnut extract and capsules are available at health food stores. You must follow label directions and dosage for it to be safe and effective. Your safest bet is to seek dosage guidance from your health care professional—a knowledgeable doctor, naturopath or herbalist.

 CAUTION: Horse chestnut is not recommended for people with liver or kidney disease. You shouldn't take this herb in combination with blood thinners such as *warfarin* (Coumadin). Safety during pregnancy and nursing has not been established. Check with your obstetrician.

➤ **Cabbage.** Savoy cabbage leaves can be very healing, particularly in severe cases of varicose veins. Take a few leaves, cut away the outer part, and iron the spine in the center...yes, with a regular iron. Since there's no setting for "vegetables," set it for "wool." The leaves should then be soft and flat. Put them on the varicose veins and bind them in place with an Ace bandage. Or, if you have support stockings that are large enough to wear over the cabbage leaves, that would work. Wear the cabbage leaves all day and/or overnight. Do this daily and watch for an improvement, along with relief.

➤ **Witch Hazel.** Studies show that witch hazel extract (available at health food stores) helps strengthen blood vessels. Dip a cotton ball in the extract and wipe the veiny area with it two or three times a day, whenever convenient. Results can be expected after two weeks. If the witch hazel causes a skin irritation, discontinue use immediately.

➤ **Herbal Oils.** To stimulate circulation, gently massage oil of rosemary into the affected area.

To alleviate swelling and inflammation, and to help relieve the pain of varicose veins, gently massage either oil of chamomile or oil of cypress into the affected area.

➤ **Vitamin E.** A natural blood thinner, vitamin E is good for circulation and helps reduce inflammation and prevent blood clots. If you prefer to get your vitamin E from food, great. Eat lots of leafy greens and soybean products, and sprinkle wheat germ on salads and cereal.

 CAUTION: Due to the possible interactions between vitamin E and various drugs and supplements, as well as other safety considerations, be sure to consult your doctor before taking vitamin E.

➤ **Oat Straw Tea.** Prepare this tea by steeping a teaspoon of oat straw (available at health food stores) in a cup of just-boiled water. Ten minutes later, strain and drink. Do this twice a day.

Once per week, take an oat straw bath. Steep one-third of a cup of oat straw in a quart of just-boiled water, strain and pour the liquid into your warm bath water. Relax and enjoy it for at least 20 minutes.

➤ **Butcher's Broom.** While you are at the health food store getting vitamin E and oat straw, you might want to check out butcher's broom, which is known to reduce inflammation of veins. The herb's two anti-inflammatory compounds—*ruscogenin* and *neoruscogenin*—constrict and strengthen veins. Follow the recommended dosage on the label.

➤ **Varicose Ulcers Poultice.** Prepare a poultice using cod liver oil and an equal amount of raw honey. Bind it in place overnight, every night, until the condition clears up.

Spider Veins

As a form of varicose veins, these small veins look like bluish-purple spider legs and are usually clustered on the legs, feet, ankles or thighs, and sometimes on the face. There are several medical procedures that can make spider veins disappear. They range from invasive needles, to noninvasive laser. All are pricey and usually not covered by health insurance.

The remedies above for full-blown varicose veins should certainly help with spider veins. Start with rosemary oil. It worked for our cousin who learned about this treatment from her yoga instructor.

AFFIRMATION

Repeat this affirmation a dozen times a day, starting first thing in the morning, every time you remind yourself to elevate your legs and last thing at night…

Healing energy is flowing freely through my veins as I move through life with joy and ease.

A Word from the Wise…

Running and Cycling May Worsen Varicose Veins

Strenuous exercise that puts pressure on the legs may make varicose veins more noticeable.

Best: Low-impact, moderate exercise, such as swimming and walking, can relieve symptoms by stimulating your circulation without increasing pressure. Consult your physician.

University of California, Berkeley Wellness Letter, 500 Fifth Ave., New York City 10010.

WARTS

For as many warts as there are in this world, that's how many wart-removal remedies there seem to be. Remedies range from sensible to something out of the Middle Ages.

No other ailment (it is a virus, you know) is as rich in folklore as warts. Through the years, we've accumulated quite a collection (of folklore, not warts).

Most recently we were told to rub the wart with a stolen egg, then wrap the egg in brown paper, and leave it at a crossroads. When someone picks up the package and breaks the egg, you will get rid of the wart and that person will get it. And one of our favorites is an old Irish remedy—collect a little mound of dirt under your right foot and kick it toward a passing hearse as you chant, "O corpse of clay, as you decay, come and carry my wart away."

The odd part about some of these outrageous remedies is that they actually work. It's a perfect example of the power of suggestion.

Below, we list some powerful suggestions that mostly fall in the sensible category. When using any of them, be consistent and be patient.

Wart Remedies

➤ **Vinegar.** Dab apple cider vinegar on the wart, and before it dries, put on baking soda, too. Dust off the baking soda after 15 minutes. Do this a half-dozen times a day, every day, until the wart disappears.

➤ **Eggplant.** Put a piece of raw eggplant on the wart and keep it in place overnight with an Ace bandage. If you can walk around with the eggplant on the wart during the day, do so. If not, put on a fresh piece of raw eggplant every night until the wart is gone.

➤ **Oil.** Smother the wart with an oil—wheat germ oil, castor oil, vitamin E oil, vitamin A or oil of cinnamon.

At the start of your day, after your morning shower, drench a cotton ball with the oil of your choice, apply it to the wart and keep it in place with a Band-Aid. Do the same thing at bedtime. Within a month of oiling the wart twice a day, it should be history.

➤ **Banana.** Cut a piece of banana peel, enough to completely cover the wart. Place the mucilaginous pulp side on the wart and keep it in place by wrapping first-aid tape or a Band-Aid around it. Sleep with it that way overnight and remove it in the morning. Repeat this routine with a fresh piece of peel every night. Give it about two weeks for the wart to be gone.

➤ **Paste.** Before bedtime, start with a half-teaspoon of baking soda in a little cup and slowly stir in drops of castor oil. Stop when it is the consistency of paste. Smear the paste on the wart and cover it with a Band-Aid. Sleep with it on and take it off in the morning. Repeat the remedy each night until the wart disappears.

➤ **Duct Tape.** Word of mouth is excellent on this wart remedy. Place a piece of duct tape on the wart and leave it on for six days. If it falls or washes off before six days, just reapply another piece of duct tape.

Next, remove the duct tape, soak the wart in room temperature water for a few minutes, and use an emery board or pumice stone to gently file down the dead thick skin on top of the wart. Leave it uncovered overnight. In the morning, place a piece of duct tape on the wart for another six days. Repeat the entire procedure every six days until the wart is gone.

There are two theories for why this works: Either the duct tape suffocates the virus, or the tape triggers a mild irritation that causes your immune system to attack the virus and win.

 NOTE: If your child has a wart and you want to use this duct tape remedy, consider using the duct tape that comes in your child's favorite color.

➤ **Rapid Wart Removal.** This remedy, taken with any of the above remedies, is thought to speed up the wart-drying process.

Prepare fresh or frozen asparagus and puree it in a blender. Eat one-fourth cup of the puree twice a day—before breakfast and before dinner.

➤ **More Than One Wart.** While this remedy harkens back to the Middle Ages, it was given to us by a level-headed lady who was as skeptical as you probably will be, yet she tried it and it worked for her. Cut an apple into as many pieces as there are warts. Assign each slice to a wart and rub that slice on its wart. After doing that, put the apple back together and bury it. When the apple rots, the warts will be gone.

➤ **Visualization.** Upon rising and at bedtime, sit up in bed (if you prefer, sit on a hard-back chair), and close your eyes for a two- to three-minute visualization.

Start by breathing out all the air in your lungs, then slowly breathing in. As you exhale, visualize a huge theater marquee with bright lights flashing the number "3" three times. Take another slow, deep breath, and as you exhale, visualize the number "2" flashing three times. Take one more deep breath, slowly, and when you exhale, see the number "1" flashing three times.

Now that you're relaxed and ready, visualize your refrigerator. Open the door and on

216

the top shelf see a colorful artist's palette. Pick up the palette, and the magical gold paintbrush that's alongside of it. Don't forget to close the refrigerator door.

Now visualize the wart and the area that surrounds it. As you hold the palette in one hand and the brush in your other hand, the brush will magically dip into the color on the palette that matches your skin tone perfectly. Take the brush and paint over the wart—keep re-dipping the brush and continue painting the wart until the wart completely disappears.

As you're looking at and admiring your clear, smooth, perfect skin, slowly count from one to three. Open your eyes, stretch and feel refreshed.

Warts on Hands and Fingers

➤ **A Success Story.** We love it when people send us success stories. Lisa Jade, a college student, had a wart on the palm of her hand. Her dermatologist tried liquid nitrogen on it. At first it was a little better, but then the pain and size increased. Lisa went to another doctor who gave her a prescription that didn't help much either. *Then, after seeing us on TV, she ran to the mall, bought our book, and tried our remedy...*

Boil a couple of eggs and save the water. As soon as the water cools, soak your warted hand in that water for 10 minutes. Do this daily until the wart disappears. Lisa said that all it took was one soaking for the pain and the wart to vanish, leaving no trace of it whatsoever.

➤ **Warts Under and Around Fingernails.** Take medical adhesive tape and wrap it around the warted finger four times. Make sure it's airless and secure, but not so tight as to stop the circulation. After a week, before bedtime, take off the tape and sleep without it. Next morning re-dress the finger again, and leave it on for another week. Keep up this pattern and by the end of the third or fourth week the wart should weaken, wither and waste away.

Plantar Warts

➤ **Washing Soda Foot Soak.** Get a basin big enough for your foot, or use a plastic shoe box. Every night, fill the basin or box with one gallon of warm water and a half cup of Arm & Hammer Super Washing Soda, and soak your foot for 15 minutes. Then rub dry the sole of your foot with a rough washcloth. At some point, little black spots will appear. They're the roots of the warts and they will come out and off, never to return. The entire process takes about two weeks.

➤ **Foot Soak and Mouthwash.** Every night, soak your foot in a basin of hot water for five minutes. Then soak a cotton ball with Listerine, apply it directly on the plantar warts, and tape it in place. (Listerine? Who discovered this? Maybe it was someone who was used to putting his foot in his mouth.) After one or two weeks, the warts should be gone, leaving your foot kissing sweet.

➤ **Oil Massage.** At bedtime each night, take one or two vitamin A or garlic capsules, puncture them, and squeeze out the oil on the plantar warts. Massage the oil on the whole area for a few minutes—do a thorough job. Then, after you've let it set for a few more minutes, put a clean, white sock on your foot and sleep that way. This, as with most wart remedies, takes about two weeks for results.

 CAUTION: Garlic oil could be irritating to the skin. Avoid putting garlic oil on areas where there are cuts.

Genital Warts

There's good news and there's bad news. The good news is that you are not alone—this is a common problem. The bad news is that it's a common problem because genital warts are quite contagious. So, refrain from intercourse until the warts disappear. *Meanwhile…*

➤ **Vitamin A and E.** Squeeze out a vitamin E and/or vitamin A capsule and apply. Because warmth and moisture encourage the growth of warts, do not put a Band-Aid on it. Just keep reapplying the oil as often as possible each day until you abort the wart.

AFFIRMATION

Cover the wart with something—a tissue, your sleeve, your hand—each time you say the affirmation, starting first thing in the morning, last thing at night and right before you drink any beverage…

I have positive feelings. Everything in my life is clear and wonderful.

WEIGHT CONTROL

Pick up something portable weighing 10, 15, maybe 20 pounds. Keep it with you for a full day. Don't make a move without it. See what it's like carrying around the extra weight. That just may be the motivation you need to lose those excess pounds.

Tips, Tricks, Tactics

Read through this section and don't scoff at anything until you've actually tried each of them. *Every suggestion can help you eat less and/or feel satisfied sooner, and lose more…*

➤ **Talk Up.** Tell your family, friends and coworkers that you intend to lose weight and you want and need their support. Explain that they don't have to cut calories or deprive themselves in front of you. All you ask is that they encourage you to reach your goal. That means they are not to sabotage your efforts by making it "okay" to pig out…"just this one time." And while you're at it, tell them how wonderful it would be for them to share in your happiness each time you hit a milestone, such as when you take a smaller clothing size.

Your assertiveness in this way will help you to help them to help you. (Read that over again until it makes sense.) It may even help the people around you to shed some unwanted, unhealthy pounds.

▶ **Weigh In.** According to a two-year study reported in *Annals of Behavioral Medicine*, researchers from the University of Minnesota tracked more than 3,000 obese and overweight adults who wanted to lose weight or prevent weight gain.

During this two-year period, the daily weighers lost twice as much as the people who weighed themselves once a week. The people who said they never weighed themselves gained an average of four pounds.

The researchers believe that more frequent weighing may be an effective tactic because it offers dieters regular feedback about their progress. Daily weighing also helps you notice small increases in weight so that you can catch an extra pound or two before it becomes an extra 10 or 20.

 NOTE FROM JOAN: This has been extremely helpful for me. As soon as I see a weight gain of one pound or two, I do something about it…I cut out treats and spend extra time on my treadmill. I never thought I'd be this kind of person, but I am and I like myself for it. So hop on that scale!

Planning Your Meals

▶ **Before Breakfast.** First thing in the morning, on an empty stomach, take one tablespoon of EVOO—yes, extra virgin olive oil. It will kick start your metabolism and help curb your appetite.

Professor of psychiatry and pharmacology Daniele Piomelli, along with his colleagues at the University of California Irvine College of Medicine, found that the fatty acid called OEA (*oleylethanolamide*) activates cell receptor molecules to regulate hunger and metabolism.

Olive oil is 85% oleic acid. During digestion, oleic acid converts into OEA and stimulates nerve cells, signaling the brain that you're full.

A University of Wisconsin study found that the body burns off heart-healthy monounsaturated fats such as olive oil, and nut and avocado oils three to five times faster than the saturated fats found in meat, dairy and processed foods.

It's a total-win situation. Take one tablespoon of (heart-healthy) olive oil and the body will burn it off quickly, meanwhile it will give you energy, cut your appetite and moisturize your skin from the inside out, while it lowers blood cholesterol and triglyceride levels.

After we learned about this tip and began sharing it, one of our friends said that Karina Smirnoff formerly of *Dancing with the Stars* keeps her incredible figure by using this ancient Russian folk remedy. Like the song says, "Everything old is new again."

▶ **Breakfast.** Eat it! If you want to lose or maintain weight, eat a fairly substantial, healthy breakfast, and your brain's "reward" center will not feel deprived and will not initiate a high-calorie food craving during the rest of the day.

According to Tony Goldstone, MD, PhD, consultant endocrinologist, and his research team at the MRC Clinical Sciences Centre at Imperial College of Science, Technology and Medicine in London, "Our results support the advice for eating a healthy breakfast as part of the dietary prevention and treatment of obesity. When people skip meals, especially breakfast, changes in brain activity in response to food may hinder weight loss and even promote weight gain."

A recent protein-for-breakfast study was conducted by scientists from Purdue University and the University of Kansas Medical Center. When participants were given additional protein for breakfast—eggs and lean Canadian bacon—they had a greater sense of sustained fullness throughout the day, compared with when more protein was eaten at lunch or dinner.

➤ **Before Lunch and/or Dinner.**

● **Tomato Juice.** Consume tomato juice about 15 minutes before you eat. The acid in the juice can give you a full feeling, making it possible to eat smaller portions than usual without feeling deprived.

● **Water and Banana.** Drink a glass of water before each meal. It helps flush your system and give you a full feeling. It can also cut down on a craving, which may unknowingly have been for water to begin with. If just the glass of water doesn't work for you, you may want to try eating half of a ripe (brown speckled) banana before you drink the water. That can be very filling.

● **Fat-Burning Formula.** Put one tablespoon of apple cider vinegar and two tablespoons of honey in a glass of unsweetened grapefruit juice. Mix thoroughly and drink it a half hour before each meal. In addition to reducing your appetite, this drink is said to help regulate your thyroid and melt fat away, too.

 CAUTION: If you take medication, check with your doctor or pharmacist about drug interaction with grapefruit.

● **Accessorize.** Right before you sit down for a meal, put on a belt, if you're not already wearing one. Tighten your belt a notch or two more than you wear it—not enough to make your eyes bulge, but just enough to make you feel full sooner than usual.

● **Better Plating.** When you are plating your meal, do it on a small plate and give yourself less food than you would if you used a bigger plate.

At the Table

➤ **Pull Up a Chair.** First of all, always eat while seated, even if you're alone in your home or office, and even if you're in a rush. By sitting at a table, you're seeing what you're eating. This mental photo of your food in front of you helps you feel fuller faster. When you stand and eat, the tendency is to shovel in and gulp down the food before you can mentally absorb the amount of food you ate. By the time your "feeling full" switch is activated, chances are you've eaten twice as much as you might have had you been seated at a table, eating in a more civilized manner.

Those of you with children, be aware that many long-term studies show that young children who eat in front of the TV, instead of with their family at the dinner table, are more likely to be overweight; teenagers who eat dinner with their families are more likely to eat healthier as adults, and less likely to smoke, drink or do drugs.

➤ **Music.** Turn off the rock music while at the table. It makes you eat faster and more. If you must have music at mealtime, make it low and slow.

➤ **Yoga.** This can be a real conversation starter, or stopper, at a dinner table. When you eat, plug up your left nostril so that you breathe through your right nostril only. It is said that this process speeds up metabolism and allows you to quickly and efficiently derive all the energy from the food you eat. And so, you don't have to eat as much as usual to be satisfied. For the sake of your social life, we recommend that you do this only when you dine alone.

Food and Drink: The Basics

➤ **Best Beverage.** Throughout the day, whenever you reach for something to drink, make it water. The average American has an extra 245 calories a day from soft drinks. We did the math—it comes to almost 90,000 calories a year and that translates to 25 (additional and unwanted) pounds.

Jillian Michaels, former trainer on the TV show *Biggest Loser*, says that proper hydration can speed metabolism by up to 3%. And adding fiber powder to water helps you feel full. Jillian explains that fiber is a great way to trick your body into producing the appetite-controlling hormone *leptin*. Benefiber and Metamucil Clear & Natural are two brands whose fiber powder completely dissolves in water. You'll think you're drinking plain water.

➤ **Portion Control.** Many of you don't need a diet as much as you need to learn portion control. If you are like one of those people who tell us they want to eat healthier and less and don't want to spend their days in the kitchen preparing food, we have a solution. Buy

220

already-prepared food, add a vegetable side dish or a salad, and you have a satisfying, guilt-free meal with enforced portion control.

There are many good brands from which to choose, with more springing up daily. Your job is to go to your supermarket, or ideally a natural foods market such as Whole Foods, or a health food store, and check out the selection of frozen or refrigerated meals.

We'll start you off by telling you about Amy's Kitchen, simply because this family-run Berliner business has been around for over 20 years, has extensive distribution and their products—ranging from gourmet to just plain down-home cooking—are tasty, have integrity, are popularly priced and help discipline you when it comes to portion size.

 NOTE: If the food you select says that it contains two servings, either share it with someone, or have it for two meals.

This information about Amy's will give you a frame of reference and a standard when foraging for food on your own.

● **Amy's Ingredients.** Everything is vegetarian. No additives, no preservatives, no GMOs (*genetically modified organisms* frequently associated with soy products) are used. The company claims, "If a child can't pronounce it, you won't find it on an Amy's label." Fruits, vegetables and grains are grown organically, without the use of insecticides and other harmful chemicals.

● **Amy's Accommodates Dietary Restrictions.** There are over 50 no-gluten-added offerings and more than 50 nondairy/lactose-free/cholesterol-free dishes. They also provide dishes that are low-fat, certified kosher, light in sodium, soy free, corn free and tree nut free.

• **Availability.** Amy's foods are in supermarkets, natural food stores, as well as health food stores and even some club stores. See a complete listing and description of their foods, along with nutritional facts at *www.amys.com*. Click on "store locator" for an outlet in your neighborhood, or call Amy's at 707-578-7270.

➤ **Prepared Food Rule.** If sugar or fructose or corn syrup are among the first four ingredients listed on a label, put it back on the shelf. It's too unhealthy and too fattening.

➤ **Frozen vs. Canned.** When it comes to vegetables, opt for frozen. Canned veggies are usually high in sodium (not good for weight watchers) and may fall short in nutrition.

When it comes to broccoli, which doesn't come in a can, we still opt for frozen, rather than fresh. We get *organic* frozen bags of broccoli florets at Whole Foods for half the price of fresh broccoli, which needs to be trimmed and washed. Also, vegetables that are flash frozen are picked at their prime. Fresh vegetables may not be so fresh. You don't really know how long they've been hanging around the market.

The bottom line here is to take the easiest way out when it comes to preparing healthy, low-calorie foods. As we said, we opt for frozen!

Vitamin D May Boost Weight Loss

In a recent study, researchers measured blood levels of vitamin D in 38 overweight men and women before and after an 11-week diet in which they consumed 750 fewer daily calories than their estimated total caloric needs.

Result: Higher levels of *25-hydroxycholecalciferol* (a marker of vitamin D status) were associated with greater weight loss while following the diet.

Shalamar Sibley, MD, MPH, assistant professor of medicine, division of endocrinology and diabetes, University of Minnesota Medical School, Minneapolis.

Binge/Craving Stoppers

➤ **Trigger Foods.** Most of us have our very own trigger foods. Just one bite triggers an out-of-control binge. Those foods generally fall into the category of sugary, fatty, high-cholesterol and/or salty. After all, who binges on broccoli?

Do you have one or more trigger foods? Think about it. Identify the foods. Realize the consequences of compulsive eating that trigger foods cause. Eliminate the trigger foods from your life and you help eliminate temptation, demoralization and other negative and unhealthy repercussions. You may also lose a few pounds along the way.

➤ **Around the House.** When you are hungry, the tendency is to reach out for whatever is at hand. While ice cream is kept out of sight in the freezer, there are plenty of surfaces in the kitchen, TV room and the rest of your home for candy dishes and bowls of chips, pretzels and other no-nos. Instead, keep the taboo treats in the back of a hard-to-reach shelf behind a closed cabinet door. Better yet, get those things out of the house. Replace them with a bowl of fruit on the kitchen table, raw, salt-free nuts in the TV room, a bag of baby carrots in the fridge and other healthful snacks that you can reach for when you feel the need to nosh.

➤ **Reflexology to Stop Sweet Cravings.** Use your index finger to draw tiny circles, massaging your *philtrum* (the indentation between your upper lip and the bottom of your nose). After about 10 seconds, your energy channel that links the brain, pancreas and spleen will have balance restored, and your craving for sweets repressed.

"Sweet Tooth" Substitutes

An overweight person went to the doctor. After a thorough examination, the doctor told the patient, "You need a bypass." "A bypass?" "Yes. Bypass the refrigerator, bypass the bakery, bypass desserts..." *These suggestions can help you submerge the urge for a sugary treat...*

➤ **A Rinse.** Dissolve a teaspoon of baking soda in a glass of warm water and rinse your mouth with it. Within a few minutes, probably by the time you're down to the last mouthful of the mixture, your taste buds will be appeased and the craving for that high-calorie, sugar-filled food will have passedl

➤ **Artichoke.** Boil an artichoke for 10 to 15 minutes and eat it—without butter. It's plenty good that way. And since it has a fructose-derived substance called inulin (not insulin), it fills the desire for something sweet.

➤ **Chew Gum.** Chew sugar-free gum for 15 minutes each hour after lunch, and if you're like the participants in a study, you will consume 60 fewer calories from sweets at snack time.

➤ **Nuts.** Eat a handful of raw almonds, cashews or walnuts or unsalted pistachios or unsalted peanuts. The healthy fat in nuts should help you lose more weight than most any other snack.

➤ **Brewer's Yeast Brew.** Stir a heaping teaspoon or two of brewer's yeast (available at health food stores) in a glass of unsweetened grapefruit juice. Drink the mixture before each

222

meal. It may help you eat less during the meal and it should help you conquer your sweet tooth completely within a few days.

 CAUTION: If you take medication, check with your doctor or pharmacist about drug interaction with grapefruit.

Helpful Herbs

These herbs (available at health food stores or check "Sources," page 309) can help curb your appetite, quell your cravings and flush out the fat cells.

Stick with one herb and be sure to pay attention to your reaction to it. Do you seem to be less hungry? Do you have more control over your desire to snack? After a few days, change to another herb and note your responses to that one, too. Keep doing this until you've tried all the herbs and know which works best for you.

For herbal leaves and flowers, prepare the tea by steeping a teaspoon of the herb in a cup of just-boiled water. After about seven minutes, strain and sip slowly. For roots, barks and seeds, bring the herbs and water to a boil, then simmer for 15 to 20 minutes and strain and drink. If sweetener is needed to make the herbal teas taste better, use stevia.

➤ **Hawthorn Berry Tea**—two cups a day—one cup between breakfast and lunch and one cup between lunch and dinner (does the heart good, too).

➤ **Psyllium Seed Husks Tea**—one to two cups daily (it's a good colon cleanser, so stay close to home).

➤ **Chaparral Tea**—three cups daily, one after each meal.

➤ **Chicory Root Tea**—one cup daily before breakfast.

➤ **Chickweed Tea**—three cups daily, one before each meal.

Metabolism Stimulators

➤ **Nature's Thyroid Booster.** Add a tablespoon of seaweed to soup, stew or salad every day. Kelp is the most popular seaweed and is available at health food stores. According to Dr. J.W. Turentine, a scientist with the US Department of Agriculture, "Of the 14 elements essential to the proper metabolic functions of the human body, 13 are known to be in kelp." One of the 13 elements is organic iodine, which rouses the thyroid gland into action, stimulating the body's metabolism and, ultimately, turning fatty foods into energy.

➤ **Metabolism Balancer.** Bergamot is a tree that bears a small orange-like fruit. Its essential oil is extracted from the fruit peel and is used in Earl Grey tea, giving it a spicy, light and refreshing taste. It is said to regulate metabolism, and may help you feel less hungry. As a bonus, bergamot also has a calming effect on the nervous system and is used as an antidepressant.

➤ **Nature's Best Diet Food.** Research reports say that bee pollen can correct imbalances in body metabolism, stimulate the metabolic processes and speed up the burning of calories. It's said to eliminate cravings and act as an appetite suppressant. The lecithin in bee pollen is known to dissolve and flush fat from the body. Bee pollen promises a lot and, from our research, we have reason to believe it delivers.

If you're interested in trying it, begin with just a few granules for the first couple of days, to make sure you don't have an allergy to it. If there's no allergic reaction, take a quarter-teaspoon for a few days. Gradually work your way up to a teaspoon or more a day. Some people get results on only a teaspoon a day; others need to work their way up to a tablespoon a day.

Aromatherapy

According to Alan R. Hirsch, MD, neurologist, psychiatrist and director of the Smell & Taste Treatment and Research Foundation, Chicago, "The stronger the flavor of the food, the stronger its power to satisfy and reduce hunger. The odor of a hearty Greek salad topped with a spicy vinaigrette dressing, a strong cheese and some anchovies will do wonders to decrease appetite in a hurry."

Dr. Hirsch's findings are based on extensive research. He advises dieters, "Sniff each bite of food quickly five times before eating. Fast sniffs signal food messages to the brain that decrease hunger and work to satisfy appetite without calories. Opt for hot foods. The heat and steam from the food send flavor molecules up the back of the throat and into the brain satiety center faster."

Dr. Hirsch says, "Don't snack between meals. Sniff! Keep a chocolate bar in your desk at work. When the urge for chocolate takes hold, sniff the candy. The smell of food can trick your body into thinking you've already eaten."

One more tip from Dr. Hirsch: "When drinking beverages, blow bubbles in the drink with a straw before sipping. By doing so, the odors of the liquid emanate into the nasal passages to satisfy hunger."

For information about aromatherapy research, along with smell and taste disorders, visit Dr. Alan R. Hirsch's Web site at *www.smell andtaste.org* or call 888-381-8040.

Gem Therapy

➤ **Amethyst.** If food addiction is your problem, you might want to consider amethyst, the stone helpful for addictive behavior, substance abuse and for any dependencies.

If you use food as an escape or avoidance technique, carnelian may be the stone for you. It is said to help you focus on the present. When you're "here now," chances are you won't want to use food as a diversion. So, wear or carry amethyst and/or carnelian to help you control a weight problem.

Motivators

➤ **Reward Stimulus.** If you're into jewelry, start a charm bracelet and with each five pounds you lose, give yourself a charm for the bracelet. Wearing the bracelet will be a constant reminder of how well you've done.

➤ **Smooching Stimulus.** Plant one on your partner...a real passionate kiss. It burns 6.4 calories per minute. Ten kisses a day and we're talking about 23,000 calories, or eight pounds a year . . . to say nothing of what it will do for your relationship.

➤ **Get Rid of the Old.** Once you've lost weight—a size or two—and have the pleasure of buying clothes that fit properly and look great, get rid of the clothes that are too big for you. You know, the frumpy ones that hide your new flaunt-it figure. Donate them to a thrift store instead of having them take up space. You never want to have occasion to wear them again...ever. It's an incentive to keep the weight off, knowing that you will have nothing to wear if you gain back the weight you lost.

Free Diet-Help Web Site

We highly recommend the Weight Loss Guide at *www.freedieting.com*. This site has diet plans, fitness plans, non-diet approaches for losing weight and calculators of all kinds (such as ide-

al body weight, ideal calorie intake, how many calories you should eat to lose weight and more) all predicated on your personal statistics (age, weight, height, gender, exercise level, etc.). Not only will this site tell you how to calculate daily calorie needs, it will also tell you which carbohydrates are good choices, and how to lose fat from certain areas.

Want to know how many calories are in your favorite foods? The site has that, too, along with the carb, protein and fat count.

We're recommending this site mainly because you can get a few days of meal plans for the most popular diets (South Beach Diet, Sonoma Diet, 5-Factor Diet, NutriSystem) and free meal plans according to calorie intake (1,200 calories, 1,350 calories, 1,400 calories, etc.). All of this information can help you find the eating plan that will work best for you.

Recommended Reading

While these tips, tricks and tactics are excellent to use on your weight-loss journey, you also need an eating plan to follow...one that best fits into your lifestyle and is in keeping with your food preferences and diet restrictions. One way to find the most-suitable way-of-life food regimen for you is to go to a bookstore (in person or on the Internet) and look in the "Health and Fitness" section for a big and varied selection of diet books. There's something for everyone. Be patient and diligent and you're sure to find the eating plan appropriate for you.

Here, to whet your appetite, are books containing doable, healthy eating plans; a book with valuable information that should be in everyone's home-reference library; and a fun book with easy, tasty, low-calorie recipes.

➤ *The Stubborn Fat Fix—Eat Right to Lose Weight and Cure Metabolic Burnout*

Without Hunger or Exercise by Keith Berkowitz, MD, and Valerie Berkowitz, MS, RD* (Rodale). This book will tell you how to lose 30 pounds in three weeks and keep it off for life!

➤ *The Perfect 10 Diet—10 Key Hormones That Hold the Secret to Losing Weight and Feeling Great—Fast!* by Michael Aziz, MD (Cumberland House). This breakthrough diet solution will help you lose up to 14 pounds in 21 days.

➤ *Nutrition at Your Fingertips* by Elisa Zied, MS, RD, CDN* (Alpha). With thousands of supplements to choose from, this highly credentialed author offers a guide to the latest findings in nutrition, including detailed explanations of vitamins and minerals, information on fats, carbohydrates, fiber and proteins, along with health weight evaluation and management, meal planning and combating disease through nutrition.

➤ *Hungry Girl—200 Recipes Under 200 Calories* by Lisa Lillien (St. Martin's Griffin). Lisa is founder of Hungry Girl, and over half a million fans receive her daily e-newsletters filled with guilt-free recipes, food and product reviews, dieting news and lots more. See what it's all about by visiting *www.hungry-girl.com*.

➤ *The One-Day Way: Today Is All the Time You Need to Lose All the Weight You Want* by Chantel Hobbs (WaterBrook Press).

VISUALIZATION/AFFIRMATION

This is not a typical visualization process. It's more of an arts and crafts assignment. Find a photo of yourself—if possible, one of you smiling. Then go through magazines and find a figure you would like to have and that's in proportion to the photo of you.

*MS = Master of Science Degree; RD = Registered Dietician; CDN = Certified Dietician-Nutritionist.

Put the picture of your head on that body, and place it where you will see it often—on the refrigerator, on your desk, in the bathroom, alongside your television set.

When you walk away from the picture, repeat this affirmation over and over, while visualizing the picture you just saw...

I am someone special. I love me and I'm creating the life I want.

A Word from the Wise...

What's Your Ideal Weight?

To determine your ideal body weight, try this simple formula. For women, start with 100 pounds for your first five feet of height. Men should start with 106 pounds for their first five feet of height. For each additional inch, add five pounds to calculate your ideal weight.

Examples: If you are a 5' 4" woman, your ideal weight would be: 100 pounds + (4 inches × 5 pounds) = 120 pounds. If you're a 5' 7" man, your optimal weight would be: 106 pounds + (7 inches × 5 pounds) = 141 pounds.

Important: The daily calorie intake required to maintain your ideal weight depends on your age, gender and physical activity level. Enter this information at the US Department of Agriculture's ChooseMyPlate.gov Web site (*www.choosemyplate.gov/weight-management-calories/calories.html*) to get an estimated number of daily calories to consume to maintain the weight that's right for you. Be sure to adjust your calorie intake if you lose or gain weight.

Barbara Rolls, PhD, Helen A. Guthrie chair and professor, department of nutritional sciences, Pennsylvania State University, University Park.

Exercise

Do it! You know you should. You know it's important. You know it will help you lose weight and be healthier. *Here are some ways to trick yourself and make it almost seem as though you're not exercising...*

➤ **Walking.** Yes, exercise burns calories. A brisk 45-minute walk burns 300 calories. Do that every day and you can lose 18 pounds in a year. (Check out "Pole Walking" in the "It Does a Body Good" chapter, page 266.)

➤ **Watching TV.** In addition to your regular workouts or walkouts, each time there's a commercial break on television, stand up, stretch and exercise, even if it's just dancing to music in the commercials. This serves several purposes—it gets the circulation going, burns some calories and, most important, it keeps you out of the kitchen!

Don't be a couch potato. Get a recumbent bicycle and sit on your couch (or a chair) and pedal as you watch your favorite shows.

➤ **Move Before Meals.** Some fitness experts believe that when you exercise right before you eat, you rev up your metabolism and it stays revved for a while, helping you to metabolize your food faster and more effectively. Exercise also helps cleanse your system by stimulating the elimination of wastes.

➤ **Fidgeting Is Good.** Did you know that finger-drumming, toe-tapping, seat-squirming and other forms of fidgeting can burn off big-time calories? In a 24-hour period, fidgeters who were tested used up as many as 800 calories, compared with non-fidgeters who used up only 100 calories for "spontaneous physical activity" during the same period of time.

226

| A Word from the Wise... |

Have a Love Affair With Exercise...Even if You've Hated It Until Now

Some people just seem to adore exercise. You see them at the gym or jogging around the neighborhood—sweating, smiling, looking fit. But if you would rather dive into a cauldron of boiling oil than work out on a regular basis, you probably wonder how other people can possibly enjoy exercise...and wish that you could, too.

Fact: You *can* learn to love exercise. Several simple behavioral changes can, within seven weeks, result in a major shift in the way you feel about physical activity.

Week One

➤ **First, Do Nothing.** The number-one obstacle to exercise is lack of time. To overcome this, commit to a one-week *predecision phase.* You don't actually exercise yet—the purpose is to prove that your schedule can accommodate three 30-minute chunks of workout time per week. How? Wake up a half-hour earlier than typical on, say, Tuesday, Thursday and Saturday...or take 30 minutes after work on Monday, Wednesday and Friday. During these times, do not make phone calls, check e-mail, pay bills or pick up clutter. Instead, just relax and imagine yourself doing different kinds of physical activities. *While you daydream...*

➤ **Open Your Mind.** Maybe you learned to hate exercise in your junior high school gym class when you were chosen last for a volleyball game or puffed around the track in an ill-fitting gym suit. That's understandable—but you don't have to let past unpleasantness poison your possibilities now. Instead, try to remember what you *did* enjoy as a youngster, such as riding a bike, jumping rope or playing softball. Or imagine doing something entirely new to you—for instance, a tai chi class or a Nintendo *Wii Fit* exercise video game. Notice how the thought of each option makes you feel. When an imagined activity gets you excited, write it down on a list.

Weeks Two and Three

➤ **Start Moving.** During the next two weeks, continue carving out your thrice-weekly half-hour periods, but instead of just visualizing exercise, do a little. Do not push yourself too hard—if you vow to "go to the gym for two hours" or "run a 10K race," you'll feel achy and uncomfortable and will want to quit. Instead, take it easy. Go for a stroll...try some stretches...splash around in a pool.

Important: During this phase, do not look for results. Do not weigh yourself, take measurements of body parts or worry about whether an exercise is intense enough. Your purpose now is simply to let go of doubts.

Weeks Four through Six

➤ **Experiment.** Now take a few weeks to try out all the intriguing activities on the list you made previously. Hike in the woods, go ice-skating, rent an aerobics video, try the Pilates class at a friend's club.

Helpful: Many gyms and recreation centers let guests pay by the visit or buy a one-week pass rather than committing right away to (and paying for) a year-long membership. *As you experiment...*

➤ **Identify Favorite Activities.** Keep track of what's fun and what's not, looking for patterns. Do you prefer working out at home, or are you inspired by the discipline of going to a health club? Do you like exercising alone or with others? Indoors or outdoors? Consider ways to enhance your enjoyment—for instance, by listening to a portable music player as you walk, watching a movie while using the Stairmaster or buying a new exercise outfit. Within a few weeks, you'll know what you like and what you don't like.

Week Seven and Beyond

➤ **Commit.** Now that you have found some enjoyable activities, it's time to choose a minimum number of workouts you'll do per week—perhaps two or three—and commit to never going below that minimum. Whenever possible, do more than the minimum. Even when you're traveling, you can fit in a half-hour walk or do some yoga poses in your hotel room.

➤ **Appreciate Your Progress.** As your exercise habit becomes more ingrained, notice the many positive changes it brings. You feel more energized and less stressed. You sleep more soundly. Your clothes fit you better, your weight is easier to control and your posture is straighter. Your muscles are stronger, and everyday tasks are easier. You feel proud of yourself and more in control of your health. Let these benefits serve as reminders of the many reasons why you now love to exercise.

New Ways to Work Out

To keep your workouts fun and fresh, try some activities that you've never done before. *Options to consider...*

➤ **Core Training.** The muscles in the center of your torso, which keep you balanced and support your spine, can be strengthened using equipment developed for this purpose.

Examples: The *bosu* is an inflated half-sphere that will challenge core muscles as you stand on it...the *kettlebell* is a weighted iron ball with a handle to grip while doing various twists, lunges and other moves. Such equipment usually is available at gyms. *Best:* Ask a trainer to help you develop a program using the apparatus.

➤ **Spinning.** Exercise on a stationary bike, led by an instructor, usually is done to music that fits the pace of the cycling.

➤ **Video Games.** You can do these at home using a game console and your television. With *Dance Dance Revolution*, you stand on a special mat and move your feet in time to music, following visual cues to perform a series of specific steps. In *Wii Fit*, you stand on a balance board and get feedback on your technique as you do yoga, strength training, aerobics and balance games.

➤ **Zumba.** This fusion of Latin rhythms and easy-to-follow dance moves creates a fun fitness workout. For classes in your area, visit *www.zumba.com*.

Mark Stibich, PhD, adjunct faculty member at the University of California, San Diego School of Medicine and expert on behavioral science who writes about longevity for *www.about.com*. He is a founding partner of Vitality Skills, a Houston-based company that works with corporations and individuals to establish habits that promote health, happiness and success.

It Does a Body Good

This extensive chapter has something or some things for everyone and for all kinds of reasons—to help prevent health challenges, to help heal whatever needs healing and to enhance your life.

Please take the time to read each entry. We're sure you will discover therapies, foods, herbs, tonics, supplements or exercises that you never heard of before. Let your instincts—that smart inner voice of yours—guide you to the thing(s) that will benefit you most.

ALEXANDER TECHNIQUE

Joan Arnold (at *www.joanarnold.com*) has been a movement professional for more than 25 years. Along with teaching dance, exercise and yoga, Joan is a certified teacher of the Alexander Technique.

The following is Joan Arnold's eloquent description of the Alexander Technique, which should give you a clear picture of how you can benefit by it and what to expect when you sign up for a lesson.

A Word from the Wise...

Joan Arnold on the Alexander Technique

The Alexander Technique is a way to move more easily. Based on the relationship between the head and the spine, its basic idea is that, when the neck does not overwork, the head can poise lightly at the top of the spine and the whole spine can lengthen in movement.

Unconscious movement habits can cause a range of body problems. Excess tension in the neck and back compresses the spine. Spinal compression can cause pain in your back, neck, shoulders, hips, knees or ankles. Since it also reduces your torso's internal volume, that puts pressure on the organs and can constrict circulation, breathing and digestion, preventing your body from working at its best. Problematic posture can undermine your overall vitality.

Our neuromuscular system is designed to work in concert with gravity. In the torso, there's an antigravity response, an upward flow that fosters buoyancy and efficient movement. Learning the Alexander Technique can help you restore

229

this natural buoyancy, which will reduce strain on one specific body part and distribute effort throughout the body. You access more flexibility, more space in the joints, fuller breathing and more resiliency, bringing more clarity, ease and focus to everything you do.

What to Expect in an Alexander Technique Lesson

Maybe you have recurring back episodes that lay you out on the couch for weeks...or your hands and wrists bother you whenever you use the computer...or you wake up at night with spasms in your legs...or you can't think straight because you're distracted by the pain in your neck and shoulders...or your attempt to sing comes out like a strained croak...or your tennis game never improves. It might be time to take a lesson in the Alexander Technique.

Because this technique is a program of movement re-education, each private session is called a lesson, the practitioner a teacher and the client a student. A student can be anyone—an athlete, a child, an arthritis sufferer, a homemaker, an executive.

An Alexander lesson—usually 30 to 45 minutes long—is an opportunity to unwind and observe how your mind and body work. In one part of the session, you lie clothed on the table and settle into a restful state as the teacher gently moves your limbs, calms your system and encourages ease and expansion. In another segment of the lesson you are more active. The teacher guides you to notice the dynamics of your body—how you sit, stand, walk or reach and offers focused, supportive coaching on how to do simple actions more easily. No matter where your problem is, you and your teacher will attend to the dynamic pattern in your entire body.

Movement then becomes the vehicle to improve your functioning. To demystify some of the body's complexity, you look at a muscle chart and miniature skeleton. As you stand or sit, the teacher helps you sense compression in your neck, release it and envision your spine lengthening. As you walk, the teacher—highly trained in the subtle Alexander touch—gives you the feeling of a lighter, more fluid stride.

That feeling then becomes your reference point when you're on your own. You recall an idea or sensation from your lesson and use that memory to cue yourself and lighten up. You learn to imbue ordinary activities—writing, speaking, washing dishes—with a spirit of observation as you notice your tendencies and explore ways to move more efficiently. You acquire a unique skill, a kind of portable body intelligence.

An Alexander lesson helps to restore your capacity for harmonious movement. Though it has therapeutic benefits, it's not a treatment such as chiropractic or massage. Like yoga or physical therapy, it is something you learn to do on your own. But it is not a set of exercises or postures. It's a method for noticing movement patterns and changing any that get in your way.

A teaching studio is a low-tech environment with a chair, bodywork table and mirror. You, the student, wear loose and comfortable clothing that allows free movement of the arms and legs. The teacher asks what problem or goal brings you there. You might discuss your medical history and what your life demands of you.

Though you should feel free to try one lesson, you will get the most out of Alexander study by taking a series. Many students begin to apply their new understanding after their first session, finding they have more choice than they realized about how they look and feel. Some people solve the problem that first drove them to study after several months, and then continue for a year or more, fascinated by the process of removing inner obstructions and refining their skills.

The success of the work depends on how you use what you learn. The goal is not to make you dependent on the teacher, but to train you, in all your interactions, to find greater comfort, confidence and peace. Given time, the Alexander Technique offers a gentle way to work on yourself for the better.

More information: Go to *www.alexander technique.com* or *www.amsatonline.org*.

ALL-NATURAL ANTIBIOTIC TONIC

One of the foremost authorities on herbal therapy in the world, Richard Schulze, ND, MH (master herbalist), has been formulating herbal medicines for more than 30 years. His natural antibiotic tonic is an original formulation, which he used in his clinic to help his patients increase circulation, detoxify their blood and promote a faster response from their immune system. No longer practicing in his clinic, Dr. Schulze now teaches throughout the US, Canada, Europe and Asia, but we have the recipe here for his amazing antibiotic tonic.

This tonic is extremely powerful because all the ingredients are fresh. Its power should not be underestimated. This formula, when added to a detoxification routine, can cure chronic conditions and the most stubborn diseases. It stimulates maximum blood circulation, while providing the best detoxifying herbs. This formula is not just for the sniffles, it has helped to turn around the deadliest infections like some of the new mutated viruses that defy conventional antibiotics. See the recipe for Schulze's All-Natural Antibiotic Tonic on the next page.

More information: To hear Dr. Richard Schulze's audio messages, and to learn about his American Botanical Pharmacy formulas, go to *www.herbdoc.com*.

AYURVEDA

From Sanskrit for the "knowledge (or science) of life," Ayurveda defines the trinity of life as body, mind and spiritual awareness. This holistic approach to healing evolved some 3,000 to 5,000 years ago among the Brahmin sages of ancient India.

We would need the rest of this book to explain the complex Ayurvedic philosophy based on one's underlying force or vital energy (prana), the seven main chakras, which are the seven spiritual centers in our body located along the spine (see description of chakras under "Chromotherapy" on page xvii), methods of disease prevention (panchakarma), examination and evaluation techniques (pulse diagnosis and examination of the tongue, voice, eyes, skin, urine, stools and general appearance) and treatment.

To give you some kind of feel for what you can expect from Ayurvedic medicine, know that practitioners and physicians recommend lifestyle interventions in nutrition, herbs, exercise, yoga, massage therapy and Shirodhara (a treatment that involves warm medicinal oil being poured over the forehead).

BACH FLOWER REMEDIES

Developed in the 1930s by English physician Edward Bach (pronounced "batch"),

■ **Recipe** ■

All-Natural Antibiotic Tonic

Ingredients

- **1 part fresh chopped garlic cloves** (offer anti-bacterial, antifungal, antiviral, antiparasitical properties)
- **1 part fresh chopped white onions or hottest onions available** (similar to garlic in benefits)
- **1 part fresh grated gingerroot** (increases circulation to the extremities)
- **1 part fresh grated horseradish root** (increases blood flow to the head)
- **1 part fresh chopped cayenne peppers, or the hottest peppers available—e.g. Habanero, African Bird or Scotch Bonnets** (promotes blood circulation)
- **Raw unfiltered unbleached non-distilled apple cider vinegar** (available at health food stores)

Instructions

Fill a glass jar three-quarters of the way full with equal parts by volume (i.e. a cupful of each) of the above fresh, chopped and grated herbs. Then fill the jar to the top with raw, unfiltered, unbleached, non-distilled apple cider vinegar. Close the jar and shake vigorously. Then, if there's room in the jar, fill it with more vinegar.

Shake at least once a day for two weeks, then filter the mixture through a clean piece of cotton fabric (old clean T-shirt) or cheesecloth, bottle it and label it.

 NOTE: Be sure that you shake the tonic a minimum of once every day, ideally every time you walk by it. All the herbs and vegetables should be fresh (and organically grown if possible). Use dried herbs only if you cannot get the fresh ingredient.

Dosage

The dosage is one to two tablespoons (½ to 1 ounce) two or more times daily. Gargle and swallow. (Do not dilute with water.)

For ordinary infections, 1 dropperful (¼ to ½ teaspoon) taken five to six times a day will do the trick.

It can be used during pregnancy (check with your doctor first), is safe for children in appropriately smaller doses (check with the pediatrician first) and, as a food, is completely nontoxic.

 CAUTION: Do NOT take this tonic if you have heartburn, gastritis, ulcers or esophagitis.

You can happily prepare a big batch of this tonic since it does not need refrigeration and it lasts indefinitely without any special storage conditions.

Bach flower remedies are dilutions of flower material. Dr. Bach believed that illnesses are "manifestations of flaws" in personality. Being convinced that a person's own nature, character and feelings play a major part in the development of disease, his approach to wellness was on a mental and emotional level. The remedies are used primarily for emotional and spiritual conditions, including but not limited to depression, anxiety, insomnia and stress.

Bach Flower Remedies (which contain a very small amount of flower material) are made

100% naturally from spring water infused with wildflowers, either by steeping in the sun or by boiling. The remedies contain 27% grape-based brandy as a preservative. Because the remedies are extremely diluted they do not have a characteristic scent or taste of the plant. Typically, the Bach flower remedies are found in health food stores in small, brown dropper bottles.

Advocates state that the remedies contain the "energetic" nature of the flower—each flower is believed to impart specific qualities to the remedy—and that this can be transmitted to the user.

Dr. Bach developed the flower remedies while he was working at the London Homeopathic Hospital, and they are often associated with homeopathy. They shouldn't be linked because the Bach flower remedies do not follow fundamental homeopathic principles.

Many times we have been in a nervous-making setting (waiting areas such as TV-show green rooms) and someone has taken out and passed around a tin of pastilles and Bach's Rescue Remedy—that has equal amounts of Rock rose, Impatiens, Clematis, Star of Bethlehem and Cherry Plum—used appropriately for treating stress, anxiety and panic attacks.

BEEF BROTH

 NOTE TO VEGETARIANS: The irony here is that vegetarians may benefit most from the beef broth properties that can only be derived from animals. So, if you're a vegetarian, before you go on to the next entry in this chapter, please read "Beef Broth" with an open mind. This broth may be an exception that's worth making.

Why Beef Broth?

Beef Broth (also known as *Bone Broth* or *Beef Stock*) is regarded as medicinal tea.

Considered a classic folk treatment (along with chicken soup, of course) for colds and flu, studies indicate that this old-fashioned, homemade stock has properties and nutrients to help boost the immune system and heal ailments that affect connective tissues, including the gastrointestinal tract, skin, lungs, muscles, blood and joints. There was a time that beef broth was referred to as "the poor man's joint supplement" (and probably one of the most beneficial).

The broth also offers nutritional support to chemotherapy patients, especially those who have mouth sores, and protein and iron deficiencies.

Beef Bones

Decades ago, before the availability of convenient cartons of beef and chicken stocks, most households had a stockpot simmering on the range more often than not.

The difference between the preparation of store-bought beef or chicken stock and this homemade stock is the addition of bones and bone marrow. Simmering bones in water for long periods of time releases many of their components for easy absorption by the human body. *The most beneficial components are…*

● **Gelatin/Collagen and the minerals and other useful nutrients contained in it.** Gelatin helps improve digestion including for those with stomach acid issues, GI conditions, lactose intolerance, celiac sufferers and for cancer patients with food-tolerance challenges.

● **Cartilage.** This is especially helpful for joint diseases including rheumatoid arthritis, and gastrointestinal diseases.

• **Glycine.** A simple amino acid that contributes to vital body processes, including detoxification by the liver. Glycine also enhances gastric acid secretion thus improves digestion. Recent studies show glycine helps infants grow properly.

• **Hyaluronic acid.** It lubricates joints and helps heal wounds.

• **Chondroitin sulfate** (yes, it's the same chondroitin used in supplements for osteoarthritis). Along with joint-pain relief, it's said to help lower cholesterol and the risk of atherosclerosis.

• **Minerals** such as calcium, phosphorus, magnesium, sodium, potassium, sulfate and fluoride. These minerals help make bones and joints strong.

Stock Tips

• **Using a stockpot or any tall, narrow pot** will slow down water loss from evaporation.

• **Roasted bones add color and caramelized flavors** to the stock.

• **Eggshells are used** because the membrane that separates the white from the shell contains four joint-boosting nutrients, which are hyaluronic acid, glucosamine, chondroitin and collagen.

• **Vinegar helps leach important minerals out of the bones.**

• **Ripe or overripe vegetables are sweeter.** Carrots, parsley and garlic cloves may also be added. Use organic veggies whenever possible.

• **Simmer on the lowest heat possible.** If the broth boils too fast, it may cause a bitter taste.

• **When the broth is taken off the fire, let it cool.** Within two hours after being taken

■ Recipe ■

Beef Broth

After weeks of experimenting with a variety of broth recipes (our cousin now refers to our kitchen as a *broth-el*), we decided that we'll stick with a basic (medicinal) beef broth recipe.

Be sure you read "Stock Tips" and "Stock Options" on this page and the next two.

Ingredients

Stockpot or tall narrow pot. Stainless steel or porcelain is ideal, not aluminum (the vinegar used can cause aluminum to leach into the broth)

3 to 4 lbs. beef bones from 100% grass-fed and antibiotic-free beef and no added hormones. The higher the quality of bones, the more beneficial the broth. (Properly prepared broth should gel after it's refrigerated. Broth made from inferior bones will probably not gel.)

Have the butcher cut bones into 2" to 3" long chunks. (The greater surface area of bone that's exposed to the water, the greater the quality and nutrient value of the broth.)

1 to 2 peeled, whole onions (ripe or overripe)

3 to 6 celery stalks (ripe or overripe)

Eggshells from 2 to 3 eggs

2 tablespoons vinegar (apple cider, red or white wine, rice or balsamic)

Instructions

1. Rinse the bones and roast them in a roasting pan for 1 hour at 400°F.

2. Transfer the roasted bones to a stockpot.

3. Cover the bones with cold water several inches above the bones.

4. Add eggshells along with their membrane linings.

5. Add 2 tablespoons of vinegar.

6. Stir the pot gently, then let it stand for 30 minutes.

7. Add 1 to 2 onions, peeled and whole. Add 3 to 6 celery stalks.

8. Slowly bring the pot of ingredients to a boil, then reduce the heat to its lowest point. Cover and simmer for about 12 to 18 hours. The longer you let it simmer, the more potent the healing properties.

9. Check on the pot every couple of hours. Gently and carefully remove the effluvium (skim the scum) that's on the surface. Replace some of the evaporated water by slowly adding freshly boiled water.

10. Once simmering time is completed, remove the bones, vegetables and eggshells.

11. If you want to spice it up, now is the time to add seasoning to taste—sea salt, pepper, garlic powder, onion powder.

Dosage

Have 2 to 6 ounces of this broth daily. Sip it throughout the day, or drink it as you would drink tea. This broth is, technically, a bone and cartilage decoction, or medicinal tea.

If you want to incorporate the broth in your meals, it can be used whenever a recipe calls for stock, or add broth to replace water in a recipe, for instance to cook beans, rice or other grains. You can add vegetables and beans and chicken and turn the broth into a stew.

 CAUTION: Whether you eat it plain, or mixed in with other foods, NEVER cook or reheat the broth in the microwave. The gelatin in the broth may become toxic to the liver, kidneys and nervous system. Warm the broth on the range.

off the fire, pour it into containers, cover and refrigerate. It should keep for about five days. It can be frozen in airtight plastic containers and kept for four to six months.

● **Before taking a portion, remove and discard the fat that settled on top.** Heat and drink or eat. Remember, NEVER cook or reheat the broth in the microwave.

Stock Options

● **There are many recipes for this medicinal stock.** If beef is not your cup of tea, you can begin with bones from poultry, lamb, pork or fish. Whatever bones you use, be sure they come from animals raised organically, or at least naturally—free-range, grass-fed, no antibiotics and no added hormones. To extract flavor and the healing gelatin, the general rule for simmering is—two hours for fish broth, all day for larger animals' bones—chicken, turkey or duck and overnight (eight to 12 hours) for beef broth.

● **Some cooks incorporate cartilage-rich parts not usually eaten,** such as the rib cage and spine, chicken feet, fish heads and beef knuckles.

● **Herbalists' recipe for this medicinal broth usually includes one or more Chinese**

herbs, such as astragalus (*huang qui*), codonopsis (*dang shen*), and lycii berries (*gou qi zi*), to increase the medicinal properties and the flavor of the broth. (See "Sources," page 309, for a Chinese herb retailer.)

Make No Bones About It

Join the many who put stock in the benefits of beef broth as a daily tonic. Invest in a stockpot, if you don't already have one, buy a bunch of bones, brew a batch of broth.

CHERRIES

Bing Cherries

Ah Bing. That's not only how we feel about the cherries, it's also the name of the Manchurian Chinese foreman for whom the cherries were named by horticulturist Seth Lewelling, when he first cultivated them in the 1870s. Little did Lewelling know that these dark red beauties are as nutritious as they are delicious.

The California Cherry Advisory Board (*www.calcherry.com*) reports that bing cherries contribute to...

➤ **Heart Disease Prevention.** According to researchers, *quercetin,* a flavonoid found in cherries, has anticarcinogenic properties that can help to prevent heart disease. Cherries are considered a nutritionally significant source of quercetin, containing large quantities per serving that surpass most fruits.

For additional heart protection in cherries, read about *anthocyanins* below.

➤ **Cancer Prevention.**

• Anthocyanins are a class of flavonoid plant pigments responsible for the color in cherries. They are also a powerful antioxidant

236

that helps protect against cancer and heart disease. Eating six cherries a day delivers 200 milligrams (mg) of anthocyanins.

• *Perillyl alcohol* is isolated from the essential oils of several plants including cherries. Animal research suggests that perillyl alcohol may help slow growth of pancreatic, mammary and liver tumors. It may also help colon, lung and skin cancer. Perillyl alcohol is under sponsorship from the National Cancer Institute (NCI), and is currently undergoing clinical trials.

➤ **Bone Health.** Cherries are also considered to be excellent sources of boron. Boron consumption, coupled with calcium and magnesium, has been linked to increased bone health.

➤ **Pain Relief.** Cherries are known to block inflammatory enzymes, reducing pain.

They are said to be 10 times as potent as aspirin for arthritis pain, without irritating one's stomach. We talk about the healing powers of cherries in the "Gout" section, page 100.

Prolong the Season by Freezin'

Buy cherries at the height of their summer season, when prices are at their lowest, and freeze them. *Here's how to do it…*

1. **Leave the stems on the fresh bing cherries,** and wash them under cool running water.

2. **Gently pat them until they are dry.** Dryness is key!

3. **Place the cherries in a plastic container** or bag and label it with the date.

4. **Place the container or bag in the freezer.** They should keep for up to three months.

5. **When defrosting, be sure to defrost in the refrigerator,** not at room temperature. The cherries will keep their firmness that way. Defrosting at room temperature may turn the cherries to mush.

 NOTE: Try eating the cherries while they're still frozen or slightly frozen. We love them that way, and you may, too. Ba-da-bing!

If you're thinking that this is it for cherries, *keep reading and find out about our recent discovery…*

Tart Cherries

This past summer, a bumper crop of bing cherries brought down their price, and life was just a bowl of, well, you know. Every day we would have some as a snack. It was at that time, Joan noticed that her blood glucose levels were consistently lower than they had been. The only new food in her diet was cherries. Of course we Googled "cherries and diabetes," and there was lots of information about cherries increasing insulin production by 50% in tests involving animals. Human studies are now well under way.

In fact, Dr. Muralee Nair, a natural products chemist, Michigan State University, conducted research with anthocyanins in tart cherries and found that they have a significant impact on insulin levels in humans.

The more we discovered about cherries, the more amazed we were. One Web site led to another which led us to Andy LaPointe of Traverse Bay Farms, in northwestern Michigan, the epicenter of tart-cherry farming.

Andy taught us all about the two main types of cherries—sweet and tart (also referred to as *sour*). Tart cherries are lower in calories and higher in vitamin C and beta carotene than sweet cherries. According to some of the cherry mavens we spoke with, while sweet cherries are very beneficial, tart cherries may prove a little more therapeutic in some ways.

Previously, tart cherries were almost always canned or frozen and used for pie filling and sauces. Now they are used in many products. Check out Traverse Bay Farms, 877-746-7477 or *www.traversebayfarms.com*, for Andy's extensive and incredibly delicious product line, including some of the best (award winning) salsas around. Andy offers a *Cherry Health Report* free of charge.

Melatonin in Cherries

Cherries are believed to be one of the most concentrated sources of *melatonin* according to research conducted by Russel J. Reiter, PhD, professor of neuroendocrinology at the University of Texas Health Science Center. He says, "We've learned that melatonin from food enters the bloodstream and binds to sites in the brain where it helps restore the body's natural levels of melatonin, which can help enhance the natural sleep process."

To help alleviate jet lag, research suggests that you should eat a serving of dried tart cherries one hour before your desired sleep time on the plane, and for three or more consecutive evenings after your arrival to help adjust your circadian rhythm. But you don't have to be a jet-setter to benefit from the melatonin in cherries. Adults with sleep-onset insomnia—usually seniors with a melatonin deficiency—may be helped by having some form of tart cherries daily.

Even though tart cherries are a seasonal fruit, they are sold year-round in dried, juice, juice concentrate, frozen, powder form and capsule form. Dried cherries are a convenient and portable way to get a melatonin boost on a plane. One serving is one-half cup dried cherries, or one cup of juice or two tablespoons of cherry juice concentrate.

For more information on melatonin and cherries, visit *www.choosecherries.com*, and for the latest, updated information on the benefits of tart cherry juice, visit *www.benefitsofcherryjuice. com*.

CLAY THERAPY

Hey, clay isn't just for kids' play or for potters. Simply put, it may be the key to restoring your health—either through ingesting or using as a compress.

We were lucky to have a clay therapy authority volunteer to introduce this healing modality to you. Perry A~, as she goes by, is the author of *Living Clay: Nature's Own Miracle* 238

Cure. She is dedicated to spreading the word about the safe, healing potential of living clay.

Perry A~ on Clay Therapy

Clay is Mother Nature's pharmacy. It is volcanic ash with all the impurities burnt out, leaving pure trace minerals. Clay is a nano crystal of highly charged electromagnetic energy from the thermodynamic heat of a volcano. It can't be duplicated in a laboratory. Only God can make clay.

Most clays have a high alkaline pH. Clay is homeostatic and as such is an adaptogen that brings balance and equilibrium to the body. A balanced body can heal itself. That is what the body is designed to do when it isn't in overload and unable to filter out the buildup of toxins and wastes in the body that begin to cause health problems. Clay's strength lies in its ability to adsorb and absorb—to suck into itself—toxins, chemicals, viruses, molds and bacteria, and then carry this out of the body.

The electromagnetic energy of the clay stimulates circulation, bringing blood flow and oxygen to revitalize cellular repair.

It sounds like a snake oil because it can help with so many things but it really can…and in a remarkable short amount of time…and with great ease, it brings about swift results.

The beauty of clay is that it is so safe. The Food and Drug Administration (FDA) gives bentonite clay a GRAS rating meaning **G**enerally **R**egarded **A**s **S**afe. (In case you're wondering why you haven't heard about this wonderful stuff before—after all, it's safe, inexpensive and effective—the clay companies cannot legally make healing claims about clay without the multimillion-dollar testing programs that the major pharmaceutical companies can afford.)

There is a long recorded history of animals in the wild instinctively seeking and eating clay to heal themselves. The medicine men of many aboriginal tribes have long used clay as part of their healing treatments.

The kicker is all clays are different, even within the same family of clays, so it is important to know your clays. The smectite family of clays is known as the healing clays. Bentonite is a smectite clay.

Although all clays have some healing potential, there are a few that are amazingly stronger than others. Some are good for internal use and others much better for external use and a few that are exceptional in both areas.

From a gentle internal cleansing, to healing wounds in half the time, to stopping acid reflux and intestinal disorders, to stopping food poisoning, to detoxing heavy metals, to healing burns, insect bites, skin rashes, acne and gum problems, to helping children with autism, to expelling internal parasites, to stopping anemia, clay is a natural replacement for most drugs and with no organ-damaging negative side effects.

Back to Joan and Lydia

More information: If you are intrigued with what you've read so far, and want to know more about the way of clay, you'll want to get Perry's book in which there is a detailed description of the five types of clay treatments—dry powder application, poultice (clay pack), hydrated topical application, liquid drink and clay bath. Perry also lists 101 ailments and how to cure them with one or more of these treatments using calcium bentonite clay. You

also may want to visit the Web site *www.living clayco.com.*

Perry A~ is willing to answer questions about clay therapy, and can be reached at 512-262-7187. For more on clay therapy, see "Stop Needless Amputations" in the "Diabetes" section, page 57.

DONATING BLOOD

Talk about giving of yourself...What better way than to donate blood?

The bonus benefit is that you will probably be healthier for doing this generous deed.

Studies show that Americans tend to consume more iron in their daily diet than is needed for good health. Women of child-bearing age get rid of excess iron when they menstruate. Men and post-menopausal women do not have that advantage, especially if they are red-meat lovers.

Having too much iron in your system can promote formation of free radicals in the body. Free radicals are believed to cause tissue damage at the cellular level, disrupting normal cell function and increasing the risk of certain chronic diseases.

Which brings us back to giving blood. When you donate a pint of blood, some of the excess iron in your body is removed in that blood. Studies have shown that men who donate blood on a regular basis have a lower risk of heart disease.

If you're concerned about giving blood and giving away more iron than you can afford to donate, fear not. Your hemoglobin level —a rough measure of your iron levels—will be checked before you're allowed to donate blood. Each time you go back to donate, your hemoglobin level will be monitored. To prevent too much iron from being removed from your body, you will only be allowed to donate every eight weeks.

According to the Red Cross organization, donating blood is a safe process. Needles and bags used to collect blood are used only once and then discarded, making spread of infection to the donor not possible.

The American Red Cross has created a huge operations network that helps direct your blood donation to the areas of the country—or the world—where they are most needed. While you can't direct your donation to be specifically routed to military personnel, you can be sure that it will be sent to the areas of most critical need.

Consider taking an hour or two out of your schedule every two months to donate blood. It will be a win-win situation.

DRY BRUSHING

Dry brushing dates back to the ancient Greeks and Romans and is used today in European spas and in many cancer treatment centers.

More than 30 years ago, dry brushing was recommended by internationally known naturopath and nutritionist Dr. Paavo Airola, who regarded it as an essential part of any intestinal cleansing and healing program. That being the case, it is understandable that it's part of therapy at many cancer treatment centers.

Dr. Denice Moffat, a certified traditional naturopath and medical intuitive, is an advocate of dry brushing and uses it in her practice. Dr. Moffat graciously agreed to share the benefits, and the before, during and after rules and

240

techniques of dry brushing, beginning with an intriguing anatomy lesson...

A Word from the Wise...

Dr. Moffat on Dry Brushing

The skin is the largest most important eliminative organ in the body, responsible for one-quarter of the body's detoxification each day.

In fact, the skin of the average adult eliminates more than a pound of waste acids daily, most of it through the sweat glands.

A few more facts: The skin is known as our third kidney, it receives one-third of all the blood circulated in the body and is the last to receive nutrients in the body, yet the first to show signs of imbalance or deficiency.

Why Dry Brush the Skin?

Detoxification is performed by a number of organs, glands and transportation systems, including the skin, gut, kidneys, liver, lungs, lymphatic system and mucous membranes. The dry brushing technique deals with detoxification of the skin and provides a gentle internal massage, stimulating the detoxification process.

Benefits of Dry Brushing

- **Helps remove cellulite.**
- **Cleanses the lymphatic system.**
- **Removes dead skin layers.**
- **Strengthens the immune system.**
- **Stimulates the hormone and oil-producing glands.**
- **Tightens the skin, preventing premature aging.**
- **Tones the muscles.**
- **Stimulates circulation.**

● **Improves the function of the nervous system.**

● **Helps digestion.**

What You Need for Dry Brushing

To dry brush, use a soft natural-fiber brush with a long handle, so that you are able to reach all areas of your body. One with a removable head with a strap for your hand is a good choice. (Health food stores usually have them, or visit *www.amazon.com* or *www.earththerapeutics.com* for a good, inexpensive brush.)

Most nylon or synthetic-fiber brushes are too sharp and may damage skin. The important thing is to find something that is just right for your skin. Once your skin becomes "seasoned," you can switch to a coarser brush.

Rules for Safe and Successful Dry Brushing

 CAUTION: Avoid sensitive areas including the face, and anywhere the skin is broken such as areas of skin rash, wounds, cuts and infections. Also, never brush an area affected by poison oak, poison sumac or poison ivy.

● **Always dry brush your dry and naked body before you shower or bathe** because you will want to wash off the impurities from the skin that result from the brushing action.

● **Always brush UP from your toes to lower back using long sweeping strokes.** Start at the bottom of your feet and brush upward. From the hands, brush toward the shoulders, and on the torso brush in an upward direction to help drain the lymph back to your heart. But

be sure to brush DOWN from your neck to your upper back.

● **Use light pressure in areas where the skin is thin** and harder pressure on thicker skin areas like the soles of the feet.

● **Skin brushing should be performed once a day,** preferably first thing in the morning. A thorough skin brushing takes about 15 minutes, but any time spent brushing prior to showering or bathing will benefit the body.

● **If you are feeling ill,** increasing the treatments to twice a day may help you feel better faster.

● **For areas of cellulite,** dry brush five to 10 minutes twice a day to achieve cellulite dissolving. For real progress, the technique needs to be done consistently for a minimum of five months. (Think of how long it took for the cellulite to accumulate.)

Easy, Fast Instructions for Dry Brushing

Read through these steps so that you get an idea of what's involved...

● **Start out with the soles of your feet,** brushing in circular motions.

● **Continue brushing up your legs.**

● **Proceed to your hands and arms** using circular motions toward your heart.

● **Brush your entire back and abdomen area, shoulders and neck.**

● **To stimulate the pituitary gland,** hold the brush on the back of your head near the base of your neck and rock the brush up and down, then side to side.

● **Do circular counterclockwise strokes on the abdomen.**

- **Very lightly brush the breasts.** Stroking your breastbone in a circular fashion stimulates the thymus gland.

- **Brush upward on the back and down from the neck.** Better yet, have a friend, spouse or family member brush your back.

 NOTE: For extremely detailed brushing instructions, visit Dr. Moffat's Web site at *www. naturalhealthtechniques.com.*

The Shower After Brushing

- **Take a warm shower with soap** (about three minutes in duration).

- **After showering, before turning off the water, end with three hot and three cold cycles.** That means turning on the water as hot as you can take it (without burning yourself) for 10 to 20 seconds, then as cold as you can handle it for 10 to 20 seconds, then hot, then cold, then hot, then cold. In cold weather, you may want to start with cold and end with hot. In warm weather, you may want to start with hot and end with cold. Select which suits you best.

  This hot-cold process will further invigorate the skin and stimulate blood circulation, bringing more blood to the outer layers of the skin. But if the hot-cold process seems too complicated, just take a warm shower.

- **After getting out of the shower, dry off vigorously with a rough towel,** and massage your skin with a pure plant oil or a combination of oils such as olive, avocado, apricot, almond, sesame, coconut and/or cocoa butter. If you have arthritis, add a little peanut or castor oil to the mix. Psychic Edgar Cayce said that this works to take out some of the pain, and we've found that to be true over the years.

242

Care of Your Brush

Clean your skin brush with soap and water once a week. After rinsing, dry the brush in an open, sunny spot to prevent mildew.

The Brush-Off from Dr. Moffat

Any well-designed program will take about 30 days for you to see and experience changes. For a thorough lymphatic cleansing, perform skin brushing daily for a minimum of three months. Please be patient and keep up the program!

GREEN TEA

Most of you know that green tea has many medicinal properties. According to the *Annals of Epidemiology,* the results of a recent study in Japan showed that drinking seven cups of green tea a day could cut the risk of heart disease by a staggering 75% and the risk of colorectal cancer by 31%. The five-year study included 12,000 test subjects between the ages of 65 and 84, and the researchers note that their impressive results may be due to the fact that these people had been drinking green tea all of their lives.

It's never too late to start drinking green tea to derive its many benefits. Its high level of *flavonoids* makes it more effective than other types of tea for boosting the immune system, decreasing cholesterol and blood sugar, reducing blood pressure, improving respiratory and digestive health, providing anti-inflammatory effects and protecting against Alzheimer's.

According to one study, drinking three cups of green tea gives you the same amount of antioxidants as you would get from eating six apples.

A Revelation in Hydration

That's the way Pure Inventions refers to their green tea and other fruit and cocoa antioxidant-rich products. Add a dropper of the green tea extract (100 milligrams [mg]) to water and POOF! green tea. No calories, no caffeine, no preservatives, no artificial sweeteners (it is sweetened with lo han and stevia extracts).

Add a dropper or two to your bottle of water for a quick energy boost while you're out and about. Have it at a restaurant, at a friend's home or wherever and whenever you want a refreshing picker-upper while reaping all of the benefits of green tea.

More information: For more details about Pure Inventions green tea flavors and other antioxidant extracts, visit *www.pureinventions.com* or call 732-842-5777.

Another benefit from drinking green tea daily, is making weight loss a little easier. There's an extract in green tea that helps fat burn at a faster rate.

 CAUTION: Some people will have stomach irritation with large amounts of green tea. If you notice stomach irritation, cut back your servings of green tea.

Matcha—The *Really Green* Tea

Got Matcha? Now that you know about the power of green tea, we would like to introduce you to matcha tea, the highest quality, most conscientiously cultivated variety of green tea.

In terms of its nutritional value and antioxidant content, one glass of matcha is the equivalent of 10 glasses of the average green tea.

When you drink matcha you ingest the whole leaf, not just the brewed water (as with green tea).

While we are comparing…regular green tea is brownish in color, but matcha, being so rich in *chlorophyll*, is a bright, beautiful green, and when mixed with water, it becomes a more regal-looking green. If you're making an effort to "go green," in addition to all of the benefits mentioned under "Green Tea," here are some more reasons to consider drinking matcha…

Benefits

- **Worth repeating—rich in antioxidants.** Matcha's higher in antioxidants than other foods known for their impressive antioxidant levels such as blueberries, pomegranates and spinach. Hey Popeye, put that in your pipe and smoke it!

- **Also worth repeating—it contains chlorophyll,** a renowned detoxifying agent that helps remove heavy metals and chemical toxins from the body.

- **Provides *catechin EGCG* (a powerful cancer-fighting antioxidant).**

 NOTE: EGCG also comes in supplement form. Check your health food store.

- **Rich in *L-theanine*, an amino acid known to relax the mind.** For this reason, matcha is also known as a mood enhancer.

More information: To learn more about matcha tea, visit *www.matchasource.com*. The site offers preparation and drinking tips, recipes, a buyer's guide including a fine selection of top-quality teas and a Matcha Starter Kit to create your own stress-relieving Chanoyu (Japanese Tea Ceremony). If you have questions, call Matcha Source (toll free) at 877-962-8242.

KOMBUCHA TEA

Kombucha (pronounced "cahm boo' shah") tea is said to provide a variety of health benefits from boosting immunity and fighting cancer to helping both diabetes and arthritis. It's made by floating a kombucha "mushroom" (which is really a special yeast patty) in sugar, tea and water. Intrigued? *Read on…*

From the Mushroom Maven

Betsy Pryor, author of *Kombucha Phenomenon— The Miracle Health Tea* (Sierra Sunrise), who introduced the kombucha to the American public in 1993, calls it "a gift from God" because of its health-giving properties. *We'll turn it over to her now…*

"The kombucha isn't really a mushroom at all. In fact, the kombucha does not exist in nature. Someone put it together. Just who, remains a mystery. Although it's widely believed that the kombucha existed as early as 220 BC in China, where it was known as the 'Divine Tea,' I believe that its origins go back much farther in time. I have a hunch that mystery-someone was Egyptian and skilled in the fine Egyptian art of fermentation.

"The kombucha mushroom is a combination of good bacteria and yeast (not the kind that causes yeast problems) that when left undisturbed for seven to 10 days, floating in a mixture of ordinary sugar, tea and water, makes an invigorating beverage containing vitamins B-1, B-2, B-3, B-6, B-12, folic acid and *glucuronic acid*, which works with the liver to bind up environmental and metabolic toxins and excrete them from the body.

"The kombucha also makes a new baby (a clone) that can be kept or given away. Legend has it that the babies of your original mom kombucha will, if treated kindly, accompany you for life."

Back to Us

It's hard to describe what the kombucha looks like. We finally agreed that it resembles a round, skinless, raw chicken-breast cutlet.

Kombucha Benefits…So They Say

Kombucha tea is said to be a super immune booster, helping the body in fighting everything from yeast infections and ulcers to psoriasis, arthritis, constipation, chronic diarrhea, prostate problems, male and female incontinence, hemorrhoids, stress, chronic fatigue syndrome, indigestion, kidney problems, gallstones, high cholesterol, acne, diabetes, multiple sclerosis, cancer, decreasing T-cell counts, hardening of the arteries, memory loss and other symptoms of aging, menopausal symptoms, PMS, impotence, wrinkles, weight problems, gout, carpal tunnel syndrome, hypoglycemia, hair loss and heaven-only-knows-what-else.

People tell us it's great for their pets, too. Putting a few eye-droppersful in their drinking water each day adds sparkle and new life to their skin, coat and disposition, and can eliminate doggy breath.

Cure-All or All Hype?

While we know people who have had miraculous health results that they attribute to drinking the tea, we also know people who started and stopped because they didn't feel they were receiving enough benefits from the tea to make it worthwhile.

So, how do you know if it will be beneficial for you? The only way is by trying it. That's why we want you to know more about it, and exactly what's involved in growing and harvesting the kombucha.

 NOTE: While reading over all the preparation details and the supplies needed, if you decide that you would like to try kombucha tea but don't want to get involved in the growing and harvesting process, see the "Something Special" box on the next page and read about ready-made, bottled kombucha tea.

How to Make It

The kombucha mushroom–growing process begins with the preparation of a distilled water, sugar and tea mixture in a stainless steel pot which is then transferred to a glass bowl. When it has cooled to room temperature, you float the kombucha tea mushroom (that someone gave you or one that you bought) in the bowl, add the starter tea that comes with the kombucha, cover it and put it in a quiet, dark, clean place for seven to 10 days. At the end of that time, take out the bowl, uncover it and—if all went well—you will see that the kombucha has cloned itself. The original kombucha has become a mom and the baby is attached to it.

You peel the mom and the baby apart, refloat the mom in a newly prepared brew and either do the same with the baby, or give it away. Then, into a glass bottle, you strain the liquid that the kombuchas were in, and refrigerate what is now your kombucha (health tonic) tea. Once it's chilled, it's ready to drink.

Ordering a mushroom: If you're still interested in preparing kombucha tea, start by ordering a kombucha tea mushroom from a trusted commercial grower.

For more information on kombucha tea read Betsy Pryor's book called *Kombucha Phenomenon—The Miracle Health Tea* written with Sanford Holst.

Supplies needed: While waiting for your mushroom to arrive, you will need to gather the following supplies…

- **2 3- to 4-quart unleaded glass mixing bowls**
- **thin, freshly laundered white cotton fabric, enough to cover the bowls**
- **a 4-quart stainless steel pot**
- **a box of green tea bags and/or black tea bags** (*NOT* organic tea, as it can cause mold)
- **a few 6-inch rubber bands**
- **a wooden or plastic spoon**
- **a 5-pound bag of white (ordinary refined) sugar**
- **a gallon of distilled water**
- **a measuring pitcher** (for quarts of water)
- **tape** (Scotch tape works fine)
- **plastic funnel**

When your mama mushroom arrives: You will receive the kombucha tea mushroom in an airtight plastic bag. The first thing you are going to do is open the bag to let your kombucha tea mushroom breathe. Make sure you don't spill the tea that's inside the bag, because you are going to need it to start the fermenting process.

Once you're ready to start the growing process, follow all the step-by-step instructions that come with the mushroom. As with most instructions, they seem more complex than they actually are. Once you get into it, it quickly becomes routine.

 CAUTION: Know all of the precautions to take when handling, growing, harvesting and storing the kombucha and tea. For

SOMETHING SPECIAL

Divine Tea in a Bottle

Want to drink kombucha without having to grow it? GT Dave began bottling kombucha in 1995 after his mother's success with drinking it during her battle with breast cancer. He was a teenager back then, and began making it from the kitchen of his house.

What started out as a desire to share this gift with anybody who could benefit from it has turned into a thriving company that makes over a dozen different varieties of kombucha products that are distributed to stores across the country. GT is committed to growing and harvesting the freshest, purest and most potent kombucha available, without sacrificing quality for the sake of profits.

If you want kombucha for a specific physical challenge, drink GT's "Original," rather than kombucha with greens, ginger or fruit juice added.

More information: Visit GT's Web site at *www.synergydrinks.com* for more information, and click on "Find a store" for a store in your area.

example, *never* expose the mushroom to direct sunlight. *Never* let metal (like your jewelry) touch the mushroom, and don't put it near microwaves.

Use green and/or black tea for the brew. *Don't* use organic tea, as it can cause mold. Herbal teas diminish the health benefits of the kombucha and some can even kill it. *Never* use honey in place of sugar, as honey can destroy some of the kombucha's healthy bacteria.

Tea Taste

Kombucha tea is a fermented drink whose taste varies—depending on weather, phases of the moon and growing conditions—from zingy and sweetish to zingy and cider vinegary. Some brews taste absolutely delicious while others will make you pucker just thinking about it. There seems to be no consistency when it comes to taste, some batches are simply better than others.

Dosage

Russian scientists who did a lot of research on the kombucha said that four ounces three times a day seemed like a sensible amount. We suggest that people work their way up to 12 ounces a day, starting with three or four ounces the first three days. As you increase the number of ounces you have each day, don't have them all at once. If you want to lose weight, have a couple of ounces before meals. If you want to gain weight, have it after meals. Within weeks, you'll get to know the amount that's best for you.

 CAUTION: Neither of us, nor GT Dave makes any claims regarding the health benefits of kombucha tea. Check with your health care professional before you embark on this or any self-help treatment.

The late Dr. Ray Wunderlich, Jr., founder of the Wunderlich Center for Nutritional Medicine, said, "With regard to the kombucha tea mushroom, the jury is not in yet for this relatively new, very old product. Just as one may choke on meat or develop hives from eating eggs, the consumer of kombucha should use caution lest any strong food such as this should prove contaminated, toxic or allergic to the individual user."

LAUGHTER

In the good old days—the 1990s—the results of a study by Dr. Lee Berk and Dr. Stanley Tan of Loma Linda University in California, published in *Humor and Health Journal*, left no doubt that laughter activates the immune system and lowers blood pressure, reduces stress hormones and raises levels of infection-fighting cells and disease-fighting proteins that produce disease-destroying antibodies. That's nothing to laugh at.

Sharing laughter can help you make new friends or improve and deepen the level of communication with old friends, family members and business associates.

Robert R. Provine, PhD, is a professor of psychology and neuroscience at the University of Maryland who did a 10-year study of laughter that resulted in the book, *Laughter: A Scientific Investigation* (Penguin). Professor Provine concluded that laughter plays a big role in mating. Men like women who laugh heartily in their presence and laughter of the female is the critical index of a healthy relationship. No kidding. Women laugh 126% more than men, but men are more laugh-getters…or so they think they are. (*Authors' note:* Women are kind and will laugh even when men aren't funny. Right, ladies?)

The professor also says that one of the best ways to stimulate laughter—and probably the most ancient way—is by tickling. Tickling is inherently social; we can't tickle ourselves. Most people enjoy tickling—ticklers as well as ticklees—because it's recognized as an indication of affection.

Men are said to be as ticklish as women, and maybe a little more so. So the next time you have an argument with your mate, don't walk out of the room. Try tickling your partner instead. Ticklish areas, in descending order, are under the arms, waist, ribs, feet, knees, throat, neck and palms.

What is all of this telling you? Make a real effort to lighten up. Be playful. Have fun. It can make a major difference in your sense of well-being and in your relationships with everyone in your life.

In this day and age, there are tons of things to tickle your funny bone. There are books, television shows, DVDs, audiocassettes, Web sites, comedy clubs across the country and the funniest of all, real life. Seek and ye shall find the humor surrounding you. Laughter is contagious. Spread it around!

Are you game? Good. Tell a joke to the next person you see or speak to. If you're one of those people who says, "I can't tell a joke," tell it anyway. It'd probably be funnier than told by someone with a slick delivery. So that you don't have the I-don't-know-any-joke excuse, take a look at one of the joke Web sites. Try *www.ahajokes.com*, *www.jokesclean.com* and *www.danggoodjokes.com*. Who knows, this may start you on a whole new career, but for the time being, hold on to your day job.

Or, to get your funny bone working, watch a funny movie. *We took a poll among friends and colleagues and got this laugh-out-loud list…*

- *Tootsie*, 1982.
- *Big*, 1988.
- *Meet the Parents*, 2000.
- *Little Miss Sunshine*, 2006.
- *The Full Monty*, 1997.
- **Movies written and directed by Mel Brooks**, like *Young Frankenstein*, 1974, and *The Producers*, 1968.

247

- **Movies written and directed by Woody Allen,** such as *Annie Hall,* 1977, and *Broadway Danny Rose,* 1984.

- **Movies with Billy Crystal,** such as *City Slickers,* 1991, and *Analyze This,* 1999.

- **Movies with Robin Williams,** such as *Mrs. Doubtfire,* 1993, and *The Birdcage,* 1996.

No Laughing Matter

If you're among the 15% of the American population with no sense of humor, you might consider joining the National Association for the Humor Impaired (NAFHI), founded by Dr. Stuart Robertshaw, professor emeritus of psychology and education at the University of Wisconsin–La Crosse and an attorney.

The benefits of joining the NAFHI are increased laughter, better health, a wallet-sized membership card, a membership certificate, an exclusive copy of the Association's Quick-Score Test of Humor Impairment (for assistance in diagnosing family members, friends or co-workers) and a "no whining" button.

A lifetime membership in the association is free to qualified members in exchange for sharing with Dr. Humor a story of the funniest moments that happened to you or someone you know. The story you submit must be a real story and not a joke or fiction.

More information: Visit *www.drhumor. com* to submit your application for a free membership, complete the form and hit the "Submit My Story" button. *Or, submit your story by mail to:* Professor Stuart Robertshaw, National Association for the Humor Impaired, 3356 Bayside Court, Suite 201, La Crosse, WI 54601. To receive your membership kit, be sure to include your mailing address.

248

Your birthright: Take advantage of one of the greatest gifts of being human. LAUGH!

MISO

Through a centuries-old double-fermentation process, soybeans and cultured grains, such as barley and rice, are transformed into miso—one of Japan's most revered culinary treasures.

For the Japanese, miso preparation is considered an art form, and those who prepare it are considered masters.

Like wine, and sometimes referred to as "wine of the Orient," miso is classified by color, flavor, aroma and texture. Sweet miso is usually light in color (white, yellow or beige) and higher in carbohydrates. It is marketed under such names as "mellow miso," "sweet miso" and "sweet white (shiro) miso." Darker miso is more distinct in flavor and somewhat saltier than lighter varieties. It's marketed under such names as "red (aka) miso," "rice (kome) miso," "brown rice (genmai) miso" and "barley (mugi) miso." Soybean misos such as "mame" and "hatcho" are also dark, salty varieties.

Many brands and types of miso—in jars, plastic tubs, squeeze containers and vacuum-packed bags—can be found in the refrigerated sections of health food stores, Whole Foods Markets and most supermarkets. Miso must be refrigerated.

With its essential vitamins and minerals and excellent balance of carbohydrates, fats and proteins, miso is one of nature's perfect survival foods. Properly stored, miso can provide life-sustaining nourishment decades after it is made.

John and Jan Belleme refer to miso as a superfood. And they should know, they wrote the book on it, *The Miso Book—The Art of Cooking with Miso* (Square One Publishers, *www.square onepublishers.com*). We thank the Bellemes for allowing us to share their miso information and recipes with you (see the next page).

As a food, miso is used to flavor and enhance the nutritional value of a wide variety of savory and satisfying dishes. As a folk remedy, it has been successfully used to lower cholesterol levels and treat digestive problems, cancer, radiation sickness, tobacco poisoning and even low libido. It also helps neutralize the effects of smoking and other environmental pollutants.

Miso Medicine

The incredible healing properties of miso, once thought of as folk remedies, have now been confirmed by modern science. *Here are some details to make you marvel...*

▶ **Enhanced Immune Function.** Misos that are made with a large proportion of soybeans and usually aged for one year or longer, such as Hatcho, barley, brown rice and soybean misos, are high in *arginine*, an important amino acid. Arginine retards the growth of tumors and cancer by enhancing the body's immune function.

Arginine also has an important positive influence on liver function, sterility in men, weight loss, hormonal balance and stimulation of the pancreas to release insulin.

 CAUTION: Arginine can promote an outbreak of herpes simplex. Avoid eating a lot of arginine-rich foods if you are prone to herpes.

▶ **Lower Cholesterol.** For many, a daily bowl of miso soup is all that is necessary to see cholesterol numbers come down. Studies have shown that consuming 25 grams (g) of soy protein per day supplies enough *isoflavones* to lower cholesterol levels. This is about the same amount of isoflavones found in one cup of miso soup. Reported cases in which cholesterol levels were high—in the over-300 range—show a 25% to 40% reduction in only three or four months. (In many cases, miso was part of an overall natural foods diet.)

▶ **Reduction of Chronic Pain.** According to unpublished clinical studies conducted by Mark A. Young, MD, former director of physical medicine and rehabilitation at Johns Hopkins Medical School, miso is effective for reducing pain. Dr. Young reports, "I have had tremendous anecdotal success recommending miso and dulse flakes (made from algae) to my chronic pain patients. Since miso soup is an excellent source of some B vitamins, beta carotene, calcium, iron and magnesium, I postulate that miso soup is likely a valuable 'pain modulator' by optimizing several critical metabolic and biochemical reactions."

▶ **Natural Antacid.** Scientists have reported that miso can act as an acid buffer due to the presence of protein, peptides, amino acids, phosphoric acid and various organic acids that are produced during the fermentation process. In the stomach, these buffers can reduce excess acidity and provide quick gastrointestinal relief.

▶ **Osteoporosis Prevention.** A bowl of miso soup with tofu, sea vegetables and a little bit of fish contains about 233 milligrams (mg) of calcium. What is more, miso is known to facilitate the absorption of calcium and other minerals. Eating miso along with other high calcium foods can be an alternative to using medications that increase bone density. In fact, the isoflavone *daidzein*, which is found in soybeans, is very similar to ipriflavone, a drug

249

■ Recipes ■

Basic Miso Soup

Yield: 2 servings

Ingredients

2 cups water
2 tablespoons water
1 tablespoon miso
1 scallion (green onion)

Optional: Add tofu, wakame (seaweed), mushrooms and/or any favorite vegetables.

Instructions

1. Boil 2 cups of water.
2. Add any or all of the optionals and simmer for 5 minutes or as long as it takes to soften the added veggies.
3. Dissolve 1 tablespoon of miso in 2 tablespoons of just-boiled water.
4. Add the dissolved miso to the just-simmered water. Once miso is added, do not boil.
5. Divide it into 2 bowls. Garnish each with slivers of scallion and enjoy!

Ultimate Miso Soup

Yield: 4 to 5 servings

Ingredients

6 cups kombu-shiitake stock (recipe follows)
1 medium onion, thinly sliced in half moons
4 shiitake caps, thinly sliced
2 medium carrots, thinly sliced diagonally
1½ cups chopped kale
8 ounces fresh tofu, cut into ½-inch cubes
4 tablespoons Hatcho miso*

---

*Although Hatcho (soybean) miso is recommended because it is highest in soy isoflavones, you can substitute any dark miso that lists soybeans as the first ingredient.

Instructions

1. Combine the stock, onion and shiitake caps in a 3-quart pot and bring to a boil. Reduce heat to low, simmer 5 minutes.
2. Add the carrots and kale and simmer 8 to 10 minutes more, or until the kale is tender.
3. Add the tofu and cook for 1 to 2 minutes.
4. Dissolve the miso in some of the broth and add to the soup. Remove from heat and steep a minute before serving.

Kombu-Shiitake Stock

Yield: 6 cups

Kombu and shiitake combine to make an especially good stock with rich flavor as well as potent health benefits. As an added bonus, preparation time is short.

Ingredients

4-5 dried shiitake mushrooms
6-inch piece kombu (dark green seaweed)
6 cups water

Instructions

1. Place the shiitake, kombu and water in a 3-quart pot and let sit for 15 minutes.
2. Place the pot over medium heat and bring to a boil. Remove the kombu, reduce the heat to medium-low and gently simmer 10 to 15 minutes more. Remove the shiitake and reserve for another use.
3. Use the stock immediately, or refrigerate in a covered container for up to 5 days, or freeze for up to 6 months.

From *The Miso Book* © 2004 by John and Jan Belleme. Reprinted with permission of Square One Publishers.

used throughout Europe and Asia to treat osteoporosis.

➤ **Radiation Protection.** In 1972, researchers discovered that miso contains *dipilocolonic acid*, an alkaloid that chelates (binds together) the heavy metals, such as radioactive strontium, and discharges them from the body. This discovery helped validate the success Dr. Shinichiro Akizuki had during World War II, treating patients and staff with miso soup and stopping the progressive effects of their radiation exposure and sickness.

 CAUTION: Miso is very high in sodium and should be avoided by anyone on a low-sodium diet.

Powerful Ingredients

The ingredients in these soups work together to enhance miso's medicinal benefits.

● **Onions.** The regular consumption of onions is associated with a significantly reduced risk of developing colon cancer. Onions also help lower cholesterol levels and blood pressure, decreasing the risk of heart attack and stroke. They have anti-inflammatory and anti-bacterial properties as well.

● **Carrots.** The richest vegetable source of powerful antioxidant compounds known as *carotenoids*, carrots protect against cardiovascular disease and cancer, promote good vision, help regulated blood sugar and enhance the immune system.

● **Kale.** Rich in phytonutrients that lower the risk of a variety of cancers including breast and ovarian, kale lends support to the immune system. It also helps combat anemia and prevent cataracts, heart disease and stroke.

● **Tofu.** Rich in soy protein, tofu, when eaten regularly, can lower cholesterol as much as 30%, lower LDL (bad cholesterol) levels up to 40%, lower triglyceride levels and reduce the formation of blood clots—greatly reducing the risk of heart disease and stroke. Tofu also alleviates the symptoms commonly associated with menopause and may inhibit postmenopausal osteoporosis.

For an excellent variety of recipes with miso as the star ingredient, and for lots more information about miso, including step-by-step instructions on the art of making it yourself, get a copy of John and Jan Belleme's beautiful book mentioned earlier in this section. Meanwhile, go to your neighborhood Asian Fusion restaurant and order a bowl of miso!

MUSIC AS MEDICINE

Listening

"M*usic washes away from the soul the dust of everyday life.*" Berthold Auerbach, German poet and author

The Sound of Music

Listening to spirited music can improve blood circulation and boost muscular strength and endurance. Your favorite music can make the most arduous task seem almost pleasant. Soothing music can keep blood pressure down, help you sleep and get you out of a funk.

According to *The Compass in Your Nose and Other Astonishing Facts About Humans* by Marc McCutcheon (Tarcher), listening to a musical score that approximates the rhythm of the resting heart (70 beats per minute) can actually slow a heart that is beating too fast. *The music found most effective in slowing an anxious heart includes...*

251

● **Venus, the Bringer of Peace** (The Planets) by Holst.

● **Mother Goose Suite**, first movement by Ravel.

● **The Brandenburg Concertos, No. 4**, Second Movement by Bach.

● **Orchestral Suite, No. 2** (Saraband) by Bach.

Singing

"I don't sing because I'm happy; I'm happy because I sing." William James, philosopher, psychologist, physician

Sing Yourself Young

"Singing exercises the vocal folds (or cords) and helps to keep them youthful, even in old age. The less age-battered your voice sounds, the more you will feel and seem younger. When you break into song, your chest expands and your back and shoulders straighten, improving your posture. Singing releases endorphins, which helps relieve pain, lift moods and clear the blues by taking your mind off the stresses of the day," says professor Graham F. Welch.

Professor Welch is chair of music education at the Institute of Education, University of London, and research adviser for the United Kingdom government's National Singing Programme, *Sing Up, www.singup.org.*

"The total person sings, not just the vocal chords." Esther Broner, professor and author

Benefits of Singing

"No one is too young to start singing, or too old to stop. There is a wide range of benefits from engaging in singing activities that apply to all ages," according to professor Welch. From the

252

professor's research findings, there are five areas of benefit—physical, psychological, social, musical and educational—all supported by scientific explanations. *Here is an abridged version of how singing does a body good…*

Physical Benefits

➤ **Improves respiratory and cardiac function.** Even when seated, singing involves dynamic thoracic activity, and major muscle groups are exercised in the upper body.

Singing is aerobic and improves the efficiency of the body's cardiovascular system, with related benefits to overall health and alertness.

Aerobic activity is linked with longevity, stress reduction and general health maintenance across the lifespan. Improving airflow in the upper respiratory tract is likely to lessen opportunities for bacteria to flourish, countering the symptoms of colds and flu.

➤ **Promotes fine and gross motor control in the vocal system.** The more the vocal system is used appropriately, such as in singing, the more the underlying anatomy and physiology realize their potential in terms of growth and motor coordination.

➤ **Enhances neurological functioning.** Singing is a key musical activity that facilitates development and interaction in diverse parts of the brain.

Psychological Benefits

➤ **Enhances the development of individual identity.** Our voices are a key component of who we are. Use of our voices reflects our mood and general psychological well-being. A confident and healthy voice links to a positive self-image.

➤ **Provides a cathartic activity.** It allows us to experience underlying emotions, such as joy and sadness. Singing also provides an outlet for our feelings, to feel better about ourselves and the world around us.

➤ **Improves interpersonal communication.** Singing improves our vocal coordination and enables us to maximize our potential to communicate with others using our voices.

The American Academy of Teachers of Singing (*www.americanacademyofteachersofsinging.org*) summed it up in their statement, "Singing fortifies health, widens culture, refines the intelligence, enriches the imagination, makes for happiness, and endows life with an added zest."

"He who sings frightens away his ills." Miguel de Cervantes, author

Take Note

Sound therapist Jovita Wallace homes in on specific sounds that will provide some of the benefits professor Welch mentioned (above). Jovita says, "Sound vibrations massage your aura, going straight to what's out of balance and fixing it."

➤ **Singing the short "a" sound,** as in "ahh," for two to three minutes will help banish the blues. It forces oxygen into the blood, which signals the brain to release mood-lifting endorphins.

➤ **To boost alertness, make the long "e" sound, as in "emit."** It stimulates the pineal gland, which controls the body's biological clock.

➤ **Singing the short "e" sound,** as in "echo" stimulates the thyroid gland, which secretes hormones that control the speed at which digestion and other bodily processes occur.

SOMETHING SPECIAL

Become the Karaoke Kid!

"Karaoke" is a Japanese abbreviated compound word—*kara* comes from *karrappo* meaning empty (as in "karate"—empty hand), and *oke* is the abbreviation of *okesutura* or orchestra. Rather than including both vocals and music, karaoke tracks only have the music. YOU provide the vocals.

You can purchase a karaoke system for home use. Load in the karaoke disc (CDG) that has your favorite songs, hold the microphone and sing while following the words that are displayed on a screen in front of you. You don't have to leave home to be in the spotlight…to be a star… to be a singing sensation.

The Singing Machine Company, in business since 1982, was the very first to provide karaoke systems for home entertainment in the US. They are recognized as the global leader in home karaoke.

Considering all the health benefits of singing, along with the fun and wholesome entertainment—alone or with family and friends—a Singing Machine is a worthwhile, affordable investment.

More information: Visit *https://singingmachine.com* to view their full line of karaoke systems, or call 954-596-1000 for stores in your area.

➤ **Making the long "o" sound as in "ocean" stimulates the pancreas,** which regulates blood sugar.

➤ **To strengthen immunity, sing the double "o" sound, as in "tool."** This activates the spleen, which regulates the production of infection-fighting white blood cells.

Tune In and Tone Up

Bob Harper, physical trainer and host on NBC-TV's *The Biggest Loser,* says that you should sing for a better workout. Singing tones abdominal and intercostal muscles and helps stimulate circulation. *By adding singing to your workout, you...*

- **Breathe more deeply.**
- **Take in more oxygen.**
- **Improve your aerobic ability.**
- **Release muscle tension.**

"Some days there won't be a song in your heart. Sing anyway." Emory Austin, motivational speaker

Sing...Sing a Song

The great thing is that you don't have to be a singer to sing. Start singing where no one is listening...in the shower, your car, your living room.

MUST-HAVE HEALTH FOOD REFERENCE

The World's Healthiest Foods—Essential Guide for the Healthiest Way of Eating by George Mateljan (George Mateljan Foundation) has been an invaluable addition to our library. George Mateljan founded Health Valley Foods, which set the gold standard for healthy, tasty, conveniently prepared foods. After 26 years at Health Valley, he then turned his energies and his resources to developing the not-for-profit George Mateljan Foundation to help people live longer, healthier lives by eating well.

It took George 10 years to write his magnificent 880-page book that's filled with great information about the world's healthiest foods, including secrets on how to select, store and prepare them without destroying vitamins, minerals and antioxidants. The nutrients in these foods can help enhance your immune system as they have his (George hasn't had a cold or experienced the flu for the last 10 years). Plus eating these foods may help you lose weight (George is now 50 pounds lighter than before he started this way of eating).

In the book, he shares a four-week plan, which takes all of the guesswork out of the healthiest way of eating. Most recipes take seven minutes or less to prepare with less than five ingredients and you can even prepare an entire five-course meal in 15 minutes! There are 500 Mediterranean-style recipes and 100 of the recipes don't require any cooking at all!

More information: Visit the George Mateljan Foundation Web site at *www.whfoods.com* for recipes, articles and videos.

OIL PULLING

Yes, oil pulling, a resurrected ancient Ayurvedic therapy. It is strange, even by our standards. But we've been overwhelmed by Web sites filled with testimonies from people who have had extraordinary oil pulling healings, starting with firmer and whiter teeth and healings of more serious challenges including diseased teeth, chronic sleeplessness, arthritis, eczema, migraines, lung and heart disease, to many kinds of cancer. Please know that we have not been able to verify any of them. But we did read the book titled *Oil Pulling Therapy—Detoxifying and Healing the Body Through Oral Cleansing* (Piccadilly Books, Ltd.) by Bruce Fife, ND, and it gave this modality credibility.

In the past, we have interviewed Dr. Fife about his work with coconut oil, and know him to be a reputable, dedicated researcher as well as the author of 18 books. After interviewing him again, this time about oil pulling, we knew it is something worth reporting, with Dr. Fife's expertise as our voice of reason.

A Word from the Wise...

Dr. Fife on Oil Pulling

Oil pulling is a tool that is useful for removing harmful bacteria from the mouth. That is its purpose. If you have an active infection in the mouth, it can pull out the offending bacteria, giving the body the chance to heal itself. It is the body that brings about the cure, not the oil pulling. If the body does not heal, it is not because the oil pulling did not work. It is because your body was unable to do the healing. If you have a health problem that may have taken 10 or 20 years to develop, it's unrealistic to expect a cure overnight. It takes time for the body to heal itself.

Also, if you are sick due to poor dietary and lifestyle habits, you cannot expect to recover until you make changes.

I have developed a program that increases the cleansing effects of oil pulling, creating a healthy oral environment and enhancing overall health. *The main points of the program are:* Healthy diet, supplemental coconut oil, fluid consumption, vitamins and minerals, dental care, maintaining healthy pH and detox. It's all good! The complete, detailed program is in my book (listed above).

The Fife Safety Factor

Oil pulling is completely harmless. All you are doing is putting vegetable oil, a food, into your mouth. You're not even going to swallow it. Women can do this during pregnancy and lactation.

Regardless of ill health or disease, you can pull oil, unless there is some physical difficulty that prevents it.

Oil pulling does not interact with any medications, so there are no contraindications.

The only precaution is to be old enough to swish the oil in the mouth without swallowing. Generally, ages five and older can oil pull.

Oil Pulling Instructions

• **The oil to use.** Most sources say to use either cold-pressed sunflower oil or cold-pressed sesame oil. I recommend either extra virgin coconut oil or the more economical refined coconut oil. Coconut oil is by far healthier than sunflower, sesame or any of the other vegetable oils.

• **How much oil.** Use two to three teaspoons of oil. The amount you use depends on what feels comfortable to you. You don't want to take too much because you need to leave room for the secretion of your saliva.

• **When to oil pull.** You can oil pull at any time of the day. The time that is most popular and makes sense is in the morning, before eating breakfast.

Oil pulling should be done on an empty stomach, especially if you are just beginning. Some people have a difficult time putting oil into their mouths because they are uncomfortable with the taste or the texture. As they pull, it may cause gagging, nausea or even vomiting, in which case you don't want a full stomach. After

255

a few days of experience, you will get used to the oil and it will no longer bother you.

- **Right before starting.** Drink some water just before you start pulling so that you are properly hydrated and can produce the saliva needed for pulling.

- **And finally...how to oil pull.** Take a spoonful of oil and swish it in your mouth. That's it. Keep your lips closed and work the oil in your mouth—push, sucking, pulling the oil through your teeth and over every surface of your mouth. Stay relaxed but keep the oil and saliva swishing constantly in your mouth for a total of 15 to 20 minutes. It seems that the longer you pull, the more effective it is.

- **When time is up.** Spit out the oil into a plastic bag. It's not recommended that you spit into the sink or toilet. Over time, oil buildup can clog the pipes.

 NOTE: When the oil and your saliva combine, the mixture will turn a milky white color. If the spit-out is not milky white, you didn't "work" it enough in your mouth, or you used an oil that is a deep yellow, like corn oil, or dark green, like olive oil. If you use a very light colored or colorless oil, expect the milky white color after a session of swishing.

After spitting out the oil, rinse your mouth thoroughly with water to remove any residual oil. If your mouth and throat feel dry, take a drink of water.

No-Nos

- **If you have dentures that are removable,** swish before the dentures are in place.

- **Do not swallow the oil.** It is full of bacteria and toxins.

- **Do not gargle the oil.** Gargling may cause you to swallow some of it, which you do not want to do, and could cause a gag reflex.

Dr. Fife Sums It Up

Oil pulling is very powerful, and when combined with a sensible diet and other health-promoting activities, it can do wonders for your health. While oil pulling may not be the answer to every health problem, it has the potential to bring about remarkable improvement for numerous conditions, including so-called incurable ones, by allowing the body to cure itself.

You could notice changes almost immediately...or not. Improvements can be gradual and subtle—so much so that you don't notice anything until one day you look back and say, "Hey, I didn't get the flu this year" or "My allergies didn't act up much this season." The most noticeable improvement will be to your oral health—fresher breath, healthier gums and cleaner teeth. That in itself makes oil pulling worthwhile.

Back to the Wilen Sisters

The very first time we oil pulled, both of us were surprised that it did not seem oily at all... not while we were pulling, and not after rinsing. We also tried extra virgin coconut oil, and it was fine, but we prefer the sunflower oil.

Each of us gets a lot done when we are pulling in the morning—we make the beds, get dressed, prepare breakfast. Get into a productive routine and the 20 minutes will fly by. Be sure to turn on your answering machine or turn off your cell phone, because one thing you can't do is talk on the telephone.

After reviewing lots of anecdotal success reports (that is, individual testimonies not yet substantiated with scientifically controlled tests using large numbers of people) and doing it ourselves, we believe oil pulling does a body good. Joan feels oil pulling gives her get up and go in the morning and Lydia feels it has cured her yawning habit in the morning. If drug companies can find a way to make money from it, then scientific studies will be done. Meanwhile, it's harmless and costs practically nothing to try, so why not give it a go?

OLIVE LEAF EXTRACT

More than a decade ago, we came across a paperback book, *Olive Leaf Extract* by Dr. Morton Walker (Kensington Books). We bought it, glanced at it, and were awed by the many ways olive leaf extract (liquid from olive leaves) does a body good. We then set the book aside, meaning to get back to it. Well, we did get back to Dr. Walker's book a couple of months ago, while researching this book and would like to share what we've learned from his book and others about the healing power of olive leaf extract.

First, some information about the incredible olive tree, its history and its gift, the leaves. Then we'll get to the many health benefits of olive leaf extract and how you can purchase it.

About the Olive Tree

The olive tree, also called "The Tree of Life," "King of the Trees" and "The Immortal Tree," was used as a medicinal plant in ancient times, as early as 3,500 BC in Crete, where the leaves were used to clean wounds.

Some olive trees live for more than 1,000 years, withstanding heat and cold and attacks from pests, viruses and bacteria. The 100-or-so compounds they contain enable them to survive adversity. Those powerful defense compounds are captured and concentrated in olive leaf extract.

The Power of Olive Leaf Extract

Fresh olive leaf extract is reported to have almost twice the antioxidant power of green tea extract and 400% more than vitamin C. Also, olive leaf extract contains up to 40 times more health-giving antioxidant polyphenols than extra virgin olive oil.

The internationally proven ORAC (Oxygen Radical Absorbance Capacity) test awarded it an antioxidant capacity almost twice as powerful as grape seed extract, and off-the-charts more powerful than the antioxidant-super-juices noni, goji, mangosteen, cranberry, blueberry and pomegranate.

Therapeutic Benefits of Olive Leaf Extract

We have found many benefits in Dr. Walker's book as well as in scientific studies. *Here are some of them…*

- **Helps strengthen the body's immune system.**

- **Helps the body deal with viral diseases** such as HIV, epstein-barr, herpes and influenza.

- **Alleviates sore throats, chronic sinusitis, skin disease and pneumonia.**

- **Eliminates symptoms of all types of infections** including yeast, fungal, bacterial, viral and other parasitic protozoan.

- **Effectively treats chronic fatigue syndrome, athlete's foot, arthritis, psoriasis—** even the common cold.

- **Helps to reduce low-density lipoproteins** (LDL—bad cholesterol).

- **Lowers blood pressure and increases blood flow** by relaxing the arteries.

- **Provides antioxidant properties** that help protect the body from the continuous activity of free radicals. (Some recent research on the olive leaf has shown its antioxidants to be effective in helping the body to fight cancers such as liver, prostate and breast cancer, but the research on this is preliminary.)

Due to its broad spectrum of natural polyphenols, and its very high antioxidant power, the testimonials from people taking olive leaf extract regularly report significant health improvements in all of the following areas, and more…

- **Allergies**
- **Arthritis**
- **Asthma**
- **Blood pressure**
- **Cardiovascular problems**
- **Cholesterol**
- **Circulation**
- **Colds**
- **Constipation**
- **Coughs**
- **Diabetes glucose management**
- **Fatigue**
- **Flu**
- **Fungal problems**
- **Gut health**
- **Hay fever**
- **Immune problems**
- **Joint aches and pain**
- **Psoriasis**
- **Skin problems**
- **Sore throats**

 CAUTION: Consult with a health care provider who understands the use of herbal preparations in place of, or in addition to, traditional medicine, and can monitor you. For instance, if you're taking medication to help bring down your blood pressure, at some point after you start taking olive leaf extract, your doctor may have reason to lower your medication dosage, or eliminate it completely. Do NOT take yourself off any medication without the approval of your doctor.

You may want to get a copy of Dr. Morton Walker's book and bring it to your doctor with the information pertaining to your specific health challenge highlighted. Better yet, take advantage of the free booklet offer at the end of this section.

A Great Source for Olive Leaf Extract

Barlean's Olive Leaf Complex is billed as "The World's Freshest and Most Beneficial Olive Leaf Extract." And in fact, lab tests proved that their extraction process maintains many more healing compounds than the standard olive leaf extracts on the market

We have recommended Barlean's products in just about all of our health books because we trust the company's integrity and happily use their high-quality products ourselves. Barlean's Olive Leaf Complex is one more of our recommendations.

What makes Barlean's Olive Leaf Complex special: In a small coastal community in Australia, there exists a peaceful and pristine family-owned and operated olive grove, planted with hand-selected trees that offer maximum therapeutic benefit.

Over a decade ago, before the Archers made even one drop of olive leaf extract, they collected 60 different varieties of olive trees from 12 countries, and planted them in their grove. From these trees they were able to make a large number of variety-specific olive leaf extracts and test each one for its levels of healing properties. Once they found the winning varieties, they planted thousands of them, and these trees still provide the fresh leaves used for olive leaf extract.

In 2008, the Barleans, producers of award-winning fish and flaxseed oils, learned about the healing properties of the Archers' product, and won the exclusive rights to sell and market Olive Leaf Complex in the US, where it had not yet been introduced despite its success worldwide.

And so, Barlean's Olive Leaf Complex is made from the fresh olive leaves grown in the Archers' grove, where they are picked at sunrise, immediately fresh pressed and bottled on site, to capture maximum nutritional potency. Dried leaves, oleuropein powders or other processed ingredients are never used. Olive Leaf Complex is a health tonic and super antioxidant with antibacterial, antiviral and antifungal properties that support a healthy immune system, healthy blood pressure, healthy joints and healthy cardiovascular system.

Barlean's Olive Leaf Complex dosage: Adults—one tablespoon per day. May be taken straight or mixed with water or juice. Children—Half of adult dosage. Do not give to children two years or younger without medical advice.

Barlean's ingredients: Fresh pressed Olea europaea varietal olive leaves, glycerin, water, natural flavors.

For diabetics and other carbohydrate-conscious individuals, in the daily dose of one tablespoon, there are 11 carbs and they are from glycerin. We questioned the carb count, and were assured that unlike typical carbohydrates, glycerin reportedly has minimal impact on blood sugar levels.

 CAUTION: Some people occasionally experience what is known as the Herxheimers Reaction or "Die-Off" Effect. This is a detoxification reaction (rather than a side effect), which occurs when the extract kills large numbers of offending microbes (toxins) in your body. Symptoms may include fatigue, diarrhea, headaches, muscle/joint aches or flu-like symptoms. The severity of symptoms will vary from person to person depending on the nature of their illness, the volume of toxins in their system and the amount of extract being taken.

Drinking plenty of water between doses will assist your body to flush out the excess toxins and reduce any reaction. While these reactions may be mildly unpleasant initially, they are a sure sign that the extract is doing its work! To reduce the intensity of any reaction you may choose to stop taking the extract for 24 to 48 hours and then restart on a smaller dosage.

When to Expect Results

According to Julian Archer, the Archer family's Ambassador of the Olive, "Each person is unique, so there's a wide range of individual reactions to olive leaf extract. Some people will experience relief from their particular health problems within 24 hours, while others will take longer to experience the benefits. Our experience with consumers in Australia indicates that the majority of people will notice a difference in their energy levels, general health or the healing of a specific illness within 30 days.

Many people notice marked improvements in their health and energy over the 30-day period and choose to use the extract as a regular health supplement."

Last Bit of Advice

Joseph J. Territo, MD, wrote the foreword to Dr. Walker's *Olive Leaf Extract* book, and closed by saying, "So here's a bit of advice: Ride the olive leaf as though it is your magic carpet to better healing and greater health."

OMEGA-3 ESSENTIAL FATTY ACIDS

One of the ways to tell what's hot in terms of what's healthy is to look at your supermarket shelves. Notice how the addition of a specific ingredient is announced on the front of one product after another, promising that the package's content is "new-and-improved" because it's fortified with (fill in the blank). In this case the blank is "omega-3"…on cartons of eggs, loaves of bread, cookies, bottles of fruit juice, even in baby formulas. And it's no wonder.

Scientific studies have found that omega-3 essential fatty acids may help prevent or reverse high blood pressure, stroke, heart disease, even rheumatoid arthritis, breast and colon cancer, Parkinson's disease and depression. They may also help eliminate menopausal symptoms and improve brain power.

The Essential Fatty Acids (EFAs)

The word "essential" signifies the fact that your body does not and cannot manufacture the omega-3 fatty acids. You are totally dependent

on your diet for them. *There are three major omega-3 fatty acids…*

• **Alpha-linolenic acid (ALA),** which is found primarily in salba, flaxseeds, raw nuts (walnuts, hazelnuts, almonds, pecans, cashews and macadamia) and dark green leafy vegetables and several vegetable oils.

• **Eicosapentaenoic acid (EPA),** which is found in cold water fish like salmon, cod, mackerel, tuna. Smaller amounts are found in organically raised animal products—free-range eggs and chickens and grass-fed beef.

• **Docosahexaenoic acid (DHA),** which is found in the same foods as EPA.

Packing in the Omega-3s

Getting back to the products in the supermarket—many of them say "fortified with EPA and DHA." Those are the two fatty acids responsible for brain development, vision, the production of certain hormones and other functions that keep you functioning. EPA and DHA are found mainly in fish, making it the most desirable, direct source of the omega-3s.

To reap omega-3s' rewards, you should be eating cold-water fish at least twice a week. More is better. Oh and uh, be sure the fish you eat has very little mercury, such as salmon, sardines or mackerel, rather than swordfish or halibut. Oh and uh, to prevent potentially harmful compounds that may be produced when grilling or frying, it's best to prepare fish by baking or steaming it.

A Word from the Omega-3 Expert

Jade Beutler is a licensed health care practitioner, former CEO of Barlean's and winner of the 2008 Ramazanov Award for Excellence in Nutritional Science (that's like the Academy Award

SOMETHING SPECIAL

Super Seeds!

There are omegas, and there are *super* omegas. When we're talking super omegas, we're talking hemp seeds (tiny, round seeds about the same size as small sunflower seeds). They have a light and pleasant flavor and aroma that is similar to toasted pine nuts.

Hemp seeds contain two naturally occurring super omegas: Stearidonic Acid (SDA) and Gamma Linolenic Acid (GLA).

SDA and GLA help your body convert the benefits of omega-3 EFAs more efficiently. Due to factors such as age, genetics, diet and lifestyle, we don't all process these good fats the same way. SDA and GLA help everyone maximize the benefits of Omega EFAs. If it's super omegas you want, turn to hemp foods for SDA and GLA.

At Living Harvest, their foods center around one main ingredient—hemp seeds, one of nature's most perfect foods. In addition to super omegas, hemp seeds contain all 10 essential amino acids (EAAs)—the building blocks of protein. They're also rich in naturally balanced omega-3 and omega-6 essential fatty acids (EFAs). Also, hemp is high in magnesium, iron, potassium, fiber and phytonutrients, plus natural antioxidants like vitamin E.

More information: If you are interested in learning more about Living Harvest's hemp products—Tempt (nondairy) Hempmilk, Tempt (nondairy) Frozen Dessert, Organic Hemp Protein Powder and Organic Hemp Oil—visit *www.livingharvest.com*. You can shop online, or click on "Where to Buy" and type in your zip code to find the stores near you that carry Living Harvest, or call 888-690-3958.

If you or your children are not diligent about eating fish on a very regular basis, or drinking hempmilk, you can all take a high-quality supplement, ensuring that you get the right amount of EPA and DHA omega-3 daily. And have we got a great supplement for you! See the "Something Special" box on the next page.

of the dietary supplement industry). The purpose of the Ramazanov Foundation is to recognize scientists and professionals working in the area of nutrition, whose dedication has contributed to significant evidence-based improvement in people's health and well-being, in an ethical way without sacrificing integrity and bending science for the sake of profit.

We turned to Jade for his expertise on the mighty omega-3s.

Why Omega-3s?: According to Jade Beutler's research, the reason omega-3s are extremely valuable for vibrant health and so effective at preventing and overcoming health conditions is because they impact the health of each and every organ, muscle, gland, ligament and tendon in the human body. If we do not consume enough omega-3s, the body will use less healthful fats—saturated, hydrogenated, trans fats—as surrogates. These unhealthful fats can

SOMETHING SPECIAL

In a Swirl

A new form of omega-3s has been created by Barlean's Organic Oils that transforms oily fish and flax oil into a fruit-smoothie consistency that tastes great. It's called Omega-Swirl and is available in several variations and flavors.

Packed with essential omega-3 fatty acids, Omega Swirl was created to nutritionally support...

- **Heart health.**
- **Healthy cholesterol levels.**
- **Joint mobility and bone density.**
- **Energy and endurance.**
- **Skin, hair and nail health.**
- **Mental health, wellness and acuity.**
- **Healthy blood glucose.**
- **Sexual and hormonal health.**

The oil molecules in Omega Swirl are so small that the digestion and assimilation is two times or 200% better than regular fish or flax oil, which helps eradicate fish burps.

That's just one of the many reasons Omega Swirl has taken the nutrition industry by storm, and was voted the Best New Product by the consumer publication *Better Nutrition* magazine. It was also voted Best Nutritional Supplement by the natural products trade publication *Vitamin Retailer* magazine.

More information: Omega Swirl is sold at health food stores and supermarkets that carry health products, such as Whole Foods Markets. Visit *www.barleans.com* and click on "store locator" to find a retailer near you.

 NOTE: Barlean's sent us one of each flavor to sample. They are seriously delicious! The Lemon-Zest variety tastes just like the lemon part of our mother's luscious lemon-meringue pie. It's that good. And there's no fishy taste or aftertaste.

cause your cells to become less fluid...more rigid and stiff.

Omega-3 fatty acids are a most powerful anti-inflammatory agent that can help reduce pain, joint discomfort and inflammation, allowing people to stay active much longer.

Omega-3s are also the most powerful and well-substantiated natural products available for the reduction of risk for heart disease. They have a profound effect on the cardiovascular system because they serve as antifreeze for the arteries, reduce platelet stickiness and prevent blood clots that lead to heart attack and stroke.

Taking omega-3 supplements: Many people wanting to supplement their diets, have a hard time swallowing large omega-3 capsules, and even if they could swallow them, many of the capsules seem to have inadequate dosages.

A lot of people are turned off by the oily taste and oily texture of flax or fish oil in liquid form. Also, many people are unable to adequately digest pure oil and/or suffer uncomfortable and sometimes embarrassing fish burps. For a great omega-3 supplement, check out "In a Swirl" above.

TAKE NOTE

Since it's impossible for us to investigate and report on the hundreds of supplement companies on the health food store shelves and online, we stick with the few outstanding companies we have come to know and trust, and we tell you about them.

Yes, clearly we are partial to Barlean's products. We started writing about their flaxseed years ago, and as they've grown, we've continued spreading the word. We are not on their payroll. We just believe in their ethics, integrity and products.

New Chapter is another outstanding company we recommend. Check out their entire product line (*www.newchapter.com*), including Wholemega, an excellent fish oil softgel.

We encourage you to look into the many other fine products on the market by researching online, calling and questioning supplement companies, and asking for suggestions from knowledgeable health food store managers.

 CAUTION: If you take a prescription blood thinner, check with your doctor before using omega-3s. Also, avoid omega-3s at least five days before surgery.

PHYSICAL TOUCH

Psychotherapist Margaret Chuong-Kim, who has worked with survivors of domestic violence and is experienced in crisis intervention and parent education, shares her research and insight on the power of physical touch here...

A Word from the Wise...

Margaret Chuong-Kim on Physical Touch

A close friend of mine mentioned to me the other day that when she and her husband first married, one of the activities she enjoyed most was having him rub her feet in the evenings. She really loved feeling the warmth of his hands and the pressure on her skin.

My friend lamented that, in recent weeks, due to an increase in the busyness in their days, she and her husband haven't had the time or energy to spend as much leisure time together. As a result, she hasn't been getting any foot rubs. She stated she's been feeling a bit grumpy and she thinks part of it has to do with the absence of these regular foot massages.

Perhaps you think this is a silly claim, that the absence of regular touch can have an effect on one's emotions. However, touch and social contact with a loved one are an important part of our physical and emotional health.

Consider the Following...

- **Skin-to-skin contact between mother and infant has been shown to benefit the baby's physical development** and contributes to a positive attachment relationship between the two. The practice of placing a diaper-clad infant skin-to-skin on the mother is so beneficial that it is now a treatment for premature babies in neonatal intensive care units worldwide.

- **A group of Korean infants under the care of an orphanage were provided with an extra 15 minutes of stimulation twice a day, five days a week, for four weeks.** This added stimulation consisted of auditory (female voice), tactile (massage) and visual (eye-to-eye) contact.

Compared with the infants who only received regular care, the stimulated babies gained significantly more weight and had larger increases in body length and head circumference after the four-week intervention period, as well as at six months of age. In addition, the stimulated infants had fewer illnesses and clinic visits.

• **Gentle touch has been shown to facilitate physical and psychological functioning,** particularly in terms of reducing stress, relieving pain, increasing the ability to cope and enhancing general health ratings.

• **Participants in one study examining the effectiveness of therapeutic touch as a treatment for managing pain** due to fibromyalgia experienced a significant decrease in pain and a significant improvement in quality of life.

• **The majority of nursing home residents suffering from dementia** including Alzheimer's disease develop behavioral symptoms of dementia, such as restlessness, searching and wandering, tapping and banging, pacing and walking and vocalization. Current treatment involves drugs, but a recent study showed that intervention consisting of therapeutic touch significantly reduces these behavioral symptoms. It's impressive that the therapeutic touch employed in the study was only provided twice per day, for three days and that each therapeutic intervention lasted only five to seven minutes.

Clearly, the importance of touch cannot be underestimated.

For more of Margaret Chuong-Kim's wisdom and expertise, visit the informative Web site *www.drbenkim.com*, where she is the contributing editor in chief.

264

Reach Out and Touch Someone

Of course you've got to use discretion and touch people in an acceptable way. Try a quick pat on the back for someone you work with, a pinch on the cheek when a friend says something amusing, a good old-fashioned hug when you're very proud of a friend or family member.

However, if you are not thought of as a touchy-feely person, a hug out of the blue from you may frighten the intended recipient. If that's the case, you should consider some kind of friendly warning like, "I feel a hug coming on."

Fact: To optimize the flow of *oxytocin* and *serotonin*—the chemicals that boost mood and promote bonding—hold a hug for at least six seconds. If that seems awkward to you, then tell the person you're going to hug about the six-second rule and then go to it—101, 102...

If you are sincere and congruent about touching someone, that touch will be appreciated by that lucky person. Actually, it will make you both feel good.

A Word from the Wise...

Give *Yourself* a Massage!

Massage is far more than a mere luxury. It may reduce the stress that contributes to heart disease and digestive disorders...relieve pain by manipulating pressure points that relax muscles...and raise levels of mood-boosting brain chemicals.

Good news: You can take your health into your own hands—literally—with simple self-massage techniques.

What to do: Always apply firm but comfortable pressure, repeating each sequence of motions for three to five minutes. Unless noted, techniques can be done while sitting or lying down. Use scented lotion or oil if desired—lavender and rose are calming…peppermint and rosemary are stimulating.

Sinus or Tension Headache

• **Lying on your back,** place the fingertips of both hands in the center of your forehead…stroke outward toward the temples… make 10 small slow circles over the temples. Move fingertips to the cheeks, where the jaw hinges…make 10 small slow circles there.

• **Place the pads of your thumbs just below each upper eye ridge (near the brow),** where the eye ridge meets the bridge of the nose, and press up toward your forehead for 10 seconds. In small increments, move thumbs along your eye ridges toward the outer edges of eyes, pressing for several seconds at each stopping point.

 CAUTION: Always press upward on the bony ridge, not into the eye socket.

• **With fingertips, make small circles all over the scalp for 30 seconds as if washing hair.** Then place fingertips at the back of the neck and make 10 small slow circles at the base of the skull.

Stomach Upset or Constipation

• **Lying on your back, place one hand flat on your abdomen** (over or under your clothing) just above your navel. Pressing gently but firmly, slowly move your hand clockwise to circle the navel.

Neck and/or Shoulder Pain

• **Sitting, reach your left hand over your right shoulder until it touches above the shoulder blade.** With fingertips, firmly knead muscles, focusing on any sore spots. Repeat on other side.

• **Sitting, place fingertips of both hands on the back of the neck at the base of the skull.** Pressing firmly, move fingers up and down along the sides of the vertebrae. To protect major blood vessels, do not massage front or sides of the neck.

Foot Soreness

• **Sitting, place your left ankle on your right knee.** Grasp the left foot with your right hand and slowly rotate the foot at the ankle three times in each direction. 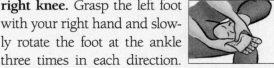 Then use your fingers to gently rotate toes, one at a time, three times in each direction. Repeat on the other side.

• **Sitting, place your left ankle on your right knee and cradle the left foot in both hands.** With thumbs, make five small slow circles—first on the instep…then the ball of the foot…heel…and pad of each toe. Repeat on your other foot.

Bonus: Performing foot massage for 10 minutes nightly may promote health overall.

Theory of reflexology: "Reflex points" on the feet are linked to various body systems and organs, which benefit from tactile stimulation.

Illustrations by Shawn Banner.

Paula Koepke, CMT, a massage therapist at the University of California, San Francisco, Osher Center for Integrative Medicine, and an instructor at the McKinnon Institute of Massage in Oakland, California, *http://paulakoepke. massagetherapy.com.*

POLE WALKING

Pole walking (also called Nordic, fitness or ski walking) is walking with special poles designed for that purpose. It developed from an off-season ski-training activity known as ski walking or hill bounding, so that skiers could keep up their strength and agility year-round. Pole walking has been practiced for decades as dry-land training for competitive cross-country skiing.

The popularity of the poles grew as hikers discovered that walking with the poles increased their power and decreased or eliminated their knee, hip and foot pains. The use of poles also brought back-pain relief to backpackers.

This dry-land combination of Nordic skiing and walking is a favorite among Northern Europeans. A dozen or so years after its introduction in Europe, an estimated eight to 10 million people pole walk as their exercise of choice. And it's no wonder when you consider that pole walking can be done indoors, outdoors and at any age. Plus, you get a full-body workout without a change in perceived exertion, or having to walk faster. There are so many benefits.

Sheri Simson, also called "the Pole Lady," shared her inspiring success story with us...

A Word from the Wise...

Sheri Simson on Pole Walking

There I was, a wife, mother of three young boys and owner of a construction company. I was over 40 years old, 30 pounds overweight, out of shape. I had cellulite in places I never knew you could get cellulite, had aches and pains all over and was tired all of the time.

In desperation, I signed up for Weight Watchers, and this changed my approach to food...for the better. While I slowly started losing weight, I still felt sluggish and out of shape. With a business to run and my boys to look after, I didn't have time, energy or extra money to join a gym or hire a trainer. The only affordable exercise, in terms of time and money, was walking, but the walking I was doing had little effect on how I looked and felt.

On one trip to my husband's homeland, Denmark, my mother-in-law gave me a pair of walking poles. I immediately put them to work and was blown away by the results they produced! Not only was it easy (at first I thought it was maybe too easy, you know—no pain/no gain) but once I got a rhythm going, my whole body felt energized, as the poles seemed to propel me forward.

I brought the poles back home and continued walking with them. It didn't take long for me to notice that walking with poles made a difference—my fat just seemed to fall off! It was amazing. Within weeks I felt stronger and definitely tighter! The funny thing was I wasn't walking any further or any faster but yet WOW —I couldn't get over what was happening to my entire body! I had so much more energy and enjoyed seeing my body take on a new shape.

I researched my new passion and discovered through documented reports from the scientific community that pole walking not only makes walking more beneficial, it also takes less effort and is easier on our bodies. *See below...*

• **We use less than 50% of our major muscles when we walk without poles**—when we use poles we use over 90%. In doing so we spread our weight out helping to lessen the load with which we hit the ground by 26%— making a big difference for those people who have back, hip, knee, ankle or feet problems.

- **Using poles while we walk naturally aligns our spine** and strengthens our core with each step—helping us to stand and sit taller.

- **We also don't have to go as far or work as hard when we are using walking poles.** We increase our cardio by 20% and our calorie burn by up to 48% without any more effort! What more could you want? Oh! and you can do it in less time too—30 minutes of pole walking is equal to 50 minutes of regular walking.

The joy at what had happened to me, and the excitement at the thought of what this European secret could do for others, helped me decide that it was my duty (and now my company's mission) to inform, inspire, empower and support people to find balance, live in peace and walk as their true selves. Out of all this, my company Keenfit was born.

Walking is an activity you already do without thinking. So relax, trust yourself and count on the rule of three, which is…either you are going to catch on after three steps, or three miles, or after three times out. Just remember to let your body do what it does naturally.

It looks easy…and for lots of people it is easy. Others may need to be patient with themselves and stick with it in order to master pole walking. And a lot of people seem to be doing just that. From the time we became aware of walking poles, until now when writing about them, they've grown tremendously in popularity. We can tell just by the results online when Googling "pole walking," and by the fact that the poles are currently being sold on television.

More information: For all the health benefits of pole walking, including how helpful it can be for breast cancer rehabilitation, and for people with Parkinson's disease, visit Sheri's Web site at *www.keenfit.com*. You'll see Sheri's before and after photos. Plus, there are videos and step-by-step instructions for how to use these poles most effectively. Or you can phone Keenfit at 877-533-6348 and ask them to send you information and/or a DVD.

REBUILDER

There's a treatment that is now Food and Drug Administration (FDA)–approved and covered by Medicare, that can help relieve pain, numbness, tingling and burning sensations and actually restore the feeling in your feet and hands, restore your balance and mobility and reduce or eliminate the need for pain medication. It's called the ReBuilder Electronic Stimulator System.

David B. Phillips, PhD, an internationally acclaimed electronic medical device inventor, set out to create a device to help his father who had peripheral neuropathy after heart surgery. Dr. Phillips discovered that nerves can be rebuilt and, in some cases, full function can be restored. In fact, Dr. Phillips' father is in his 80s now, walks just fine, has no pain and works every day in the quality control department of his son's company.

The ReBuilder is based on the fact that nerves are electrical in nature and respond to specific electrical stimulation that duplicates a healthy nerve signal.

The ReBuilder can be used in the comfort of your home. Each treatment takes a half hour, during which you can just sit back and relax. Throughout the session gentle massaging pulses work to totally eliminate or ease symptoms, and symptoms are reduced for hours afterward. Permanent benefits accumulate with continued use.

267

It's an amazing nonsurgical, noninvasive alternative to surgery or pain-masking medication. And, unlike surgery and medication, there are no side effects! Well, maybe one side effect…it causes the brain to release *endorphins*, putting you in a much happier state of mind.

The ReBuilder can be used on the lower back, hands, shoulders and feet. The conditions it's mostly used for are neuropathy, arthritis, peripheral vascular, peripheral artery disease, reflex sympathetic dystrophy, restless leg syndrome and sciatic nerve pain. But anyone can use it to enhance circulation.

The ReBuilder is now the first line of defense for peripheral neuropathy caused by chemotherapy. The Cancer Treatment Centers of America announced that 94% of their patients achieved excellent results—less pain, return of feeling in their feet, better balance, better sleeping at night and elimination of their pain meds.

More information: See the ReBuilder Web site, *www.rebuildermedical.com*, which includes video interviews with Dr. Phillips, a demonstration, testimonials and details on the company's 30-day money back guarantee.

If you prefer to speak with a person, the company has full-time, licensed medical professionals on staff headed by Brian Sheldon, the company's president and licensed practical nurse. They will help you in any way possible, including through the Medicare process. (We know from experience, they are very patient.) The toll-free number is 866-725-2202.

SALBA

Salba is a nutrient-packed, ancient seed from the *Salvia hispanica* family of mint plants, reborn and spectacularly cultivated. This little seed

is now grown in Peru's ideal climate and environment, under strictly controlled conditions, which are reported to be the finest on the planet.

Unlike any of the other grains, salba has undergone intense, long-term human nutritional studies. Salba has health and medical claims that no other grain can claim.

Salba's Super Powers

Mitch Propster, founder and CEO of Ancient Naturals (formerly Core Naturals), bills salba as "Nature's perfect whole food." True, his company is selling the product, but he's selling it because he is so sold on it. We think you will be, too, after learning about all that salba has to offer. *Gram for gram…*

● **Salba has eight times more omega-3 fatty acids than salmon.** In fact, omega-3 fatty acids are found more abundantly in salba than in any other naturally occurring whole food source. Salba has an amazing four to one ratio of omega-3 to omega-6.

● **Salba has four times more fiber than flaxseed.**

● **Salba has six times more calcium than whole milk.**

● **Salba has seven times more vitamin C than an orange.**

● **Salba has three times more antioxidants than fresh blueberries.**

● **Salba has three times more iron than spinach.**

● **Salba has 15 times more magnesium than broccoli.**

As if all of that weren't enough, salba also has folate, B vitamins, potassium, zinc, selenium and vitamin A. Salba is gluten-free and kosher.

Health Benefits

Dr. Vladimir Vuksan, professor of endocrinology and nutritional sciences, faculty of medicine, University of Toronto, has devoted over two decades searching for, finding and testing dietary therapies, including ancient whole grains.

Dr. Vuksan has rediscovered and been studying Salba, with impressive and promising results for diabetics, as well as for everyone else.

Total Health Magazine reports that Dr. Vuksan's studies provide irrefutable evidence that consumption of salba results in a simultaneous reduction of blood pressure, body inflammation and blood clotting, while balancing after-meal blood sugar.

As a result of such overwhelming health benefits, salba is the only seed that is patent-pending, defining salba as a functional food with therapeutic benefits for the prevention and treatment of various diseases, especially cardiovascular disease, diabetes and obesity.

In addition to salba being high in antioxidants, fiber, vegetable protein and micronutrients (calcium, magnesium and iron), this grain is the richest whole food source of *omega-3 alpha-linolenic acid*, which has been shown to be converted to EPA, the heart-protective omega-3 found in fish oil.

This translates into the following health benefits...

- **Promotes cardiovascular health.**
- **Supports joint function and mobility.**
- **Provides a great source of fiber for digestive health.**
- **Assists bowel function and regularity in a gentle way.**

How to Eat Salba

Salba comes in several forms—seeds, ground, oil, gelcaps. Salba does not have a discernable

■ Recipe ■

Salba Gel

Salba can be used in cooking and baking. This simple preparation of seeds in water, can be used in recipes in place of eggs.

- **Pour 2 cups of warm water into a container that has a tight lid.**
- **Add ½ cup of dry salba seeds.**
- **Put the lid on and shake vigorously for 10 seconds.**
- **Wait one minute, then shake again for another 10 seconds.**
- **Let the container with the gel remain at room temperature for at least four hours, or overnight to germinate.** (Nutrients from germinated seeds are up to 10 times more bio-available.)
- **Store the gel in the refrigerator.** It will stay fresh for up to two weeks.

flavor. The seeds are good tossed on salads, cereal, yogurt, in sauces, smoothies and burgers. Ground salba is easy to use in food preparation—up to 25% of the flour used in any recipe can be replaced with it. Also, salba gel, a simple preparation of salba seeds in water (instructions above) can be used in place of eggs in food preparation.

Once you start using salba, you will find that you can add it to just about any food you prepare without altering the taste of the dish.

There are also delicious products containing salba—chips, salsa, tortillas, pretzels, bars which make great snacks. Salba products should be used in addition to, not in place of, your daily recommended dose.

■ Recipe ■

Salba Date Balls

Yields: 40 to 60 date balls

Our thanks to Ancient Naturals for giving us permission to include this recipe for a super healthy treat that's gluten-free and no sugar added.

Ingredients

3 cups dates (pitted)
3 cups water
¼ cup Salba ground seeds
5 cups crisped rice cereal (e.g. Rice Krispies)
1 cup walnuts (crushed)

Instructions

1. Bring dates and water to a boil.
2. Cook on low for 5 minutes, then remove from heat.
3. Mash boiled dates with potato masher. Let cool.
4. Add Salba ground seeds to date mixture and mix well.
5. Add crisped rice cereal to the mixture and mix well.
6. Roll the mixture into 1-inch balls.
7. Spread crushed walnuts on a baking sheet and roll the balls to coat them with walnuts.
8. Refrigerate overnight.

   These no-bake, gluten-free date balls are a perfect, easy-to-prepare, healthy treat for when company is coming.

Typical Dosage

For adults, two level tablespoons daily. That's 15 grams (g), supplying more than 100% of the recommended daily intake of omega-3 and omega-6 in a perfectly balanced ratio.

For children, typical dosage, depending on the age and size of your child, is up to one tablespoon daily.

Since it is rich in fiber, you may have to be near a bathroom the first time or two that you take any appreciable amount. It has a cleansing effect, and that's a good thing.

 CAUTION: Diabetics should continue taking their medication, carefully monitoring their blood sugar and working with their health care provider. Hopefully, blood sugar numbers will improve and medication dosage can be lowered with a doctor's supervision.

Where to Buy Salba

All forms of salba are available on the Internet at Salba Smart Natural Product's Web site, *www.salbasmart.com*, or call Salba Smart Natural Products at 303-999-3996. Also check your local health food stores and natural food markets such as Whole Foods.

SMUDGING FOR SELF-CLEARING

Lucky for us, "Britain's top writer on alternative therapies" and well-trusted expert in natural medicine, holistic living and contemporary spirituality, Jane Alexander, agreed to share her in-depth knowledge of smudging. *Here are her words and instructions…*

A Word from the Wise…

Jane Alexander on Smudging

If you're not familiar with it, smudging is the common name given to the Sacred Smoke

Bowl Blessing, a powerful cleansing technique from the Native American tradition. Smudging calls upon the spirits of sacred plants to drive away negative energies and put you back into a state of balance. It is the psychic equivalent of washing your hands before eating.

These concepts are not new-fangled nor are they airy-fairy New Age nonsense. Native American tradition dates back millennia and most traditional cultures, from the Zulus to the Maoris, from the Chinese to the Balinese, have age-old forms of cleansing and blessing rituals. Even the West retains relics of it, although we have long forgotten the true purpose behind many of our rituals and ceremonies. The incense wafting through a church or temple is cleansing the atmosphere just as surely as the medicine man's bowl of sacred smoke, or smudge is cleansing.

How Smudging Works

The answer lies in the subatomic world of subtle or spiritual energy. Homes and bodies are not just made of purely physical matter; they also vibrate with subtle, invisible energy (you might know it as qi or chi, prana, quwa, etc). Cleansing a space or our bodies with techniques such as smudging clears away all the emotional and psychic "garbage" that may have gathered over years. It's like spiritual spring-cleaning.

Smudging is so wonderful. Truly. Try it and you'll become a convert, I'm almost willing to bet. I love it because it's the simplest yet most incredibly effective form of space clearing available. It takes just five minutes to learn the basics and you're off. Plus, it really works!

My most powerful experience of smudging came when I visited shaman Leo Rutherford in London. I had moved out of the city quite a while before and had totally lost the "street savvy" sense you have when you live in a big city. Consequently I was feeling pretty nervous about stepping out into an unknown (and slightly rough) neighborhood on my own at night. Leo must have guessed my apprehension, because he said, "Hold on, Jane. Just need to give you a quick smudge before you go." I stood, in my coat and with bag in hand, in his hallway while he wafted smoke around me with a huge eagle's feather. It felt like having an energy shower—tingles ran all over my body in waves. I breathed deeply and it was as if someone had fired up every one of my chakras. I gave Leo a hug, totally forgetting my fears. I walked along the dark streets feeling invincible. It was as if I had a cloak of power surrounding me.

I use smudging to cleanse myself (particularly if I've had a lousy day or have had to deal with difficult or unpleasant people). I use it as a prelude to all kinds of spiritual and magical work (it's like a spiritual power shower). I use it to cleanse my home and office. I use it to mark the seasons and as part of other rituals. Basically I use it all over the place, at all kinds of times—it is totally adaptable and practical, a really user-friendly soulful tool."

Basic Smudging for Self-Clearing

The following directions come from my book, *The Smudging and Blessings Book* (Sterling)—a quick, do-it-yourself guide to getting started. Go to *www.exmoorjane.com* for more information and books, including *The Illustrated Spirit of the Home* (HarperCollins), which gives instructions on basic *space* clearing using smudging.

There are many ways to use smudging. Here is a simple way to get started. As you become more proficient, you may find you want to use different words or actions. That's fine— just be guided by your intuition.

271

CAUTION: If you have asthma or any respiratory challenges such as chronic obstructive pulmonary disease (COPD), smudging may NOT be for you. If you insist on trying it, experiment very cautiously.

You will need: A smudge stick…matches…a small ceramic or stone bowl or a large shell (as a place to rest the smudge stick)…and a large feather. (Most health food stores and Whole Foods Markets offer bundles of sage smudge sticks. Also, check "Sources," page 311, for another place that sells smudge kits.)

Instructions

1. Light the end of your smudge stick and let it burn for a few minutes until the tip starts to smolder. You may need to fan the flames for a while to get the smudge really smoking. Then extinguish the flame so the smudge stick smokes.

2. Call on the spirits of the smudge to cleanse and protect you, saying, "Sacred Sage, drive away any negativity from my heart—take away everything unworthy and impure."

3. First waft the smoke toward your heart. Hold the smudge stick away from you and use the feather to waft the smoke toward you. Then take the smudge smoke over your head, down your arms and down the front of your body. Imagine the smoke lifting away all the negative thoughts, emotions and energies that have attached themselves to you.

4. Breathe in the smudge, visualizing the smoke purifying your body from the inside.

5. Now bring the smoke down the back of your body toward the ground. Visualize the last vestiges of negativity being taken back into the earth, away into the air.

6. Repeat your smudging once again, this time calling on the spirit of Sweetgrass in this way, "Sacred Sweetgrass, bring me the positive energy I need to do this work. Help me to come into balance. Purify my soul." As you smudge, imagine yourself being surrounded by gentle, loving energy. Breathe in positivity, courage and love.

7. When your smudging has ended, douse the smudge stick with water.

Making a Sacred Smudge Bowl

Native American shamans do not always use the smudge sticks. Equally common is a loose smudge mixture, which is placed in a bowl or shell and lit. It is easy to make, and also has the advantage that, as you become more experienced and intuitive, you can alter your mixture to fit each individual ritual.

You will need: Your choice of dried herbs and resins and a bowl to mix them in, a shell or smudge bowl, self-igniting charcoal blocks, candle and matches, feather, sea salt.

Instructions

1. Sit down with all your ingredients. Light your candle and center yourself. Ask the spirits of the plants you are using to give you their help.

2. Take a bowl or large shell—it needs to be able to withstand the heat of the burning charcoal. Ensure it is clean and cleansed by washing it in water to which you have added a little sea salt.

3. A basic smudge mix would include a tablespoon of crumbled sage (either sagebrush or culinary sage) plus a teaspoon each of cedar bark and lavender. Mix the herbs together in a bowl.

4. Place a charcoal block in your bowl or shell and light it. Wait until the charcoal stops sparking and has turned white-grey.
5. Add a few pinches of your smudge mixture. It will readily smoke.
6. Use your smudge bowl in exactly the same way as you would your smudge stick—hold up the bowl and use a feather to direct smoke toward you, someone else or out into the area in which you are working.
7. You will need to add more smudge from time to time.

Closing Thoughts

I hope this introduction to smudging helps you. Do take the time to try this wonderful ritual. If nothing else, I think taking five minutes out of a hectic day to center oneself, breathe and just be, has to be therapeutic.

Also see "Smudge Your Space Clear," page 291.

A Word from the Wise...

Reiki: The Energy That Heals

Reiki (pronounced "RAY-key") is a healing art traced to spiritual teachings from Japan in the early 20th century. The name combines two Japanese words, *rei* (universal) and *ki* (life energy). Reiki practitioners often use the technique to help ease clients' anxiety and stress... chronic or postsurgical pain...menopausal hot flashes...menstrual cramps...migraines...and nausea and fatigue from chemotherapy.

How it works: The traditional principle is that the practitioner taps into a universal life energy that exists within and around us... then channels this energy to the client, enhancing the body's innate healing abilities. The modern scientific theory is that reiki promotes profound relaxation, increasing levels of pain-relieving, mood-boosting brain chemicals called *endorphins*.

What to expect: During a typical 60-minute reiki session, the client (fully dressed) sits in a chair or lies on a massage table. The practitioner places his/her hands, palms down, on or just above a dozen or so different spots on the client's body, holding each position for several minutes. Clients become deeply relaxed, and some perceive sensations of warmth or tingling at the spot being treated.

Cost of treatment: About $50 to $100 per session.

How to find a practitioner: Reiki has no formal licensing process, so locating an experienced practitioner is largely a matter of word-of-mouth.

Helpful: Get a referral from a local hospital that has an integrative medicine center.

Bottom line: While no large-scale clinical trials on reiki have yet been done, studies show benefits from various touch therapies. There are no negative effects from reiki. If you have a serious health problem, try reiki as an adjunct to standard medical treatment. Some people say that reiki works only due to a placebo effect—and that could be so. However, practitioners often encounter clients who are skeptical at first...but who, after experiencing reiki firsthand, report that the therapy has helped them.

Aurora Ocampo, RN, CNS, clinical nurse specialist at the Continuum Center for Health and Healing, Beth Israel Medical Center, New York City, *www.healthandhealingny.org.*

TAI CHI

Throughout our country, groups of people gather in parks and other peaceful public areas to start their day by doing tai chi (pronounced "tie-chee"), a simple, westernized form of the classic more complex Chinese exercise.

While we do not teach tai chi in this book, in several chapters we do recommend it as a worthwhile discipline. Therefore, we owe it to you to give you a better understanding of this gentlest of martial arts, and how it may benefit you.

The following information is from the American Tai Chi and Qigong Association (online at *www.americantaichi.org*)...

Tai chi is defined as a mind-body practice that originated in China as a martial art. A person doing tai chi moves his body slowly and gently, while breathing deeply and meditating (tai chi is sometimes called "moving meditation"). Many practitioners believe that tai chi helps a vital energy called qi (pronounced "chee" and means "air" or "power") flow throughout the body.

Brief History of Tai Chi

While accounts of tai chi's history often differ, the most consistently important figure is Chang San-Feng (or Zan Sanfeng), a Taoist monk in 12th-century China. San-Feng is said to have observed five animals—tiger, dragon, leopard, snake and crane—and to have concluded that the snake and the crane, through their movements, were the ones most able to overcome strong, unyielding opponents.

San-Feng developed an initial set of exercises that imitated the movements of animals. He also brought flexibility and suppleness in place of strength to the martial arts, as well as some key philosophical concepts.

274

Core Philosophy of Tai Chi

One of the core concepts of tai chi is that the forces of yin and yang should be in balance. In Chinese philosophy, yin and yang are two principles or elements that make up the universe and everything in it. They also oppose each other. Yin is believed to have the qualities of water—such as coolness, darkness, stillness and inward and downward directions—and to be feminine in character. Yang is believed to have the qualities of fire—such as heat, light, action and upward and outward movements—and to be masculine. In this belief system, people's yin and yang need to be in balance in order for them to be healthy, and tai chi is a practice that supports this balance.

Three Basic Components of Tai Chi

When tai chi is performed, these three major components are working together...

➤ **Movement.** When doing tai chi, individuals feel the ground with their feet, sink their weight to the ground and maintain good body alignment to promote stability and balance. Movements flow from one to another, with body weight shifting from the right leg to the left leg to balance the empty and full feeling. The movements make up what are called forms or routines. Some movements are named for animals or birds, such as "White Crane Spreads Its Wings." The more complex style of Tai Chi has up to 108 movements; the simplest style uses 13 movements.

➤ **Meditation.** While performing the gentle and slow tai chi movements, individuals keep their mind calm and alert, concentrating on the inner self.

➤ **Deep Breathing.** With the flow of the movements, individuals exhale stale air and toxins from the lungs, inhale lots of fresh air, stretch the muscles involved in breathing and release tension. This process supplies the entire body with fresh oxygen and nutrients.

Health Benefits of Tai Chi

It will…

• **Provide an aerobic, low-impact workout that is weight bearing as well.** (Weight-bearing exercise has been shown to fight off bone loss.)

• **Improve physical condition,** muscle strength, coordination and flexibility.

• **Give you better balance and a lower risk for falls,** especially in elderly people.

• **Ease pain and stiffness,** such as from arthritis.

• **Provide the health benefits of meditation,** such as better management of stress and stress-related conditions.

• **Enhance sleep.**

• **Improve overall wellness.**

In Asia, many consider tai chi to be the most beneficial exercise for older people, because it is gentle and can easily be modified to accommodate a person's health limitations.

 CAUTION: Tai chi is a relatively safe practice, however there are some cautions…

• Tell your health care provider if you are considering learning tai chi for health purposes (especially if you have a health condition for which you are being treated, if you have not exercised in a while or if you are a senior citizen).

• If you do not position your body properly in tai chi, or if you overdo it, you may get sore muscles or sprains.

• Tai chi instructors often recommend that people not practice tai chi right after

they eat, or when they are very tired, or when they have an active infection.

• If you have any of these conditions (hernia, joint problems, back pain, sprains, a fracture or severe osteoporosis) or you are pregnant, your health care provider should advise you whether to modify or avoid certain postures in tai chi.

Tai chi is not only very effective for various health issues, it's also very easy to practice. You can do as little as one 15-minute session a day anywhere that suits you, and you do not need any special clothes or equipment.

More information: Visit the American Tai Chi and Qigong Association Web site at *www. americantaichi.org.* It is a national nonprofit trade organization based in Virginia.

To find a tai chi teacher or class in your area, at the Association's home page, click on the "Tai Chi and Qigong for Health Information Center" link in the middle of the page. Then click on "Tai Chi Qigong Class Locator" in the left-hand column.

A Word from the Wise…

Strong, Calm and Confident with Tai Chi

Why do millions of people around the world practice tai chi? Because it is a wonderful way to integrate and nurture mind, body and spirit—to hone mental focus, build muscles and bones and foster self-confidence. To practice the meditative movements here, repeat each sequence for five minutes daily. Stand with feet shoulder-width apart, knees slightly bent, toes slightly angled out, posture erect (or sit in a sturdy chair). Move slowly and gracefully…match the rhythm of your deep breaths to your movements.

 CAUTION: Check with your doctor before beginning any new exercise routine.

Gathering of Heaven and Earth

In Chinese medicine, earth and sky represent yin and yang, powerful healing energies.

1. Start with hands in front of chest at heart level, several inches apart.
2. Open arms wide…begin to bend knees out to sides.
3. Sink into knees as far as is comfortable while reaching down and bringing hands together, as if arms were encircling and gathering up earth energy.

4. Straightening legs, bring hands up toward heart.
5. Now, open arms wide…reach up and bring hands toward each other, as if encircling and gathering sky energy.
6. Lower hands, bringing them past face to heart level. Repeat sequence.

276

Hands Like Clouds

In this movement, each time your hand drifts past your face, follow it with your gaze, imagining it as a tranquil, billowy cloud. Relax your shoulders…rest your mind.

1. Start with hands in front of heart, several inches apart.

2. Turning torso slightly to the left, lower your right hand to waist level …move both hands to left side of body.

3. Raise right hand and lower the left hand, so hands pass each other.

4. Turning torso to the center, bring right hand past face like a drifting cloud…bring left hand past center of body at waist level.

5. *Repeat on other side:* Turn torso and move hands to the right, left hand at waist level. Raise left hand and lower right hand. Turn torso to center…let left hand drift past face as right hand passes at waist level. Repeat sequence.

Illustrations by Shawn Banner.

Roger Jahnke, OMD, a board-certified doctor of Oriental medicine, lecturer and author of two books, including *The Healer Within* (HarperOne). He is director of the Institute of Integral Qigong and Tai Chi, *www.feeltheqi.com,* and CEO of Health Action, a wellness consulting firm, both in Santa Barbara, California.

Healthful Hints

This chapter is filled with an assortment of helpful advice and *"I didn't know that!"* tips that help make our lives a bit easier…and can help you too. We suggest that you read through it, discover the items that will support your good health, incorporate suggestions for food preparation and share it all with others.

AN APPLE (OR TWO) A DAY

Researchers studied students who ate two apples a day and compared them with students who didn't eat any apples. The apple eaters were less stressed, had fewer headaches and were more emotionally stable. Apple eaters also seem to have clearer skin, fewer colds and are not as troubled by arthritis. Start eating those apples! For tips on how to clean apples, see page 283.

ANTIBIOTICS

If you are taking a doctor-prescribed antibiotic be sure to also take acidophilus (available at health food stores). Antibiotics have no discretion—they destroy the good as well as the bad bacteria. Acidophilus replaces the beneficial bacteria. It can also help prevent intestinal infections and decrease the chance of diarrhea by 40%, while on antibiotics. Capsules should provide one to two billion viable acidophilus cells. No, you don't have to count them. Read the label carefully.

If you prefer eating yogurt instead of taking acidophilus capsules, be sure the brand you choose clearly states that it contains probiotics (such as Stonyfield Farm, Yoplus and Activia).

 NOTE: Take acidophilus right *after* you've eaten and at least two hours *before* or two hours *after* you take an antibiotic. That way you won't diminish the effectiveness of the antibiotic while reaping the benefits of the acidophilus.

AVOCADOS—WHEN ARE THEY RIPE?

Give it the five-finger test. Let an avocado rest in the palm of one hand and put the fingers of your other hand on the side of the avocado. Gently press in. If it feels as though the pit inside is detaching itself from the meat of the fruit, then the avocado is ripe.

Also, when you remove the little stem of the avocado and the little circle that was under the stem is bright yellow, you can expect that it will be a perfect bruise-free fruit, ripe and ready for eating.

The reason we tell you this is because avocados are an amazing superfood, worth adding to your diet. They are a vitamin E powerhouse...they are an excellent source of *glutathione*, an antioxidant that helps to prevent cancer, heart disease and aging...they provide the compound *beta-sitosterol* that helps lower cholesterol levels...they are rich in carotenoid *lutein* to protect against macular degeneration and cataracts...their high levels of folate protect against strokes...and certain nutrients such as *lycopene* and *beta carotene* are better absorbed when eaten with avocado. We rest our case.

BAND-AID REMOVAL

➤ **Baby Oil.** Soak a cotton ball with vegetable oil or baby oil and dab it all over the Band-Aid. The Band-Aid will peel off painlessly.

➤ **Hair Dryer.** Let a hair dryer blow warm air on the Band-Aid for a minute or two. The heat will melt the sticky stuff, making it possible to peel off without pain.

278

CITRUS TIP

You've probably heard or read the word "bioflavonoids," but do you know what they do and how to get them?

What they do is promote the absorption of vitamin C and they reinforce the walls of small blood vessels that deliver nutrients to individual cells.

You get bioflavonoids from the white layer of skin that you usually peel off citrus fruits and throw away. Do not be so quick to throw it away. Instead, eat some of that bioflavonoid-rich (usually bitter tasting) white skin known as the pith.

COLD WEATHER DRESSING

Opt for mittens rather than gloves. They'll keep your hands warmer. Another way to keep your hands warm, surprisingly your feet too, is by wearing a hat.

And, thin layers of clothing will keep you warmer than one heavy layer. Your body heats the air that's between the layers and insulates you from the cold.

Many people think a good stiff drink will warm them. Wrong! Alcohol dilates blood vessels and that results in a loss of heat.

USING COMPUTERS SAFELY

The National Institute of Occupational Safety and Health (*www.cdc.gov/NIOSH*) advises all computer users to...

• **Position the screen at eye level,** about 22 to 26 inches away.

- **Sit about arm's length from the terminal.** At that distance, the electrical field is almost zero.

- **Face forward and be sure that your neck is relaxed.**

- **Position the keyboard so that elbows are bent at least 90°F** and you can work without bending your wrist.

- **Use a chair that supports your back,** lets your feet rest on the floor or footrest, and keeps thighs parallel to the floor.

- **If you can step away from the computer for 15 minutes every hour,** it can help prevent eyestrain.

"EGGS-CELLENT" ADVICE

There is a lot of controversy in the health community about whether or not it's safe to eat raw eggs. Raw eggs could contain salmonella bacteria that cause food poisoning. Salmonella is usually found in the yolk, but the egg white is not totally immune from this kind of contamination. Statistics show that about one in 30,000 eggs have this bacteria. Are you willing to take the chance? Eggs cooked to at least 160°F will kill bacteria that can cause food-borne illness.

➤ **Where to Keep Them.** When you buy eggs, keep them in your refrigerator in the carton they came in. If any salmonella exists, the egg section in the refrigerator door will not keep them cold enough to discourage the salmonella from multiplying, especially if the door is opened often.

➤ **Safety First.** Throw out eggs that are cracked. They may be contaminated. Better safe than salmonella.

FEET-SOAKING MADE EASY

We find that the best way to soak each foot comfortably is in a plastic shoe box. It's neater and more comfortable than a basin.

GARLIC SMELL REMOVER

➤ **Take the Smell of Garlic Off Your Hands** by rubbing celery, tomato or lemon on your hands.

➤ **Our Favorite Garlic Smell Remover.** Pretend a piece of silverware is a bar of soap and wash your hands with it under cold water. It works like magic.

This tip can also be used for onions.

GET WELL SMELL

➤ **Freshly Baked Bread.** Try to imagine the smell of homemade bread just taken out of the oven. The thought alone can make you feel warm inside. The actual smell of freshly baked bread is said to have the power to make you feel better and get better faster.

➤ **Fresh Eucalyptus.** The scent of fresh eucalyptus leaves is also very healing. If you can't get the fresh leaves, use the essential oil.

GINGER AT THE READY

Several remedies call for gingerroot. Up until now, we've been freezing chunks of gingerroot and grating a piece whenever we need it. We just learned a better way to keep ginger. Buy a large piece of gingerroot and when you get it home, peel it, slice it in pieces, each about the size of a quarter, and place the pieces on a tray in the freezer. Once they're frozen solid, place the ginger quarters in a plastic container and put them back in the freezer. Whenever a remedy or recipe calls for ginger, take out the amount of frozen pieces that you need. They will thaw in a few minutes at room temperature.

 CAUTION: Ginger acts as a blood thinner, so check with your doctor before using it if you are taking a prescription blood thinner. Also, stop using ginger three days before any surgery.

BETTER HAND WASHING

Washing your hands may be your single most important act to help stop the spread of infection and stay healthy, reports the Centers for Disease Control and Prevention (CDC) (*www.cdc.gov*).

Yes, you have been washing your hands for—well, forever. But are you doing it properly so that you wash away germs? Be particularly diligent about hand washing after being out in public during the cold and flu seasons and/or after being in contact with contaminated surfaces (e.g. on public transportation, any desk in your office, handling money).

Most Important Times to Wash Your Hands Are...

- Before preparing or eating food.
- After using the toilet.
- After changing diapers or cleaning up a child who has used the toilet.
- Before and after tending to someone who is sick.

- After blowing your nose, coughing or sneezing.
- After handling an animal or animal waste.
- After handling garbage.
- Before and after treating a cut or wound.

Hand-Washing Instructions From the CDC...

- **Wet your hands with clean running water and apply soap.** Use warm water if it is available.
- **Rub hands together to make a lather** and scrub all surfaces.
- **Continue rubbing hands for 20 seconds.** Need a timer? Sing the "Happy Birthday" song twice through.
- **Rinse hands very well under running water.**
- **Dry your hands using a paper towel or air dryer.** If possible, use your paper towel to turn off the faucet.

If soap and water are not available, use alcohol-based gel to clean hands. *When using an alcohol-based hand sanitizer...*

- **Apply product to the palm of one hand.**
- **Rub hands together.**
- **Rub the product over all surfaces of hands and fingers until hands are dry.**

HOT DRINKS

Throughout this book, we tell you about the healing properties of herbal teas and we hope you are reaping their benefits, but... be sure to let tea or coffee or any other hot beverage cool off for four or five minutes before drinking it. Researchers estimate the risk of getting cancer of the esophagus (the muscular tube through which food passes from the throat to the stomach) may be increased five or more times in people who drink very hot drinks on a regular basis.

Researcher David C. Whiteman, Australia's Queensland Institute of Medical Research said that this is not the first time we've been warned. Whiteman quoted the advice of the famous Victorian cookbook writer, Mrs. Beeton, who prescribes "a five- to 10-minute interval between making and pouring tea, by which time the tea will be sufficiently flavorsome and unlikely to cause thermal injury."

HOT WEATHER ENDURANCE

To stay cooler in the warmer months, take an additional 250 milligrams (mg) of vitamin C every day.

ICE PACK SUBSTITUTE

If you need an ice pack but don't have one, you can use a package of frozen vegetables. Bang it with a hammer to break up the clumps of veggies, making it flexible and easy to work with.

IMMUNE SYSTEM STRENGTHENERS

When you're finished reading this chapter, be sure to read the "It Does a Body Good" chapter, page 229, for more immune system strengtheners.

➤ **Aloe Vera Juice.** The main active ingredient in aloe vera is *acemannan,* which is thought to bolster the immune system's effectiveness. Take an ounce of aloe vera juice before each meal daily. It may also help digestion.

➤ **A Cold Bath.** Stepping into a cold bath or under a cold shower for a few minutes every day can improve circulation as well as the immune system.

➤ **Sauerkraut.** Eat a portion of salt-free sauerkraut (available at health food stores) every day. The raw, fermented cabbage is rich in selenium, which is known to help strengthen the immune system.

LEG SHAVING

➤ **Ingrown-Hair Prevention.** Go *with* the grain and shave down from your knee to your ankle. Going *against* the grain can cause ingrown hairs.

➤ **Prevent Dry Legs.** Throw away the shaving cream, lose the soap. Shave with oil instead—sesame, peanut or sunflower—and have a leg up when it comes to smooth and silky skin.

LEMONS—THE BIG SQUEEZE

➤ **Juice Up.** You will get almost twice as much juice from a lemon if you roll it on the counter after it sits in hot water for a few minutes, or after you zap it in the microwave for about 20 seconds…30 seconds at most, or it can explode.

➤ **Pit-Free.** To get the juice without the pits, wrap a wet piece of cheesecloth around the cut side of the lemon and strain the juice as you squeeze it out.

MEDICATION IDENTIFICATION

When you have a prescription filled, even if it's a reorder, or if you buy over-the-counter pills, check to be sure you got what you wanted. Go to *www.webmd.com/pill-identification* and type in the name, shape and color of the pill. It will not only identify the medication, there will be all kinds of information about it, including people's reviews about its effectiveness.

MEDICINE MADE EASY

➤ **Yucky-Tasting Stuff.** If you have to take something unpleasant, whether it's an herb, a pill or cough syrup, numb your taste buds first by sucking on an ice cube for a couple of minutes.

If you're going to have herbal tea, the heat of the tea will counteract the numbness of your tongue. In that case, just make up your mind to acquire a taste for the herb.

➤ **Popping Pills.** You know that awful feeling when a pill or capsule doesn't go down smoothly? The late Dr. Hans H. Neumann, Connecticut public health physician, once suggested to us that after taking pills or capsules you follow with a bite of banana, chew it well and swallow. He said, "The banana helps to coat the esophagus and push the pill into the stomach for quick absorption."

The late Dr. Ray Wunderlich, Jr., respected physician and founder of the Wunderlich Center for Nutritional Medicine, suggested liquids with texture such as tomato juice or other vegetable juices make pill-swallowing much easier.

METAL REMOVERS

Part of the pollution we breathe every day, especially those of us who live in smoggy big and/or industrial cities, are heavy metals—cadmium, mercury, lead, copper and more.

Vegetables rich in sulfur—sweet potatoes and cabbage, for example—can help detoxify our systems of these metals. Eat them often, at least several times a week.

NATURAL MEDICINES DATABASE

If you're serious about doing medical research as a health care professional, or as a person with a health challenge, and your emphasis is on natural ingredients and products, consider signing up for the Natural Medicines Comprehensive Database (NMCD), which is updated daily.

You can subscribe to this online service one month at a time, or for a year, two years or longer. The subscription fee is reasonable and the return in terms of reliable, current, valuable information is priceless.

Included in the subscription…

● **A disease/medical condition search,** which indicates the natural products that might be effective for a particular condition.

● **Ratings on safety and effectiveness for more than 1,100 natural medicines.**

● **Product information on more than 49,000 brands**—objective information about any individual ingredient or brand name combo product.

● **A natural product and drug interaction checker** that shows potential interactions between any natural product and any drug. It automatically checks for interactions with each product ingredient.

- **Patient-handout information** in consumer-friendly wording.

- **Monthly warnings sent by eUpdate.**

The company responsible for the NMCD is Therapeutic Research—a completely independent research and publishing organization. The fact that they accept no advertising is your guarantee that they provide objective, evidence-based information to subscribers. There is also an annual 2,300 plus page NMCD book.

More information: Call 209-472-2244 or go to *www.naturaldatabase.com.*

NO SWEAT

During those dog days of summer, when you have to do something physically taxing in a non–air-conditioned location, chew a chunk of honeycomb (available at health food stores). The honeycomb can actually cause a drop in body temperature, keeping you from feeling the heat.

 CAUTION: If you have a suspected sensitivity to bee products, do NOT chew on honeycomb. Also, asthmatics should NOT have honeycomb.

ONIONS WITHOUT TEARS

➤ **Freeze Out.** Put onions in the freezer for 20 minutes and then you can tearlessly chop 'em, dice 'em, mince 'em, slice 'em.

➤ **Match.** Keep a kitchen match in your mouth—sulfur side out—while you work with onions.

➤ **Goggles.** We put on goggles when working with onions. We think it is the most effective method of preventing tears and bitterness in the eyes.

To remove the smell of onions, see "Garlic Smell Remover," page 279.

PESTICIDE REMOVAL FOR FRUITS AND VEGETABLES

Jay Kordich, known as "The Juiceman," shared with us his method for removing poisonous sprays and pesticides from produce. Fill the sink with cold water and add four tablespoons of salt and the fresh juice of half a lemon. This makes a diluted form of hydrochloric acid. Soak most fruits and vegetables five to 10 minutes; soak leafy greens two to three minutes; soak strawberries, blueberries and all other berries one to two minutes. After soaking, rinse thoroughly in plain cold water and enjoy.

An alternative to The Juiceman's method is to soak produce in a sink or basin with a quarter cup of distilled white vinegar. Then, with a vegetable brush, scrub the produce under cold water. Give them one final rinse and they're ready to be eaten.

PINEAPPLE RIPENER

Usually, the bottom of a pineapple gets ripe and even overripe while the crown with its spikey leaves stays green. To remedy this, turn a pineapple upside down and keep it that way. To test for ripeness, pluck a little leaf. If it comes out easily, the pineapple is ready for eating.

PROBLEM SOLVING

Laura Silva Quesada, healer, international lecturer and president, The Silva Method (*www.silvamethod.com*), claims you can create a state of ultra-awareness by questioning yourself. As you're going to sleep and are in a completely relaxed state, ask yourself whatever it is you want answered. Laura says to phrase it this way, "If I knew that answer, what would it be?" Or, "If I had the solution, what would it be?" Or, "If I knew the path to take, which path would I take?"

According to Laura, when you're in a relaxed state, these questions open up your mind to creative problem solving.

RECOMMENDED REFERENCE BOOK

If you are a spur-of-the-moment cook and cannot always run out for needed ingredients, *The Food Substitutions Bible* from David Joachim (*www.fireflybooks.com*) is a must-have. This very-accomplished author has included more than 5,000 substitutions for ingredients, equipment and techniques. Every substitution includes exact proportions and directions for making accurate and reliable replacements.

RECYCLING PLASTIC BAGS

The printing on plastic bags—like the kind you get at the grocery store—can contain lead. The same holds true for the printing on most plastic bags that loaves of bread are packaged in. If you use a plastic bag with printing on it, be sure the printed surface does not touch food. When you recycle the bags, don't turn them inside out. The food can absorb the lead; then the lead would be absorbed by whoever eats the food.

RING REMOVAL

When your finger is a little swollen and you can't take off a ring, put your hand in ice-cold water. The cold water will cause your finger to contract and the stuck ring will come off easily.

SALAD SAVVY

Prepare a salad as close to mealtime as possible. The longer a salad stands, the more vitamins are lost and the less value the food has.

Home Health Hints

AIR POLLUTION FIGHTERS

Since "Home is where the heart is," you've got to protect your heart along with your other organs by making sure your home is well-ventilated and as pollution-free as possible. *These suggestions can help...*

Plants

After extensive research conducted by the National Aeronautics and Space Administration (NASA), it was concluded that specific common house plants can dramatically reduce toxic chemical levels in homes and offices.

If you're thinking to yourself that your home isn't polluted—after all, you do open up the bathroom window when you use that tile spray—take a look at this list of common toxins lurking in your living quarters...*benzene* (found in inks, oils, paints, plastics, rubber, detergents, dyes and gasoline); *formaldehyde* (found in all indoor environments, including foam insulation, particle board, pressed wood products, most cleaning agents, paper products treated with resins, including grocery bags, facial tissues and paper towels); and *trichloroethylene* (TCE, which is found in dry-cleaning processes, printing inks, paints, lacquers, varnishes and adhesives).

We will spare you the details on the serious harm these chemicals can do. *Instead, here's a list of the top five plants that proved effective in reducing the levels of the common toxin...*

- **Spider Plant** (*chlorophytum comosum "vittatum"*)—very easy to grow in indirect or bright-diffused light.
- **Peace Lily** (*spathiphyllum* species)—very easy to grow in a low-light location.
- **Chinese Evergreen** (*aglaonema* "silver queen")—very easy to grow in low-light.
- **Weeping Fig** (*ficus benjamina*)—fairly easy to grow, but requires some special attention. Needs indirect or bright-diffused light.
- **Golden Pothos** (*epipremnum aureum*). This is very easy to grow in either indirect or bright-diffused light.

Didn't see any plant you like? *Here are an additional five plants also recommended by NASA as air cleaners…*

- **Gerbera Daisy or Barberton Daisy** (*Gerbera jamesonii*).

- **Janet Craig dracaena** (*Dracaena deremensis* 'Janet Craig').

- **The Snake Plant or mother-in-law's tongue** (*Sansevieria trifasciata* 'Laurentii').

- **Warneck dracaena** (*Dracaena deremensis* 'Warneckii').

- **Pot Mum or Florist's Chrysanthemum** (*Chrysanthemum morifolium*).

NASA recommends placing 15 to 18 of these plants in an 1,800 square-foot home to clean and refresh the air. Most of us living in apartments or houses with much less space need just one plant in each room. Place plants where air circulates. Once you have the plants, don't be surprised if you or members of your household don't complain any more of sore throats and stuffy noses that were caused by contaminants.

Protection from Harmful Chemicals

➤ **Fireplace Alert.** Do not feed the fire in your fireplace with colored magazines and colored newspapers, as they contain lead and when burned emit dangerous levels of lead. It can be extremely harmful, especially to children in the house.

➤ **Dry-Cleaning Clothes.** Still having your clothes dry-cleaned and not using an eco-friendly dry cleaner? Tsk! Tsk! The chemicals used in the cleaning process are potent and can affect people in different ways. One common complaint involves the thyroid, making people feel sluggish.

To protect yourself from inhaling dry-cleaning chemical fumes, never hang just dry-cleaned clothes in your closet with the plastic cover over them. Ideally, take off the plastic cover and find a way to air out the clothes (on your terrace, in your yard, on the roof) before bringing them into your home. Once the chemical smell disappears, the solvents have evaporated. That's when you should bring your clothes in and hang them in your closet.

➤ **Much Better Shower Curtain.** Use a shower curtain that is made from polyester, nylon, cotton or hemp. Ideal is a shower curtain whose label clearly states *PVC-free!*

According to the Center for Health, Environment & Justice (*www.chej.org*), PVC (polyvinyl chloride) plastic, commonly referred to as vinyl, is one of the most hazardous consumer products ever created. PVC is dangerous to human health and the environment. Our bodies can get contaminated with poisonous chemicals—mercury, dioxins and phthalates—which are released during the PVC lifecycle.

New shower curtain smell? That's the smell of those poisonous chemicals off-gassing (releasing gas into the air) from the PVC. One study conducted by the EPA (Environmental Protective Agency, *www.epa.gov*) reported that vinyl shower curtains can cause elevated levels of dangerous air toxins, which can persist for more than a month.

We read that Target and Bed, Bath and Beyond are phasing out PVC. Ikea and Crate and Barrel currently have PVC-free shower curtains.

If you haven't already done so, go check the label on your shower curtain. If it's vinyl (PVC), take down the curtain and replace it. Stay clean, stay green!

COOKWARE CARE

Recent research suggests that we need to be as concerned about using copper or ceramic cookware as the much-maligned aluminum cookware. *We suggest that you avoid using this type of cookware, but if you cook with it, here are some ways to help minimize the harmful effects...*

● **Copper.** As for copper cookware, some inexpensive brands have copper as the cooking surface, and that can leach out in unhealthy amounts. Copper cookware is okay only if it has a stainless steel cooking surface.

● **Ceramic.** Worst of all is ceramic, from which lead can leach into the food it holds. Lead—even low levels—can be seriously toxic, especially to children. To prevent possible lead poisoning, the FDA advises against the use of ceramic cookware from China, Mexico, India and Hong Kong. If you are using ceramic cookware, do not cook or store acidic foods like tomatoes, orange juice or vinegar in it. And don't put ceramic in the dishwasher.

● **Cast Iron.** If you use cast iron pots and pans for cooking, the food will absorb some of the iron and, in turn, you will, too. This is particularly beneficial for women who are menstruating and lose iron each month. It can, however, be harmful to people who do not need the additional iron. Know your needs and cook with caution.

● **Lead-Testing Kit.** If you have doubts about the safety of your dishes and other items in the home, especially if they're used by children, you may want to purchase a lead-testing kit.

A Word from the Wise...

Are You Cooking the Health Out of Your Food?

Inflammation is the body's natural, temporary, healing response to infection or injury. But if the process fails to shut down when it should, inflammation becomes chronic, and tissues are injured by excess white blood cells and DNA-damaging free radicals.

Result: An elevated risk for heart disease, cancer, diabetes, osteoporosis, arthritis as well as other diseases.

Here, Richard E. Collins, MD, "the cooking cardiologist," tells how to prevent chronic inflammation.

His advice: Consume a diet that is rich in immune-strengthening nutrients...and use the cooking techniques that neither destroy food's disease-fighting nutrients nor add inflammatory properties to it.

Smart Ways with Vegetables

Deeply colored plant foods generally are rich in antioxidants that help combat inflammation by neutralizing free radicals.

Examples: Healthful flavonoids are prevalent in deep yellow to purple produce...carotenoids are found in yellow, orange, red and green vegetables.

Exceptions: Despite their light hue, garlic and onions are powerful antioxidants.

Unfortunately, these nutrients are easily lost. For instance, boiling or poaching vegetables causes nutrients to leach into the cooking water—and get tossed out when that potful of water is discarded. The high heat from frying causes a reaction between carbohydrates and amino acids, creating carcinogenic chemicals called *acrylamides*. And even when healthful techniques are used for food preparation, overcooking destroys nutrients. *Better...*

● **Microwave.** This uses minimal water and preserves flavor (so you won't be tempted to add butter or salt). Slightly moisten vegetables with water, cover and microwave just until crisp-tender.

● **Stir-fry.** In a preheated wok or sauté pan, cook vegetables over medium-high heat for a minute or two in a bit of low-sodium soy sauce.

● **Steam.** This beats boiling, but because steam envelops the food, some nutrients leach out. To "recycle" them, pour that bit of water from the steamer into any soup or sauce.

● **Stew.** Nutrients that leach from the vegetables aren't lost because they stay in the stew sauce.

● **Roast.** Set your oven to 350°F or lower to protect vegetables' nutrients and minimize acrylamides.

Best Methods for Meat

When beef, pork, poultry or fish is roasted at 400°F or higher, grilled, broiled or fried, it triggers a chemical reaction that creates inflammatory *heterocyclic amines* (HCAs)—in particular when food is exposed to direct flame and/or smoke. At least 17 HCAs are known carcinogens, linked to cancer of the breast, stomach, colon and/or pancreas.

Safest: Roast meat, poultry and fish at 350°F. Avoid overcooking—well-done meats may promote cancer. Also, be sure to avoid undercooking to prevent food poisoning.

If you love to grill: Buy a soapstone grilling stone, one-and-a-quarter inches thick and cut to half the size of your grill. (The stones are

sold at kitchen-counter retail stores and at Dorado Soapstone, 888-500-1905, *www.doradosoap stone.com*). Place it on your grilling rack, then put your food on top of it. Soapstone heats well, doesn't dry out food and gives the flavor of grilling without exposing food to direct flames or smoke.

If you eat bacon: To minimize HCAs, cook bacon in the microwave and take care not to burn it.

The Right Cooking Oils

Do you cringe when the Food Network chefs sauté in unrefined extra-virgin olive oil? You should. This oil has a very low smoke point (the temperature at which a particular oil turns to smoke) of about 325°F—and when oil smokes, nutrients degrade and free radicals form.

Best: Sauté or stir-fry with refined canola oil, which has a high smoke point. Or use tea seed cooking oil (not tea tree oil)—its smoke point is about 485°F.

Try: Arette Organic (*www.amazon.com*) or Republic of Tea (800-298-4832, *www.republic oftea.com*).

Rule of thumb: If cooking oil starts to smoke, throw it out. Use a laser thermometer (sold at kitchenware stores) to instantly see oil temperature—so you'll know when to turn down the heat.

Richard E. Collins, MD, director of wellness at South Denver Cardiology Associates in Littleton, Colorado. He is board-certified in cardiology and internal medicine, has performed more than 500 cooking demonstrations nationwide and is author of *The Cooking Cardiologist* (Advanced Research) and *Cooking with Heart* (South Denver Cardiology Associates). *www.southdenver.com*

CLEANING TIPS

➤ **Liquid Foods as Cleansers.**

• **Tea and a mirror.** Cold tea is supposed to shine your mirror. I just tried it with a cold, wet tea bag. I wet the mirror with it, then wiped it with a paper towel, and it's as clean as can be.

• **Potato water and silver.** Potato water, the water that's left in the pot after cooking potatoes, is a popular old folk remedy for many ailments. But it also cleans silver. Simply soak tarnished silver in potato water for a couple of hours.

➤ **Dusting Tip.** Before you take out a vacuum cleaner, use a damp cloth to dust. The vacuum's exhaust blows the dust from one place to another.

➤ **For Ant- and Worm-Free Wood.** Squeeze out the gel from the leaves of an aloe vera plant and use it as a varnish on the woodwork and wood furniture in your home, to protect the wood from worms and white ants.

➤ **Trash Compactor Deodorizer.** Three to five drops of oil of wintergreen in your trash compactor will make it tolerable until it can be emptied.

➤ **Home Sweet-Smelling Home.** Boil a few cinnamon sticks in a quart of water. By the time the water is almost boiled away, your whole house will be bathed in the lovely scent of cinnamon.

➤ **Married Men and Housework.** According to a four-year study of married couples, men who did housework were healthier than those who didn't. It seems that willingness to use a little elbow grease is representative of one's ability to deal with marital strife and life's pressures. Okay, fellas, get out the vacuum!

Help for Household Blunders

Below, friends and coworkers share their more memorable household blunders and their solutions...

➤ **Shrunken Sweater.** Soak for at least five minutes in a mixture of hair conditioner (use one to two tablespoons) and lukewarm water. Do not rinse. Roll the sweater up in a towel to remove excess water. Then lay it on a dry towel, and gently pull the sweater to reshape.

An oddball alternative: Wear the damp sweater—preferably over an extra layer—until it is dry.

➤ **Stinky Wet Clothes.** If you have left washed clothes in the washing machine too long, send them through the rinse cycle again and add one cup of white vinegar.

➤ **Overflowing Toilet.** One new home owner had a plumber reconnect the basement sink and toilet, which the previous owners had disconnected. During a storm, water gushed out of the toilet and flooded the basement.

Solution: The plumber installed a check valve—an inexpensive device that helps to prevent backflow.

➤ **Objects Dropped Down the Drain.** Cover the nozzle of the hose on a wet/dry vacuum—not a regular vacuum cleaner—with the leg from a pair of panty hose. Stick the nozzle into the drain opening, and turn on the vacuum. After the object has been retrieved, run water into the drain to refill the trap.

➤ **Bleach Spots on Furniture.** A friend's husband cleaned a living room fan with bleach. When he turned on the fan, bleach sprayed all over the room. The navy blue sofa now has permanent bleach spots. My friend covered them

289

using a decorative throw blanket, but fabric paints, available online and at craft stores, could also make the spots less conspicuous.

➤ **Bleach Spots on Clothing.** If it is a garment you really love, try using color remover—usually found near the clothing-dye supplies in department and grocery stores—on the entire garment, and then re-dye.

Alternative: One friend ended up with an artsy T-shirt by carefully spattering more bleach on the garment.

➤ **Scratched Hardwood Floors.** A coworker colors in scratches with matching permanent marker.

➤ **Stuck Candle Wax.** Freeze wax-covered candle holders, and then carefully chip off the wax.

Wax on a tablecloth: Place a paper towel over the hardened wax and under the tablecloth, and then iron the top towel. The iron should be at a medium, not hot, temperature.

➤ **Crayon On Walls.** Apply WD-40, rub the crayon mark with a damp sponge. After the crayon is removed, clean the area with soap and water, and dry with a paper towel. WD-40 is a multipurpose item. Some people have used it to remove nail polish from hardwood floors…camouflage scratches and remove Rollerblade marks on linoleum or ceramic tile floors…and get gunk off piano keys.

Marjory Abrams, chief content officer, Boardroom Inc.

HOME SWEET HOME

Feng Shui

Feng shui (it's pronounced "fung shway") is an ancient Chinese practice, at least 5,000 years old, believed to utilize the laws of both Heaven (astronomy) and Earth (geography). The goal is to balance your environment's energy flow known as qi or chi (pronounced "chee") by color selection and furniture placement so that you may live in harmony with your surroundings and enjoy good health, less stress, good luck and well being.

While researching feng shui, and looking around our apartment, one minute we were elated and the next minute we were ready to pack up and move. *Warning:* It can make you crazy!

The following basic feng shui tips will let the energy flow better around your home, hopefully producing small gains, with the chance of spectacular gains as you perhaps stimulate an area you didn't even know was there or needed stimulating.

➤ **Health and Family Areas.** The East corner of your home is the health and family area. Books about healing, herbs and nutrition are excellent for this area. We mention this just so you know where to keep this book you're currently reading.

In addition to the East corner of your home, each individual room has a health and family area—the left middle section of the Bagua, which is too complex to explain here. If you're really interested in going all the way with feng shui, see "More information" on the next page.

Meanwhile, back to basics…

➤ **Front Door.** Put something you love in your line of sight when you open your front door. This will make coming home feel more welcoming.

➤ **Doors.** Oil your doors so that they don't squeak. This will also decrease irritated feelings.

➤ **Bedroom.** Open your bedroom window(s) for at least 20 minutes a day, allowing stale chi (energy) to leave your bedroom and be replaced with fresh chi. It is said to bring good fortune to you. Okay, so you may have to dust a little more often, but hey, the good fortune will more than make up for the time you spend dusting. All that good fortune? Hire a maid!

➤ **Water Fountain.** A water fountain in your home is used to attract whatever you want in your life.

➤ **Window View.** If you look out any of your windows and see an unpleasant (permanent) view, place a mirror on the opposite wall, sending the image back outside.

➤ **Good Health.** To us, an apple, whether it's real, or porcelain, glass, wood or a watercolor painting, represents good health.

Buy yourself a gift that is your symbol of "good health" and display it in a prominent, often-seen place in your home. Each time you see it, visualize optimum health.

More information: Consider taking a feng shui class, a workshop, reading a book or two. We recommend *Feng Shui* by Richard Craze (HarperCollins). Or hire a professional feng shui consultant. For a directory of classes, workshops or consultants visit *www.fengshuidirectory.com.*

Smudge Your Space Clear

Through the years, we've heard many success stories about smudging (the practice of burning herbs for emotional, psychic or spiritual purification). *Here are just a few of those stories…*

A real estate agent in New York City could not sell a desirable apartment. A holistic practitioner smudged the apartment, rid it of its negative energy, and the following day, the apartment sold for the original asking price. Also, we heard about a couple who moved into a new home where they just couldn't get a good night's sleep. At their wits' end, they took a friend's advice and smudged each room in their home. They've been getting great ZZZZZ's ever since.

Smudging not only cleanses people, it can also clear a room or area of any old or stagnant energy. All rooms need cleansing…just as much as they need physical cleaning. If your life feels stuck or things just aren't going according to plan, you may just find that simple space clearing solves the problem. Clearing the space around you is also an important part of any ceremony.

You will need: A smudge stick, matches, a small ceramic or stone bowl or a large shell and a large feather. (Most health food stores and Whole Foods Markets carry bundles of sage smudge sticks. Also, check "Sources," page 311, for another place that sells smudge kits.)

 CAUTION: If you have asthma or any respiratory challenges such as chronic obstructive pulmonary disease (COPD), smudging may NOT be for you. If you insist on trying it, experiment very cautiously.

Instructions

1. To cleanse the space in which you are working, light your smudge stick as described in the "It Does a Body Good," chapter under "Smudging for Self-Clearing," page 270, and smudge yourself and anyone with you.

2. Then, walk around the room wafting smoke into each corner. Call on the spirit of Sage to drive away all negativity from the room. Then repeat, asking the spirit of Sweetgrass to bring harmony and balance to the room.

3. Go to the center of the room and stand quietly for a few moments. Turn to the East of the

room and fan smudge smoke out into that direction four times with the feather, saying: "Spirit of the East, Great Spirit of Air, cleanse and inspire this space."

4. Turn to the South and smudge four times, saying: "Spirit of the South, Great Spirit of Water, strengthen and bring peace to this space."

5. Now turn to the West and smudge four times, saying: "Spirit of the West, Great Spirit of Fire, energize and protect this space."

6. Turn to the North and smudge four times, saying: "Spirit of the North, Great Spirit of Earth, ground and cleanse this space."

7. Return to your original position in the center of the room and look upward sending smudge up to the ceiling four times, saying: "Great Father Sky, guard this space from above."

8. Now finally squat toward the floor and send smudge down to the floor four times, saying, "Great Mother Earth, nurture this space from below."

9. Put your smudge stick in the bowl or shell and stand quietly with your eyes shut. Visualize the great spirits you have summoned standing guard around your room. You could imagine them as the great archangels or the four animal spirit keepers of Native American tradition (Buffalo—North; Eagle—East; Coyote—South and Grizzly Bear—West). Visualize the loving energy of the Mother and Father Spirits above and below you. Offer thanks to all of them.

10. When your smudging has ended, douse the smudge stick with water.

 NOTE: You should also smudge anything you will be using for your blessing or clearing—crystals, candles, flowers, stones, etc.

Home-Grown Love

There is a notion that sprouting an avocado pit will spread love throughout your home. Why? Because the avocado is ruled by Venus. It will also give you the joy of watching greenery grow. And it's easy. All you need is an avocado pit, a tall glass of water, a few toothpicks and a sunny windowsill.

Wash off any bits of avocado meat that are on the pit. Determine which end of the pit is narrowest. The narrower point is where the stem and leaves will grow; the wider end is where the roots will grow.

Stick four or five toothpicks evenly spaced around the middle of the avocado pit (which we'll now refer to as the seed) and place it on the glass of water, making sure that the wider end of the seed is in the water and the narrower end is pointing up to the sun. Place the glass on a sunny windowsill. Check on it daily, refilling the glass so that one-third to one-half of the seed is in water at all times.

 NOTE: Most avocado seeds grow, but you may want to start with two or three avocado pits in separate glasses of water to guarantee that at least one will sprout.

Your patience will pay off when the roots begin to grow, followed by the stem and leaves. When the plant is about 12 inches tall, transfer it to an eight-inch pot and cut one-half inch off the growing tip to encourage more fullness.

Stained Glass Light

Stained glass windows, lamps and chandeliers refract light and create rainbows that add to the positive flow of energy in the house.

"I Might Need It One Day"… And Other Common Excuses For Clutter

Most people want to eliminate clutter, but many never quite manage to get the job done. They know that throwing away the stuff they no longer use would make it easier to find the things they do need…that de-cluttered lives are more focused and less anxiety-ridden…and that less clutter means lower levels of dust and allergens in the home. They simply cannot convince themselves to take action.

The most common excuses for not getting rid of clutter and how to move beyond them…

"I Might Need It One Day"

Some people are unable to throw anything away out of fear that they might need it later. In truth, the vast majority of items saved because "I might need it one day" are never needed. They just pile up and get in our way. *Example:* Your sister gave you a new electric coffeepot as a present. You hold on to your old one "just in case."

This might-need-it mentality sometimes stems from a subconscious fear about the future. Those who were raised in poverty or who lived through the Great Depression are particularly prone to such thinking.

What to do: Establish a "one-in, one-out" routine. When a new magazine arrives in your home, throw away an older issue. When you purchase a new piece of clothing, select an old piece of clothing to discard.

"It's Too Important to Let Go"

Our possessions can become intertwined with our memories. We assign sentimental value to items linked to events of our past, then find it psychologically difficult to discard them.

Some of these objects are related to our family's history, creating a sense that we have been "entrusted" with them and are obliged to keep them. Others, such as sports trophies and term papers, are related to accomplishments that required considerable effort on our part or that of our children.

What to do: Consider where objects with "sentimental value" have been stored. If these things have spent years untouched in boxes in the attic or gathering up dust in the back of a closet, they must not be as important as we think. Truly important possessions are kept in more prominent locations. If you are not willing to put an item on display somewhere in your home, throw it away. (If this object is a piece of family history, first ask other family members if they wish to take it off your hands.)

Your memories and sense of accomplishment will not be diminished by the loss of a physical item related to the event—nor is it an insult to your dear, departed grandma to get rid of the porcelain figurines that she once loved, but you do not.

"It's Worth a Lot of Money"

Don't confuse the amount that something costs with what it is worth to you. The fact that you paid $3,000 for a massage chair or a pool table is irrelevant if this item is never used. In fact, an unused item has negative value to you—not only do you derive no enjoyment from it, but it takes up valuable space in your home.

What to do: Try to sell unused "valuables" through an online auction site, such as eBay, or through consignment stores. Recovering a portion of your costs will mitigate the psychological pain of getting rid of something expensive.

"My House Is Too Small"

Some people will claim that they do not have too much stuff—they simply have insufficient space. In reality, the size of your home is the least flexible factor in the clutter equation. If your small home is bursting at the seams, it is much easier to get rid of some things than it is to move into a larger space. Until you de-clutter, your possessions will just make your small home feel smaller.

What to do: Understand that the size of your home provides a limit to what you can acquire. Don't rent a storage locker or waste living space on unnecessary things.

"I Don't Have Time to Get Organized"

Organizing can be a major chore, taking several days or longer.

What to do: Think of getting organized as a way to save time. In the long run, organization makes it easier to locate things and eliminates "panic cleaning" before guests visit.

Also, divide big jobs into more manageable tasks. *Example:* Each day, take 10 minutes to walk around your home filling one trash bag with trash and another with items to give to charity. Do this for one week, and you'll see what a big impact this has on clutter.

"It's Not the Problem My Spouse Thinks It Is"

Perhaps clutter and disorganization just don't bother you—but wouldn't doing away with it be easier than arguing with your spouse about it? Clutter can foster considerable tension in relationships.

What to do: Ask your spouse for his or her vision for a room, then share your own vision. Perhaps you see your living room as a comfortably cluttered space where you watch a ballgame, but your spouse sees it as a place to entertain guests. One solution could be to move the TV to another room and keep the living room neat for guests.

"It's Not My Stuff"

Do friends and family members treat your home like a storage facility? Do your grown children still keep childhood possessions in their old rooms?

What to do: Decide if it is okay that your home is used by others for storage. If it is, you must learn to live with the clutter. If not, politely ask these other people to come and claim their things by a certain date.

Peter Walsh, an organizational consultant based in Los Angeles who was featured on the TLC program *Clean Sweep.* He is author of *It's All Too Much: An Easy Plan for Living a Richer Life with Less Stuff* (Free Press). His Web site is *www.peterwalshdesign.com.*

Pets...Keeping Them Healthy

FOR DOGS AND CATS

Tune in to your pet to evaluate his or her needs. Use common sense when determining treatment dosage, taking into account the size of your pet. After treatment, pay careful attention to your pet's reaction. As with humans, if symptoms persist, seek professional help.

First-Aid Kit for Pet Owners

First off, the ASPCA Poison Control Center (*www.aspca.org*) advises pet owners to invest in an emergency first-aid kit for their pets. *The kit should contain...*

- **A fresh bottle of hydrogen peroxide,** 3% USP (to induce vomiting).
- **A turkey baster, bulb syringe or large medicine syringe** (to administer peroxide).
- **Saline eye solution.**
- **Artificial tear gel** (to lubricate eyes after flushing).

- **A mild grease-cutting dishwashing liquid** (for bathing your animal after skin contamination).
- **Tweezers** (to remove stingers, ticks).
- **A muzzle** (to protect against fear or excitement-induced biting).
- **A can of your pet's favorite wet food.**
- **A pet carrier.**

Always consult a veterinarian or a poison control hotline for directions on how and when to use any emergency first-aid item.

Remedies for Common Ailments

➤ **Diarrhea.** Mix one teaspoon of carob powder (available at health food stores) in a glass of water and give it to your pet in the morning and the evening. If your pet's condition is not abating, give him the carob powder in water several times a day.

➤ **Ear Mites.** When your pet seems to have itchy ears, take a flashlight and look inside them. If you see crud in the ear that resembles coffee grounds, chances are your pet has mites.

295

Puncture vitamin E capsules, squeeze out the oil into each of your pet's ears, and gently rub it in. Then take cotton swabs and carefully clean out the oil along with the coffee grounds. Repeat the process three days in a row. The vitamin E oil will suffocate the mites and help heal the itchy ears.

▶ **Itching.** To give your pet relief from an itch, dab on some apple cider vinegar.

▶ **Worms.** It is unanimous—garlic gets rid of worms and eggs, and prevents them from returning. Use common sense when it comes to dosage. One clove of garlic a week seems to be about right for puppies. Grown dogs, depending on size, should have two or three cloves a week.

Mince the garlic and mix it in your pet's food—a little at a time. A couple of garlic pills daily also seem to be effective wormers.

 CAUTION: Large amounts of garlic can be harmful to dogs (see page 301). Three to four times a week is usually well tolerated.

Skunk Odor Removal

▶ **Tomato Juice.** If your pet gets sprayed by a skunk, put on rubber gloves and bathe him in tomato juice. You'll need a lot of tomato juice even though you can dilute it with water.

▶ **Vinegar.** It might be more economical to bathe your pet in distilled white vinegar diluted with water—one part vinegar to 10 parts water. Being careful not to get the solution in his eyes, sponge his face with the vinegar. Do not rinse off the vinegar with water. The smell will return. Even by letting the vinegar dry naturally on him, you may have to give your pet one more treatment before the smell is gone forever.

Fleas

Since fleas are a big problem for pet owners, we asked alternative-thinking veterinarians, animal trainers and animal groomers how they take care of their own pets. All agreed that they never use chemical flea collars or sprays on their pets. Some collars and sprays are said to contain very strong ingredients that can cause all kinds of physical problems including heart trouble, allergies and nervous system disorders.

▶ **Do-It-Yourself Flea Collar.** There are herbal flea collars available at some pet shops and some health food stores. If you're feeling ambitious, you can prepare a homemade flea collar for your pet.

Find a durable and comfortable collar—a leather strap or heavy-but-smooth twine—and soak it in pennyroyal oil (available at health food stores) for 24 hours. Then tie it around your pet's neck and fleas will flee.

 CAUTION: Do NOT use pennyroyal if you or your pet is pregnant. In near-lethal dosages the oil could act as a menstrual-flow stimulant and induce miscarriage.

▶ **Flea Repellents.** Fleas have a keen sense of smell. *Here are remedies known to successfully assault their little noses...*

• **Lemons.** Cut up two lemons into small bite-sized pieces (peel and all). Place in a pan with a quart of water. After it boils for an hour, take it off the burner and let it steep overnight. In the morning, strain and use this liquid to sponge down or spray your pet. While fleas will be repelled by the smell of citrus oil, the people who live with the pet find it pleasant. The lemon water will also help heal flea bites on your pet's skin.

• **Brewer's yeast.** Your pet's diet is said to play the most effective role in repelling fleas, specifically the addition of vitamin B-1 (thiamine) to the menu. Brewer's yeast (available at health food stores), a rich source of B-1, is highly recommended. A daily dosage gauge—one rounded tablespoon for 50 pounds of pet.

The way it's thought to work is that vitamin B-1 produces an odor on your pet's skin. We can't smell it, but it supposedly sickens the fleas.

To prevent brewer's yeast from causing gas, feed it to your pet in moist food and in small amounts.

Pet owners, you may also want to take a daily dose of brewer's yeast to protect yourselves from fleas.

• **Garlic.** We heard about someone who rubs vegetable oil on his dog's skin, then massages in some garlic powder. True, the poor pet smells like a salami sandwich for a few hours, but because of the garlic, he's flea-free for a few months.

• **Cedar.** Fleas hate the smell of cedar, one of the reasons that storage closets are lined with cedar. See that your pet's living quarters contain cedar shavings or chips. Put them in a cotton bag, or sew them into padding or a pillow. Just make sure that your pet can't get at them if he has a tendency to chew things up.

• **Outdoor doghouse.** Put fresh pine needles in or around the house to help keep fleas away.

➤ **Ridding Your Home of Fleas.** Fleas breed and hatch in carpeting and on furniture.

• **Vacuum.** Every other day, vacuum the areas where your pet hangs out and sleeps. Put on a pair of white socks and slowly walk through your home. Fleas will be attracted to your body warmth and electromagnetic energy. When they jump on your feet, the white socks will make them easy to see. Then get out the vacuum cleaner!

To make sure you kill the fleas and eggs that you suck up in the vacuum cleaner, place some chemical flea powder (the strong kind that you would not use on your pet) in the bag before vacuuming.

• **Brewer's yeast.** Since fleas hate the smell of vitamin B-1, sprinkle brewer's yeast, a rich source of the vitamin, on the carpeting, furniture and other pet hangouts.

• **Laundering.** Once a week, wash your pet's bedding.

Traveling with a Pet

➤ **Peppermint Oil.** While traveling with your pet, his/her drinking water may have a different taste than his at-home water and he may not want to drink it. But you can prevent this problem. Starting a few days before you travel with your pet, put three or four drops of peppermint oil in his daily water. Remember to pack the peppermint oil, so that when you're traveling you can continue putting it in your pet's water. That way, it will smell familiar and he will drink it just as he did at home.

Loving Your Pet

➤ **Nurturing with Crystals.** According to gemologists Joyce Kaessinger and Connie Barrett, animals respond to stones just as humans do. They had a cat and wanted to bring home a kitten. To avoid going through the usual long and unpleasant "getting used to each other" period, Joyce put rose quartz—a stone of nurturing and love—all around, including

297

where the cats slept. In only two days, the older cat was mothering the kitten.

 CAUTION: Be sure each stone you use is big—too big for your pet to swallow.

► **Pet/Owner Bonding.** By encouraging your pet to eat the last few crumbs on your plate, it is said that you are attuning him to your vibes and strengthening his relationship with you.

Money-Savers for Dog and Cat Owners

We love our pets and want to make sure that they live long, healthy lives. *Here are ways to ensure that they do just that—without breaking the bank in the process...*

● **Catch diseases early.** Watch for changes in a pet's routine, such as more panting than usual or additional water consumption. These can be early signs of disease—which may be easier and less costly to treat than at later stages.

● **Feed them a high-quality diet.** You'll keep your pet healthy *and* save on vet bills. The first ingredients on the label should be animal proteins—not byproducts, grains or vegetables.

● **Have grooming done midweek.** Many salons charge 20% less for work done Tuesday through Thursday.

● **Consider pet insurance.** The cost is about $16/month for cats and $22/month for dogs. Go to *www.petinsurance.com* or *www.pet-insurance-information.com* to find out what is covered.

Charlotte Biggs, former chief governance officer, Pet Care Services Association, Colorado Springs.

FOR DOGS

Arthritis and Lameness

► **Bone Meal Tablets.** Start slowly— one a day for a medium-sized dog, and gradually regulate the dosage in accordance with his reaction and needs.

► **Glucosamine.** Just as it works for humans, glucosamine may also help relieve your dog's painful joints. Ask your vet to recommend a quality product (with or without chondroitin), the method of delivery (pills or liquid) and the daily dosage.

► **Alfalfa Tablets.** Three alfalfa tablets a day—have been known to make a dog's arthritic limp disappear.

Cough

► **Garlic Cure.** If your dog has a cough, give him a couple of garlic capsules every three hours until the cough subsides. And for Pete's sake, tell him he must stop smoking!

Digestive Issues

► **Gas.** Rub apple cider vinegar on a dog's stomach—where the hair is sparsest— and within a half hour, the dog should be more socially acceptable company.

► **Diarrhea in Puppies.** If your puppy has diarrhea, feed him cottage cheese for a couple of days—nothing else, just cottage cheese. It's an effective cure for this puppy condition called *coccidiosis*. Before you use this treatment, you may want to clear it with your pup's vet.

Eyes, Ears and Teeth

► **Ear Care.** Once a week, dip a cotton ball in mineral oil and carefully wipe the insides of your dog's ears. This process helps prevent infection.

 NOTE: Some breeds, such as poodles and terriers, have hair growing inside the ear. Get a groomer to teach you how to pluck the ear hair to prevent wax and dirt from accumulating.

➤ **Eye Inflammation.** If your dog loves to ride in the car with his head out the window, from time to time his eyes may get a little inflamed. Take a soft, lint-free cloth, dampen it, and carefully clean his eyes. Then drop a drop of castor oil in each eye. Do it twice a day until your dog's eyes are normal.

Incidentally, it's not a good idea to allow any pet to ride in a car with his head out the window. It's downright dangerous.

➤ **Teeth and Gums.** Do not limit your dog's diet to soft foods. Canned food, table scraps and other soft food do not clean tartar from the teeth. A build up of tartar can cause gum infection and soreness. Make sure your dog's diet is supplemented with dry food, hard dog biscuits or large bones.

➤ **Bad Breath.** Mix some sprigs of fresh parsley into your pet's moist food, then add that to your pet's dry food. Once he downs it, his breath should be greatly improved. Also, if you're up for it, brush your dog's teeth every day to alleviate unpleasant breath.

Feet

➤ **Protection When It Snows.** Walking your dog on snowy sidewalks, strewn with commercial snow-melting products, can be dangerous to your dog's health. The chemicals in those products burn his paws. The dog licks his paws to soothe them, licking the chemicals that can make him sick. Right after you have

walked your dog, wash his paws with a mixture of one teaspoon of baking soda to one glass of water. The baking soda solution will relieve the burning from the chemicals.

Coat Health

➤ **Shiny Coat.** The addition of a couple of tablespoons of baking soda to your dog's bath and rinse water will make his coat soft and shiny.

➤ **Dry Skin.** We heard about a dog who had chronic dry skin for years. Nothing helped, until the owner started mixing a tablespoon of safflower oil into the dog's food every day. A week later, the dry skin condition had cleared up completely.

➤ **Stop Shedding.** If there's no end to your dog's shedding, massaging the coat with olive oil once a week has been known to limit the shedding to the appropriate seasons.

Housebreaking

➤ **Until Puppy Is Housebroken.** If your puppy is still leaving puddles on your rug or carpet, put wheat germ on the wet area. It will dry leaving no stain and no smell. All you'll have to do is vacuum it up.

Weight

Jill Elliot, DVM, knows how much you love your pet, but don't show your love by feeding her more than she should be eating. Dogs (cats, too) are healthiest when they are at a normal weight.

Dr. Elliot tells below how to determine whether your pet is too fat, too thin or just right. The best way to judge this is by running your hands over your dog's body. You should be able to feel a thin layer of fat between the rib cage and the outside of the dog's body, and you should feel an indentation (a waist) behind the rib cage as you move your hands backward on the dog's body. When you run your hand down your dog's back, you should feel a nice flat back, not a protruding spine or hips.

If the ribs and spine are prominent, the dog is too thin. If there is a lot of fat between the ribs and the outside of the body or there is no waist, your dog may be overweight.

The dog of perfect weight has a decent amount of fat between her skin and her ribs, hips and spine, and you can actually feel the bones. When viewed from the side, her stomach is tucked in, with good muscle coverage. From above, her waist is evident, and again, her muscle is visible.

Being overweight is especially dangerous in dogs with elongated body types because of the extra strain it places on their back. Being overweight is one of the most common causes of all back and joint problems. It can also predispose your dog to other health problems. So, achieving the ideal weight is not only great for your dog's overall health, but it will help prevent common diseases from occurring even if your dog may be predisposed to them.

Next time you want to feed your dog more than he should be eating, remember that overweight pets have many serious diseases especially musculoskeletal problems, and it can also lead to diabetes in both dogs and cats.

Poisonous Substances for Dogs

As a veterinarian with practices in New York City and New Jersey, Dr. Jill Elliot has dealt with many poisoned pets. Her advice and information are worth heeding.

Speaking from Dr. Elliot's years of experience, dogs are like children—they are curious, and you need to keep harmful substances out of their reach. As your dog's medical mentor, you need to make sure you keep the following things in a safe place where your clever pal can't access them.

➤ **Most Human Medicines**—including medicines for heart disease, high blood pressure and hyperthyroid, antidepressants, aspirin and so on.

➤ **All Narcotics**—including marijuana, hashish and hallucinogens. If your dog ingests a narcotic, he may need in-patient medical treatment until fully recovered.

➤ **Xylitol.** While *xylitol*, a sugar alternative, may be good for your waistline, it may be deadly for your dog…even a miniscule amount. Xylitol is rapidly growing in popularity and being used in more and more products, such as sugar-free puddings, hard candy, gumdrops, chewing gum, many diabetic foods, baked goods and even toothpaste.

When a dog ingests xylitol, he develops a sudden drop in blood sugar levels, which can result in loss of coordination, a seizure and sometimes even worse. Symptoms occur in as little as 20 minutes after ingesting xylitol, or it can take as long as 12 hours.

Read labels and when xylitol is included in the list of ingredients, be sure there is no way your pet can get at it.

➤ **Products Containing Organophosphates (OP), Carbamate and Chlorinated Hydrocarbon (CIHC)**—such as flea- and tick-repelling collars. These collars have poisonous substances that are supposed to be on the dog's skin and not ingested. Ingesting them can cause neurological problems that may require in-patient care, depending on the severity of the condition.

➤ **Bleach** can be very harmful if swallowed or even licked. It can burn your dog's esophagus and stomach lining as it's swallowed. Never induce vomiting in this instance. Give your dog lots of water and milk to help dilute the bleach.

➤ **Chocolate and Caffeine**, depending on the amount ingested. If your dog consumes either of these, it is okay to induce vomiting, but he may also need medical treatment. The ingredients in chocolate and coffee products that make them so dangerous for canines are *methylxanthine alkaloids* (compounds that are part of the natural molecular makeup of these products), particularly *theobromine* and caffeine. Unlike humans, dogs do not possess the enzyme necessary to break down theobromine. Because of this, theobromine will continue to accumulate in your dog's body over time if he

is allowed to continue to consume chocolate. While he may not get sick the first time he eats it (however, hyperactivity will probably be pretty evident due to the sugar and caffeine), eventually your dog will become toxic with chocolate and could ultimately die from this toxicity. Err on the side of caution and avoid allowing your dog to have chocolate altogether.

Some over-the-counter drugs also have these ingredients, so be very careful with these substances around your dog. Vomiting and/or diarrhea will usually happen within two to four hours after eating the chocolate or coffee product. Your dog will also show signs of extreme nervousness and perhaps even have tremors and seizures or excessive urinating. Prognosis is good if you catch the problem within two to four hours of your dog's ingesting the substance. Don't induce vomiting if your dog is having a seizure; just get him to a veterinarian quickly. However, you should get your dog to a veterinarian even if he has vomited up the substance. Be safe rather than sorry.

➤ **Onions and Garlic**—depending on the amount eaten, can cause anemia. Your dog may need a blood transfusion and in-patient care. Garlic can be given cautiously whole, or as liquid three to four times a week.

Some people give garlic to their dogs because there is some belief that it can be a powerful parasite repellent. Also it has a very good effect on digestion in small amounts.

➤ **Zinc**—found in nuts, bolts and pennies minted after 1983. This can cause anemia if the substances are ingested.

➤ **Lead** is found in some coins, old paints and toys. If your dog swallows things such as coins or toys, he may need surgery to remove the foreign body, and hospitalization for in-patient care.

Bottom Line's Treasury of Home Remedies and Natural Cures

➤ **Rat Poison** can be very dangerous—even in small doses. If you see your dog ingest rat poison, induce vomiting and give him activated charcoal within 15 minutes; this will help minimize the effect. Then take him immediately to the veterinarian for observation.

If you don't see your dog ingest the poison, be advised that she may look normal for 24 to 72 hours before showing signs of poisoning (bleeding from anywhere including nose, rectum, mouth/gums, urinary tract, etc.). By the time you see these signs, it may be too late to save your dog. Seek immediate care if you think she has eaten rat poison, and whenever possible, bring the name of the rat poison with you to the veterinarian.

 CAUTION: If you think your pet has ingested ANY AMOUNT of a toxic substance, it is crucial that you take immediate action. Always have the number of the nearest animal hospital or a local animal poison hotline posted somewhere obvious in your home. The veterinarian will tell you if what your dog ate was poisonous or could cause a problem, and will advise you of what treatment is needed (or if you need to seek immediate medical attention). If the substance was not dangerous to your dog, this call will relieve your concern. It is always better to err on the side of being overly safe rather than sorry.

Keeping Dogs Off the Furniture

➤ **Sound and Glare Deterrent.** To train your young dog to stay off the couch and chairs, put sheets of aluminum foil on the seats. When your dog jumps up on it, surprise! The crumbling noise and the dazzle will frighten your pet into keeping her feet on the ground.

➤ **A Concoction Deterrent.** Mix one-fourth cup oil of cloves with one tablespoon of paprika and one teaspoon of black pepper. Pour the mixture into one of those stamp-moistener tubes and dab it all over furniture legs and around the edges of rugs. The scent will discourage the puppy from going where he's not wanted. If he isn't trained by the time the scent wears off, mix up another batch of the solution and reapply.

Separation Anxiety

Homeopathic veterinarian Dr. Jill Elliot (*www.nyholisticvet.com*) knows that we live in a world where people have to work and shop and run errands outside their home. This is Dr. Elliot's observations and advice.

If you come home to chewed up furniture and personal belongings; elimination messes on your floors; trenches dug in your yards, gardens, rugs or floors or you hear your dog howling loudly enough to shake buildings, your dog is most likely suffering from separation anxiety. This seems to be one of the most common mental health issues in dogs. Dogs are pack animals, and that means they are not meant to be left alone. If your dog is the only dog in the household, you become his pack.

Different dogs do different things to show you how they feel. Some become very destructive to your things, others howl and moan, while still others hunker down for the long haul to wait for your return. The bottom line is that they are all waiting to be reunited with their pack, and that means you. This problem may be more evident in dogs that were formerly abandoned, but it can happen even in a dog that was well raised. The solution lies with you and the choices you make to remedy the situation.

What often happens is that caregivers with dogs who have this problem will reinforce the problem by some actions they actually think are helping. For instance, you get ready to leave (your dog knows the signs that say you are leaving), so you start making a big to-do about it. You promise to return soon, you hug and kiss and keep talking to your dog, delaying your departure while trying to reassure your dog of your return. By doing this, you are only reinforcing the problem. The more you try to reassure your dog as you try to slip out the door, the more you tell him he has something to worry about. A better way to handle leaving is simply to say good-bye and leave.

One way to overcome the problem is to leave for short time periods and return again. Maybe on days off from work, you can leave for 15 minutes and then return. Leave for longer periods each time until your dog comes to realize that you are not going to abandon him.

Leaving your dog home with some great mind-stimulating toys can also help. Challenging toys are ones that make your dog think or try to get something out of the toy, like a piece of food inside a Kong toy (a toy with a hollow center). These types of approaches can keep your dog stress-free and both of you happy.

FOR CATS

Remedies for Common Problems

➤ **Cat Box Deodorizer.** To go a long time between litter box changes, clean out the solid waste every day and add the contents of a 16-ounce box of baking soda to your kitty litter. While adding four teaspoons of dried mint is optional, it would make it fresher. Also, stir the kitty litter often to aerate it.

➤ **Cuts and Scratches.** Clean up the wound with tepid water. (You may have to cut some hair to get to it.) Then puncture a vitamin E capsule and squeeze the oil onto the cut or scratch. If your cat licks off the vitamin E, just apply some more.

➤ **Fur Balls.** Make sure you feed your cat roughage—dry cat food or fresh grass—along with a daily teaspoon of vegetable oil, to enable him to pass the fur balls with the stools. Roughage and the daily dose of oil can help prevent large fur balls from forming.

➤ **Prevention of Urinary Problems in Male Cats.** Adding one teaspoon of distilled white vinegar a day to your cat's water may help prevent the formation of kidney stones that can eventually cause all kinds of urinary problems. A diet of low-ash cat food is also said to help.

Food

➤ **Dry Dog Food Is a No-No.** We were told on good authority that a cat will not survive on a diet of dry dog food. A cat doesn't need all that bulk, but does need more vitamins and protein than dry dog food provides.

➤ **One Meal at a Time.** Moist cat food that's left out half a day can sour, get moldy or grow harmful bacteria that can seriously sicken your cat.

➤ **An Appetite Delight.** Save the liquid from canned tuna fish for when your cat doesn't seem to like the food you're serving him. The tuna gravy may turn out to be the cat's meow.

Saving Your Furniture

➤ **Furniture-Scratching Deterrent.** If you have dark woodwork and a cat who likes to use it as a scratching post, get out the chili sauce. Cats are repelled by the smell of it. Rub the chili sauce on the woodwork, then buff it off and watch your cat stay away.

➤ **Keep Off Furniture.** To keep a cat off the couch or your favorite armchair, cram mothballs between the pillows, in the seams—wherever possible. Not too many or you won't want to sit there either.

FOR EXOTIC PETS

➤ **Canaries—Sick and Molting.** Along with its regular seed feed, give the sick bird sponge cake that has been dipped in sherry. No matter how little of the sponge cake the bird eats, keep feeding it to him daily. We were told that this remedy, weird as it seems, can bring a canary back to health and fine voice in no time.

 CAUTION: Check with your vet before trying this remedy.

➤ **Goats—Fly Repellent.** Feed goats a quarter of a cup of apple cider vinegar daily. Not only will they like the taste, they will love the results. It will keep flies away from them and even from their droppings.

➤ **Hens wtih Lice.** Are your pet hens plagued with lice? A couple of times a week, mix three tablespoons of sulfur into their feed and the lice will lose their lease in the henhouse.

➤ **Horses—Shiny Coats.** Add crushed oats to hay as part of the horse's diet, and his coat will get a lustrous sheen.

➤ **Parakeets—Fatigue.** On a daily basis, add three drops of liquid vitamin C to the bird's drinking water and feed her sunflower seeds after you've put them in the blender. Hopefully, you'll notice a difference in her energy level within a month.

➤ **Pigs with Worms.** Coal—like the kind you find in your Christmas stocking if you've been naughty—helps rid your pig of worms. Let your pig pig-out on a few chunks every now and then.

PET OWNER FOOD-FOR-THOUGHT

Have you observed a correlation between what's going on in your life and your pet's illnesses?

Psychologist Lloyd Glauberman (see *www. mindperk.com*) is an expert in behavior change and the creator of a form of hypnosis that helps people gain access to the incredible untapped power of their subconscious mind. He suggests, "Next time your pet is sick, take a good, long look at your present situation. Your emotional problems may be manifesting themselves in your pet. In some instances, the pet will not recover until its owner straightens out his or her life."

For your sake and the sake of your pet, lighten up so that both of you can thrive.

A Word from the Wise...

Diseases You Get from Pets: Simple Steps to Stay Safe

In recent years, the drug-resistant bacteria *methicillin-resistant Staphylococcus aureus* (MRSA), which used to be found exclusively in humans, has turned up in pets. Humans can acquire MRSA (often pronounced "mersa") during a hospital stay, then pass it on to their pets, where it can live for several months before being passed back to humans that have close contact with the pets. Dogs and cats both appear to be potential carriers of the bacteria, which can cause severe skin infections, pneumonia and even death in both humans and pets. For protection, always wash your hands after handling a pet, and don't let a pet lick your face. Take your pet to the vet if he/she has any sign of a skin infection.

Other diseases that you can get from your pets...

Dogs

➤ **Roundworms.** *Toxocariasis* is an infection acquired from the roundworm parasite that lives in the feces of infected dogs. Roundworm eggs find their way into the soil and can be ingested after gardening in infected soil or petting a dog that has been rolling around on the ground. Once ingested, the eggs develop into worms that migrate around the human body. Roundworm infections are more common in arid areas, where the eggs can survive in soil for years.

Human symptoms: Mild infections may not cause symptoms. More serious infections may cause abdominal pain, cough, fever, itchy skin and shortness of breath.

Human treatment: Antiparasitic drugs.

Dog symptoms: Diarrhea, weight loss.

Dog treatment: Deworming medication.

Prevention: Wash hands thoroughly after working in the garden or petting your dog.

➤ **Hookworms** are in the feces of infected dogs. Hookworm larva can penetrate the skin and develop into worms that tunnel under the skin, creating itchy red tracks.

Human symptoms: Itching, rash, abdominal pain, diarrhea, loss of appetite.

Human treatment: Antiparasitic drugs.

Dog symptoms: Diarrhea, weight loss.

Dog treatment: Deworming medication.

Prevention: Avoid bare-skin contact with soil or beaches where dogs may have defecated.

➤ **Leptospirosis** is a bacterial infection that affects the urinary tracts of dogs and other animals that acquire the infection through their noses or mouths after spending time in habitats shared by raccoons and other wildlife. Humans acquire it when an open sore or mucous membrane comes in contact with the bacteria.

Human symptoms: Some infected people have no symptoms. Others have high fever, severe headache, chills, vomiting and sometimes jaundice.

Human treatment: Antibiotics.

Dog symptoms: Lethargy, loss of appetite, jaundice.

Dog treatment: Fluids and antibiotics.

Prevention: Wear gloves when working around soil or a habitat shared with raccoons. Avoid swimming or wading in water that might be contaminated with animal urine.

Cats

➤ **Ringworm** is not a worm but a fungal infection named for the circular rash it causes on humans. Ringworm is transmitted via direct contact with an infected animal's skin or hair.

Human symptoms: Ring-shaped rash that is reddish and often itchy.

Human treatment: Antifungal ointment.

Cat symptoms: Hair thinning and loss.

Cat treatment: Antifungal ointment.

Prevention: Keep your cat inside to minimize the risk for skin parasites.

➤ **Toxoplasmosis.** Some felines shed a potentially infectious organism in their feces that can be particularly dangerous if ingested by pregnant women and people with compromised immune systems. Cats typically become infected when they eat infected prey, such as mice or birds. Humans can accidentally ingest the parasites after cleaning out a litter box.

Human symptoms: Most people never develop symptoms. Those who do may have headache, fever, fatigue, body aches.

Human treatment: Certain medications can reduce the severity.

Cat symptoms: Often no signs.

Cat treatment: Antibiotics.

Prevention: Pregnant women should avoid cleaning litter boxes. Keep your cat indoors.

➤ **Cat Scratch Fever.** This is a bacterial disease caused by *Bartonella henselae*. The organism usually is carried by fleas that live on the cat.

Human symptoms: Swollen lymph nodes, fever and malaise.

Human treatment: Antibiotics.

Cat symptoms: Most cats don't show any signs of illness.

Cat treatment: Flea medication.

Prevention: Promptly wash and disinfect any cat scratches.

Birds

➤ **Psittacosis.** Some birds carry bacteria that cause a bacterial respiratory infection in humans, acquired when they inhale dried secretions from infected birds.

Human symptoms: Fever, chills, headache, muscle aches and dry cough.

Human treatment: Antibiotics.

Bird symptoms: Typically no symptoms, though some birds show signs of respiratory illness, such as lethargy and discharge from eyes and nasal airways.

Bird treatment: Antibiotics.

Prevention: Use extreme care in handling any pet bird showing signs of respiratory illness.

Jon Geller, DVM, a veterinarian at Veterinary Emergency & Rehabilitation Hospital in Fort Collins, Colorado. Dr. Geller writes for numerous pet magazines and answers dog owners' questions online at *www.dogchannel.com.*

Sources

For years we have known and dealt with most of the companies and services advised here. The few other companies have come highly recommended from people we trust. Even so, before you place your order, find out about guarantees, return policies and whatever else you need to know to make you a happy shopper.

If you prefer shopping from a catalog in hand, rather than scrolling through pages on the computer, call and ask if a printed catalog is available. There are some super catalogs among these companies—e.g. Magellan's (for travelers), UPCO (for pet owners), Gaiam (great gift items). Some companies also offer free online newsletter subscriptions.

In addition, be sure to check out the helpful services described on page 317.

At the time of publication, the contact information here was accurate, but addresses, telephone numbers and Web sites do change frequently.

Natural Foods and Beverages And More

Amy's Kitchen, Inc.
(Natural and organic frozen foods)
1650 Corporate Circle
Petaluma, CA 94954
707-578-7270
www.amys.com

Damascus Bakeries
(Pitas and wraps)
56 Gold Street
Brooklyn, NY 11201
800-367-7482
www.damascusbakery.com

Deep Foods, Inc.
(Tandoor Chef—Kofta Curry)
1090 Springfield Road
Union, NJ 07083
866-672-3378
www.tandoorchef.com

Dreamfields Foods
(Healthy pasta)
301 Carlson Parkway, Suite 400
Minnetonka, MN 55305
800-250-1917
www.dreamfieldsfoods.com

FiberGourmet, Inc.

(Healthy pasta and crackers)
545 W 37th Street
Miami Beach, FL 33140
786-348-0081
www.fibergourmet.com

Gardein Protein International Inc.

(Plant-based meat-like foods)
200-12751 Vulcan Way
Richmond BC V6V 3C8
Canada
877-305-6777
www.gardein.com

GG Scandinavian Bran Crispbread

2121 Boundary Street
Suite 207
Beaufort, SC 29902
855-507-7442
www.brancrispbread.com

Gold Mine Natural Food Co.

(Macrobiotic foods, organic grains, beans, seeds)
13200 Danielson Street
Suite A-1
Poway, CA 92064
800-475-FOOD (3663)
www.goldminenaturalfoods.com

Matcha Source

(Matcha green tea)
2779 Forrester Drive
Los Angeles, CA 90064-3447
877-9-MATCHA (628242)
www.matchasource.com

Millennium Products, Inc.

(GT's Kombucha Tea)
PO Box 2352
Beverly Hills, CA 90213
877-RE-JUICE (73-58423)
www.synergydrinks.com

308

Natural Health International, Inc.

(Original Himalayan Crystal Salt)
224 6th Street
San Francisco, CA 94103
888-668-3661
www.himalayancrystalsalt.com

NuGo Nutrition

(NuGo fiber bars)
520 Second Street
Oakmont, PA 15139
888-421-2032
www.nugofiber.com

Pure Inventions, LLC

(Green tea and other antioxidant extracts)
64B Grant Place
Little Silver, NJ 07739
732-842-5777
www.pureinventions.com

Salba Smart Natural Products, LLC

PO Box 3009
Littleton, CO 80161
303-999-3996
www.salbasmart.com

Traverse Bay Farms

(Cherry products, other fruit items)
7053 M-88 S
Bellaire, MI 49615
877-746-7477
www.traversebayfarms.com

YC Chocolate

(Sugar-free dark chocolate)
320 Cleveland Avenue
Highland Park, NJ 08904
800-433-2462
www.ycchocolate.com

Nutritional Supplements, Vitamins and More

American Botanical Pharmacy

From Dr. Richard Schulze
(Botanical formulas, tonics)
4114 Glencoe Avenue
Marina Del Rey, CA 90292
800-HERB-DOC (437-2362)
www.herbdoc.com

Barlean's Organic Oils LLC

(Olive Leaf Complex, Omega-Swirl)
4936 Lake Terrell Road
Ferndale, WA 98248
800-445-3529
www.barleans.com

Freeda Vitamins

(Kosher certified, 100% vegetarian, sugar-free,
    salt-free, yeast-free, gluten-free, lactose-free)
47-25 34th Street, 3rd floor
Long Island City, NY 11101
800-777-3737
www.freedavitamins.com

Life Extension Foundation

(Nutritional supplements)
5990 N. Federal Highway
Ft. Lauderdale, FL 33309
800-544-4440
www.lef.org

New Chapter, Inc.

(Nutritional supplements)
90 Technology Drive
Brattleboro, VT 05301
800-543-7279
www.newchapter.com

Nutrition Coalition, Inc.

(Willard Water, more)
PO Box 3001
Fargo, ND 58108
800-447-4793
www.willardswater.com

Swanson Health Products

(Nutritional supplements)
PO Box 2803
Fargo, ND 58108-2803
800-824-4491
www.swansonvitamins.com

Sylvan Bio

(Red yeast rice)
90 Glade Drive
Kittanning, PA 16201
866-352-7520
www.sylvaninc.com

Herbal Products and More

Blessed Herbs

(Major selection of single-ingredient
    liquid extracts)
109 Barre Plains Road
Oakham, MA 01068
800-489-HERB (4372)
www.blessedherbs.com

Chinese Herbs Direct

(Internet's largest Chinese herb store—raw
    herbs, herbal formulas, teas)
2675 Skypark Drive, Suite 102
Torrance, CA 90505
877-252-5436
www.chineseherbsdirect.com

Flower Power Herbs and Roots, Inc.

(Free in-store herbal consultations)
406 E 9th Street
New York, NY 10009
212-982-6664
www.flowerpower.net

Great American Natural Products

(Herbs, oils, teas)
4121 16th Street N
St. Petersburg, FL 33703
727-521-4372
www.greatamerican.biz

Herbally Grounded, LLC
(Learning Center and store)
4441 W Charleston Boulevard
Las Vegas, NV 89102
702-558-HERB (4372)
www.herballygrounded.com

HerbalProvider.com
(Himalayan Herbal Healthcare products)
1143 N 1430 W.
Orem, UT 84057
801-225-6160
www.herbalprovider.com

Indiana Botanic Gardens, Inc.
(Herbal remedies since 1910)
3401 W 37th Avenue
Hobart, IN 46342
219-947-4040
www.botanicchoice.com

Penn Herb Co., Ltd.
(Herbal remedies, vitamins)
10601 Decatur Road
Philadelphia, PA 19154
Phone Orders: 800-523-9971
Customer Service: 215-632-6100
www.pennherb.com

San Francisco Herb Company
(Quality herbs, spices, more)
250 14th Street
San Francisco, CA 94103
800-227-4530
www.sfherb.com

Aromatherapy, Flower Essences and More

Aroma Thyme
(Aromatherapy products, essential oils)
888-AROMA-99 (276-6299)
www.aromathyme.com

Flower Essence Services
(Flower essence therapy products)
PO Box 1769
Nevada City, CA 95959
800-548-0075
www.fesflowers.com

Bee Products

C.C. Pollen Co.
High Desert Beehive Products
3627 East Indian School Road, #209
Phoenix, AZ 85018
800-875-0096
www.ccpollen.com

Therapeutic Clay

The Living Clay Company
(Information on clay, clay for purchase)
12209 Twin Creek Road, Unit G
Austin, TX 78652
800-915-CLAY (2529)
www.livingclayco.com

Alternative Products, Gems and Gifts

Crystal Way
(Crystals, gemstones)
2335 Market Street
San Francisco, CA 94114
415-861-6511
www.crystalway.com

Gaiam—A Lifestyle Company
(Eco-friendly, organic products)
833 W South Boulder Road
Boulder, CO 80027
877-989-6321
www.gaiam.com

Gemisphere
(Therapeutic quality gemstones)
2812 NW Thurman Street
Portland, OR 97210
800-727-8877
www.gemisphere.com

Incense Warehouse
(Smudging products—sticks and kits)
3 Newbridge Road
Hicksville, NY 11801
888-288-2977
www.incensewarehouse.com

Mystic Trader
(Unusual gifts from around the world)
1334 Pacific Avenue
Forest Grove, OR 97116
800-634-9057

Prairieland Herbs
(Environmentally friendly food, flowers, gifts)
13505 South Avenue
Woodward, IA 50276
515-809-7022
www.prairielandherbs.com

TickleMePlant.com
(A plant that moves when tickled)
60 Hurds Corner Road
Pawling, NY 12564
845-350-4800
www.ticklemeplant.com

Health Products and More

Apothecary Products, Inc.
(Pharmacy supply items)
11750 12th Avenue S
Burnsville, MN 55337
800-328-2742
www.ezydose.com

Battery Operated Candles
412 W 10th Street
Kansas City, MO 64105
800-879-0537
www.batteryoperatedcandles.net

Bayer HealthCare LLC
Diabetes Care
(A1CNow SELFCHECK)
555 White Plains Road
Tarrytown, NY 10591-5079
914-366-1800
www.bayercontourusbmeter.com

CKB Products Wholesale
(Useful products for your life)
8900 Directors Row
Dallas, TX 75247
888-CKB-BUYS (252-2897)
www.ckbproducts.com

Core Products International Inc.
(Back Saver Wallet, Tri-Core Pillow, more)
808 Prospect Avenue
Osceola, WI 54020
877-249-1251
www.coreproducts.com

Corn Bags for Hot and Cold Therapy
www.corn-bags.com

Crocs Rx
(Footwear for diabetics)
6273 Monarch Park Place
Niwot, CO 80503
877-238-4404
www.crocs.com

InterCure, Inc.
(RESPeRATE device to lower blood pressure)
220 Meridian Blvd.
Suite 07735
Minden, NV 89423
800-220-1925
www.resperate.com

Keenfit
(Walking poles)
2684 Casa Loma Road
Kelowna BC V1Z 1T5
Canada
250-769-9241
www.keenfit.com

311

LA Outback

(Didgeridoos)
2750 E. Vincentia Road
Palm Springs, CA 92262
760-992-5982
www.laoutback.com

Magnatech Labs, Inc.

(Therapy magnets)
74818 Velie Way, #9
Palm Desert, CA 92260
800-574-8111
www.drbakstmagnetics.com

National Allergy Supply Inc.

(Nickel Solution Kit, more)
1620-D Satellite Boulevard
Duluth, GA 30097
800-522-1448
www.natlallergy.com

Omron Healthcare, Inc.

(At-home blood pressure monitor)
1200 Lakeside Drive
Bannockburn, IL 60015
866-216-1333
www.omronhealthcare.com

ReBuilder Medical Technologies, Inc.

(ReBuilder Electronic Stimulator System to
relieve numbness and pain due to diabetes
and other conditions)
636 Treeline Drive
Charles Town, WV 25414
866-725-2202
www.rebuildermedical.com

The Singing Machine Company Inc.

(Karaoke machines)
6301 NW 5th Way
Suite 2900
Fort Lauderdale, FL 33309
954-596-1000
www.singingmachine.com

312

Yomega Corporation

(Yo-yos)
1950 Fall River Avenue
Seekonk, MA 02771
800-338-8796
www.yomega.com

Zona Plus

(Device for lowering blood pressure)
12554 W. Bridger Street
Suite 108
Boise, ID 83713
866-669-9662
www.zona.com

Skin Care Products

LaROCCA Skincare

10061 Riverside Drive
Suite 449
Toluca Lake, CA 91602
818-748-6114
www.laroccaskincare.com

Dental Care Products

Bioforce USA

(Secure, zinc-free denture cream)
6 Grandinetti Drive
Ghent, NY 12075
800-641-7555
www.bioforceusa.com

Vitality Products, Inc.

(Tooth soap)
60 Main Street
Mountaindale, NY 12763
www.toothsoap.com

Weight Loss

Free Dieting—Weight Loss Guide

www.freedieting.com

Travel Products

Magellan's Travel Supplies
(Worthwhile travel tips and
advice on Web site)
PO Box 3390
Chelmsford, MA 01824
888-450-7715
www.magellans.com

Pet Food and Products

ASPCA Poison Control Center
888-426-4435
www.aspca.org

Halo Purely for Pets
(Holistic pet care products)
12400 Race Track Road
Tampa, FL 33626
800-426-4256
www.halopets.com

NY Holistic Vet
Dr. Jill Elliot
212-741-4000
www.nyholisticvet.com

UPCO
(Great selection of pet products)
3705 Pear Street
Saint Joseph, MO 64503
816-233-8800
www.upco.com

Vegepet
(Prepared vegan food for cats
and dogs, more)
2240 Encinitas Blvd.
Suite D-224
Encinitas, CA 92024
800-870-PETS
www.vegepet.com

Advice on Alternative Therapies And Healthy Living

About.com: Longevity
http://longevity.about.com

Jane Alexander
(Smudging information)
www.exmoorjane.com

Joan Arnold
(Alexander Technique)
1 Union Square W, # 708
New York, NY 10003
917-699-0239
www.joanarnold.com

Dr. Gerald Epstein
(Mental imagery for healing emotional and
physical issues)
351 E 84th Street
Suite 10-D
New York, NY 10028
212-369-4080
www.drjerryepstein.org

Feng Shui Directory of Consultants and Schools
888-490-6687
www.fengshuidirectory.com

Health Concepts
From Ray D. Strand, MD
(Nutritional medicine)
PO Box 9226
Rapid City, SD 57709
800-500-6803
www.raystrand.com

Dr. Ben Kim
(Health tips, news, recipes)
3035 Appleby Lane
25003
Burlington, ON L7M OV8
Canada
415-578-4628
www.drbenkim.com

Ask Dr. Mao
("The Natural Health Search Engine")
www.askdrmao.com

MindPerk, Inc.
(Self-improvement products—books,
   DVDs, CDs)
10291 S 1300 East, # 109
Sandy, UT 84094
800-457-2523
www.mindperk.com

Natural Health Techniques
From Dr. Denice Moffat
(Dry brushing, more)
1069 Elk Meadow Lane
Deary, ID 83823
208-877-1222
www.naturalhealthtechniques.com

The Silva Method
From Laura Silva Quesada
(Mind-body healing)
PO Box 2249
Laredo, TX 78044-2249
800-545-6463
www.silvamethod.com

Second Opinion
(Guide to health and wellness)
5305 Oakbrook Parkway
Norcross, GA 30093
800-791-3445
www.secondopinionnewsletter.com

Institutes and Clinics

Center for Personalized Medicine
www.centerforpersonalizedmedicine.com

The George Mateljan Foundation
www.whfoods.com

Journey Healing Centers
844-756-2654
www.journeycenters.com

314

Mayo Clinic
www.mayoclinic.com

Whitaker Wellness Institute
4321 Birch Street
Newport Beach, CA 92660
866-944-8253
www.whitakerwellness.com

Associations and Organizations

Action on Smoking and Health
701 4th Street NW
Washington, DC 20001
202-659-4310
www.ash.org

Alcoholics Anonymous (AA)
475 Riverside Drive, 11th floor
New York, NY 10115
212-870-3400
www.aa.org

American Diabetes Association
1701 N Beauregard Street
Alexandria, VA 22311
800-DIABETES (342-2383)
www.diabetes.org

American Horticultural Therapy Association
610 Freedom Business Center, #110
King of Prussia, PA 19406
610-992-0020
www.ahta.org

American Reflexology Certification Board
2586 Knightsbridge Rd. SE
Grand Rapids, MI 49546
303-933-6921
www.arcb.net

American Sleep Apnea Association
1717 Pennsylvania Avenue, NW, Suite 1025
Washington, DC 20006
888-293-3650
www.sleepapnea.org

American Sexual Health Association
PO Box 13827
Research Triangle Park, NC 27709
919-361-8400
www.ashastd.org

American Tai Chi and Qigong Association
2465 J-17 Centreville Road, #150
Herndon, VA 20171
www.americantaichi.org

Arthritis Foundation
PO Box 932915
Atlanta, GA 31193-2915
800-283-7800
www.arthritistoday.org

Association of Reflexologists
5 Fore Street
Taunton Somerset TA1 1HX
England
01823 35 1010
www.aor.org.uk

Asthma and Allergy Foundation of America
8201 Corporate Drive, Suite 1000
Landover, MD 20785
800-727-8462
www.aafa.org

California Cherry Advisory Board
1521 I Street
Sacramento, CA 95814
916-441-1063
www.calcherry.com

Center for Health, Environment & Justice
PO Box 6806
Falls Church, VA 22040-6806
703-237-2249
www.chej.org

Centers for Disease Control and Prevention
1600 Clifton Road
Atlanta, GA 30329
800-232-4636
www.cdc.gov

Diabetes Action: Research and Education Foundation
PO Box 34635
Bethesda, MD 20827
202-333-4520
www.diabetesaction.org

Environmental Protection Agency
1200 Pennsylvania Avenue NW
Washington, DC 20460
202-272-0167
www.epa.gov

Foundation of the American Academy of Ophthalmology
(Seniors EyeCare Program from EyeCare
    America)
415-447-0386
www.aao.org (click on "Find an M.D.")

International Diabetes Federation
166 Chaussée de la Hulpe, B-1170
Brussels, Belgium
32-2-5385511
www.diabetesatlas.org

National Association for the Humor Impaired
3356 Bayside Court, Suite 201
La Crosse, WI 54601
608-385-3922
www.drhumor.com

National Cancer Institute
9609 Medical Center Drive
Bethesda, MD 20892-9760
800-422-6237
www.cancer.gov

315

Substance Abuse and Mental Health Services Administration (SAMHSA)

1 Choke Cherry Road
Rockville, MD 20857
877-726-4727
http://www.samhsa.gov

National Coalition Against the Misuse of Pesticides

701 E Street SE, #200
Washington, DC 20003
202-543-5450
www.beyondpesticides.org

Beyond Celiac

(Formerly The National Foundation
for Celiac Awareness
124 S Maple Street
Ambler, PA 19002
215-325-1306
www.celiaccentral.org

National Institute for Occupational Safety and Health

1600 Clifton Road
Atlanta, GA 30329
800-232-4636
www.cdc.gov/NIOSH

National Sleep Foundation

1010 N Glebe Road, Suite 420
Arlington, VA 22201
703-243-1697
www.sleepfoundation.org

Partnership for Prescription Assistance

888-477-2669
www.pparx.org

Services

American Board of Medical Specialties (ABMS)

The ABMS is an organization of 24 approved medical specialty boards. Just call the toll-free number, provide the doctor's name and the ABMS will verify, at zero charge, whether the doctor is board-certified in his/her specialty.

353 N Clark Street, Suite 1400
Chicago, IL 60654
Phone Verification: 866-ASK-ABMS (275-2267)
312-436-2600
www.abms.org

Federal Citizen Information Center (FCIC)

The FCIC is a trusted source for answers to questions about consumer problems and government services. You can get the information you need by calling the toll-free number below, or online through FCIC's family of Web sites also listed below...

800-FED-INFO (333-4636)

- USA.gov (or in Spanish at GobiernoUSA.gov)
- Pueblo.gsa.gov
- Kids.gov
- Consumeraction.gov

Natural Medicines Comprehensive Database (NMCD)

If you want to do medical research as a health care professional, or as a person with a health challenge, and your emphasis is on natural ingredients and products, consider subscribing to the online NMCD, which is put together by Therapeutic Research and updated daily. You can subscribe to this service one month at a time, or for a year, two years or longer.

Included in the subscription: A disease and medical condition search that indicates the natural products that might be effective for a particular condition; ratings on safety and effectiveness for more than 1,100 natural medicines; product information on over 50,000 brands; a natural product and drug interaction checker; patient-handout information written for consumers and monthly warnings sent by eUpdate.

209-472-2244
www.naturaldatabase.com

World Research Foundation (WRF)

For a very reasonable fee, cofounders Steve Ross and LaVerne Boeckmann will research—using 5,000 international medical journals and more—holistic, alternative, complementary and traditional treatments for a specific health condition. Therapies range from ancient techniques to the latest technologies.

Also for sale are tapes and videos on specific ailments and rare or little-known therapies. If you want to research a topic on your own, at the Web site click on "Info Packets," and you will then be able to click on an A-to-Z selection of ailments. The Foundation's library in Sedona has more than 30,000 books, periodicals and research reports and is available to the public free of charge.

PO Box 20828
Sedona, AZ 86341
928-284-3300
www.wrf.org

Index